TURNING POINTS
in Washington's Public Life

George Scott, Editor

Jonathan Dembo • Daniel Jack Chasan • Mason Morisset

Howard McCurdy • Don Burrows

ISBN   978-0-9722765-2-8

For more information on upcoming books on state government, or to place an order, go to **www.civitaspress.net.**

This book was printed in the United States of America.

Contents

By 1920 there were a fifth of the population in seven counties, including the three largest. Being one was said to be worth 100,000 votes in a statewide race. Small wonder our two longest-serving U.S. senators, Warren Magnuson and Henry Jackson enjoyed a total of 89 years in Congress, and Arthur Langlie was the first three-term governor. The Swedes, Norwegians, Danes and Finns' persistent individualism and political independence are still a part of the state's reputation.

Seattle's protracted life as a raucous seaport city continued from the Gold Rush to the Twenties. The Great Depression brought an influx of displaced farmers, out of work loggers, radicals, and intensifying clashes between the newly empowered industrial and craft unions in a combustible mix some called "circus politics." From 1938 to 1968, the North End's burghers prevailed in electing four of their own as mayor. Seattle became the quiet, provincial ""Queen City if the Northwest"– until the explosions of the 60s pushed it on the path to cosmopolitanism, and being a liberal "San Francisco of the north."

Tells how attempts by presidents Roosevelt and Truman to coordinate the development of the Columbia River and its Basin were sabotaged from within their administrations. Major federal bureaus resisted a CVA replicating the Tennessee Valley Authority. Cries of "states rights" rang out, as public and private power advocates battled, and the Northwest's Republican governors fought its powerful Democratic senators to a standstill in 1956. The 30-year duel ended when relentless demands for more power in the 1960s forced the antagonists to cooperate.

Washington was second only to Michigan in union membership by the 1950s. From the "International Workers of the World" (the "Wobblies") who fought the forest company's Loyal Legion of Loggers and Lumbermen also producing spruce for airplanes in World War I, to the baseball bat versus cargo hook combats of Dave Beck's Teamsters and Harry Bridge's Longshoremen in the 1930s, the decline of Labor and the swelling of Public Employee unions in the 1960s, Labor has been has been a dramatic and contentious part of the state's public life.

Washington has tried and failed to pass an income tax or comprehensive tax reform eight times in the last 65 years. Being one of the five states without an income tax has become part of our identity, and to many, a badge of honor. The intricacies of a flawed system based on the sales tax, a levy on business' gross (rather than profits), and over 40 other taxes takes twice as much from families of four earning less than $20,000 a year as from those above $120,000, raising questions about Washington vaunted reputation for "progressivism."

In the Medicine Creek Treaty of 1856, imposed by first Governor Isaac Stevens, native Americans ceded most of the land west of the Cascades in return for permanent reservations, and half the salmon runs. Settlers ignored it, and state agencies harassed the Indians until Supreme Court Justice George Boldt reaffirmed the agreement a century later. Four decades of litigation, and arguments between sports, commercial and Indian fishermen over a declining fishery still punctuate present-day Washington.

By the 1940s Washingtonians had felled most of our first growth timber and fished out salmon runs. The Columbia River was being turned into a series of lakes, as mining residues, sulphur from paper mills and chemicals were sluiced into the Puget Sound. The 1971 legislature opened the environmental era in passing six laws, from Shorelines Protection to the Nuclear Siting Act that became national paradigms. Has litigation over the spotted owl, and the tangling of state codes and local ordinances dampened enthusiasm for "the environment," or made us more determined to sustain it?

The legislature gave Washington women the vote in 1912, eight years before national suffrage. (The 19th Amendment passed in 1920). Two women were immediately elected to the state House, and the first to the Senate in 1924. None were left in the upper chamber in 1973, but by 1999, 43 percent of Washington's legislators were women, the highest ratio in the nation. By 2005, they held five of the nine Supreme Court seats, and all five Majority leadership posts in the Senate. The state has set precedents: a second female governor, and both United States senators are women. The tenor of politics has changed.

They were begun in 1914 to give the public a means of overturning, substituting for, or amending laws too much tailored by special interests, to fill oversights and confirm or reject constitutional amendments The signatures of eight percent of the voters in the last gubernatorial election are required to place an initiative on the ballot, and four percent for a referenda. Voter initiated laws have a minimum life of two years before they can be amended by the legislature. Some now argue their purpose has been subverted by the most powerful lobbies, who hire professional signature gatherers, or challenge lawmaker's acts they find inadequate to financial wants. From abortion to water rights, citizen action increasingly takes the most controversial and significant issues out of the hands of the legislators.

Popular Democracy, 1914-2009:	*Proposed*	*Passed*	*Certified*
Initiatives from the people	*1,063*	*132*	*64*
Initiatives to the legislature	*466*	*28*	*10*
Referenced bills and Constituamendments	*51*	*48*	*39*

It is the ultimate political battle, with members and majorities' fates fixed by the redrawing of district lines to insure "one man one vote" districts of equal size after every decennial census. For decades the mandate was ignored, as rural legislatures fought to keep their leverage against the burgeoning cities. In the 1960s the Supreme Court told legislators they could transact no other business until it was done. The matter went to the high bench, who appointed an outside "master," beginning a new GOP era in the House. In 1983, the task was finally turned over to a bipartisan commission with one "public" member. The ability to gerrymander has been dramatically reduced. But the tendency of the four partisans to trade "safe" seats to protect incumbents has arguably lessened competition.

Prologue
<hr/>

The Past is Prologue

History, as the wise from Socrates to Santayana remind us, is a sequential if not always understandable evolution. No where is this more evident than in the path-breaking, arresting events peculiar to Washington's "freestyle" politics. These pivotal landmarks in our past are also portents of our future. Our selection criteria for *Turning Points* were the subjects' dimensions, the illustrative value of an event, and its ongoing impact in the State. We wrote these chapters for those fascinated by the Evergreen State's quick coming of age, and its penchant for extraordinary events. They are for upperclassmen badly in need of concise, contextual treatments of major happenings as well as specialized reading graduate students in history, political science and public policy, those looking to careers in public service or politics, and those seated.

The authors, two historians, two lawyers, a political science professor, and an economist-administrator, have served with the last seven governors, on legislative staffs, as a departmental director, and a legislator. We have taught, researched, managed, litigated, published, and practiced state politics an average of 25 years. Our topics span the Twentieth Century, from the impact of Scandinavians who bought the one-way $100 tickets offered by the Great Northern Railway from the Midwest, and got off in Spokane or at Seattle's King Street Station, to those who participated in the 30 year struggle between advocates of public or private power to develop the Columbia, to the ongoing "salmon wars."

Twenty percent of Washingtonians work for government, and it is now the largest determinant of how we live. This was not so 150 years ago. In 1853, when Washington Territory was born as a colonial outpost of Congress, it held 30,000 native Americans and immigrants, in equal numbers, spread across a huge expanse from the Rockies to the Pacific, and some hoped, into British Columbia. It was hardly "governed." Transportation was by canoe and later, small steamers along the coast, inland up the westward flowing rivers to the Cascades, and by horseback east of them. The Territorial budget was under $2 million for the first two years, (about $30 million in today's dollars). The State is now the largest "corporation" in Washington, with over 110,000 employees (including teachers), and had a biennial budget of $43 billion (in 2007-09). It serves 6.5 million citizens through 300 agencies, boards and commissions.

Washington is the most geographically diverse state in the nation. The 260 inches of rain that fall each year on the west side of the Olympics diminish to less than six on the Hanford Reservation near the Tri-Cities. The economy east of the Cascade divide originally rested on mining, railroading, agriculture and wheat. Tree fruits sprouted in the Columbia Valley in the 1920s, nuclear energy in World War II, and of late world-class wines. On the wet side of the mountains, timber and fish were overtaken in World War II by services and retailing, aircraft and military manufacturing. Government is third. Federal dollars have made the two research universities, five regional ones, and 32 community colleges educate over 250,000 students, and are critical components of the economy. Technology has pervaded the landscape since the 1970s, led by Microsoft.

Culturally, before 1900 a few arrivals came from New England, and most from the Midwest, salted with large contingents of Scandinavians displaced by the 100 degree Summer-to-Winter temperature changes in the colder states. Any stroller on a college campus can sense the future. Japanese, Chinese, Vietnamese, and expatriates from the Malay Peninsula are 15 percent of student bodies, and as is usually the case with immigrants, are arguably more engaged than native Washingtonians. This, and rise of women to senior positions in all fields has suffused if not supplanted the moirés of the heirs of the Northern Europeans, Protestants, Jeffersonian Democrats and their philosophical brothers, small government Republicans. Washington is now the least churched of the states, increasingly diffuse, and driven by the post-Great Society values around Puget Sound.

The stabilizing burgher and rural mentalities prevailing prior to the Vietnam War have been overridden by advocates of a supplemental welfare state generated in Olympia. The coming of state paid health insurance, subsidized mortgages, spreading of the facilities budget to local government and historic restorations, buy-ins for dramatically expensive sports emporiums, and tax relief for private enterprises to "compete" with other states has confused, diluted and strained Washington's ability to meet its primary missions. An archaic tax system has been made more unfair by professional signature gatherers working for well-heeled major lobbies wielding initiatives to get what the legislature denied them, citizens frustrated by inability to pin responsibility on the proliferating public agencies, and nativists hooked on simplistic solutions. Witness the end of our minimal inheritance tax in the 1980s, and repeal of graduated car license fees, the only state revenues based on "ability to pay." The chronic gap between what citizens want and what they are willing to pay for has widened, as expectations race ahead of affluence.

Coincidentally, the State's bonded debt limit, and owings, have risen from four to seven percent of the operating budget in three decades, and the operating budget has an ongoing deficit of billions, federal stimulus dollars notwithstanding, for three biennia.

The migrants crossing the Columbia from the south, and streaming down the passes into Western Washington after the 1840s turned a territory into a state in 40 years. The westward-shifting struggle from the 1880s to 1920 over whether Walla Walla, Ellensburg, Yakima, and then Seattle, Vancouver, Tacoma or Olympia would be the capitol has faded into lore. In the 19th Century population was east, and west of the Cascade divide and politically offsetting. After 1889, the "cow counties" in the southwest and northwest conspired with the east side to contravene Tacoma and Seattle.

The symbols of the East-West schism from the "Depression Decade" to the 1960s were legislative brawls over prohibition, for a "fair share" of highway monies, rural-small school subsidies, dams, reclamation and flood control for the Columbia and its basin. They have been partially mooted by an independent Highway Commission, education formulas and formulaic federal funds, but have not staunched more pervasive disagreements. "Protecting the environment" means different things on the two sides of the Cascades. So does the "right" to an abortion and "family values," if we contrast those of the 40,000 souls attending Seattle's annual gay parade, those marching against the military, or protesting lowering barriers to international trade, as opposed to Republican run Eastern Washington's need for an entrepot.

Historian Frederick Jackson Turner famously declared the "end of free land" as Washington became a state in 1889. The massive waves of newcomers since 1980 are a more monumental "Turning Point" conditioning the first half of the 21st Century in the Evergreen state. Accelerating urbanization on the Coast, condensation of the suburbs on an arc from Vancouver through Redmond to Bellingham in the last three decades has driven their traditional politics left, reinforcing the liberalization of Seattle since the 1960. Democrats from both venues had had overwhelming majorities in both houses since 2005, and Washington is a modified one-party state for the foreseeable future, with "Pugetopolis" dominant.

The momentous questions are, will the state continue its drift of the last 20 years away from innovative environmentalism, continue to avoid structural problems like the outdated Constitution and outworn revenue system, and recognize regional attitudes outside King, Pierce and Snohomish counties? Washington's withering "progressive," heritage is tangled in statism, and a race to imitate the previously abhorred patterns of the larger, older states. Urban anonymity seems to be supplanting individual commitments, creativity and collective responsibility – the real demise of the values of "the Westward Movement."

George W. Scott, Ph.D., Editor

Chapter 1

Scandinavians in Washington Politics

George W. Scott

> *"Be agreed among yourselves, you Swedish, Norwegian, and Danish men and women, help and support one another…. I do not wish to say that the Scandinavians should form a power all to themselves or be a state within a state…. On the contrary, it is the sacred duty of the emigrants who wish to make this country their… home… to become assimilated… to learn the English language and to… uphold the spirit and institutions of the Republic. The sooner this comes about, the better."*
>
> From a farewell speech by Paul Hjelm-Hansen at Alexandria,
> Minnesota, September 4, 1869.[1]

Patriotism and the Politics of Ambivalence

An "insistent drive for Americanization provided a central and unifying theme for the Scandic immigrant community in Washington." The sons of Norway celebrated on July 17, and Swedes at Midsummer festivals, but both "felt compelled to state and restate arguments" on the 'Glorious Fourth' [of July], "in support of their claim of being more patriotic, more devoted, …more 'American' than those who were native born."[2] Filiopietistic Scandinavian-American historiography, partly put to rest in the 1920's by Turnerians like O.E. Rolvaag and Theodore Blegen in Norwegian-American Historical Studies, was resuscitated by ethnologists in the 60's, and is still with us.[3] In practice, the drive to acculturate translated into even less grass roots political activity in the new Northwest than the Old one. A cultural ambiguity about involvement abided in Washington, resulting in a remarkable inversion of the conventional

A large Nordic family and their small home. Circa 1920

political pyramid. Nordics were not in partisan or in organizational politics or local government in predictable numbers, and held less than 7 percent of legislative seats at their peak, yet held the most powerful statewide and congressional incumbents from 1939 to 1957.

The Midwest: Way Station of Acculturation

Swedish immigration to the U.S. reached a crescendo between 1880 and 1890 at 478,041, when 73 percent of them still lived in the Old Northwest. The cold clear climate, lakes and forests felt like home. Nearly half settled in Minnesota, where by 1930, 11 percent of the population was Swedish. For them land was wealth, and the Homestead Act made it free for the working. By 1938, a fifth of the state's rural population was Swedish farmers. So were 70-80 percent of their countrymen in Wisconsin, Illinois, Iowa, and the Dakotas. Late Nineteenth Century Scandinavian-American historians give thin distribution, lack of perquisite service with the Union Army in the Civil War, orthodox Lutheranism, insularity ("Little Swedens" and Norways), and the near absence of English and lawyers among Nordics as reasons why they were "a less potent factor in American [public] life."[4] The rural environment, social conservatism in the sense of "respect for the law," and the Irish and Catholics being Democrats reinforced Nordic's Republicanism. Sten Carlsson believes up to 90 percent were "voting cattle" for GOP bosses.[5]

There was a parallel insurgent strain. John Lund (1854-1930), Minnesota's first "Swede" congressman, and later governor (1899-1901), deserted the GOP for the Silver Fusionists, then the Democrats. His Republican successor John Johnson spent four terms in the state house, as a less aligned second generation emerged. Johnson would not have gotten a third term – as a Democrat in 1904 – without crossover votes. The farmers became Teddy Roosevelt Bull Moosers in 1912, until crop prices crashed at the end of World War I, and then made the Farmer-Labor Party the main opposition. The GOP began nominating "Swedish" lawyers to compete, and did – until the Depression. Still, "open appeals" for the Scandinavian vote, heard in Minnesota as early as 1883, worked only intermittently until 1910, when Norwegians and or Swedes were 13.5 percent of the state, and all Scandics 30-35 percent. By the Thirties "Minnesota did not care about the nationality of the governor so long as he was Scandinavian." Between 1931 and 1936, "decidedly radical" Floyd Olson won three terms as a Farmer-Laborite. In 1946, Luther Youngdahl's election as governor signaled the return of many Farmer-Laborites to the GOP, and the stamp of insurgency was no longer perquisite to election. Regardless of party, from 1892 when Knute Nelson became governor to 1983, all but four of the state's executives and predictable numbers of elected officials at all levels have been Scandinavians.[6]

On to Puget Sound: The Driven and the Drawn

A generation later Nordics flooded into Washington, the Minnesota of the West in like numbers, but "ethnic" politics were not visible. Half had been acclimated in the Midwest, and suffered "no appreciable cultural shock." Yet pressure to naturalize was higher on the Pacific Coast. Aliens could not own land or vote. Most would cease to be Scandinavian citizens a decade after departing Europe. And this was land's end. The leading Washington Posten in pressing for aggressive citizenship, also embodied the ethnic press' self-conscious, telltale, almost defensive attitude about Scandinavians' slight presence in public affairs.[7]

They began arriving here in volume in the 1870's, reaching 8 percent of Seattle's population in 1910, in a "second stage" Westward Movement that virtually "submerged the previously established culture."[8] Depletion of prime land, the agrarian depression of the 90's, draught and grasshoppers and 140 degree Summer to Winter temperature changes drove most who came. The rest were drawn and the topography of Puget Sound, which resembled Scandinavia: Seattle's Lake Washington was compared to the Baltic Sea. Homesteads in the Midwest sold at ten to fifteen times more per acre than on the Sound, supplying capital. Opportunity knocked. Reconstruction of Seattle after its 1889 fire, ship wrighting after the onset of the Alaska Gold Rush in 1897, and meeting the surging demand from California for logs, wheat and salmon were things Nordics could do.[9] In 1876, Andrew Chilberg, soon to become the first Swedish-Norwegian consul in Seattle, founded the privately funded Scandinavian Immigration Society. Guidebooks like Ernst Skarstedt's Oregon Och Washington abetted railroad agents scouring rural Scandinavia. Scandics' drive to succeed soon bore fruit, and farm and trade associations took the word East. New "letters from America," now from the Pacific Slope, arrived in Europe. Net emigration to Washington rose six times by 1890, to 357,232.

The Evergreen State now had the most Scandinavians in the nation. Half the 15,078 Danes, 52,624 Norwegians and 56,079 Swedes were "natives," half "foreign born."[10] Contrary to the Midwest, 73 percent of them aggregated in just seven counties from the Columbia River to the Canadian border West of the Cascades, and in Spokane County. Few clustered, and half became urban.[11] They declined as a fraction of the populace after 1920, while becoming more dominant among the "foreign born," peaking in 1940 at 32.4 percent, also the highest share in the nation. Seattle had over 75,000 Scandinavians in a population of 350,000 in these two decades, a potentially decisive electoral bloc.

The Ballard Microcosm: 'Doers' and 'Joiners'

Seattle's notable exception to the tendency to disperse was Ballard. Just five miles North of the 'end of the line,' the Great Northern's King Street Station, it was known as "Snoose Junction," or "Swede Town" through the 1950's.[12] A Ballard High yell went: "Lutfisk, lutfisk, lefse, lefse, all for Ballard, yah, sure, you betcha!" Seattle was one of six cities designated for the "Year long Scandinavian Celebration" opened by Iceland's head of state at Seattle Center in the 1960's. Seattle's Mayor went there in 1979 to declare the observance of May 17 (Norwegian Independence Day) "in perpetuity." The largest Scandinavian community in the West is home to the nationally unique Nordic Heritage Museum.

An exhaustive study of early Ballard and Seattle Nordics found those who moved oftenest, were English speakers and literate, rose fastest and were quickest to naturalize and vote.[13] Yet till well after the turn of the century their political impact was marginal. Of the 13,919 men in Seattle registered for the 1892 general election, just 381, or 2.7 percent were found to be Scandinavian immigrants, who were 8 percent of the populace. Patsy Adams Hegstad discovered thirteen Scandinavian political clubs, and a "wide variety of political activities." Peter Wickstrom led

THE NORDIC MUSEUM

In the 1950s, the Swedish Club in Seattle was the largest Scandinavian organization in the nation.

rallies of the county's Scandinavian Democratic Club, and A.J. Lee the Republicans, among "many additional examples."[14] T.W. Lake was mayor of Ballard, Andrew Chilberg County Assessor, the Secretary of the Board of Public Works and two Road Supervisors Nordics. So were the city Treasurer, auditor, and city councilman Peter Rude. Otherwise, the near absence of Nordic names on the rosters of public officials and in the parties suggests more social 'doing' and 'joining' than serious politicking. Midwestern Scandinavian historians' contention that economic security was a perquisite to politics also rings hollow in the Northwest. Nordics came with as much as most here had, and swiftly joined the mainstream.[15] In 1900, 37.8 percent of Seattle's Nordics were laborers; most single women were domestics. More remarkably, four of ten were in the 'higher categories' of professionals, owners, managers and white collar or skilled workers. The First Scandinavian-American Bank was one of the city's largest, and small businessmen made ethnic appeals.

Being 'joiners' simultaneously sped Americanization and sustained language habits and homogeneous social institutions. The nineteen Scandinavian churches, social, mutual aid, musical, literary and labor fraternities were clannish. Seattle's Svenska Klubben (founded 1892), had a 250 voice choir at the 1909 Alaska-Yukon-Pacific celebration, and in 1950 was the largest club of its kind in the nation with 6,000 members. It held light operas, masquerade balls, festival dances, and Mid-Summer's Day joint picnics with other societies on nearby Mercer Island drawing 5,000. Christmas brought on a smorgasbord and lutfisk och grot. The Sons of Norway, begun in 1903 as the Leif Erickson Lodge, emphasized sports, especially skiing and gymnastics. There were orders, medical aid and benefit societies, song and glee clubs. Good Templar (temperance) lodges included Seattle's North Star, the Grays Harbor Light in Hoqiam, Enight in Tacoma, and Scandia in Bellingham and Spokane. The fortunes of Tacoma's Valhalla Lodge, organized in 1884, mirrored the city's. It grew from 20 members to "plush times" in 1946, when Valhalla's share of a picnic with other lodges netted $400.[16] The Dillingham Commission's Report listed Scandinavians in fourteen other fraternities in the state, including the Red Men, Maccabees, Woodmen, Odd Fellows, Masons and Eagles, suggesting Nordics were 'into' American social orders as much as their own.[17] The amazing social energy of second and third generation Nordics, and their closer proximity in urban settings on the Pacific Coast opened the way to powerful political alliances. Yet these institutions have been as apolitical as any in Washington.

Each of the seven 'Scandinavian counties' had ethnic newspapers. Word of candidate endorsements would have traveled fast. "Foreign language newspapers gave second ranking Tacoma its character."[18] The 1890 city directory lists the Vestra Posten as the "only Swedish newspaper in Washington, Oregon, Idaho and Dakota. By 1913, Tacoma Tidende (1890-), competed with five other weeklies and a monthly. The "City of Destiny" had a Swedish Brotherhood for Americanization, and the traditionalist alternative, the Swedish National Association for Unity and European Culture. The ethnic societies' fate was in the wind when minutes began to appear in English in the mid-Thirties. The "Wet Side of the Mountains" had long since been studded with Vasa Halls, Lief Erickson monuments, and redoubts like Bothell's "Norway Hill." The sense of community lingered long after the controversy over values and language began to die with the third generation in the 1940's. It was never a case of new nationalism versus old.

If there were few Midwestern-type clusters, the ability to elect legislators and county officials was as great, because of concentration in just seven counties. But Pacific Coast Scandinavians never saw themselves as a "majority" group as they may well have in the Upper Midwest, or even as a significant minority in their communities. "Popery" was never a unifier. Emigrants to the Northwest had left cohesive communities and a conservatism bred of land and bolstered by orthodox rural parishes in states with the highest church attendance in the nation for one with the lowest. Hegsted identified only 13 percent of Scandics as regular churchgoers once in Seattle. They dispersed faster, into a larger population. The freer milieu seems to have amplified Nordics' legendary independence to the point of precluding political organization, as liturgical schisms segmented their churches. Seattle's Vestra Posten, applauded a new Scandinavian Republican Club in Seattle, but wondered if the members had "merely shifted their factional and individual differences to the organization." Washington Posten's editor listened to the reasons why a Scandinavian League for Political Action could not be formed, and decided Nordics could not agree on fundamentals. Other foreign language editors bemoaned a 'stubbornness.'[19] "You can always tell a Swede ... but you can't tell him much," Swedes proudly rejoined.

As importantly, the State's vaunted political independence took a two decade hiatus just when Nordics could have been expected to enter into politics. An inhospitable Republican old guard was in the saddle from 1908 and 1932, blunting many a Scandinavians moderate and insurgent inclinations. Until 1929, they continued to give the GOP credit for prosperity, for lack of a viable alternative. The divided Democrats elected one congressman, one U.S. Senator (twice), and held no more than 12 of 145 seats in the legislature between 1919 and 1933. Nordic progressives favored prohibition, agrarian relief, the labor movement, and increasingly, public power. Their conservatives in Seattle and Spokane were for Al Smith for President, and against prohibition. The split climaxed in 1930 in the progressive's favor with a successful referendum for public utility districts.[20]

Ole and the Legislators

As few as four, and no more than seven percent of the 3,000 people serving in the state legislature in its first hundred years (to 1989), were Scandinavians. Senator Lewis Foss of Tacoma was first in 1892. They became visible as Republican Progressives in the 1909 session.[21] Senators Avrid Rydstrom and Hans Fatland of Pierce County (Tacoma, and environs), representatives John Rudene and Nels Anderson of Skagit, Samuel Bugge of San Juan, and Seattle's assertive Ole Hansen voted for a direct primary and industrial insurance. Kitsap County, on the Olympic Peninsula West across the Sound from Ballard had the heaviest concentration of Nordics of all the "Scandinavian" counties in 1910, with 17,647, centering on Poulsbo's Finns. Their typically "non-partisan" Citizens Club was to "stimulate thought," and Peter Iverson, the Norwegian State Senator from the

Seattle Mayor Ole Hansen seized on the 1919 Red Scare to run for president.

23rd District beginning in 1915, a paradigm Republican Progressive of the period. Literally "between the devil and the deep sea," he fought the "Sawdust Gang" at home as Chair of the

Committee on Logged Off Lands, and a "very conservative, if that is the right expression," majority in Olympia. Against the "Blue Laws of old," but sympathetic to the WCTU, Iverson voted to refer a 1914 initiative by the "liquor element" to the people, and damned the lobby for trying to "fix the law so that women could not vote so much." Ex-loggers could be made into farmers if the State produced "stumping powders" at half the fourteen cents a pound Californians got. Governor Lister vetoed his bill for lack of $50,000 to build a factory. Inverson persisted, trying to protect solo fishermen with a State Fish Commission, and a closed season on the trawlers roaming Neah Bay and the San Juan Islands.

Iverson's solace was knowing his Progressivism put him on the side of "right thinking people." "It must be remembered," he lectured a constituent, "that all the rights are not always on the side of the one who hasn't got the money, those who have the money have a right as well, and what we want to do is legislate fairly for all concerned." His conservative instincts led to lame excuses for voting against four-year terms for county officials in 1919. "Constitutional questions," "unsettled times," and voting to present the issue as a referendum sufficed.[22] The debt-pressed and increasingly thin-skinned publisher of the Poulsbo Record, (later the Kitsap County Herald) was castigated in 1920 for backing progressive U.S. Senator Miles Poindexter, who was defeated. With the laconic realism of North Country, Iverson had long since reconciled himself to political fate. "My Dear Christie Boy," he wrote his son in 1915, "I have studied often about human ingratitude and stupidity. We have to deal with the world as it is."[23]

As a member of the House (1909-11), Ole Hansen attacked vice-prone Seattle, and backed the Bull Moose in 1912. The Seattle Argus was nonetheless skeptical when Ole ran for mayor in 1918: "Do we have [a candidate] who claims to be a Swede when addressing Swedes, a Norwegian when addressing Norwegians, and an American when talking to everybody else?"[24] His "No special privileges" rhetoric unnerved some down towners, even if "a fair, square, business administration" was promised – until a General Strike broke out February 6, 1919. The Central Labor Council's sympathetic strike with workers in the suffering post-war shipping industry stalled Seattle. Ole imagined a "Bolshevik revolution," inspired by Joe Hill's (i.e., Joel Hagglund's) radical International Workers of the World (or "Wobblies.") The I.W.W. was "... fighting the best government yet conceived by man.... You shall obey the law or you shall go to jail." The strike collapsed in three days, but made Ole a "national figure." Extolling "Americanism" inflamed his ego into a short-lived campaign for President in 1920, one soon snuffed out in smoke-filled rooms. Ole was a "Cincinnatus" [sic], with a tendency to be a moralist. His signal act was the city's purchase of its Street Railway, a civic cancor later made a spring board by another Norwegian – and Cincinnatan – Arthur B. Langlie.

The Scandinavian reputation for empathy with Labor and the Left, born of Northland hardships, may also have had a chilling effect in the Twenties on the political ambitions of Hansen's peers.[25] There could be no doubt about the Scandinavian presence in the age of "normalcy." The Norse-American Centennial (1825-1925), that filling the University of Washington Stadium June 28, 1928, featured U.S. Senator Hans Norbeck of North Dakota, and drew Mayor Bertha Landes and Governor Roland Hartley. The Swedish Tercentenary overflowed Seattle's Civic Auditorium July 9-10, 1938. Sponsored by the Swedish Businessmen's Association, Tabernacle, Svenska Posten, "The Nordic Hour," the First Swedish Methodist and Baptist churches, the "All Swedish Day" wound up at Woodland Park.[26]

Hans Norbeck, Unived States Senator from North Dakota and his wife visited Seattle in the Summer of 1928 to speak at a Scandanavian celebration in Husky Stadium.

Roosevelt's New Deal for Washington.

In 1932, FDR caught up a cast down country, and won a majority of Washingtonians for the Democrats for sixty years. The President got 57 percent of the popular vote, all the Democratic congressional candidates were elected, all 25 of the contested State Senate seats taken, and 70 of 99 in the State House. The New Deal sharpened the participatory paradox: outstanding Scandinavians began to capture high office in Washington as nowhere else, while most of their kinsmen were largely invisible in public life.[27] Few Nordic names can be found on Democratic organizational rosters, or those of the Washington Commonwealth Federation and the Old Age Pension Union, spear carriers of the left on Puget Sound. The Depression had overturned politics, but the few Nordic radicals who filed for office did miserably. Embarrassed foreign language editors continued to scourge the left-wingers and question their pedigrees and. Nordics "vacillated."[28] Adjusting to the Left's domination of Democratic politics in the coastal cities where most lived would take time.

The few continuing Nordic political clubs were ostensibly neutral until New Deal's intent became obvious. Seattle's Swedish Non-Partisan Progressive Club, begun in 1933, was to "cultivate interests … in matters of civic importance and to establish for the Swedish American colony its proper respect and position as a factor in government." It at once boosted the public schools, a shift from property taxes, and "stricter economy in governmental administration." In 1936, the club moved left, endorsing the Democratic candidates for congress and state office.

It also came out for Councilman Langlie, a mayoral aspirant – and against his charter amendment trimming police substations in favor of prowler cars. Both were defeated.[29] The 34 members agreed to "cooperate as much as possible" with the Scandinavian-American Democratic Club. Convinced by 1936 that the Depression would linger and that Democrats alone were tackling it, most Scandinavians swung with the nation behind FDR. Their small ethnic political clubs were absorbed by the New Deal. In 1938, the rise of the first major "Scandinavian" candidacies in both parties in Washington caught the eye of now third and fourth generation Nordics.

Sou'Westers: Andy Winberg

Danes, Icelanders, and especially Finns drifted down the Coast. The Sunday Oregonian compared scenes at Finnish settlements on the lower Columbia River to "the thousand lakes between the White Sea and the Gulf of Bosnia." "Like the cowboy has his lariat, the Finn has his sauna." By 1903, the purifying effects of the hot vapors rose in places like the "Little Kalama" and Butte Hill districts north of Woodland. Finn Hall was built on the Lewis River in 1912. A Farmers Cooperative Trading Company incorporated there in 1917, lasted 40 years. The 1900 census lists 6,000 Washington born Finns. Half were in Seattle or Aberdeen/Hoquiam, in fishing, lumbering, Grays Harbor County, the Scandinavian haven of Southwest Washington for seventy years.[30]

If Peter Iverson was a prototypical Progressive Republican, Aberdeen's Andy Winberg was the ultimate 'joiner,' and "Mister Democrat" on the Harbor. Born in Nordfjordied, Norway, and orphaned at 6, Winberg migrated to Warren, Minnesota in 1903. He arrived in Cosmopolis as a baker in 1907, and was a Labor Council official fifty years. The foreman at the Siese Bakery went on to manage the Real Estate Department of Aberdeen Federal Savings and Loan. The Sons of Norway, Moose, Elks, Odd Fellows, and Rotary were his civic starts. Winberg chaired the first committee for a Public Utility District, and the School Board. He was a freeholder drafting a new city charter by 1926, headed the United Good Neighbors, the Goodwill, Salvation Army, and bond drives – in both wars. In partisan politics by the New Deal, Winberg presided over the Grays Harbor Democratic Central Committee for twelve years, chaired the Nine County Democratic Council, and sat on the State Executive Board. He directed Governor C.D. Martin's local campaign in 1932, and was president of the Scandinavian-American Democratic Club of Grays Harbor when it came to aid of the left-besieged Governor in 1936. Martin made Winberg a trustee of Grays Harbor College for eight years. Governor A.D. Rosellini put him on the Seattle World's Fair Committee in 1955.[31]

The Harbor's Scandinavian-American Democratic Club apparently peaked in 1936, claiming to be the "largest" of its kind in the region, and probably the State, with over 300 paid members.

Winberg lost the leadership of the State Federation at Seattle's Swedish Club in May, 1937 by one vote, becoming First Vice President. Resolutions for Roosevelt's "court packing plan," an Alaskan Highway, full power development, "socialized medicine," inclusive Social Security, and equalization of state school funds passed. In 1939, Second District (Norwegian) Congressman Mon Wallgren's Olympic National Park bill was added. Organizer Oscar Asplund was on a first name basis with U.S. Senator Homer T. Bone, who atypically sat the fence on the Court plan.[32] If "six hundred" attended the convention in 1936, the Federation shrunk quickly. The minutes of the 1939 meeting at Aberdeen show six delegates for Grays Harbor, the most on the Coast. Winberg's resignation as President in 1941 foretold the demise of the elusive Federation, absorbed by the Democratic Party, and the War.[33]

In 1942, another group, the "United American Scandinavians" unsuccessfully 'begged' Seattle's "Swedish" Congressman Warren G. Magnuson to speak at their "Sixth Annual Convention" on the Fourth of July. An appeal by the State Finance Director of the Democratic National Committee to "give us a little help among the Scandinavian people" by speaking at the Swedish Club also fell on deaf ears. The UAS may have been the "Scandinavian-American Democratic Club," incorporated in 1937, not to be confused with the "United Scandinavians of Washington, "United for Progressive Democracy," who celebrated their "Fifth Annual Christmas Party" in December, 1941. Magnuson would surely have been present at one of the gatherings if they were by then more than splinter groups.[34]

On November 6, 1946, the Grays Harbor Washingtonian headlined, "GOP Sweeps the Nation" – but all the county's Democrats survived. Andy Winberg had been a State Representative since 1943. While asserting "the deepest respect for (Norwegian) Governor Arthur Langlie," he voted against the Governor's farsighted forest management reform and his corporation tax in 1951. During three terms in the Senate the New Deal regular was a respected, if secondary player. On his death in 1965, (Norwegian) U.S. Senator Henry Jackson wrote Winberg's widow that the "Native of Norway... espoused in his adopted land the great traditions of freedom and social justice which are the heart of Norwegian culture."[35]

Two Giants and a Gypsy: FDR's Congressional Offspring

Aberdeen Lawyer Martin Smith switched parties in 1930. Traveling the nine counties of the Third Congressional District (Southwest Washington) in April, 1932, he found "overwhelming sentiment in favor of change ... ." Democrats, "many of who are former Republicans like myself" he wrote Bone, and agreed with him and Governor Roosevelt, particularly on the power issue. Bone converted, becoming U.S. Senator. Smith served as a left-wing congressmen from 1933 to

1943, his record as superficial as his "thorough Scandinavian ancestry." The President put Smith on the U.S. Tariff Commission in 1943, at the urging of his colleagues.[36]

Knute Hill was Smith's counterpart in the Fourth Congressional District, which straddles the Columbia River and a hundred miles of Central Washington. Born of Norwegians near

Madison, Wisconsin, he was a "Lincoln Republican, like my parents." "Of this," he later wrote, "I am not ashamed, for to me Jeffer[sonian] Democracy and Lincoln Republicanism are one and the same...."[37] A temperance lecturer while a mill worker, he evolved into a seminarian, lawyer, farmer, principal, Grange lecturer and publisher. "What We Stand For," in the lead edition of his Benton County Free Press, of May 7, 1920, revealed a man of substance: "Insist on truth...courtesy...[be] open to conviction...[practice] obedience to the law and [the] Constitution.... Condemn the mob spirit," he counseled. "We shall persevere."

WASHINGTON STATE ARCHIVE
Congressman Knute Hill in the late 1930s.

A booster of Governor John Johnson (D) while in Minnesota, and Philip LaFollette for President in 1916, Hill's race for Congress in the Fourth District failed in 1920. He began again "at the bottom of the ladder" as a Republican State Representative in 1926. After twice fighting off reactionary Governor Roland Hartley, he was reelected as a Democrat in 1930.[38] In Congress after 1933, Hill proposed melding Wisconsin's employer reserves approach with Washington's merit rating industrial insurance system, and kept faith a "significant realignment was taking place." Congress might be helpless to change the way bourbon Democratic Governor Clarence Martin administered relief, but this was no time to split liberals. "If and when the Democratic party is captained by reactionaries, it will be time enough to form a third party." FDR's Secretary of Agriculture, Henry A. Wallace, did just that a decade later, faulted the President for forcing farmers to face the world market, and into supplementing their incomes with relief payments which supposedly went to buoy the operations of futures traders.[39]

Hill's mother was a Quaker. He spoke for the America First Committee. "The people just won't stand for a war party...." he wrote Seattle's left-leaning Congressman Hugh DeLacey in February, 1941. "So possibly your idea of a People's Party is the only alternative." "Hitler's unprovoked invasion of the U.S.S.R. will convince Representative Hill that FDR's pledge to the allies is the only hope of escaping a Nazified war," DeLacey correctly surmised, following the Left's reversal.[40] Hill took his 1942 defeat stoically, having gone "all over the Coast" speaking for a steel plant in Everett. "It just could not be prevented," he wrote Henry Jackson. Farmers were "on the rampage and [former Senator C.C.] Dill and I were in the path of the storm...."

More accurately, Hill's essentially conservative district, like Smith's, was now profiting from and supporting the War. Isolationists were passé.[41]

Northwestern Washington's Monrad C. Wallgren was the luckiest, and least talented member of the House class of '33. Appointed to the U.S. Senate "…at the suggestion of others high in the [Democratic] party" in 1940, he ousted Governor Langlie in 1944, and is the only person to hold all three of the State's highest offices. The Wallgrens were "washed … right out of Texas and into Puget Sound," by the Galveston flood of 1900. Mon graduated from optometry school in 1914, became a lieutenant in the Coastal Artillery, then melded into his father's Everett jewelry store. Impressive in appearance, a forceful speaker, master storyteller and joiner, and easily met at veteran's and service clubs, he was local icon after winning the national Amateur Backline Billiard Championship in 1929.

Wallgren is remembered for triggering the State's longest environmental clash with a 1939 bill creating a "Mount Olympus National Park." It stalled in the House Committee on Public Lands, but a second version, also drawn and pushed by Eastern environmentalists and scaled down to 640,000 acres, passed.[42] FDR later added 250,000 acres by proclamation, and Harry Truman enlarged the Park still further. Wallgren also introduced legislation letting the War Department authority to relocate the Japanese-Americans (S.444), while opining the "waste of manpower." As late as January, 1945 the now Governor was 'visibly perturbed' at letting them return home from relocation camps before the war was over.

"We Are All Products of the Old World" Senator Henry M. Jackson[43]

Wallgren's successor as Second District congressman was Henry Martin "Scoop" Jackson, whose moniker came from a comic strip character while he was a paper boy for the Everett Daily Herald. A Stanford, and U. of W. Law graduate of 1935, he was elected Snohomish County Prosecutor at 28, in 1938, in a challenge of "corrupt" Democrats. This began 45 years as one of Washington's four exceptional statesmen. (The others: first governor John Rogers, the 35th, Daniel Jackson Evans, and Senator Warren Magnuson).

Hitler's invasion of Norway in March, 1940 was not Jackson's road to Damascus. He voted against Lend Lease, ostensibly because an amendment requiring Great Britain to put up collateral failed. By 1942, however, he had taken up the Democratic maxim, "STAND BY the Commander-in-Chief," and then never wavered on defense. Resistance to Lend Lease, hardly on "procedural grounds," is explicable only by lagging isolationism in his rural counties, filled with many Scandinavians, and Jackson's cultural conservatism.[44] The congressman's Norwegian Constitution Day (May 17), speeches over the years interpret Norwegian sentiment through the prism of an American's experience. In 1948, he explained how Washington with its progressive traditions could understand Norway's determination to be "one of the great spiritual arsenals of democracy," in "maintaining their independence against authoritarianism."[45] Cherishing Norway's freedom of speech, its "elaborate system of laws," centralized legislation and social democracy, the perhaps most anti-Soviet member of Congress came to see his countrymen as victims of Hitler and Stalin.

Another anomaly in a career of integrity also came early on, and is attributable to Jackson's emphatic decision to become a professional politician. Defying Speaker Sam Rayburn, who told him to "dismiss any idea" of going into the Armed Services, Jackson enlisted in the Army in 1943, making the front pages of New York papers. Washington Posten was among the 26 local presses receiving releases carefully spelling out why he was giving up a $10,000 salary for one of $600. How a congressman with no military experience could be useful after basic training by doing four days a week at Tacoma's Camp Lewis is yet to be fathomed. He never got to Italy to serve under his friend General Mark Clark, and was out well in advance of another political necessity, the 1944 election.[46]

Jackson was nothing if not systematic. The evidence is, Scandinavians were not predisposed to traditional ethnic politics or engaged in normative numbers in his constituency, or in his post 1940 races. They were a bonus to be tended. The Reverend H.L Foss, President of the Pacific District of the Norwegian Lutheran Church of America who had held pastorships across length of the Second District, was one of those getting special attention.[47] In 1944, The Sons and Daughters of Norway, totaling 610, were specially mailed. So were the Snohomish District's Federation of Women's Clubs, (Mrs. Henry Backstrom, President) – and the Townsendites, Grangers, Labor, the Railroad Brotherhoods, the Old Age Pension Union, Small businessmen, and other "racial groups" – of which there was only one. Then all 54,000 registered voters in the County were canvassed at the Precinct level. Returns against Payson Peterson his (Norwegian) Republican opponent (for six elections), now ran two to one to six to one.[48]

In 1946, every Democrat in Washington, Idaho, and Oregon was defeated, save one. And by 1950, Jackson was roaming the State, as U.S. Senator Harry Cain self-destructed. Jackson for Senator Clubs were CO-chaired, on a "non-partisan" basis, and backed only him. No one doubted Jackson's "discipline of thought," nor did he forget the swing voter. Seated in the Senate despite Eisenhower's victory in Washington, he stayed on the Merchant Marine and Fisheries committees (1941-), was on Indian Affairs ('44-'47), Appropriations, and Joint Atomic Energy (1947-52). His "majors" in the Senate were chairing Government Affairs (1973-78), and the Permanent Subcommittee on Investigations, where he served under Joe McCarthy, resigning early. He presided over Interior and Insular Affairs (Energy and Natural Resources after 1977), (1964-1980). Jackson played lead roles in energy policy, resource development, and environmentalism, garnering the Sierra Club's John Muir Award in 1969.

Overseeing Armed Service's Arms Control Subcommittee took him into perilous waters over nuclear testing and human rights. By the Sixties the "Senator from Boeing," as liberal anti-war advocates tagged him, was redefining liberalism as the way he wanted to be treated, as "A person of independent mind, committed not to any political orthodoxy, but to the proposition that the political task is to use our knowledge for creative and constructive purposes..." He was someone seeking "little gains when opportunity offers, instead of crying out, 'We are right and they are wrong...'" Jackson dispatched his critics as "faulty strategy ... idealists (i.e., left liberals), who "forgot "The Sino-Soviet argument ... [was] one over means, not ends – over the best way to dig a grave for the West." The Republicans' "misfortune" was to be in power in a period of crisis, exactly

JOURNAL OF THE WEST

From left: U.S. Senators Warren G. Magnuson (State Representative 1933-1935), Congressman, First District, 1937-1944, United States Senator (1944-1981) and Henry M. Jackson, Snohomish County Prosecutor (1938-1941), U.S. House, Second District (1941-1953), and U.S. Senator until his dealth in 1973, were the State's preeminent politicians.

what they were not up to: "Republican leaders are great when what is needed is not thinking but tenacity."[49]

Jackson placed himself squarely in the middle, he was consistently liberal in all other ways. The Jackson straddle was the best of all worlds for a politician. Who could fault votes for the Navy, and Labor ("a bulwark against radicalism in hard times"), for both "guns and butter"? When old friend John Kennedy handed the Vice Presidency to Lyndon Johnson in 1960, Jackson dutifully became the chair of the Democratic National Committee. This led to presidential tries in 1972 and 1976 where his reserved Norwegian demeanor fell flat on television.[50] Honored at home in 1982 with 69 percent of the vote, he was strong enough to send $100,000 to the State Democratic Central Committee to lift the Democratic legislators, who won back the State House, and gave the rest of his war chest to charity.[51] His heart failed a year later.

"Our Little Swede Congressman From Seattle,"
Senator Warren Grant Magnuson[52]

An illegitimate child born at Moorhead, Minnesota, April 12, 1905, who was adopted by a Swedish family three days later, acquired even more seniority. Warren Magnuson, a 1929 U. of W. Law graduate, joined the legislature in 1933, was King County Prosecuting Attorney in 1934, and in Congress by 1937. On the Naval Affairs Committee, Magnuson began a career founded on agility and magnanimity. He escaped unharmed while presiding over the Democrat's riotous 1936 state convention at Aberdeen, and with Jackson and Wallgren, avoided the convocations of the left's Commonwealth Builders, and Washington Old Age Pension Union. Magnuson sent more money to Bremerton's Puget Sound Shipyard in one year (1940) than it received in the previous ten, and led rearmament, while denying it. Left-wingers were told he was at "Work for a Navy of sufficient size … to protect our far flung coastline and insular possessions but not to function in an aggressive way."[53] Promoted to Lieutenant Commander, he spent the Winter of 1943 with Admiral Nimitz on Hawaii or the carrier Hornet. Magnuson's suggestion to Governor Langlie, also a naval reservist, that they go in together, was more for coverage than companionship. Ironically, it was Langlie who appointed Magnuson to Mon Wallgren's Senate seat in December, 1944, to give him seniority over his class. The tea-totaling Presbyterian and the imbibing, genial, freewheeling bachelor could not have been more different.[54]

Jackson was the systematizer, Magnuson the arranger. Businessmen enjoyed the man they had to work with for 23 years as chair of the Commerce Committee (1955-78), and father of consumer affairs laws, notably that on children's' flammable clothing. Magnuson was known for the innovative National Science Foundation (1950), the first tax-supported research, long before taking over Appropriations (1978). Authoring the Public Accommodations Section of the 1964 Civil Rights Act, battles (with Jackson) for a Columbia Valley Authority and Hells Canyon Dam on the Snake River, a $.65 minimum wage (1945), against arbitration of disputes (1949), and two years trying to repeal the Taft-Hartley Act define his orientation. Less honorably than Jackson, he steered clear of the Army-McCarthy dispute, then joined in censuring the senator and signed a resolution urging the committee chair to pursue Communists. The only significant split in 28 years of partnership with Jackson was over the latter's leading President Nixon's ABM missile program. Magnuson was President Pro Tem and the senior United States Senator when defeated in 1980.

His non-pariel ability to capitalize on incumbency and power can be seen in cameo in his overt playing of the Scandinavian card. Oscar Asplund's 1936 suggestion he be designated chair of the "Foreign Language Division" of the State Democratic Party was welcomed. The $400 raised for FDR's reelection by the Scandinavian-American clubs came, Asplund insisted, from "one of the most active Democratic organizations in the State." As president at the clubs' peak in 1937, he set out to "enlist Scandinavian people in the Democratic Party."[55] Magnuson was quick to find jobs for Scandinavians just out of the University in the Bureau of Fisheries, the Geodetic Survey, and Forest Reserve. Asplund was invited to become one of coterie Magnuson intelligence operatives, and sent him monthly bylines for forwarding to Scandinavian newspapers. The Congressman romanced Asplund at the President's inaugural. Both senators, Wallgren and Hill later signed a letter to Commissioner of Fisheries Frank Bell to advance Asplund from a job "lower than his ability." Magnuson personally leaned on Bell "on several occasions."[56] In 1939, Asplund heard that the model Viking ship he had sent FDR was in "a very prominent position" in the East Room. His "Scandinavian-American Brain Trust in the Fisheries Department" felt threatened by a "noisemakers" and "brain twisters" faction, even as he was disclaiming "quarrels in any of our clubs." Jealousy over patronage, they split the "Progressive Scandinavian-American Democratic Club." Their promotion of Langlie for mayor also irked Asplund's regulars.[57]

All six congressmen got the Democratic National Committee to foot a tour by Chicago's Bertha Delin, a prominent IRS attorney. Among other stops, she spoke at Seattle Scandinavian-American club before 200. Magnuson's plea to get National Democratic chief Jim Farley (the needed "big name") to the "statewide picnic" of the clubs at Vasa Park in Seattle in 1938 failed. The prior year, he dutifully reported, Wyoming's Governor Miller and "16,000 Scandinavian-American Democrats had attended."[58] Magnuson proudly told Crown Prince Gustaf he was on the Executive committee for the Swedish Tercentenary, in inviting him to a state with "at least a half a million Scandinavians, of whom over 50 percent are of Swedish extraction."[59] September 12, on "The Nordic Hour," Magnuson underlined that Washington had more Scandinavians in its delegation that any state, (four of six). Nordics heard they were the "possessors of the most progressive and soundest political heritage of any people," and "awakening to the realization that you have a definite place in the political life of the community." The telling Scandic trait was a "stubborn determination … to want the good things of life and want them now." Magnuson's pat response to critics who complained he was "Socialist" for supporting the New Deal was also a self-description: "What has been a New Deal to America is old stuff to Norway, Sweden, Denmark and Finland."[60]

Don Magnuson answered the question of what a Scandinavian name was worth 1952. Unknown except for articles in the Seattle Times, he won the state's Congressman At Large seat and held it a decade. The liberal Democrat was overshadowed in ability as well.[61]

Nordic High Noon: the Gubernatorial and Senatorial Duels of 1956

Arthur Langlie became Washington's leading Republican for twenty years. He profited from Seattle's urge to be rid of its lingering Gold Rush hangover, the radicalism fracturing the Democratic Party in the 1930's, and the largesse of the New Deal. Buttressed as Seattle's mayor (1938-40) by Governor Martin's revenue sharing, and by New Deal dollars, he replaced the city's dilapidated Street Railway, and was reelected with 76 percent of the vote in March, 1940. Mansion, while not unaware the worries of Democratic chieftains shared about Langlie's potency, was "happy to cooperate" in getting the Reconstruction Finance Corporation to turn the Street Railway into electric trolleys.[62] Breaking almost even in Seattle allowed Langlie Governor in November by 5,000 votes of a million cast.

Arthur B. Langlie, pictured in 1941, was governor (1941-1945; 1949-1957) and ran for the U.S. Senate in 1956.

Langlie's alcoholic Norwegian father came to the Olympic Peninsula via Minnesota via North Dakota in 1905, to become grocer. Abstinent Arthur was a University of Washington undergraduate six years, doing stints as a logging camp rigger and a "bindle stiff" in the wheat fields of the Polouse at $6 a day. Out of the Law School in 1926, he conducted a quiet civil practice for nine years, until drafted for the City Council by the New Order of Cincinnatus. The Order was a non-partisan reform vehicle for progressive Republicans and Bourbon Democrats under 35 sidelined by the New Deal. In 1935, Seattle's North end WASPS, among them many prospering Nordics who had gravitated to the high ground, outvoted the commercial and industrial Southern sectors, labor, and the left. For three years Langlie and two other Cincinnatans tangled with a corrupt police department, collecting evidence of a "wide open town." As County Prosecutor at the time Magnuson had a blurred if not blind eye. Losing the mayoralty in 1936 taught Langlie the reformer the liabilities of economizing, and turned him a pragmatist as well as a moralist.

The nation's second youngest governor at 38, He pursued moderation and the Republican progressive's efficiency ethic as assiduously as his ethnic Democratic contemporaries hove to New Deal liberalism. A new Department of the Budget emerged. Purchasing was centralized. Employment Security extended the definition of "injury" to occupational diseases. Republican regulars grumped over appointments of mugwumps and the broadening of civil service by executive fiat. Reforming forest management proved a lost cause against the state officials, all of whom were Democrats, some having a piece of the action.[63] After the outbreak of war, the Governor reflected the nationalism of the electorate before Congress' Tolan Committee in Seattle in 1942. "Every precaution should be made to be humane ... but the people feel this is no time to worry about hurt feelings" among Washington's 38,888 Germans, Italians, Japanese, and Nisei. Most of them lost everything while in Idaho detention camps. The governor's time in the next two years went to preparedness – bond, rubber, salvage and blood drives.

After the Republican surge of 1942, taking Langlie out in 1944 was critical to the Democrats. Magnuson was from Seattle, and most popular, but chested his cards. Knute Hill was shunted out, leaving Wallgren unopposed. Confident and lazy, he did not get underway until August: "I'm running for Governor," he said, "because the people of this state will overwhelmingly vote to reelect Franklin Roosevelt." Langlie's "do-nothing administration of isolationism" could not "best cooperate" with Washington, D.C. Instead, "What this state needs Wallgren can get."[64] Privately, he was bored, and his wife Mabe (Mabel) homesick and eager for the water of Eastern Washington's Soap Lake for her arthritis, or their Palm Desert haunts. Langlie, one of the seven governors campaigning for internationalist Tom Dewey, was defeated by World War II. Boeing had expanded 100 times, pulling in working class Southerners, and tripling the state's blacks. The Governor had correctly backed a liberal soldier vote bill: Democrats harvested three quarters of their votes. And the turnout rose from 46.3 percent in July to an unexcelled 84.5 percent in the general election. Wallgren won by 28,283 votes.[65]

Wallgren's ineptness was evident once he was closer to his constituents. He ignored the departing governor's invitations to budget hearings, carelessly named a cabinet, avoided detail, offended state officeholders, and was partisan. After 1947, he fell victim to a Republican Legislature who investigated perks at parks and the governor's yacht, lending credence to a tougher Langlie's charges of "mismanagement" and "cronyism" in 1948. Wallgren's indecisive and defensive campaign lost by 29,000 votes. His Administrative Assistant later reasoned he had risen to fast.[66] Harry Truman nominated his senatorial colleague to chair the National Security Resources Board. Tellingly, Magnuson backed the Public Utility Districts' Executive director, as the state's other senator, Harry Cain, led an onslaught. Wallgren was finally confirmed as head of the Federal Power Commission in 1950, and served a year.

Langlie initiated the first State Board Against Discrimination, courageously fought for a corporate income tax, almost single-handedly reigned in effected welfare deficits, and executed an unwanted but politically necessary takeover over of the world's largest ferry system. His welfare Initiative 178 neatly summed his 'work ethic' and tenacious anti-Communism. The governor watched with satisfaction the work of Washington's version of the House un-American Activities Committee, the legislature's "Joint Fact Finding Committee on Un-American Activities," which lead to the dismissal of three University professors. He had already swung the anti-Communist cudgel in becoming Washington's first three-term governor in 1952. The victory was made possible because the Tom Dewey's GOP governors nominated Dwight Eisenhower. At the Chicago national convention, it was Langlie who moved the "Fair Play Amendment," undoing Senator Bob Taft's illusion of control of the floor as well as committees. Governor Earl Warren, a Norwegian married to a Swede, released his 70 California voters for the general. Washington's 22 put Ike over the top.[67]

The New Deal's legacy led to Langlie's demise at Magnuson's hands four years later. The ex-chair of the National Governor's Conference, the senior Republican governor, and man "most like Ike,"[68] could not say no the President. The classic Langlie-Magnuson U.S. Senate race of 1956 epitomized the inability of progressive Republicans and states righters to compete politically with New and Fair Dealers. Voters believed "We're Stronger with Magnuson in the U.S. Senate," and, "No man has done more for Washington ... " and were not dissuaded by Langlie's attacks on "the myth that is Magnuson," an image he insisted publicity had built. The Governor's moralistic slashes at Magnuson's personal life eroded his own best asset, caught in the theme "High office demands high principle." The war against Magnuson and Jackson over a Hell's Canyon High Dam on the Snake, Labor's outpouring against "Right to Work" Initiative 198, and Eisenhower's weak price supports, unequal to the Democrat's promise "parity" for stagnated farmers, bled the Governor white. Jackson duly nominated Magnuson for President at the Democrats' conclave, then campaigned two months in the hustings for his ally.[69] The seniority Langlie had bestowed in 1944 now haunted him. Washingtonians knew they could be "visibly pro-Ike," and "substantially Democratic," and continue to enjoy federal largesse. The Republicans' national keynoter won only the state's smallest county, ending his career as chairman of the McCall's Corporation in New York.[70]

Langlie was first undercut by the clash of the three Scandinavian Republicans who ran to succeed him as governor. All were from Tacoma, dividing Pierce County, the state's second largest. Thirty-six year old Don Eastvold had been a State Senator. He attracted attention as a Eisenhower advocate at the convention, and, applauded by the Governor as having the "highest qualifications," became Attorney General in 1952. Liquor, women, and real estate speculation soon eroded his image.[71] Don and his father Seth, for twenty years the dynamic and autocratic president of Pacific Lutheran College, were each other's undoing. Regents discovered a reason to depose the President when they found $1 million from the Rockefeller Foundation had gone into Don's speculative development at Ocean Shores.[72] Then Langlie, stupefied by the Attorney General's seduction of one of his secretary, turned to five term Congressman Thor Tollefson. Eastvold made a "critical analysis ... [of] the failures of certain [executive] departments," and announced he would fire 90 percent of the governor's appointees.

Thor Tollefson was fourteen when his immigrant father died in 1915. He supported his family in the mills and shipyards, not returning to high school until 1922. He finished in two years, was class valedictorian, student body president and a three-sport letterman. A graduate of the U. of W. Law School in 1930, Tollefson, like Jackson, began his rise as County Prosecutor in 1938. He was the sole Republican on even more Democratic turf. Being pro public power (but not against the privates), for the Hells High Dam, bending over backward for labor, (he opposed Taft-Hartley), on the "Merchant Marine and Fisheries Committee, a devout Lutheran, anti-Communist, and "middle of the road person" could never make Tollefson secure. Veritable dynasties of Tollefson families campaigning in Pierce County may have.[73] Still the county's only Republican after the 1946 election; his popularity surged to the point where he carried the 6th Congressional District by 24,000 votes in 1952, when Eisenhower was taking it by 1,000. Two years later Tollefson become the first congressional chair from either party from the state since 1932.

Tollefson families from and in "the Land of Thor,"[74] who had lived in Pierce County since the 1890's numbered 370 by the 1970's. For instance, Julius Tollefson of the Sons of Norway, Norden Lodge No. 2, was the "longest continuous member … in the U.S.," and headed the 1925 celebration of 100 years of Norse immigration. Thor was master of Ceremonies for the Lodge's Golden Anniversary in 1954. His brother Harold Tollefson was mayor of Tacoma in 1955, Ronald Tollefson a city councilman in 1957, and mother Bertha "Mother of the Year" in Tacoma in 1958.[75]

Pressured by "our governor and his friends" and the daily papers to commit, and simultaneously not to give up his seat to a Democrat, he delayed a decision even longer than Langlie. Despite a "slight lead" in a February, 1956 poll, Tollefson's heart was never in the gubernatorial race. He bowed out in mid-July.[76] Langlie was left with Lieutenant Governor Emmett Anderson, a clubman and Republican Mon Wallgren.[77] Eastvold covertly backed the winner, Albert D. Rosellini, still the state's only other "ethnic" governor. Rosellini later mused, "Tollefson was the only Republican possibility who worried me. Thor could attract Democratic votes. He had done so repeatedly."[78]

An Inverted Pyramid: Scandinavians in Washington's Politics 1889-1989

In many ways the political milieu on the Pacific was almost opposite the Midwest. Scandinavians aggregated into fewer counties in Washington, but clustered less. Half lived in coastal cities, where traditionalism dissolved the closer the logger, fisherman or farmer was to the port. The clan was as often a club. And in this least churched state, it was often a place to meet. Cultural Protestant morality and anti-Communism were the hallmarks of most elected Nordics. Most of their leading figures took office as Republicans, but Magnuson and Jackson more than equaled their power. English was not a handicap for the second and third generations in the West. Nor was a lack lawyers: every Scandinavian entering statewide or congressional office save four was one. Six of the eight in high office were degreed by same school in a decade.

Scandinavians did lead in "Americanization" in the Northwest, largely ignoring organized ethno-politics, perhaps in part out of aversion to politics as practiced by the Irish, Germans, and Southern Europeans from the urban Northeast to Chicago. Here, there was no other sizable ethnic group to react to. Filings and outcomes at the county and legislative levels lend no credence to an "ethnic" as much as natural inclinations aided their confreres. The extraordinary showings of the talented cadre of Scandinavian political leaders in state and congressional races from 1932 to 1957 was not due to partisan activism or a base of local offices by kin, but to forceful their personalities. Word-of-mouth among the parallel clans, social clubs, and ethnic media facilitated the phenomenon. The Nordic's psychology of integration dictated that their "reformist proclivity" be exercised not as "radicals," who were relegated to the fringe, but in the mainstream. Assumptions in Washington, as late as 1952, that names ending in "son" or "sen" were "worth 100,000 votes" in statewide races are nebulous. There was a bonus – if one's opponent was not also a Scandinavian.

In Norwegian-Americans and the Politics of Dissent 1880-1924, Lowell Soak confirms that Ethno-cultural motives "operated independently of the intervening influence of the states' political culture…" in the Old Northwest[79] On the Pacific Coast, ethnic appeals were indirect; the primal need was to fit in, not be set apart. On the Pacific Slope ethnic politics was as tenuous as the Turner thesis. This was not a "frontier," it was largely urban, almost entirely American. Still independent and often contrarian, Scandinavians resisted joining parties. Political clubs were as much for discussion and socializing. They did not try for or hold public office in projectable numbers, contrary to Midwestern historians' presumptions of inclusive involvement. The Depression, in overturning the old order in both parties, opened the way for exceptional individuals, as the 18 to 48 year tenures of Tollefson, Langlie, Magnuson and Jackson testify. The essential impact of these nationally significant "Scandinavians" on their state was to ingrain and sustain personality-driven, weak-party, independent politics.

Charting An Inverted Pyramid: Scandinavians in Washington's Politics 1889-1989

A. Federal and State electees. Grand Total 186

Party	U.S. Senator	Cong.	Gov.	Lt.Gov.	Treas.	Atty Gen	SPI	Aud	Sec.St	Tot.off.
R	0	1	1	0	1	0	1	0	1	5
D	5	4	1	0	0	0	0	0	9	

Possibly Scandinavian:

Party	U.S. Senator	Cong.	Gov.	Lt.Gov.	Treas.	Atty Gen	SPI	Aud	Sec.St	Tot.off.
R	0	1	0	1	0	1	0	4		
D	0	1	0	0	0	0	0	0	1	

Totals all other candidacies:

23	62	19	14	20	14	13	8	13

B. The Legislature. Possible total incumbents 2,423

Possibly Scandinavian:

House	74	78	152
Senate	31	10	41
Percent:	4.3	3.6	7.9

C. Nordic Nominees Compared to all Candidacies, in the Seven "Scandinavian Counties" (Whatcom, Skagit, Snohomish, King, Grays Harbor, Kitsap, Spokane), in

Selected General Elections.
1916: 11/97 **1922:** 10/99 **1936:** 11/106 **1940:** 3/33 **1948:** 6/31 **1952:** 16/102 **1956:** 16/93

Total general election nominees, all parties:	634*
Total Scandinavian nominees:	73
Percent:	11.5%

*Perhaps one fourth of the Scandinavian filees were on minor party tickets prior to 1948, and virtually none thereafter.

D. County Officials in Two "Scandinavian Counties," 1889-1989*

	Snohomish	Skagit
Commissioner	0 0 0 8	2 1
Assessor	5 0 2 4	0 0
Assessor	4 1 2 0	0 0
Treasurer	0 4 1 1	
Prosecutor	2 1 0 1	
Clerk	5 2 3 3	3 0
Totals:*	R D Other	R D Other
	24 0 9	17 5 1
Percent:		6.1

*Coroner and sheriff excluded as requiring special qualifications.

E. Selected Statewide Nordic Candidacies, "Scandinavian Counties"

	Snohomish	Skagit	%	King	Pierce
1916: St. Auditor					
C.W. Claussen (R)*	9,067	4,758	50	39,527	19,473
Otto A. Case (D)	6,536	3,508	32	10,726	14,789
Two others	3,258	1,234		3,586	2,543
1920: U.S. Senate					
2) Republican Primary					
Wesley L. Jones (R)	5,173	2,565		21,488	7,352
Three others:	4,806	2,820		20,939	6,194
1940: U.S. Senate					
Mon Wallgren (D)*	24,555	9,210	53	129,497	44,716
Stephen Chadwick (R)	14,469	8,295	47	97,753	29,149
1952: U.S. Senate					
Henry M. Jackson (D)*	35,927	10,918	56	72,202	67,328
Harry Cain (R)	18,554	8,554	44	47,643	42,895
1952: Governor					
Arthur B. Langlie (R)*	25,509	10,847	55	164,511	52,119
Hugh B. Mitchell (D)	29,301	8,782	44	197,830	58,958
1952: Congressman At Large					
Don Magnuson (D)*	29,224	9,061		172,239	57,298
Al Canwell (R)	22,963	9,782		172,236	48,586
1956: Governor					
E. Anderson (R)	23,973	997,444	-	47,740	
A. D.Rosellini (D)	37,168	1,092,775	-	65,509	

Chapter 2

All of a Peace: Seattle's Mayors and the Civil Matrix, 1938-1968

George W. Scott

"A Seaport Town"

Seattle's pioneer period (1852-1889) ended abruptly. Rebuilding after the 1889 fire, the arrival of the Great Northern Railway in 1893, and the discovery of gold in the Yukon in 1897 drove its population from 42,000 to 237,000 by 1910. At the turn of the century half of Seattleites lived within a mile of downtown,[1] a robustious seaport of sailors, loggers and suppliers, with a tenderloin of liquor and skin traders too profitable to suppress. Mayors got one, then two year terms, though few were reelected, and there were 37 in the 49 years between 1889 and 1938. Hiram (Hi) Gill personifies the era. He was elected in 1910 on the promise to make – really keep –Seattle an open town, with one difference: gambling and prostitution were to be confined to "south of the line" (Yesler Way). "This is a seaport town ain't it?" he rhetorically asked.[2] Gill chose the perfect Police Chief for the task. Charles "Wappy" Wappenstein was soon reportedly taking in $10 a month per prostitute for "protection" to keep his officers from raiding their brothels. "I may have let things get away from me," the Mayor confessed after his recall in 1911, when "Wappy" was on his way to Walla Walla. The "things" included an immense 500 room sporting house to overlook the city from Beacon Hill, for which the City Council had vacated a street and granted a 15 year lease.[3] Gill was also accused of colluding with the Seattle Electric Company and the Boston firm of Stone and Webster who had been forced to lower their rates

A car of the Seattle Municipal Street Railway, a raging controversy for two decades, during regrading.

because of competition from Seattle City Light. He Gill also fired popular Superintendent James D. Ross (1872-1939).[4]

His 1911 recall was a "turning point" that began a close run battle between the forces for "sin" and "decency" lasting 50 years. Women had voted for the first time, and 20,000 of the 23,000 registered did. Gill's corruption coalesced the Clean City Organization, The Public Welfare League, the Municipal League and the Ministerial Federation. Accordingly, the chameleon ran for a "closed town" in 1914 and won, in large part because the Employer's Association alienated Labor by endorsing his opponent. Then Washington passed a "dry" law in 1916, four years before the nation. To the startlement of some, the mayor personally led raids on restaurants, liquor stores and even the Rainier Club, causing $20,000 damage, and offending even Prohibitionists. To cover himself with Labor during a waterfront strike he refused to back the employers' attempt to get an "open shop." And after the "Everett Massacre" left four dead in November, 1916, he declared that the sheriffs had fired "without right or justification into the crowd on the boat [the Verona], and were the murderers...not the I.W.W.'s"[5] The mayor was "diselected" in 1917 after a trial for accepting police protection money from bootleggers, in the surge anti-strike patriotism came on the heels of the nation's entry into World War I. Gill visible accomplishment was proving restricting vice was impossible.[6]

Moral and economic issues were joined by public ownership of utilities, and the incoming tide for prohibition. Those in the Progressive Movement (1901-16), never agreed on an agenda, and weakened their causes with different and often conflicting priorities, as illustrated by two mayors of that era. Self-made surveyor George Cotterill (1865-1958), arrived in Seattle in 1883 with $5 in his pocket, and soon was second in command to the dynamic City Engineer R.H. Thompson, and constructed the city's first sewers after 1892. He lost his first race for mayor in 1900, being identified as a Democrat on Republican turf. Displaying the same persistence with a smaller constituency, he became one of the three Democrats in the 42 man State Senate in 1906, backing the direct primary, the Lake Washington Ship Canal, shorelines for city parks and suffrage. He lost to Gill in 1912, but his fervent stand for "local option," a device he hoped would control alcohol, drew the moral crusaders and middle class and women.

Cotterill was in the older Populist tradition: "Reform consisted of a battle against vice and monopoly. He vetoed Councilman Austin Griffith's Welfare Board, a vehicle for the Progressives' eagerness to concert and improve city social services, and their desire to move to new issues. Cotterill feared the 'civil rights' portion of the ordnance limiting arrests without warrants would make it harder to clamp down on vice. After America's entry into World War I in 1917 his troubles were the reverse of Gill's, being too tolerant of street speeches by Socialists and union organizers, and to strident on prohibition. He redoubled the folly when criticized for a riot that destroyed the Pioneer Square offices of the IWW and Socialists by forbidding street gatherings, closing saloons, and suspending publication of the idiosyncratic Seattle Times."[7] Seattle police made 17,078 warrant less arrests (a third of which were dismissed), creating new opportunities for graft to the untrained force. Erstwhile admirers felt he had violated free speech and assembly. Cotterill did not seek reelection.[8]

The new majority of voters apparently for a "clean" city were at odds over how police power should be exercised. Progressive and prohibitionist Austin Griffiths was Gill's Police Chief in his second term. Progressives fought for home rule, participative democracy via new charters (the cities' constitutions), "efficiency," and "socialization of urban life" through municipal ownership and ameliorative social services.[9] Seattle's burgeoning middle class was now comfortable enough for the civic "Social Gospel" to be attractive. After 1910 the Municipal League, perhaps under the illusion that Gill's defeat had ended corruption, turned to "constructive policies rather than political reform. "Civic consciousness" would lead to municipal light and transportation, and "welfare:" public markets, hospitals, baths, lodging, employment bureaus and playgrounds. Its voice was the short-lived Seattle Sun, which appealed to "salaried and wage-earning homemakers."[10] The tenets of 19th century Populism were absorbed by the middle class progressive reformers who found a home with Teddy Roosevelt's Progressives, only to be squelched by President Taft's regular Republicans in 1912. Uncomfortable with the Gill and Cotterill extremes, in 1914 a Municipal League referendum tried strengthen civil service, remove "public welfare" from the mayor's office, substitute a 30 member city Council, and return to the ward system (ostensibly to end "log-rolling' by nine members elected at large). "With our citizens enlightened, there is no reason why the various wards should not choose men of the highest type …. The day of the political machine is past."[11]

Some Progressive were not so ebullient. Labor, noting the Chamber of Commerce was for the new charter, and afraid its edge in mobilizing members spread across the voting "wards" which helped it elect city councilmen would be lost, organized a special committee to fight the change. The First Presbyterian Church's Reverend Mark Matthews, the towering point man for the religious front,[12] suspected return to the ward system would bring saloon men to power. Griffiths ran for mayor against the utilities monopolies, and to confirm an issue already supposedly 'settled' by the recall and Cotterill's election: a "closed" town. He placed fourth, and the division of moral and economic reformers allowed Hi Gill to come back.[13] The referendum's smashing defeat made plain the upper middle classes were willing to lead, but labor and the lower middle class would not follow.[14]

The voter's 1911 decision to own municipal street cars to compete with the traction company proved a disaster for both. In 1916, Gill opposed it on practical grounds, as he did the expansion of City light beyond the city limits: there were too few customers. Competitor Austin Griffith's promotion of morality and economy remained constant, as outdated as the latter may have been in his campaigns into the Depression. Democrats and Progressives had "an emphatic mandate to bring health to a suffering people." If they did not, "a radical party will come within the next [few] years …."Drift, dribble and dole leads to disaster." Business and professional men needed no convincing, but he had little appeal for Labor and the lower middle class. "Fighting "police arrogance," "raids and round-ups" done in the name of national security, and the "smug moralists" trying to forestall prohibition was not popular in wartime. He lost in the 1918 primary. The "Street Railway" deteriorated for another 20 years, becoming a perennial political pincushion.[15]

A want of "normalcy" set in once the War was over in 1919, and the mayoral cycle of corruption and cashiering repeated. Advertising Dentist Edwin J. "Doc" Brown's regime (1922-26), was the 20's edition of Gill's first term. This brought on Bertha Landes, the first female to be mayor of a major city, who set her own anchor among the downtowners.[16] In 1921, as President of the Seattle Federation of Women's Clubs, she orchestrated a week-long Women's Educational Exhibit for Washington Manufacturers impressively staffed by 1,000 women that was a balm to the spirits of businessmen in the grips of the post-war recession. In 1926, after a term on the Council, she defeated Brown by 6,000 votes, then began a "municipal house cleaning," asking citizens to blow the whistle on bootleggers, offering $1 for reports of reckless drivers and appointing professionals who ran a scandal-free administration. Despite the endorsements of the major newspapers, the Central labor Council, the Prohibition Party and Women's organizations, she lost to Frank Edwards a well-bankrolled unknown in 1928. "Sex prejudice," and resistance to "petticoat rule," the idea that a city's status was hurt by having a woman at the helm were transparent.[17] Seattle's abiding ambivalence about social maoris and what was good for business was just as evident. Edwards, the "businessman mayor" delivered on his promise to "open up the town again." Edwards was recalled in 1931, after City Light Superintendent J.D. Ross was fired (for the second time).

The Great Depression's imitation of Hi Gill was demagogic half- Harvard educated defense lawyer John F. Dore, elected mayor in 1932. The Depression was nearing

its bottom, and the Banker's Clearing House soon refused to extend the city any more credit, forcing it to issue payroll warrants cashed at discount. Dore clamped down with pay cuts and curtailed city services. He tried to close the police detective division to put more patrolmen on the beat, ordered the release of petty offenders of personal recognizance, banned city employees from taking autos home, and asked the Council to lid all salaries at $3,000 – except his. The violent West Coast strike of Harry Bridge's longshoremen in 1934 added to public discomfort, and divided resurgent Labor as seriously as it had Populists and Progressives. Dore's use of mounted police also put off Labor. His successor, lawyer Charles L. "Charlie" Smith actively entered the maritime strike on the side of management, serially fired police chiefs, and soon faced a recall.

SMA

Left to right: City Auditor M.H. Strouse, with Cincinnatus councilmen Fred Hamley, Arthur Langlie. David Lockwood and Mrs. F.F. Powell in 1935.

When he was not fighting the Council or the Board of Public works, he stormed about Communists "infecting the unions," and called for "finger printing every man, woman and child in the country" to discourage crime. The Municipal League decided Smith failed his pledge to rid the city of Chinese lotteries and assorted sin, and near the end of his term called for his impeachment. He did not survive the 1936 primary.

Flamboyant Mayor John F. Dore (right) and Artic explorer Richard Byrd in the mid-1930s.

The left-leaning Bridges drove business into the arms of the Teamster's Dave Beck, who offered stability in return for higher wages. He bluntly told the Chamber of Commerce, "There can't be any such thing as a labor union without coercion. The word 'peaceful' and the word 'picketing' don't go together... Industry wants to be controlled by labor unions."[18] Dore decided business had deserted him, and swept back into office in 1936 as Labor's champion. He unhorsed the police by selling their mounts, and the Teamsters proclaimed the "New Dore." The Seattle Star, until then his most fervent backer, offered an epithet: "the revolving Dore."

Unlike the Progressives, the New Deal took little interest in urban reform. Big city bosses were its power base, and FDR was preoccupied with the national crisis The middle classes' outlet in Seattle was the New Order of Cincinnatus, the city's only "municipal party." Founded in 1933, it adopted the public service credo of the Roman farmer-soldier-statesman Lucius Quintus Cincinnatus. The New Order attracted 1,000 professionals in two years, moderate Republicans shut out of partisan politics by the New Deal, and Jeffersonian Democrats unsettled by it. The age limit was 35. The "Oath for Candidates for Public Office" written in 1934 was Progressivism tinctured by the Depression and disgust: "To work for the reduction of government expenses, unneeded employees, and "absolute cleanliness and honesty."[19] They organized on para-military basis and paraded in green hats, singing "Stout-Hearted Men." The Order's three novice nominees for the City Council in 1934 collided with 30 others, including two state legislators, two Communists, and "enough dark horses for a circus parade." Accountant David Lockwood won the sixth and last spot in the primary without editorial endorsements on the canvassing of

Cincinnatus enthusiasts, and led in the general election. The Seattle Central Labor Council and the new Washington Commonwealth Federation, an amalgam of liberals from Technocrats to Trotskyites, endorsed opponents: the Cincinnatans were "tools of a Fascist dictatorship."

The Order's nominees in 1935, attorneys Arthur Langlie 35, and Fred Hamley 31, argued City Light employees should be in civil service, and Superintendent Ross should not be given power to negotiate the takeover of Puget sound Power and Light: the $95 million asking price was too high. Grafting on a grand scale was implied: Why had the Council majority interred Lockwood's inquiry into the city's garbage contract? The two Cinncinatans led, followed by their new ally Mrs. F. F. Powell, who ran 10,000 votes ahead of the top incumbent. She and council chair John Carroll helped launch the trio's nightly inspections of vice in collaboration with the Council of Churches that found 60 speakeasies, gambling dens and hooker havens. Police Chief Walter Kirtley reflected the voters' abiding ambivalence about vice. Conditions were "better than in the past," he insisted, then lapsed into a "lengthy dissertation" on how all ordinances called for liberal construction. The Chief was not about to arrest anyone he could not convict. "Pillars of the church," he noted, were just as equivocal. They pled for enforcement, then that their properties – on which illegal activities took place – not be abated.[20] The Cincinnatan's answer was protecting the chief from pressure with a five year term.

Given the "strong council-weak mayor" system adopted at the turn of the century, department heads turned their attention to the nine councilmen as their budgets were revised downward. Opting to trim rather than tax, Lockwood extracted $564,000 from a $2,027,000 deficit for 1936, a substantial amount in addition to absorbing a $335,000 debit carried forward from 1934.[21] Tactics like substitution of prowler cars for police sub-stations began a recall campaign by the North End Federated Clubs, and John Carroll's retirement put Cincinnatus back in to the minority. "As long as a mugwump organization is a hopeless minority of dedicated reformers," Lorin Peterson wrote in the Day of the Mugwump, "its problems are relatively simple." With success, "the single-mindedness, the easy blacks and whites of the campaign vanish, and in their place come the confusing demands of power and its wise exercise."[22]

Undaunted, the Order ran Langlie against Dore for mayor in 1936. Dore courted his former patrons in business: "You can't attract tourists to a Sunday School town. I'll make a San Francisco out of it." Exploiting his "ostreperous eloquence," he hired halls for one-man 90 minute exhibitions. Langlie conceded a three-way race: "The ex-mayor who disappointed you – The present mayor [Smith] who has disgusted you – or a Cincinnatus mayor with a real program backed by a sympathetic City Council."[23] Dave Beck doubted Dore, but was offended that Langlie chose not to negotiate with an emissary. In hours Teamsters were on the street for

MAYORALTY ELECTION
PRIMARY
SEATTLE: 1938

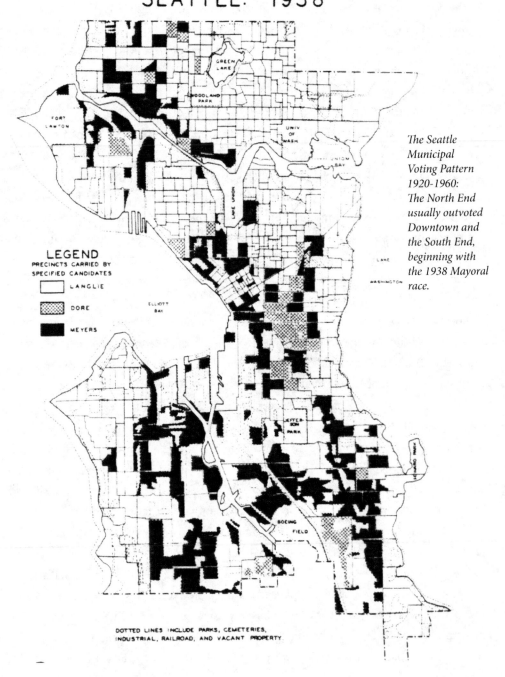

LEGEND
PRECINCTS CARRIED BY
SPECIFIED CANDIDATES

LANGLIE

DORE

MEYERS

*The Seattle
Municipal
Voting Pattern
1920-1960:
The North End
usually outvoted
Downtown and
the South End,
beginning with
the 1938 Mayoral
race.*

DOTTED LINES INCLUDE PARKS, CEMETERIES,
INDUSTRIAL, RAILROAD, AND VACANT PROPERTY.

the mayor. Langlie lost by 7,000 votes, and Dore set out to pay his debt. "Brother Dave Beck was the greatest factor in my election, and I say again I am going to pay back my debt to Dave Beck and the Teamsters in the next two years, regardless of what happens."[24] That Summer police stood by in a protracted strike as Beck's "plug-uglies" helped unionize the PI. There was more turmoil as the Teamsters began a "March to the Sea" to blunt Harry Bridges' and the Longshoremen's "March Inland." By 1938 Seattleites knew debts, mismanagement and the city's fiscal condition would soon stop the streetcars in their tracks. Riders had fallen by half, payments were seven years in arrears, the operating deficit $4.5 million, and receivership imminent. On his death bed at Providence Hospital days before the general election the broken man confessed he had been misled on a refinancing plan.[25]

The "Day of the Mugwump" was over when Cincinnatus lost two council races in 1937, but its climax came when Langlie ran for mayor a second time the following Spring, asking a " shouting repudiation of the misrule that has been Seattle's lot." His opponent was Lieutenant Governor Victor Aloysius Meyers was the epitome of the era's burlesque politics. In a previous mayoral race he had campaigned atop a beer wagon, until a wheel fell off on Fourth Avenue. Now he strode up it dressed as Gandhi in gold-rimmed glasses and a white robe, trailed by a goat on a golden chain. Meyers' inability to transfer his popularity as an uplifting New Dealer,[26] Langlie's had no partisan identity, and a 30 year demographic shift insured Meyers' downfall. Just 15 percent of Seattleites now lived within a mile of downtown. Property values had doubled despite the Depression, especially on Capitol Hill and the new houses on the hillsides North of the Ship Canal, home of the burgeoning middle class. The steady Northward shift of the population became the calculus to municipal politics. The burghers could stand corruption and confusion. "Circus politics," "radicalism" and chaos were beyond their ken. World War II prosperity soon quelled the class clashes of the 30's. By 1950, 79.7 percent of the city was single family dwellings. Seattle was second of 31 major cities in seniors, first in median education and college graduates, and a placid provincial center.

Arthur Langlie and "The Queen City of the Northwest"

The gauntlet was thrown down to Beck over wage increases for the city's garbage contractor. The Cincinnatans believed he had connived with Diamond Truck Transport to get "scale," then ask for higher rates. "The sole question is," Langlie's draft veto message read, "shall the City ... be brought to its knees by the Teamster's union and its threat to stop garbage collection ... ?" "Frank [beforehand] discussions" between councilmen were the new mode.[27] While still on the council, Langlie moved a no strike clause. The contract was vetoed, rewritten, and repassed – with just three nays. His position consolidated, Dave Beck now took only a passing interest in municipal affairs. But his detractors, Langlie chief among them, kept him center stage for 20 years, winning votes as bulwarks against this disturber of the burgher's new-found peace.[28]

Draining the law enforcement swamp took another 25 years. Langlie knew the force was "very corrupt," and taking in an estimated $160,000 a month in graft. Any pressure on vice and gambling except was to keep it "below the [Yesler Way] line." Cincinnatus' granting of five year terms for the police chief ironically left Langlie with Dore's. The chief admitted collecting protection money had "been for years just as much a part of a policeman's way of life...as any other thing he does..." Episodes in the mayor's office, where he complained of "too many prostitutes," framed his predicament and the chief's technique. The Chief asked Langlie if he wanted them closed down. Langlie said "Some of them." The chief: "All or none." Langlie: "All right then, close them." The ladies moved to new locations. Langlie: "This makes you look foolish." The Chief: "Do you want them opened up again? He [the Mayor] just looked at the ceiling.... Well, I guess you want them opened up again, and I left the office." The Chief claimed he would follow any policy set down, "but never got one in writing."[29] "Bad" morals was "good" business, and opinion still divided. Langlie also knew Times was right; "Numerous worthy and responsible citizens pass judgment [on an administration] solely in accord with what they believe to be the city's moral status." Unable to stop vice or gambling, he and his successors solace was the "arrest and fine" system – which had the virtue of bringing another $400,000 a year to the city. Gambling was likewise regulated so as to bring revenue to the city rather than to policemen.[30]

Confrontation turned to consensus, but New Deal dollars were needed to solve the perennial headache. The Mayor was "quite blue" when the Reconstruction Finance Corporation's legal staff almost derailed a $10.2 million refinancing of the Street Railway by making it "too...involved for legislative consumption."[31] The agency soon relented on supervisory control as well. The tracks were torn up, and the electric "trackless trolley" busses symbolic of the unfolding era rolled in late 1940.

Cincinnatus' reformers became pragmatists. Hamley was still the mayor's alter ego as Water Superintendent, authoring a budget that went to the Council the day after is inauguration, and passed in five. Langlie took advice not to propose specific budget cuts in 1940, and simply set $600,000 as the council's goal.[32] With peace pervading city hall, the trolleys humming, and city finances buoyed by the defense buildup, he campaigned little, trying to be reelected for the $75 filing fee. He got 77.2 percent of vote, becoming the second mayor to be reelected in 20 years. Langlie won the Governorship in November by 5,000 votes out of a million cast by holding 49.3 percent of Seattleites, in the face of a third term for FDR.[33]

Bill Devin: "The Mayor Who Finished Making Seattle Respectable"

A new municipal majority was coalescing, and Langlie's popularity molded appeals. Bill Devin, his appointee as police judge[34] was the fifteenth and last to file for the unexpired term. He had changed record keeping to end ticket fixing, persuaded the legislature separate criminal from traffic offenses, and pled for the chronic alcoholics he saw, for whom "nothing is being done." Devin insisted he was a "realist," not a "crusader," and had "no intention" of 'shut[ting] down the city' as critics claimed, adding, "the forces of corruption never relax." Seattle had "tasted the fruits of good … government," and wanted them to continued. He lost to Democratic County Auditor Earl Millikin, who captured the partisan and some of the puritan vote on the same premise: build on Langlie's foundations, and end the "queer gimmicks of government" that made Seattle the "laughing stock of the nation."[35]

Milliken, a Kansan, teacher, Army reserve artillery captain, Mason, and former President of the Northwest Football League socially fit the middle class image. He was undone by the CIO's upset over renomination of Langlie's police chief, inability to bring the department under control, and vacillation, including leaving town while the debate over the chief was going on.[36] Congressman Warren Magnuson's confidant reported after the 1942 primary, a precursor to the

SMA

Mayor William F. Devin selling war bonds in "Victory Square" between Fourth and Fifth avenues and what is now Rainier Square and the Fairmount Olympic Hotel, in 1942.

Republican come back in the Fall, "Once again we had the usual Millikin race with everything wrong with it last year ….There is a good chance he will be defeated …. He was very kind and appointed men in the Langlie camp to offices [so] they would not run against him. They [sp] thing left for him …[is] to conduct himself as he would get the Democratic vote behind him. He missed every chance to sock Devin and Langlie." Another, Mark Matthewson, agreed. "From the Republican side I think there is a very definite change even in this [First Congressional] District as evidenced by Devin's overwhelming majority. The city election got down to a vote for or against Beck …." A third surmised, "As between …Beck and Earl…I do not know that there is a great deal of choice. Earl is…honest…though frankly he has been rather ineffective, and at the beginning did some foolish things …. Bill Devin is personally an awfully nice fellow …."[37]

Devin predictably said it was encouragement from civic stalwarts "that prompts me to take a part in politics that I would not otherwise do." He was no longer a novice, resolving "to reclaim ... government from the hands of the racketeers and leeches ... ."and "condonation for a price."[38] He denied Labor was an issue, was for collective bargaining and impartiality, (both Langlie stances), and in the next breath asserted, "Dave Beck's control of my opponent began secretly before the [1940] election ... .setting the Teamster chief apart as "spokesman for a small group of selfish minded leaders ... ." a signal to Beck's enemies in the rank and file. "We just got rid of one stooge as mayor, and now they want to hand us another," Beck growled.[39] Devin won by 20,000 of 108,000 votes. The State and city might be among the nation's most unionized; but as to Labor, it was surely the most divided. The Teamsters Promotion League continued to vocally back Democrats, but did less to get out the vote – and gave to incumbents. Its leader warred with A.F. of L. counterparts and sided with the building trades, making the Central Labor Council more conservative.[40]

WASP morality and positive human relations was the motifs of Devin's five terms at City Hall (1942-1952). Adversaries were always "controlled by interests detrimental to the city's welfare," in contrast to the majority, who wanted "good, clean, honest government."[41] William Franklin Devin, son of a Missouri Presbyterian minister, is captured by his genteel aphorisms: "The Communities, the village, and the cities are still the abiding place of American Democracy ... " "Honesty is the first and paramount requisite of any public official," "The spirit of give and take," balanced budgets, and "efficient and courteous service," the essence of public life.[42] Seattle, long the way station of mariners, adventurers, and lands' end for emigrants had turned inward, but still had "little sense of identity." Bill Devin was there to reinforce its character. As chair of the Civilian War Commission, the mayor promoted preparedness and Victory Gardens "Victory Square" on Union Street between the Olympic Hotel and the White Henry Stewart Building opened in May, 1944, and his noons were spent greeting veterans and selling war bonds. Strikes were unpatriotic. "Good government" and the "old pioneer spirit" were the means of job creation. His biweekly radio homiletics dwelt on "test [civil defense]," the need for 'mother-in-law' apartments, the citizens' "responsibility to avoid the reefs and shoals of financial disaster ... class prejudice and partisanship, to provide protection against raider from without and saboteurs within ... to deal fairly, justly and courteously with all on board." The Council was to act in the "spirit of co-pilots. In a city throbbing with 19 shipyards, the Boeing boom, 100,000 in-migrants, and a new wave of soldier-induced vice, charges of "smug complacency" and "a futility of inactivity" fell on deaf ears. Seattle had no longer had a need to be the "New York of the Pacific." [43]

Devin made major progress in empowering the executive, initiating professional law enforcement, in race relations, and "full scale" planning. For four years he was unable to either appoint a new police chief, or get two-thirds of the Council to remove the incumbent, and settled for an Advisory Commission.[44] In 1946, a the new city charter, the first serious revision in 56 years was approved, [As late as 1941 the voters approved a referendum forbidding the mayor to remove any member of the Board of Public Works (directors of the largest departments mid-term, or the chief until the Council had heard formal charges].[45] He named George Eastman, the first chief chosen on merit, and brought in police science professors to give credence to mayoral appointment of the chief, a police academy, Records Bureau and motorization. In effect, the "tolerance policy" was simply more tightly defined. "Sporadic" enforcement ended, and "large scale" prostitution and gambling were "repressed." Policing "small card games" and the like was a waste of manpower. Major crime did drop 17 percent in his decade, then shot up 51 percent in the next 1953-54. By then, Seattle now had the lowest police ratio of the five major West Coast cities, but had "simply not kept up."[46]

Demographic and racial changes and the affluence impelled by World War II were silently eroding the burgher-business-civic matrix. Between 1940 and 1958, King County grew 73 percent, and industrial jobs 192 percent. Blacks were one percent of the population when Boeing and the Shipyards began to draw migrants from the rural south, but Boeing's engineers union resisted hiring blacks until near the end of the war. By 1950 there were 15,668 in Seattle, up 413 percent. Protests came from whites, and complaints of discrimination from blacks, as they dispersed North along Capitol Hill. Langlie realized Devin was "sitting on a powder keg relative to the race problem."[47] The Mayor's response was the Civic Unity Committee, linked to the NAACP and the Urban League, and sensitively led by George Greenwood, President of the Seattle First National Bank. A "persuading approach" by "respectable, reliable" people which would have met with derision at a later date worked. The original C.U.C. had just two blacks, but managed to defuse violence, educate, resolve incidents, and repatriate Japanese-Americans from internment camps in 1944.[48] In 1950, Devin reminded the Council about the lack of low income housing as not "morally or politically" acceptable, and made the first call for federal aid as the only alternative. The strongest tribute to Devin's social conscience is in relations with defeated Japan. At the height of the war Devin could "think of no enemy more adroit and clever at deception than … the Jap," yet he was one of the first mayors to visit Tokyo in 1946, chaired the Seattle-Kobe Sister City Committee, and found special satisfaction leading the Japanese-American Mayors' Conference.[49] He was honored in 1953 by the American Conference of Christians and Jews for humanitarian work.

Devin's instigation of a Planning Commission was as important. A professional director was hired in 1945, and a Comprehensive Plan adopted in three years. But the city's fiscal capacity was unchanged. As chair of the Home Rule Committee of the Association of Washington Cities trying to capture "a reasonable and uniform share of … revenue," the Mayor spoke to deaf ears in Olympia. In the Devin decade, the Cedar River Watershed was acquired, $50 million spent on the Alaskan Way Viaduct, and Seattle's take over of Puget Sound Power and Light within its boundaries ended a distracting 30 year war.[50]

The Mayor's fifth run in 1952, another referendum on "good government," "truth and falsehood," augured well. His District Organizer was Joel Pritchard, a prototype of the talented young Eisenhower Republicans.[51] But Assistant Federal Prosecutor and former Superior Court judge Allan Pomeroy managed to win by 3,000 votes. Television was not Devin's medium, and as Fred Baker, also Langlie's advertising counsel put it, "Just being honest, Christian, able, sincere is not enough. Too many people subconsciously, or consciously want something else." The public was weary of militant decency. Baker added, "Many of your [Devin's] friends no longer vote in the city." Upwardly mobile bourgeoisie was now moving onward and outward – to Eastside suburbs. The Municipal News mourned the passing of a "Golden Era," and "a remarkable performance."[52] The establishment, from Rabbi Raphael Levine, to Stimson Bullitt, to the Governor Langlie nodded.

P.I. MOHAI

The exception that proved the rule. 'Democratic' Mayor Alan Pomeroy served a single term in the 1950s.

Gordon Clinton: The Matrix at High Tide (1956-1964)

Allan Pomeroy was willful, and trapped in the 'weak mayor' system. The Council refused his partisan appointees. He stubbornly vetoed their ordinances, made personal attacks, and was truculent. Nothing was accomplished.[53] In 1960, the Seattle Times and the Post-Intelligencer ran features on Gordon Clinton, a 35 year old former Deputy Prosecutor and FBI Agent, ignoring two primary opponents. Like Langlie, Clinton demanded the mayor's donors list be public, and resurrected the police issue. A futile request to the council for 50 more officers a week before the final election served only as a reminder of the Pomeroy's impotence. His ads about "Devin's hand-picked boy," and pitting "The people and Pomeroy vs. the clique" were only half correct. The Eisenhower-inspired Young Republicans of King County, marshalled "1,000 young men for Clinton," as Joel Pritchard collaborated with David Lockwood, Fred Baker, and the county GOP.[54] The other possibility, Ford dealer and World's Fair leader Joe Gandy, was in many ways his opposite. But "both present [ed] prominence to a small but influential group of men who really run Seattle" as the Argus affirmed. Clinton's 89,111 to 80,608 victory was clinched by predictable North End pluralities. His election was a passing of the baton from the sons of Cincinnatus to another coterie of Republican reformers soon to make Dan Evans governor.[54]

The police issue refused to die. Clinton moved to full delegation, pledging not "consult" with the Chief's subordinates. "That has not always been true in the past."[55] Despite the mayor's policy "of charging those people with every possible criminal offense," in April, 1958, there were just 24 vice arrests. Police manpower was minimal.[56] Clinton quietly began to consolidate "certain" county and city police functions the World's Fair in 1962, and suspended the tolerance policy on gambling in 1963, when an undercover investigation indicated "abuses." Afflictions of a different dimension were emerging. When juvenile delinquency went to the unheard of level of 1.7 percent of public school students, the mayor assembled a Metropolitan Youth Commission.

Mayor Gordon Clinton (center), the last of the WASP establishment's designated hitters makes his adjustment to the oncoming era. (ca 1960)

Clinton "would never be classified as a dynamic leader." His less than aggressive "do it by committee," avoid controversy, and turn the other cheek approach was a milder version of Devin.[57] "The mayor's office [has] ... an obligation to suggest new programs," he insisted, and he did so by perfecting the system. In 1957, David Levine was again Council president, as he had been in the late 30's, and as crucial an asset to Clinton as he had been to Langlie. An administrative analysis they commissioned yielded 200 recommendations, but just $3 million in savings, suggesting city operations fiscally tight, if not optimally arranged. Booz, Allen and Hamilton's appraisal echoed "nationwide acclaim" for the utilities, an "enviable" traffic safety record, a balanced budget, cooperation, and the "unusual amount of interest" shown by Seattleites, and obscured structural the deficits of the "weak mayor" system, and lack of specialized staff.[58] At the Municipal League's insistence, planning and personnel were moved under the mayor, incrementally strengthening the office.

The Mayor met weekly with the Muni League's executive, tactfully visited councilmen, doing relaxed negotiating and acting as a conduit for civic ideas. Citizen committees were now "best practice," The council had to and to react. The bottom-up legislating is best seen in the birth of METRO (The Municipality of Metropolitan Seattle). The League first raised the possibility of regional governance in 1951. Clinton named attorney James Ellis, who proved Seattle's most proficient civic builder as committee chair, and he convinced the 1957 legislature to pass the benchmark Urban Renewal Enabling Act.[59] Joel Pritchard led a speakers bureau for METRO, and 5,000 volunteers went door to door in March 1958. Clinton and his advisors overreached: placing mass transit under Metro's umbrella as well inflated the local control shibboleth, and stoked fears of an omnipotent Seattle. Raw sewerage was feeding floating islands of algae on the north end of Lake Washington. Narrowing METRO's boundaries and nominally restricting it to a sewer utility aimed at cleaning up the lake enabled a second referendum to pass in September. Within three years Clinton asked METRO to take on the transportation and garbage functions. In April, 1962 he boosted a $360 million light rail system straddling the Lake. Its double the next year was the community's largest loss in a generation.[60]

The "Queen City" Dethroned?

At mid-century, Bill Devin saw no threat from deterioration or suburbanization. Two thirds of the houses in Seattle had been built since 1920, and the census classified just 1450 acres, or 2 square miles out of 91, as "blighted," and remarkably, just .9 percent were classified substandard, those in the arc southeast of the Central Business District. On Clinton's watch, downtown's was fixation on losing its dominance was exacerbated by fears of decay. The matrix, up to then intent on holding taxes down, reversed itself to become pro-freeway, pollution control, and development. The Central Association, formed in 1958, worked hand in glove with city's planning staff to promote capital projects. Every one of business' "Big Ten" was on the board, and Clinton was in its office so often, " ... it is difficult to distinguish whether he is a public servant or one of our private members."[61] "Lesser Seattle's" reflex to suburbanization was a "Greater Seattle."

Clinton proposed a "full time" "workable" renewal program in 1958, ingenuously premising "no great expense of public funds or serious dislocation of families." The Federal Housing and Home Financing Administration (predecessor to HUD) unexpectedly concurred in the proposal, and a largely business Urban Renewal Advisory Board of 42 was charged with meeting federal mandates under a ten year plan. "Renewal" first meant eliminating blight. Most of the 15 percent of total acreage to be "redeveloped" was in the path of the Seattle Freeway; 30 percent of it was to be rehabbed, 55 percent "conserved." "Slum prevention was largely a matter of code enforcement," the mayor explained in enlisting a chair, and "imagination" the essential ingredient.[62]

Incorporating SURE, (Seattle Urban Renewal Enterprise), legalized the city's partnership with downtown. In April, 1960, an $89,000 planning grant was in hand, and later $2 million to reshape the Yesler-Atlantic neighborhood. The impressive Jackson Street Community Council began redoing 32 blocks, then a smaller parcel on Cherry Hill. Clinton, 21 civic groups, and the Central Association backed SURE's new housing code. The age of locally chosen, federally funded and stipulated social service had begun in Seattle. The Urban Affairs Coordinator Clinton contracted in January, 1958 as a funnel for federal funds metamorphosed into an "Urban Renewal Division" by 1963.

To their credit, Clinton and the Central Association pushed new parks and recreation prior to the Vietnam riots. Council budget chair Dorm Braman compressed the departments' 1960-66 capital requests into an unprecedented referendum for $323 million. Business backed it; after all, 90 percent of bond costs could be paid over 30 years from the general fund. Clinton gave over his campaign to selling them, and in an analogue of Langlie's 1940 walk in, Democrats helped swell a team "swamped" with volunteers. The Teamsters and the King County Labor Council endorsed his opposition, but with Dave Beck of the scene, Labor's business agents were behind Clinton. The Times found "no convincing reason … for replacing the city's … tested leadership." The bonds were adopted, and for the last time, everyone was reelected.

Anticipating the prosperity of a Worlds' Fair further warmed relations between downtown business and labor leaders. Conceived as an economic stimulant in 1951, then as an "antidote" to suburbanization, and next to arrest urban decline, the cameo Fair was billed as an "international event" by opening day in 1962. Business' last-staged gala celebrated a lingering sense of community, masking the undercurrent of change. The Fair's aerospace and technology themes allowed Seattleites to think of it as an extension of the past.[63] It fact, facilitated the onrushing metropolitanism of the 70's.

Dorm Braman and "The World of Tomorrow"

It fell to "Dorm"[64] Braman, an "intuitively intelligent" high school dropout to cope with a city unseen in the Fair's theme. A World War II Navy Commander overseeing timber procurement, and then North end Lumber dealer was the council's budget chair after 1958, and embodied its conservatism. "We vote money to expand programs … only when it seems unavoidable and inevitable," he declared. Elected mayor in 1964, and facing an empty larder and an imploding Central Area, he complained, "All our problems stem from not having enough money." The "builder's" attempt to broaden the tax base ran into the same wall his predecessors' hit at the hands of the rural-dominated legislature. Braman's fate was to complete what Langlie had begun, making the city a 'creature' of Congress as well as the legislature.

Skeptical about an Economic Opportunity Act when voted by the Council, Braman was wise enough to know events had moved "past the point" for a debate over the legitimacy of federal aid. "The need to do something was so great," and the nation was wealthy enough to shape its cities' futures he reasoned.[65] The opponent of the Open Housing Ordinance defeated at the 1964

The Space Needle, symbol of the 1962 World's Fair with the grounds in front of it.

election promised action and jobs months before enactment of the federal Civil Rights Act of 1965, began a Citizens Service Bureau, an experimental Youth Corps, and enlarged the Human Rights Commission. His forbears' faith in unity persisted: otherwise the remedies offered were "fruitless."[66]

Downtown was now the object, not the initiator of action. The problem was finding the true leaders of the boiling Central Area, as opposed to rioters "who… constitute a wall barring any communication with those of us trying to do something about their problems." Braman gathered a Special Citizens Committee to air charges the "police brutality" first heard in June, 1961, then ordered a separate investigative unit reporting to the chief and mayor.[67] He helped write a Human Rights Training Course, complete with role playing and a rumor clinic, and spent "unlimited" time in the Central Area. It was a two way street, he wrote minority leaders.

"If we are to look coldly and impartially at police brutality, we must also expect the same attitude toward black brutality [which] will also take place … "[68]

"The sheer weight of the figures" between 1963 and 1969 were shocking: robbery was up 110 percent, aggravated assault 465 percent, forcible rape 93 percent. Policemen rose from 206 to 1,109, with 250 more cut for lack of funds. The "Little" city halls in the neighborhoods did little to quell the avalanche of criticism. "Nerve-wracking" waves of anger had "taken much of the glitter and satisfaction out of my job," the mayor soberly admitted to University Rotarians in 1969. "Guerrilla warfare" by the few seemed to offset his investments in mutual trust. The "growing consensus … among informed authorities" was "that the day of the big city is about over. As Mark Sidran, later to be Corporation Counsel noted, "Political institutions do not attract the participation of dissidents, even when they are middle class." [69]

Braman's considerable legacies are converting the Fair into "Seattle Center," strengthening the executive office, and mass transportation. Knowing the need for specialization, in the man who had opposed the Open Housing referendum in the Spring of 1964 as "not a proper solution," and resisted school "bussing," now insisted on leading the way, hiring a Staff Services Department to close the gap between planners and implementers, and rearing a Citizens' Service Bureau. Community Development merged the Urban Renewal, Housing Code Enforcement and Building Abatement operations. Human Rights, the Neighborhood Youth Corps, the Civil Service, Library and Transit Commissions, and critically, budgeting and a new management control system were put under him, further redressing power.

The beloved trolleys were now 35 years old. Ridership, which had doubled to 12.5 million passengers a month by 1943, half of all traffic, declined six percent a year after 1946, as the automobile took over. Seattle Transit fell into the red in 1957. Braman was the leading advocate of a METRO/Forward Thrust rail system, and his keenest disappointment its defeat in 1963. The middle class was now as fractured on transportation as the Central Area was socially. Braman, "the father of mass transit," claimed Seattle had at least "shaped the transportation policy for the nation," when he left for the 'other Washington' to be Assistant Secretary of Transportation for Urban Systems and Environment in 1968. He had learned "Its not true that you make a successful city the same way you make a successful business." The key was services, not profit, and "trying to serve the needs of the people as they express them."[70] A "Management Systems Office," Department of Community Development, a Department of Human Rights, were established in 1969, and in 1970, a "youth Programs Division "Dorm" Braman's perspective changed radically in the face of the urban-racial crisis. The 'seaport town," the Seattle of quiet gentility that urban realities had caught up with, was had been forced to face metropolitanism. He was the city's Dan Evans.

"Freedom" marchers on Fourth Avenue, Seattle, in the late 1960s.

The Civic Matrix in Retrospect

The paradox that emerged in 1938 lasted a generation: Democrats continued to dominate Seattle's partisan wars, while her mainstream mayors and council were conservative and largely 'Republican.' Still, weak parties and civil service never erased the partisan undertones of mayoral politics. Loyalties were understood. The Times' Ross Cunningham, one of the civic matrix, was close to correct in arguing that the only people who thought city elections were partisan were the partisan pros.[71] After 1942, Democrats charged non-partisanship was a "form of Republican domination," and sometimes boycotted the Municipal League's Candidate Evaluation Committee, but the ongoing alchemy of mugwump successes seconded by the business and professionals sustained the non-partisan illusion. Cincinnatus waxed into an interlocking civic directorate whose life cycle paralleled the four mayors. They were chosen and financed between the Smith Tower and the Times on John Street, and between Third and Sixth Avenues. Business' political "Big Ten" took turns presiding over the Chamber of Commerce, the Washington Athletic and Rainier Clubs, and were regulars at the "Monday Luncheon Club" which met weekly from 1935 to 1960 at the Olympic Hotel to discuss the city. The mayors often sat in. Ross Cunningham told the Post-Intelligencer's political reporter Stub Nelson, "If I knew of a good man for mayor, I could get him elected."[72] The "Club" was the nominating committee.

Next to this "fluid coalition of influentials," was the Municipal League, "a potent force for good government …" which peaked in the 1950's with 4,900 members, 800 on committees, and staff of seven, with a conservative but not partisan stance. It favored incumbents, and from 1940 to 1964 just five were defeated. Its vanguard, lawyers like Harold Shefelman and Jim Ellis began to fall away after 1960, when the law became as much a demanding business as a profession.[73] Expansion and professionalization of the staff at City Hall all but obviated the League's research function, and its membership and influence fell four-fifths in 20 years.[74] Publisher William Blethen's had loomed over the less partial and anemic Post-Intelligencer. Its influence was strongest in non-partisan races, where it sonorously favored "tested leadership," as Cunningham, Langlie's first Administrative Assistant in Olympia, rose to Editor of the Editorial Page. He and the paper's traditionalism died in the 80's.

The (Protestant) Seattle Council of Churches profiled middle class preoccupation with policing and 'closing' the town. Its endorsement of Langlie in 1935 and Mrs. F. F. Powell his female counterpart (1935-1955), began a close association. Those who felt the Council had "no place in politics," were overruled by activists who insisting that "where a clear moral issue is involved the Council must act."[75] Volunteers from the Council's network were essential to the four mayors' campaigns. In 1960, Clinton's manager asserted churchmen "constituted the bulk of [his] campaign organization," and fretted when the press counted 25 ministers at a campaign breakfast.[76] By then ecumenicity was "Bustin' Out All Over" as the Council's Executive Director put it. Urban issues and Vietnam brought in liberals often at odds with their parishioners on these issues to the fore, marginalizing the Council as a force in local politics.

In 1967, a new reform cycle rose. Braman's and citizens' groups advice to the council on the telescoping urban crises seemed unavailing. The council's calling of a 67-year-old former state

UWA

Forty years on: Camden Hall (R) and Peter Lesourd, the non-partisan leaders of Choose and Effective City Council (CHECC), the 1970's rendition of the New Order of Cincinnatus.

senator as interim mayor was too much. Even the Argus, downtown's putative civic voice asserted the "…Members of the business and professional community could find no better investment in Seattle's future" than to refresh the "sluggish and inefficient" body. Young Turk lawyers formed the bipartisan Choose An Effective City Council (CHECC). In two years, CHECC elected Phyllis Lamphere, Tim Hill, Bruce Chapman and John Miller to the Council, using Cincinnatus' now conventional "doorbelling" and media techniques – only to find the 'middle class consensus' had disappeared. Six years later the Argus was again complaining the Council was "sluggish." "What is left for these reformers to do?"[77]

In retrospect, the City's last annexation – of Lake City in the Northeast corner in 1954 – that drew in Dorm Braman, was the demographic divide on the road to metropolitanism. The middle class soon split, as the disadvantaged decided pressure was the way to win at City Hall. "The good of the community as a whole" ethic fell to the demands of its fractions, each with its definition of "good government." "Downtown was in a sense just another neighborhood."[78] By 1967, professional families were fleeing to schools in the homogeneous, Republican suburbs. Amalgamated Seattle, with its racial, ethnic and sexual minorities, cashiered its last Republican legislator in 1984.

Seattle reflects the three major changes in city government since the 1940's: increasing suburbanization and heterogeneity, and enlarged expectations of government's role. The upheavals of the late 60's and the federal interventions of President Johnson's "Great Society" programs are the dividing line into a new age. The city's per capita net spending in real dollars in the 50 years before 1990 rose 485 percent, mostly since 1969, the population 30 percent.[79] Labor, "moral," (i.e., police), and class issues gave way to the urban crises. The cities, (and counties), once utility operators, law enforcers, library and park providers, now do everything but defense, all but erasing a two-century tradition of differentiated three tier government.

Arthur Langlie, Bill Devin, Gordon Clinton and Dorm Braman mirrored a bourgeois political culture lasting a generation. Three of the four mayors were born within a decade, and all lived in a six mile radius in the North End. They were Scouters, Protestant churchmen, only accidentally politicians, and initially mild partisans distasteful of campaigning. Three were lawyers who practiced ten years before entering public life. Langlie, Clinton and Braman were World War II naval officers. Devin and Clinton were

SEATTLE POST-INTELLIGENCER COLLECTION
Mayor Dorm Braman tried vigoursly to integrate the city.

police judges, and presidents of the American Municipal Association. Langlie alone had 'further political ambitions,' and remains the only mayor of Seattle in a century in higher elective office, although three have tried.[80] The more conservative Braman, Lake City lumberman and devout Christian Scientist, shared their adaptability, optimism, the generation's belief in civic unity and civil rights. Each was more progressive than his councils, and their power had come to equal its by the time upheaval overtook both. Seattle's 30 year civic peace closed as quickly as her infancy. Demand for the mayor's strenuous public service ethic remains steady. A comparable generation of civic leaders is absent.

Chapter 3

Culmination of the Great Columbia Power War:

The CVA, Governor Arthur B. Langlie and Eisenhower's "Partnership"

George W. Scott

The Columbia River, fourth largest in North America, is the nation's prime hydroelectric source with an elevation drop of 2,650 feet. The huge potential of this coronary artery of the Northwest economy, made politics and electric power synonymous, paired off every major economic interest, and divided state and the federal executives for thirty years. Presidents Roosevelt and Truman and their congresses brought federal dominance, without unifying control. Eisenhower and his governors were as crucial as the competing federal bureaus in keeping a Columbia Valley Authority buried after 1949, but unable to assure 'states rights.' In keeping public opinion divided, insured Hells Canyon Dam, the last monument to federal multi-purpose planning would never be, and their own demise, in 1956. New and Fair Dealers knew North westerners wanted dams, the "Modern Republicans" that they did not want control. Blinded by ideology, both sides ignored the contradiction, and compromise.

Prefiguring The New Deal

Public power rooted in the Northwest just four years after Washington's admission to the union. Tacoma was the first large city to go public, in 1893; in 1902 Seattle City Light took over distribution. Both proved efficient, and an impetus to the Populists and Progressives, then Grangers, Labor, and liberals' earned paranoia of railroads and utility magnates. A "preference" for municipals buying federally generated power was the signal clause of the Reclamation Act of 1906. The publics' advance slowed because they could not afford to build lines to the "bus bar," even as demands for inland navigation and flood control drew congress into dam construction. The Federal Water Power Act of 1920 created the Federal Power Commission as licensor, and limited non-federal owners to fifty years, tightening congress' grip. Local Public Utility Districts (PUDs) were sanctioned by initiative in 1930, in the face of the Great Depression. The Army Corps of Engineer's "308" report premising multi-purpose dams for reclamation from Canada to Astoria arrived in 1932 with New Deal.

JOURNAL OF THE WEST

Harold Ickes and his wife. FDR's Secretary of the Interior was a formidable advocate for public power.

FDR turned the federal government from passive partner to pacesetter. The Tennessee Valley Authority, and the Grand Coulee Dam, begun in 1933, were to be models. The Public Utilities Holding Company Act of 1935 gave the new Securities and Exchange Commission regulatory power, and buttressed state counterparts. As Grand Coulee neared completion in 1940, Roosevelt designated Bonneville Power Administration marketer and distributor of power, rate setter, and direct supplier to the PUD's, settling who would wholesale and distribute. The BPA was now in charge, but had two masters operationally more pivotal than the president: Congress for appropriations, and the region's congressmen, whose constituencies were deeply divided on power questions. BPA was the publics' ally to 1953. But four of its six heads came from the Northwest, and its regional in-breeding and character were obvious. The best weathervane of sentiment, the agency was ever more neutral.

The private utilities felt unequal competition, and feared nationalization. Seattle's Puget Sound Power and Light, Portland General Electric, Pacific Power and Light, Spokane's Washington Water Power, and the Idaho Power Company, on the one hand, and the PUDs and Cooperatives on the other, used obstruction and litigation as weapons in what each side saw as a duel to the death. To reclaim their New Deal losses, in 1940 the privates promoted an initiative requiring public referenda on PUD acquisitions. The Electric Companies Advertising Program in was begun in 1941, the National Association of Electric Companies in 1945, their Public Information League Program (PIP) in 1949.

President Franklin Roosevelt on one of his several trips to the Grand Coulee.

The struggle was intensified by a touch-and-go race with supply. Defense drove demand after 1941, the consumer after 1945. The average home took 1220 kilowatts in 1935, and 11,000 in 1967, three times the national average. Cries for reclamation, navigation, and flood control were spurred by disastrous floods on the Columbia in the summer of 1948, and the "dry" years of 1951-52, when clocks lost time, lights dimmed, and industry slowed. Lacking coal or oil, the Northwest became dependent on "the River," and the Columbia displaced the TVA as a national controversy.

Fair Deal Come Apart

Its nucleus was Washington state, home of the main stem. U.S. Senator Monrad C. Wallgren rode with F.D.R. in 1944, ousting Republican Governor Arthur B. Langlie. He then named Hugh B. Mitchell his administrative assistant since 1933, to his seat. Mitchell made his mark as Langlie's nemesis, promptly introducing Truman's Columbia Valley Authority in 1945.

But President Truman lost Interior's imperial Harold Ickes, FDR's crucial and longest serving cabinet member in 1946. Fifth columns in his cabinet went on the march. The CVA was ignored, but not killed by the GOP 80th Congress of 1947-49. In 1948, Reclamation, and the Corps of Engineers split the Army's "Main Control Plan," and created a Columbia River Basin Fund to pay for them, repeating their divide and conquer strategy of 1933. Scholars correctly give them credit equal to all other opponents for stalling the CVA. The window of opportunity the President, Democrats, Labor, the Grange, and public power had against the private utilities and Republicans to complete public control closed by the outbreak of the Korean War in August, 1950.

Counterpoint: Rise of The Republican Governors

The Northwest's governors were the cats paws that kept it shut. They were led by Arthur Langlie, Washington's first three term governor, whose career coincided with the coming of the all-electric age in the Northwest. Elected in 1941, he was the only GOP statewide official Evergreen State. Impressed by Seattle City Light as a mugwump mayor after 1938, he helped Democrats defeat the Utilities' initiative to require referenda on PUD bonds in 1940. An apprentice partisan, Langlie was able to avoid being tied to GOP presidential nominee Wendell Willkie, but was defeated in 1944 by an extraordinary "soldier vote" and turnout. The New Deal had in fact crested in the Northwest in 1942. After the 1946 election six of seven Northwest governors, and after 1950 seventeen of its twenty-two its congressmen were Republicans. They met the region's strongest senators on the Potomac after 1953, Democrats Henry Jackson and Warren Magnuson, and Oregon's Wayne Morse, head on.

By the time Langlie returned to the governor's chair for two more terms in 1949, the Northwest had become the capitol of the light metals industry. Fourteen aluminum plants were using half the Columbia's output. Two hundred and fifty seven dam sites had been identified on the main stem and tributaries, twenty one authorized, seven were underway. He rejoined the conclusive battles in April, with a sharp blast against an "super agency without checks and balances."

The Army Corps of Engineers failed to foil F.D.R.'s T.V.A. with the "Pick-Sloan" plan. The "Weaver-Newell" ("308") design derailed the less facile Truman. The division of sixty projects into "spheres of interest" with Reclamation was so quickly contrived some of the dams would flood others. Langlie led Douglas McKay (Oregon), C.A. Robins (Idaho), Vail Pittman (Nevada) and Robert Bonner (Montana) in blanket approval before the House Interior Committee. Every state official, except Treasurer Tom Martin who was acting executive, came to rebut the Governor, whom the Speaker of the House Charles Hodde called "the lone voice of an Evangelist." Chairman Whittington, a Southern Democrat, interrupted Mitchell's testimony to say the CVA would "create a super agency." Mitchell was could concede only that the directors and an advisory committee be local. Remove the 'defect' of central control, and its proponents would have "no further interest….The issue is as simple as that," Langlie declared. No amendment could make CVA acceptable, discussion a waste of time. The concrete was literally setting.

Just in time: The Grand Coulee Dam was completed in 1940, with World War II on the horizon.

Truman's bill substituted "Administration" for "Authority." Undersecretary of the Interior C. Girard "Jebbie" Davidson, its father, testified there was no 'super agency,' simply a reordering of existing ones for effectiveness. Saying the three presidential directors were expected, but not required, to engage in regular "consultation and interchange views" with locals mollified the governors not at all. Langlie saw an "unregulated utility ... a ... complete and unprecedented departure from the dual federal-state form of government," precluding states from negotiating for ownership.

Davidson crisscrossed the Northwest to "inform" the electorate. Mitchell as President of the League for a CVA, enlisted the AF of L, the CIO, Grange, completing the fateful drawing of partisan lines. "Your position is unrealistic and without any solid basis in fact," Mitchell abrasively wrote the governor and the private power lobby. "Real progressives," Langlie retorted, worried about "power politics" on the Potomac penetrating peoples' lives.

The Pacific Northwest Development Association, the industrial, engineering, transport and mining associations, chambers of commerce, and the militant private utilities were the backbone of the opposition. The Oregon Farm Bureau, and legislature, the Idaho Grange, and livestock, reclamation and conservation, and four out of five groups in the Basin joined in. Forty-eight page booklets pictured the region's eighty-six major dams and thirty-two irrigation operations as progress itself. The CVA was "far beyond socialism," Langlie gravely told the Association in 1950, quoting the Socialist Party's platform rejecting it for lack of democratic controls. This was a "completely negative" and "unthinking" alignment of forces athwart the development of the Northwest, Mitchell countered. "The governors of Oregon, Idaho, and Washington are foolish men."

TIME MAGAZINE

Washington's first three-term governor, Arthur B. Langlie, (1941-1945, 1949-1957) led his Republican contemporaries in the Northwest in opposing the CVA.

No "Middle Way"?

Caught in a killing zone between the armies of the intent and the irate, Washington's congressmen sought a modus vivendi. Senator Magnuson offered a new version, and covered his flank by joining Senator Harry Cain (R, Washington), in his. Tacoma's Thor Tollefson, the only open Republican advocate, was convinced his Western counterparts would "vote overwhelmingly for a CVA before being…crucified on the cross of private power." He and Congressman Walt Horan (R-Wenatchee) offered the "308" plan as an amendment to the Omnibus Public Works Bill. Senator Wayne Morse of Oregon, then a Republican, thought it a "valuable framework," and went on record against the CVA, only to become a Democrat and its other chief patron.

The only via media, Horan's Columbia Basin Interstate Commission, was the doomed idea of a Minority member. "Not persuaded" by the 'super-government' arguments against Mitchell's 1945 bill, Horan reminded Langlie the Interstate Commerce Clause gave congress authority over rivers. Those who were for the status quo were for federal control. The C.I.C. vested home rule authority in the four Northwest governors, who were each to name a director, and send their chiefs of conservation as an advisory council with veto power. The "policy and administrative council" placated the Army and Interior by leaving construction with them. A "Basin Account" for power revenues to repay the capital costs of new construction undercut both a key argument for the CVA, and the governors unsolvable problem, the need for enormous investment. If federal control was Langlie's prime reservation, he should have embraced this "middle way." He did telegraph fourteen senators asking its inclusion in the "308" package. Mitchell read "too rigid limitations on the President's appointive power." The "composite" was "too conservative to satisfy the radicals, too liberal for the reactionaries, and doesn't promise enough special privilege to anyone," Horan sighed.

State "Alternatives"

At its worst, the fight over control justified delay. Langlie wanted the Ice Harbor and Hells Canyon dams restudied when Truman had tried to fund them in 1950. The radical decline in the Columbia salmon fishery was a genuine concern. He and Idaho's governor Len Jordan, with an eye on the last, asked the CBIAC for a defensive plan – review of each project, while Oregon's McKay played peacemaker. When Jordan referred to the "federal or nothing zealots," he was not alone. Two years later Langlie urged the Senate to restore the House's excisions from Albini Falls, Detroit, Lookout Point, Chief Joseph, the Dalles and Ice Harbor, with no mention of a Basin Account.

The Columbia Basin Interagency Committee, formed as a clearing house in 1946, was a prototype of the fronts the bureaus eagerly agreed to delay the CVA and the loss of their projects, and was the best argument for it. And their rivalries had left them in such disarray before congress they were driven to support the CBIAC. The chair rotated between the five major agencies involved. Unanimous agreement was required. The Hoover Commission concluded it "... failed to solve any of the important aspects of the problem... the dominant members have been unwilling to permit interagency committees to settle their differences." Langlie insisted the CBIAC had never been given a chance: if other interested parties could be "fused" the assertion it was nothing more than a debating society would be disproved. The idea it was "functioning effectively and harmoniously" was the first of his illusions. Governor J. Bracken Lee of Utah, resisted pleas for involvement. His state's role in whatever plan is adopted... is so slight as to be insignificant." The CBIAC lacked the "punch" to effectively oppose the CVA. On Langlie's motion and after two years, the CBIAC brought eighteen page mouse, adding a time table for reclamation to the "308" plan, and a plea for eight more dams "at the earliest practicable date." By 1953, even he was forced to admit the "recurrent lack of unanimity between federal agencies ..."

The CBIAC's second alternative, an interstate compact like those operating in Missouri, Delaware and Potomac Valleys at limited levels, was circulated in the 1953 and 1955 legislatures. Langlie grasped it as means of "checks and balances," and oversight. His Director of Conservation, Jack Rogers, who chaired the CBIAC through the thirty drafts before submission, conceded it would make formation of a CVA "difficult or unnecessary." The compact was ratified in Idaho, Nevada, and Utah, passed the senate in Montana, and died after hearings in Washington and Oregon. Friends of public power looked askance on the pretext upstream states might preempt the water of those downstream, although the latter approved the pact. As 1956 dawned, the governors were mulling over their eighth report. Eisenhower's chief advisor on his Water Resources Policy Commission saw the CBIAC gave the states a way to monitor federal agencies, but no motivation to do more.

The Columbia River and its 2,500 square miles basin: Note that the drawing is reversed east to west, with Mt. Rainer east of the Columbia.

Lacking direction from the BPA after Dwight Eisenhower's election as President in 1952, Langlie and Idaho's Jordan had organized the "Northwest Governor's Power Policy Committee," an executives' replicate of the CBIAC It first met in Olympia in October, 1953, to, in the words of Montana's J. Hugo Aronson, "bring order out of chaos." "If we don't come up with answers instead of just raising questions" Oregon's Paul Patterson observed, "we are going to be criticized." Langlie, tacking to his advisor Holland Houston, was preoccupied with finding the "engineering acts." If found, "the result will amaze even the most optimistic among us." "Engineering leadership" could create an "orderly process," and overcome the "degrading influence of politicians."

A stillborn State Power Commission was his answer to the BPA. Langlie asked for one in his 1949 inaugural, so Washington could initiate projects and protect its economic position. Five directors were to acquire facilities and lines by lease, contract, or purchase, or condemnation, or by taking over federally originated projects. The governor's insistence the public versus primary squabble was not primary was belied by the thesis of Holland Houston's prospectus: public power was so "entrenched" as to need no advocates, the privates should be strengthened to "maintain a yardstick." A "controllable" agency was to take the place of an "uncontrollable" one. Both sides lobbied for it. The Supreme Court had nullified the PUD's condemnation of the Skagit County properties of Puget Sound Power and Light, and saw a way to jointly condemn. Unbeknownst to the governor the privates had all but thrown in the towel. PSPL and WWP. were negotiating with the PUDs, and wanted a face saving way to go out of business on the best possible terms. The SPC. came close to being the death of private power in the state of Washington.

The Speaker and Minority Leader cooperated, and the SPC. passed the House 84-13, March 3.

UNIVERSITY OF WASHINGTON ARCHIVES
One of the cavernous concrete tubles to convey water to the 'Great Columbia Plain.

"With a State Power Commission," the Governor proudly told a Spokane Civic group, "we can bring order out of chaos." In January, 1951, he was still holding off appointments, until "someone comes down here and shows me its needed." The conspirators had built in a loophole. A case where there was no PUD in the county of a private company had not been covered. Spokane's WWP was now trying to sell out to PUDs for a windfall. The "commissioners and their Wall Street collaborators" were trying to foist a public instead of private monopoly. The "age old problem of freedom versus tyranny" had been brought on by those the governor had sought to protect. The "Spokane Power Bill" requiring a referendum on any sale, was the cause celebre of the 1951 session. The SEC stepped in to block the transfer in January, 1952.

Role reversals were complete when Langlie helped P.S.P.L. The PUDs were to be bought off by having the S.P.C take over its facilities, and letting them distribute. When heard before the State Public Service Commission in August, 1952, both U.S. senators and all four Westside congressmen testified against; public power and the Democratic State Central Committee applauded. The Seattle Times commended Langlie contributed some "splendid statesmanship" as it now editorially drove W.W.P away from an unfriendly takeover of P.S.P.L., whose capital it wanted. He was "happy" the company had decided to stay in business for itself.

In November, he bludgeoned Mitchell as thinking the states resources "belonged to the gigantic, expanding, grasping federal government." The challenger exposed himself by sponsoring a power intertie to California, and ties to the Americans for Democratic Action as fear of Communism surged.

"Creeping Socialism" or "Partnership" ?

Dwight Eisenhower's natural resources speech in Seattle, October 10, 1952 promoted "Partnership," to end "Empire building," and Reclamation's "whole hog" theories. The closest definition it got was the President dedication of McNary dam in 1954. The threat was federal monopoly: projects should be "freely chosen by the citizens of each area, with the federal government drawn in as a cooperating partner where this seems necessary or desirable." In the first fifteen months of his administration there were "no new starts" on the Columbia, to allow locals to assume their share, according to now Secretary of the Interior Douglas McKay. Public advocates saw pressure to increase rates by giving dam sites to the privates, and reflective of the F.P.C.'s attitude on apportionment of costs.

McKay, and the twenty-three GOP governors had gotten Eisenhower nominated, had convinced him on "partnership," and were the lynchpins if it was to work. Arthur Langlie, senior among them, was the prototype and point man in clash of philosophies. Time's September 3, 1956 cover story on him declared, "No senatorial hopeful personifies more clearly Ike's kind of candidate" of the national convention keynoter. Langlie wanted the SPC to lead the way. The Republican legislature mandated the commissioners' consent to form an operating agency, or to construct. "If California and Texas can get their offshore oil lands, Langlie said, "I don't see why we can't have our dams." Once paid for they and their revenue should revert to the states.

The SPC. wanted to co-wholesale Bonneville's power, and asked for "all firm seasonal energy." Undersecretary of the Interior Ralph Tudor, with whom Langlie had conferred at length, equivocated: 'For Sale' signs were not on federal dams, unless "some responsible public body such as a state, comes in with a concrete proposal to purchase ... such a proposal will be approached with an open mind." BPA Administrator William Pearl was as protective as his forbears. No money was to be made at federal expense. Obliviously, the commissioners moved on the Priest Rapids dam proposed by Grant County PUD. Central Washington's Congressman Hal Holmes, was irritated when the Governor appealed to Tacoma colleague Thor Tollefson to block any variation from "308." The S.P.C. ignored the application, and filed its own in July 1953. The PUD rejected joint application suggested by the SPC. "The Democrats are obstructionists. They are not really interested in building dams," the governor exploded, "they are only trying to obstruct the progress we are making by trying to take on something that is ... beyond them ... carrying the partnership principle too far." The obverse was the case.

Congress granted a variance, and in October, the PUDs invited anyone in. Fourteen PUDs and seven small cities activated as an "operating agency" in January, 1954. Langlie's last chance was reaching Olympian Jerry Kuydendall, chair of the Federal Power Commission, whom he had gotten appointed through Eisenhower's Chief of Staff Governor Sherman Adams. Senator

Magnuson, sure the SPC would subvert public preference, announced October 20, the P.U.D. would be licensed. The coup was a "Memorandum of Agreement" allowing engineering to proceed. If the S.P.C. got the license, it was to reimburse the PUD, if not, the PUD would share its power.

Langlie insisted to the 1955 legislature the S.P.C. was equal to the project; the PUD's and municipals should "meet their own needs." More was "a violation of sound principles of government." In fact, both sides were unprepared. Langlie needed a $1 million loan, the PUDs the right to contract power over long periods and bonding capacity. The Supreme Court brought down the curtain in sustaining a restraining order forbidding the Commission to supersede the PUD. Priest Rapids told why "partnership" was not to be. The states lacked capital; the federals would not give up dams or revenue. Ideology precluded cooperation or real compromise. The SPC impractical. "We don't know yet what 'partnership' means," Kinsey Robinson, president of Washington Water Power admitted.

River of No Return

The CVA was now a bogey, having died in 1949, but its twin, a "high head" Hells Canyon dam on the Snake came to a boil once the Democrats regained congress in 1955. The states righters were astir as the 1952 governors conference. "Now we finally have an administration willing to go along," Langlie noted, "dumbfounded as the support for Hells Canyon and the attempt to force pubic ownership in an area where people don't want it." McKay, now Secretary of the Interior, declared public preference created monopolies in large areas, and withdrew a "Petition of Intervention" against Idaho Power Company. The Secretary sought a good faith "middle way" without advocates, or sophistication. His thinker was Under Secretary Ralph Tudor, as Truman's Oscar Chapman had relied on "Jebbie " Davidson. The administration was divided: Kuykendall was for an end to "whole hogism "– but for multipurpose.

Houston and Langlie claimed upstream storage was "overemphasized," and unnecessary. Congress' cost was to be $356 million. Three low dams by the Idaho Power Company for $133 million would generate 783,000 kilowatts (as opposed to 800,000 for Hells). It was a "politicians dam," Langlie insisted in the six year struggle. Technology had advanced the date when steam and atoms could absorb larger loads. He, Oregon's Paul Patterson, Montana's Aronson, and Idaho's Robert Smylie asked congress to review the Army's "531" document, which contained Hells. The Army compliantly revised its approach of 30 years in a restudy urged by the governors and the administration, concluding for three "run of the river" dams with 13.5 million acre feet of storage, half the original amount. The environmental impact on America's second greatest canyon were only lightly considered. Patterson and Langlie breakfasted with the President, who "satisfied" with Northwest power, left for Augusta. Langlie spent the rest of the day with Adams, McKay, Budget Director Rowland Hughes, and the congressional delegation to get a "maximum interpretation" of partnership – meaning money for John Day and Rocky Reach dams.

The Northwest Democratic senators' tactical mistake was forcing a vote in July 1956. The antagonists had the public "hopelessly divided." Before congress, Patterson offered the soundest arguments, Smylie the "slickest," and Langlie the "most absurd" Wayne Morse thought. "The Three musketeers of resistance to the twentieth century" were "highly provincial."

As Mckay congratulated Langlie for his "Hell's Canyon speech" before congress, the "Idaho-Oregon-Washington Hells Canyon Association" condemned his version of "pseudo-partnership," and asked the legislature to investigate the use of public funds to promote a private company's projects outside the state. Democratic senators won the public relations fight with a new iteration serving people or 'economic royalists.' Hells, despite denials on both sides was a public-private fight, was by the same people, for old reasons.

The CVA and Hells Canyon, the Northwest's most abiding, exciting, and crucial arguments, are also its best examples of where politicians were not pragmatic. The CVA was an operationally superior idea. On the axial issue of federal control, Langlie speculated that if all nine proposed regional authorities were effected, the question would be whether congress or twenty-seven commissioners had the most influence. The CVA did not carry an "element of Fascism," it was the lesser evil. Congress could be counted on to contain it. This was one of the few in politics issues where there was only one only viable "middle Way," and Horan's CIC was inferior. The need for three of four governors to agree, and turnover, precluded policy continuity.

Eisenhower's governors, more than helping defeat the CVA, kept it interred. A 1956 Roper poll found North westerners preferred the 'partnership' concept three to one, and rejected "federal control of their utilities" two to one. But in losing the political war, they arrested the region's return to two party politics. "Partnership," arguably Eisenhower's largest domestic failure, a philosophically driven abstraction lacking substance. The governors who nominated him led the President to invest heavily in proven be cul de sacs. Washington's little BPA, the State Power Commission, an uncapitalized artifice, nearly embalmed private power. Provincialism in the state capitols was no worse than that of the self-serving bureaus, or the rigidity of CVA advocates.

"Engineering facts" argued by politicians who only vaguely understood was at an apogee over Hell's Canyon, the only defeat of the Democratic senators whose places in a majority the governors sought in 1956. Morse crushed "Give away McKay," who like Horan had tried to walk a "middle Way" with no turf. "Majority opinion" was claimed where there was only confusion on the issues. Langlie's 1956 loss to Magnuson reminded that a "Voice of political conscience" cannot compete with a "Voice of political service."

To meet demand, finance dams and nuclear power, public and private power producers were forced to cooperate. President Kennedy spoke at

UWA   *Hanford in 1961*

Ironies abound in the crusades of federal activists and states' righters. Both sides denied what was most obvious, a philosophic, private versus public development fight, with different 'yardsticks.' Thousands drawn to the Northwest by an electrified, diversified economy came to grieve the loss of much of the spectacular Grand Coulee gorge. Reclamation greened millions acres of desert on the "Great Columbia Plain" as loggers finished stripping the wet side of the Cascades of old growth forest. Indians lost Celilo Falls, tribal fishing and sacred grounds, to be paid three decades later under the Indians Claims Act in money harder to hold than water. Sappers within stalled Truman's CVA. In setting the public against "autocratic control," Eisenhower's governors kept it interred, without stopping federal dam building. Their arabesques damaged "partnership" more than the CVA. Hells was hardly the intended paradigm of partnership. The Democrats captured a national media on "waste" versus development, which would now see the issue in an environmental light. Conservatives saved the continent's second deepest crevasse, from liberals, for the wrong reasons.

Combat closed only when options were gone. The Columbia River was a series of lakes by 1960, the year the Washington legislature passed an Atomic Energy Act. This new necessity for power, also birthed on the stream, has been controverted thirty years, beliefs defying reality, even as dependency on the atom deepened. If the nuclear alternative to dams and the age of ecology had come a generation earlier, would the protagonists' roles and outcomes have reversed? There were two "generation" gaps.

Chapter 4

Organized Labor in Washington State, 1885-2005

Jonathan Dembo

This chapter serves as a concise anatomy of the critical turns of Washington's labor history. As understood in this chapter, the labor movement is limited to organized trade unions and their regional and state organizations. It excludes such quasi-labor organizations such as the Farmers Alliance, and the Washington Education Association. This chapter will give a glimpse into both the political and economic activities of the unions and relate them to national and international events.

Washington State is among the most geographically diverse and politically volatile in the union. The "Cascade divide" splitting the state between East and West creates distinct differences in climate, geography, population, economic activities and political affiliation between the regions. The divide assures deep splits in both parties, and the emergence of two distinct geographic-political "cultures."

Still, it is possible to generalize about Washington State to a limited degree. The state has been unusually egalitarian both politically and economically compared to other states. It has never had political machines, or heavy industry. Yet, it has had one party government over long periods of time and industries that had overwhelming political and economic influence. Massive federal support for economic and social development has left a deep mark on the state and on the labor movement. These are among the major factors that produced an unusually strong labor movement and a continuing populist/progressive strain in the life of the state.

Historians have produced a number of fine works on various aspects of Washington State labor. Unfortunately, they have tended to concentrate their attention on a few colorful or notorious incidents, organizations, and issues. In particular, they have examined and reexamined the Industrial Workers of the World, the Seattle General Strike, and the prominence of political radicalism in the labor movement. My purpose is to add continuity and perspective to these scattered efforts and, with original research, to connect the interstices in our knowledge of the early history of the Washington State labor movement.

In writing Organized Labor in Washington State 1885-2005, I have drawn very heavily on my dissertation The Washington State Labor Movement, 1885-1935,[1] which I later published as Labor and Politics in Washington State, 1885-1935.[2] Both focused on the rise of the Washington State Federation of Labor (WSFL), the statewide affiliate of the national American Federation of Labor (AFL). It is important to remember that then, as now, a significant portion of organized labor in Washington State including locals of AFL-affiliated international unions, did not affiliate with the state or the national federations. First, the Knights of Labor (K of L), then the Western Federation of Miners (WFM), then the Industrial Workers of the World (IWW), then the Congress of Industrial Organizations rose to rival the AFL for the hearts of union men and women. Meanwhile, the so-called Railroad Brotherhood unions existed independently with the other international unions and federations. At the same time, numerous local unions of AFL-affiliated international unions remained independent of the WSFL. At times nearly half of the AFL-affiliated locals in Washington State remained independent of the WSFL.

For purposes of this chapter, I have divided the labor history of Washington State in the twentieth century into two parts.

Part I: Baseball Bats and Cargo Hooks: Labor Comes of Age traces the history of the movement from the formation of the Labor Movement in the 1880s, to the establishment of the WSFL in 1902, to the reunification of the AFL-CIO and the establishment of the Washington State Labor Council in 1957. It covers the rise of the IWW – known familiarly as the "Wobblies" from the attempts of its foreign language speaking members to pronounce IWW ("I wobble wobble") – and the continuing challenge of a phalanx of syndicalist, anarchist, and socialist parties and splinter groups, such as the Bolsheviks (later the Communists) to the WSFL. It also covers the WSFL's efforts to maintain a non-partisan political course keeping close ties with the mainstream Democratic and Republican parties. It covers the crisis of World War I, the Seattle General Strike, and the postwar depression. It describes how changing technology affected organized labor from the 1920s to the 1940s and focuses on the confrontation between Teamster

Dave Beck 'the businessman's unionist' and his labor opponent, Longshoremen's leader Harry Bridges, an accused Communist and illegal immigrant. It also deals with the causes of the Great Depression that followed the Wall Street Crash of 1929 and labor's responses to it, including the establishment of the Congress of Industrial Organizations (CIO) and the competition that ensued between the CIO to organize industrial workers in Washington State eventually won by the WSFL. It covers the rapid changes that occurred during World War II and the settlement of the great ideological disputes that had split the labor movement over the past half century. It ends with the end of World War II and the emergence of the United States as the preeminent world power. In 1902, when the first reliable statistics become available, the labor movement in Washington was weak and isolated, representing approximately 7.2% of the state's non-farm labor force. The WSFL represented only 2.01% of the non-farm labor force, 2,520 members. By the end of the period, in 1956, the labor movement in Washington represented over 400,000 union members, comprising over 51% of the non-farm labor force in the state. The WSFL claimed to represent over 129,000 union members.[3]

Part 2: Labor Rules traces the long slow relative decline of the movement from the unification of the AFL and CIO, in 1957, to the beginning of the 21st century. Labor Rules explains the continuing strength of the movement despite its relative decline to a small portion of the work force. It covers the jailing of Teamster Boss Dave Beck and Longshoremen's Leader Harry Bridge's historic productivity agreement with the longshore employers. Labor Rules shows how divisions over the role of communists in the CIO weakened the "industrial" unions and led to the triumph of the AFL's "craft" unions. It covers labor's role in Washington politics from the New Deal to the decline of "labor unions," and the rise of civil service and public employee unions. It concludes with a discussion of labor's accomplishments since the 1950s and its slow, steady decline as a force in Washington State economics and politics. It attempts to foresee labor's future, given a decline of unionism and the rise of foreign competition and technological change in the extractive industries in the Northwest. It ends with the International Association of Machinists contract with Boeing in 2005 and legislative action requiring public employees to join unions. During this period, membership in Washington labor unions remained stable at about 400-500,000 members. Unlike unions in other states, there was no wholesale decline in membership. However, between 1956 and 2005, the non-farm labor force in Washington grew from to 803,000 to 2,724,000. As a result, the percentage of the non-farm labor force organized by Washington unions declined from 48.7%, in 1957, to 18.6% in 2001.[4]

The decade 1880-1890 revolutionized Washington Territory. In it Washington evolved from a rural to an urban-dominated area. The rise of the urban population reflected the growth

The Anti-Chinese riots, Seattle 1885

of Washington's manufacturing industries. Between 1880 and 1890 the number of persons employed in manufacturing increased from 1,147 to 20,366, a phenomenal rate of increase and many times greater than the national average. It was this urban-industrial shift which set the stage for the rise of the labor movement in the decades to come.

A central cause of this growth was the construction of the transcontinental railroads. These huge private projects attracted a steady stream of low cost immigrant labor from all parts of the United States, Europe, and Asia. Massively subsidized by federal land grants, they offered high wages and steady work. Other immigrants found jobs in the farms, coal mines, lumber camps and mills, and fish canneries which acquired their land from the railroads or which relied on the railroads to purchase or export their products to the world. This wave of immigration led to the rise of an industrial working class, which, by the early 1880s had begun to organize unions in the urban areas and in both the lumber and mining industries. The relatively high wages and the likelihood of continuing growth attracted immigrants to the state.

Following completion of the Northern Pacific Railroad on 8 September 1883, however, a severe depression ravaged the Pacific Northwest. Several thousand laid-off railroad workers flocked into Seattle and Tacoma looking for work. Their presence transformed the Pacific Northwest from a labor deficit to a labor surplus region and inspired some employers to cut wages and reduce conditions of employment. To continue to operate some employers hired Chinese immigrants who worked longer hours for lower wages than European immigrants or native born workers. Moreover, they did not complain so much about poor living and working conditions. Among the unemployed workers' movements began to grow to resist further Chinese immigration and to expel Chinese already in the region. Workers in San Francisco had already established Anti-Chinese organizations.

The growing economic crisis and related rise in racial tensions led to the establishment of the first labor federations in Washington Territory. As economic and racial tensions rose, organizers of the Knights of Labor, a rapidly growing national labor federation, found ready acceptance of their ideas in Washington Territory. The K of L, which first appeared in the Newcastle coal mines in 1881, divided the world into "Producers" and "Non-Producers" and unlike traditional trade unions accepted employers, small businessmen and farmers, as well as wage earners as members. They aimed to create a farmer-worker "producers" alliance. They opposed pure trade unionism, on the grounds that workers organized trade unions to protect the selfish interests of the workers rather than to promote the common good and excluded Blacks and other racial minorities.

In the early 1880s the K of L proved far more successful than the trade unions in attracting membership in Washington Territory. The trade unions responded by developing non-partisan political activities that aimed to improve life for the entire community, not just wage earners and to develop political alliances with farm and professional groups, a characteristic that has remained with the labor movement unto the 21st century. Since the 1880s, the craft unions have resisted affiliation with any political party even when they generally supported that party. And they were hampered by the absence of a state-wide body to develop policies and coordinate political campaigns and lobbying efforts.

The K of L blamed the rising unemployment of native born and immigrant White workers on the over-supply of cheap Chinese labor. Despite the opposition of business, civic, and government leaders, the K of L helped to organize "Chinese Must Go" movements in the Seattle-Tacoma area. Between the fall of 1885 and the spring of 1886 the K of L inspired the unemployed workers to organize strikes, boycotts, and physical attacks on the Chinese in the coal mines, forcing the mine owners to fire their Chinese workers. They succeeded in expelling nearly every one of the Chinese living in Seattle or Tacoma.

Although many business, social and political leaders opposed the anti-Chinese movement, the leaders of the new working class favored it. Jacob Weisback, a labor leader, was elected mayor of Tacoma on an anti-Chinese ticket. Later, in the spring of 1886, the Seattle K of L chapter began to organize a "people's party" to elect a labor-sympathizer, W. H. Shandy, as mayor. The Peoples Party, a populist coalition, represented the first significant political reform movement in the Territory. The Peoples Party coalition included trade unions, middle and lower class elements, as well as anti-Chinese groups. It disavowed socialism and anarchism, but attacked machine politics and monopoly control.

The business, civic and professional groups in the community that opposed the eviction of the Chinese then organized the Loyal League, insisting that the main issue was loyalty to the Constitution. Employers began to fight the unions. The coal operators, for example, recognized unions only as beneficial societies to entertain their members or to pay their funeral expenses. They denied them the right to negotiate over wages or working conditions; and they began to use spies, lockouts, blacklists and armed guards to enforce their will. They even supported a competing mine workers union.

The K of L reacted with a series of occasionally violent strikes and boycotts in their search for union recognition. In 1886 and between 1888 and 1889, those battles repeatedly disrupted the mines of Western Washington. They were aided when Shandy won the Seattle mayoralty election in 1886 defeating the Loyal League's candidate, A. A. Denny, the Seattle pioneer. Subsequently, the Populists endorsed the Democratic candidate for governor, Charles Vorhees, who went on to victory. In King County 10 of 17 Peoples Party candidates were elected.

The K of L's political success was short-lived. In 1887, a split developed among the labor supporters of the Peoples Party. Some trade unionists opposed cooperation with all "producers" feeling that non-labor groups would betray their labor allies in a crisis. In Seattle and Tacoma, a labor faction broke away from the Peoples Party and formed a separate United Labor Party based on Henry George's National Union Labor Party. They refused to compromise with non-labor groups and demanded government ownership of railroads, more paper money, free coinage of silver, abolition of contract labor on public projects, abolition of child labor, and a graduated income tax, culminating in the 1896 elections. The lack of unity proved a disastrous turning point for the reformers. The Republicans swept the elections. In Seattle, the trade unions vowed never again to organize an independent political party.

Chastened by their defeat at the polls, the two labor factions – the K of L and the trade unions – turned their attention to their economic organization. In April 1888, they joined the Cascade coal mining unions to form the first central labor body in the Territory, the Western Central Labor of Union of Seattle and Vicinity (WCLU). The WCLS, later, renamed the Seattle Central Labor Council (SCLC) continues in operation as the King County Central Labor Council (KCCLC). The trade unions in the WCLS also included the Cigar Makers, Printers, and Iron Molders unions. The two main organizers of the WCLU were two young civil engineers, Otto F. Wegener and C. O. "Dad" Young, both of whom had been prominent in the anti-Chinese movement. Wegener soon dropped out of the labor movement, but Young joined the Tacoma Steam Engineers Union and served as its legislative agent. He played an important leadership role in the establishment of the Washington State Federation of Labor (WSFL) and served as an American Federation of Labor (AFL) organizer in the Pacific Northwest from 1904 to the end of his life in 1944. By then, membership in the trade unions exceeded that of the K of L, but the K of L continued to wield considerable influence. The unit-voting rule prevailed in the WCLU and the other central labor bodies later established in Spokane, Tacoma, and other cities in Washington. This allowed the K of L assemblies to have equal votes with the trade unions even as their memberships declined.

The lack of representation equal to their numerical strength in the central labor bodies probably contributed to the growing conflict between the trade unions and the K of L. This came to a head in 1888. A feud developed between the K of L members and the Miners Union members working at the Oregon Improvement Company's (OIC) Newcastle mine on the eastern shore of Lake Washington. About 60 "discordant" K of L members struck the mine but 150 or 200 Miners Union members, with the covert support of the OIC, refused to join the walkout. This led to a confrontation between the two sides which left one dead and as many as nine wounded. In August 1888, the Northern Pacific Coal Company took advantage of this union dispute to bring in 400 Blacks to break the strike at its mines and Roslyn, Washington. This broke the back of the K of L in the coal mines and prevented the Miners Union from organizing until after the turn of the century. In the wake of the conflict in the mines, relations between the K of L and the trades unions deteriorated further, with the K of L declining in numbers while the trades unions waxed. Economic recovery after the depression of the early 1880s also undercut the appeal of the labor movement.

The sharp Depression of 1893-1894 hurt both the trades unions and the K of L already in a weakened condition. The WCLU nearly collapsed. In an effort to recoup, the K of L again struck the OIC coal mines in the summer of 1894. By the fall of 1894, however, the strike collapsed and the K of L never recovered from the blow.

A few years later, a new group emerged to challenge the trade unions. With the failure of the K of L many nonferrous[5] metal miners in the Pacific Northwest and Rocky Mountain regions began to move into the Western Federation of Miners (WFM). The WFM, unlike the K of L, was a trade union. Unlike the trade unions affiliated with the AFL, however, it was an industrial union. That is, it favored organizing all the workers in a single industry into a single union regardless of the workers' craft. It also favored Socialism. In the early 1890s, the WFM achieved a number of remarkable successes among native-born miners in the Idaho panhandle and among smelter men at Northport and Tacoma in Washington. In 1896, they became one of the few industrial unions in the AFL. This did not last long, especially after the AFL refused to support a WFM strike in Leadville, Colorado in 1897. When the WFM created a subsidiary, the Western Labor Union, to organize western workers in competition with the AFL's international unions a break became inevitable.

This inspired the WCLU to take action. In 1898, it joined several other central labor councils and local unions to organize the Washington State Labor Congress, the first statewide labor organization in Washington's history. Its thrust was to lobby the legislature and so encourage enactment of the Populist Party's platform. Equally, the WCLU's craft unionists hoped the Congress would blunt the appeal of industrial unionism represented by the WFM. The Congress sent its own representative to lobby the 1899 legislature in behalf of its legislative agenda, including the direct election of United States senators and passage of a women's suffrage amendment to the Constitution among other proposals. While failing to pass a majority of its bills, the Congress did succeed in passing legislation establishing a State Labor Bureau and a Labor Lien Law.[6] Organized labor has sent its lobbyists to every state legislature since that time and has never failed to win some improvement, however slight, for its members.

The turn of the 20th century saw the emergence of the Socialist Party of America (SPA) and its affiliate, the Socialist Party of Washington (SPW). However, the cooperation between the national and state organizations was fraught with tension. Whereas moderates by moderates, who favored democratic reform of the economy, dominated the SPA, the left wing, who favored revolutionary change, dominated the SPW. The SPW was drawn leftward by competition from several local factions, including the Social Democratic Party and the local branch of the Socialist Labor Party, each more radical than the other. These parties made some inroads among union members but failed to gain majority support from the unions. The attraction of the socialists persisted throughout the early decades of the twentieth century, but their tendency to break down into quarrelling factions became quickly evident when the SPW split.

The trade unions, continued to lobby the legislature for improved labor legislation. There were no dramatic improvements, but labor won incremental gains that collectively seem very impressive, most notably the Workmen's Compensation Act of 1911, which was among the earliest in the nation. The Workmen's Compensation Act for the first time provided monthly benefits from state funds to workers injured on the job while they were incapacitated. Employers, who contributed according to the number of workers and the accident rate for their industry, funded the program. This was a major benefit to those workers in the state's most dangerous industries, including the logging, lumber and shingle industries, which had very high accident rates. Tying the fees to the accident rate the law had a significant effect in encouraging employers to emphasize and encourage safety in their plants.

At its fourth annual conference in January 1902, Washington State Labor Congress could point to some significant organizational achievements. By that time, labor historian Harry Call later estimated that there were 160 local unions, with 15,000 members in Washington. Of those, 114 local unions and 5 central labor councils had affiliated with the Congress.[7] This exaggerated the size and strength of the WSFL, but clearly the craft unions had established a strong foothold. In a total non-farm labor force of approximately 286,000 workers, the WSFL had organized approximately 2.01%. Between 1902 and World War I, it never represented more than 4% of the work force.[8] But because it was organized, this small percentage was able to have a much larger economic and political influence than mere numbers alone suggest.

The most important action at the Congress in 1902 was the battle over affiliation with the AFL. Opposition to this move was very strong. Advocates only won approval to change the name of the Congress to the Washington State Federation of Labor (WSFL), and agreement to submit the decision to a referendum of the membership. The advocates of affiliation were stronger, and a hard fight lasted more than two years. Ultimately, the WCLU voted in favor of the referendum in 1904 and the Spokane Central Labor Council followed suit in 1905. The titanic struggle left strong pockets of opposition from industrial unionists, several socialist factions, and K of L remnants in most of the labor organizations. Only continuing factionalism within the socialist ranks prevented them from uniting to oppose AFL affiliation successfully.

The lack of adequate statistics on union membership in Washington State has long handicapped labor historians. For my dissertation, I produced union membership figures for the period 1902-1935, but these statistics were limited to the WSFL and affiliated unions. I have updated those figures with nearly complete statistics for both WSFL and its successor, the Washington State Labor Council WSLC memberships (1902-2005).[9] Except for 2000-2005, these data come directly from the labor organizations themselves; the 21st century statistics are based on labor union statistics compiled by the Bureau of Labor Statistics. By the middle of the first decade of the 20th century, the WSFL had successfully organized its core constituency, the craft trade unions, and had begun to win gradual political and legislative gains. They had also successfully fought off the calls from the Socialist Party of America and its various factions to affiliate with them and thus harness the state's workers in behalf of socialist political goals. These successes were by no means permanent and depended upon constant vigilance from the leadership to prevent individual unions or members from affiliating with political parties. New challenges also arose to the continued dominance of the WSFL. The first decade of the 20th century also saw the rise of the Industrial Workers of the World (IWW) otherwise known as the "Wobblies." The IWW was formed in 1902 by break-away syndicalist factions from the WFM and the SPA. The Wobblies like most syndicalists opposed political action of any kind. Syndicalists believed that an organization of workers should replace both governments and employers. They also opposed specialized craft unions, or the idea of separate international unions for workers in different industries. Their quixotic core belief was that if everyone joined "one big union," there would be no further need for politics, government, separate craft or industrial unions, or employers. The One Big Union would take over the world. They believed that if they prepared properly a revolutionary moment would arise at which point they workers of the world would arise and sweep away the old order through a general strike. The Wobblies were largely young, male, unskilled, immigrants from eastern and southern Europe. They had English speaking leaders but most of them did not speak English, were not citizens and did not understand American politics. Nor, living in isolated lumber, mining camps or fishing they had an opportunity to learn about the American political system. Many were expatriates from the oppression from Kings, Kaisers, or Czars; and had participated in anti-imperialist revolutionary movements in their homelands. The IWW managed to make some gains in Washington between 1902 and 1919 especially where absentee owners used company housing, medical care, and transport as a means to control their isolated work forces. The Wobblies resented such "benefits" and despised those satisfied by such incremental gains. The Wobblies believed that the goal of labor was to overthrow the bosses and take economic control of the State in behalf of the working people. They felt trapped by in their jobs and saw little prospect of real improvement under the existing capitalist economic and political system. They even supported sabotage of businesses as a way to force employers to bend. Despite their revolutionary proposals and tactics, the Wobblies initially won some sympathy among the wider public for their "Free Speech" campaigns against employers and governments that obstructed their organizing efforts.

The IWW and the Western Federation of Miners (WFM) diverged in their political goals and methods. They both envisioned organizing giant industrial unions that would incorporate all the specific crafts working in them and both aimed for achieve utopian goals by transforming their causes into a political crisis in the wider society. Both also opposed the WSFL's craft union structure which favored highly skilled workers competing within small local markets. Subsequently, the WFM migrated into the Socialist Party of America, and individuals in it later affiliated with the Bolsheviks during and after World War I. The IWW kept itself free of political entanglements, and engaged in a campaign of sabotage and economic disruption, hoping to create or take advantage of the resulting crisis to assume political power for the workers.

In most places in the United States neither the WFM nor the IWW managed to gain more than a toehold in any industry. Their "Free Speech" campaigns against the anti-syndicalism laws in several localities in Washington were widely publicized and attracted widespread public sympathy, but their policies of sabotage and working to rule to force employers to concede to their demands, brought on the enmity of employers and widespread criticism. World War I led to the undoing of the Wobblies, the Socialist Party of American and to its various radical offshoots. To date, neither the socialist left, nor their Bolshevik and Communist successors have ever regained the level of support they obtained from the labor movement in the years before World War I. The Socialist Party of America was the first to suffer. When the war broke out in 1914, every one of the socialist parties in Europe abandoned pacifism and patriotically supported their nations on the war. American socialists also split on the war with German-American socialists opposing American entry into the war on the side of the Germans and Anglo-American socialists supporting American support for the British, French, Russian allies and calling for American entry into the war. The socialists split into an ever smaller group of warring factions and never reunited after the war. The IWW also suffered from the war, but the crisis for them came after America entered the war, when they launched a campaign to gain control of Pacific Northwest lumber workers especially those involved in the production of wood for making military aircraft. Whereas before the war, the federal government had been only mildly concerned with the IWW or the socialist parties in peacetime, once the war broke out, Woodrow Wilson's administration unleashed a ferocious and concerted anti-IWW campaign to keep the lumber industry out of IWW hands. To reduce the appeal of the IWW to the workers, the federal government established and recognized a company union for the lumber industry known as the Loyal Legion of Loggers and Lumbermen to represent lumber workers. The Loyal Legion, or "4Ls" as they were known, promised its members fair pay and conditions for the duration; the workers immediately abandoned the IWW; and the IWW effort collapsed the 4Ls soon followed. Popular disapproval, government repression, imprisonment, exile, death soon eroded the appeal of the IWW. The growing attraction of bolshevism after the Russian Revolution in 1917, also hastened its demise by diverting labor and socialist groups away from the unsuccessful domestic groups to the new and apparently successful Russian

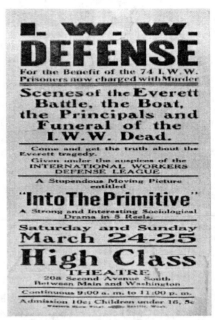

SMA

"Radical" International Workers of the World riding a tugboat from Seattle were met by trigger happy sheriff's deputies at the Everett docks. The impromptu Seattle General Strike of 1919 collapsed in four days, but unions grew stronger.

revolutionaries. At the same time the IWW and other labor radicals and socialists who opposed American involvement in World War I, became the targets of federal, state, and local legal attacks on the ground that they were interfering with the war effort. The economic recession which followed quickly in the wake of the war and which led to drastic cuts in employment in the Pacific Northwest prevented any quick recovery. It was not until the 1930s that lumber and sawmill workers organized effectively or that socialist ideas received a sympathetic hearing in the labor movement. The WSFL joined actively in the campaigns against the IWW and the anti-war socialist parties.

By 1919, the economically and politically conservative leaders of the Washington State Federation of Labor had come to dominate the organization. In the 1920s, they linked politically with the Farmers Alliance, the Grange, the Washington Education Association, and progressive Republicans to win substantive reforms like workmen's compensation improvements, the eight hour day, specific legislation for women and minors, election reform, tax reduction and a wide variety of health and safety legislation placing the state at the forefront in these areas.

Thus, the Seattle General Strike of 1919 was essentially an unrepresentative event. Rather than representing a forward step on the path most Seattle workers wanted to follow, it represented a momentary detour or diversion from that path. Furthermore, by adding to the existing fears of employers and other conservatives the fear of revolution, it strengthened those who opposed labor.

Why this Seattle General Strike occurred when and where it did requires some explanation. The Seattle General Strike occurred at a time of dramatic change for the trade unions in Washington, a time when union members sensed great opportunities in the future but feared the approach of hard times. The statistics show WSFL membership increasing dramatically during World War I as wartime government spending gave a great boost to the economy. It reached new highs each year during the war and growth continued during the first months of peace. By 1919-1920 WSFL membership reached 55,257 organized in 263 locals, or 9.56% of the state's total workforce of about 578,000.[10] Most of the new members worked in the Puget Sound region especially in the wartime shipyards that proliferated there. Seattle shipbuilders and other employers working on generous government contracts did not struggle against union organizers to the same degree as if they were working on commercial contracts because the government contracts covered all of their costs and guaranteed a profit. New locals won recognition in many previously unorganized firms. Union coffers were full, but many unions experienced a shortage of experienced leaders for the first time as the unions attempted to service their thousands of new members with an organizational structure designed for a much smaller membership. This was an especially serious weakness in view of the dramatic world events occurring in the last days of World War I and the early postwar period. The Bolshevik Revolution, then underway, the collapse of the German and Austrian Empires and the rise of revolutionary movements in those regions stirred the new members of the unions in Washington State as never before. The events encouraged the more hopeful or gullible workers to put their trust in the more radical voices. IWW organizers, radical socialists, industrial unionists, and Bolshevik or communist sympathizers were only too happy to encourage the belief that world revolution awaited only a single spark to ignite.

At the same time, it was clear to labor and business leaders and the general public that the wartime boom could not go on when the wartime contracts ended and that the local economy would soon begin to suffer. More experienced or sensible leaders might have counseled against a general strike except for the fact that in January 1919, most of the experienced leaders of the WSFL-affiliated Seattle Central Labor Council had left town to attend a national meeting in Chicago.[11] In their absence, the inexperienced junior union leaders seized the opportunity to call a general strike in sympathy with a strike by the

Seattle shipyards workers, which was scheduled to begin 1 February 1919. The shipyard workers hoped to force agreement on a new contract before the ending of the wartime contracts. To support them the Seattle Central Labor Council voted to call a city-wide general strike for 6 February. The vote represented a rank and file insurgency that lacked responsible leadership or coordination. Most critically, the strikers failed to spell out any practical goals for the strike or to prepare for a long term struggle. Instead of rallying to the union banner, the public ignored the call for revolution and enjoyed the holiday from work. When senior union leaders heard what was going on, they rushed back to Seattle and quickly reasserted control. The strike collapsed by 9 February.

The relative success of the WSFL in the 1920s came from a more sophisticated understanding of American politics. Under the leadership of President William F. Short, a former mineworker, the WSFL was devoted to working within the American economic and political system and in ensuring that union members received fair pay and benefits for their labor. Most Americans and most union members were not recent immigrants from imperialist Europe. Most did not work in dangerous, poorly paid industries or live in company housing. They spoke English and had at least a basic education. They had access to public education and medical care. Many, if not a majority, owned their own homes. If they had a disagreement with their boss they knew that they had a good chance of finding another job. At the very least, they expected that their children would benefit from their hard work. The American people were never radical; nor were the people of Washington.

By the 1920s, AFL craft unions had won a firm economic niche for themselves in the economy of Washington State. Their main failing was that, except for a brief period during World War I, they never succeeded in organizing the bulk of the industrial workers. The United Mine Workers and the International Brotherhood of Teamsters were the only large industrial unions in the AFL or the WSFL. The AFL and WSFL were handicapped in organizing industrial workers because industrial workers earned far less than the skilled craft workers. They were not able to afford the kind of union dues paid by well-paid, skilled AFL workers and the AFL craft unions. To organize them, the craft unions would have had to subsidize their organizing efforts to a very great extent, and transfer many of their own members to the new industrial unions. Most of the major unorganized industries contained pockets of craft workers who were already members of AFL unions. Electricians, plumbers, bricklayers, and other craft workers claimed jurisdictions in some or all of these industries. An AFL effort to organize the unorganized industrial workers would lead to perpetual jurisdictional conflicts within the AFL. Thirdly, industrial workers were generally recent immigrants from eastern and southern Europe, largely Catholic or Orthodox in religion, and frequently spoke English as a second language if at all. The AFL craft unions derived their memberships primarily from native born and older immigrant groups from Germany, England, Scotland and Ireland, and other Northern and Western Europe. There were vast cultural differences between the craft and industrial workers.

Hope that Labor's economic gains from World War I might be permanent proved ephemeral. In the post-World War I economic recession most of the workers in the shipyards and other wartime industries lost their jobs and union memberships collapsed. After reaching a peak of over 55,000 members in 1919-1920, WSFL membership fell to 20,253 in 1923-1924, when the WSFL represented only about 3.32% of the state's workforce. After that WSFL membership stabilized and even recovered somewhat, but it generally remained under 4% of the workforce during the 1920s.[12]

Technological change was disastrous to other unions. As oil, gasoline, and hydroelectric power began to supplant coal for heating, transportation, and power production in the Northwest, coal prices fell and mine owners pressured workers to improve productivity and accept cuts in pay and conditions. Year by year in the early 1920s coal miners' wages and conditions deteriorated. Finally, when United Mine Workers District 10's contract with its employers expired at the bottom of the postwar depression in 1921 United Mine Workers District 10 struck the owners. The industry was in very bad shape and the result a foregone conclusion. Washington coal was expensive to mine. The alternatives – oil, gas, and hydroelectric power – were cheaper to produce, cleaner and more flexible to use, and more modern. To stay in business, Washington coal producers needed to cut labor costs. By 1923 District 10, once the backbone of the WSFL, virtually collapsed. Miners who returned to work after the strike did so without contracts. District 10 existed until after World War II, but never again won employer recognition; the industry as a whole also declined steadily and eventually disappeared shortly after World War II. In the 1920s, the development of radio threatened to put musicians out of business. The public increasingly turned to free radio performances instead of attending concerts, theaters, or night clubs for their musical entertainment. Broadcasters turned increasingly to recorded music in place of live musicians, and the pressure on organized musicians grew intense. The Seattle Musicians Union local attempted heroically to resist the trend but to no avail. In a strike lasting more than a decade, from 1921 to 1935, they failed to slow the trend away from live musical performances, and returned to work without a contract.

b) The weakness of the WSFL in the 1920s was a symptom of a growing economic crisis more than a century in the making. The crisis was largely the result of a national economic policy that affected workers, farmers, and merchants throughout the nation, and even throughout the world. During the American revolution, American non-importation agreements – the refusal of Americans to consume products made in England – gave a strong but temporary boost to American manufacturers. After the Revolution, the refusal of the Europeans, especially the British, to give American producers access to their markets, caused trade to languish and also gave an impetus to domestic American manufacturers. During the French Revolution and the Napoleonic Revolution, between 1789 and 1815, both sides interfered with American shipping and impressed American seamen into their navies. This also encouraged Americans to manufacture goods that they could not import from Europe. In reaction to this interference with American trade President Jefferson imposed an embargo on trade with the belligerents. This further increased the incentive for Americans to begin manufacturing goods that they could no longer obtain abroad. During the War of 1812 trade continued to languish as both American and British navies captured one another's trading ships. Each one of these events, placing limits on importation of goods from Europe raised the cost of imported goods and therefore encouraged domestic manufacturing. American manufacturers responded by successfully making and marketing domestically made products on a very wide scale.

The rise in domestic manufacturing became so marked that by 1818, large numbers of New England men and women had left their farms and found jobs in the new industries. Most found work in cotton and wool spinning trades and in the manufacture of clothing and shoes, primarily for sale to southern planters. Following the war, the return of trade to its traditional routes led to rising bankruptcies and unemployment in the new American industries; thousands of workers found themselves destitute. Congress responded, in 1819, to protect American manufacturers by placing import tariffs on competing goods from abroad. This proved so successful in protecting the manufacturers and jobs that Congress increased the tariff in every Congress but one (1914) from then until 1931 (Smoot-Hawley Tariff). Each year, the rise in tariffs protected American manufacturers by making competing foreign products more expensive. By the 1920s, American import tariffs were so high that very few foreign producers could sell their products in the United States; consequently, they could not earn dollars to buy American exports. Recovery to pre-World War I levels was impossible. Revolution in Russia led to her isolation from the international trading system. Financially destitute because of the war, Britain and France limited international trade within their empires, and lacked the resources to make major purchases from America. To a certain extent, the international trading system was able to limp along during the 1920s funded by private American loans to Germany and Austria, which allowed them to pay reparations to the British and French. The reparations, in turn, allowed the British and French to repay debts from World War I to the United States. American exporters, such as Eastern Washington wheat farmers and Western Washington lumber producers found their markets drying up as foreigners lacked the resources to buy American products.

The collapse of Wall Street in 1929 further undercut the world trading system. When the market fell, American bankers no longer had the money to lend to the Germans and Austrians. They in turn could not continue to pay reparations to the British and French, who defaulted on their war debts to the United States, and were unable to purchase American exports. Congress tried to solve the problem with the Smoot-Hawley Tariff of 1931, the highest tariff yet. After more than a century of raising tariffs, Congress had made it harder for trade to resume. Other nations responded by imposing tariffs of their own, further constricting trade and economic activity, and causing unemployment to rise to catastrophic levels throughout the world. Conditions were so bad in Germany and elsewhere that people lost faith in democracy itself. The breakup of the pre-1914 World into rival self-isolating economic systems, worsened the economy, and aborted recovery.

The 1929 stock market crash and the Depression of the 1930s struck organized labor in Washington when it was already in a weakened and disheartened state. Politically, conservative Republicans dominated the state legislature and Congress and Labor gained Little politically during the later 1920s. However, the seeds of renewal and strength had already begun to sprout in the unlikeliest places. In the mid-1920s, a young Seattle laundry truck driver began to emerge as a dynamic leader of organized labor. Dave Beck convinced the leadership of the International Brotherhood of Teamsters to let him try to organize the teamsters' over-the-road truck drivers. The over the road truck drivers first appeared in World War I when congestion on the railroads forced Seattle shipbuilders to import welding supplies from Portland in trucks. But the postwar growth in highway construction and tremendous technological improvements in trucks and their carrying capacity made it possible for drivers to greatly expand their markets, traditionally the distance a teamster could travel to deliver a load and return in one day. By the mid-1920s a teamster could easily travel Seattle to Portland, Oregon, with a load of cargo and return in the same day; by the 1930s he could travel almost anywhere in the state and return the same day. Beck realized he could organize the teamsters on a regional basis without traveling from his base in Seattle. Further, he saw that he could use the strength of this jurisdiction to organize other trades in regions thousands of miles from his base in Seattle. Beck's bargaining position was immeasurably strengthened because cost of transportation labor was a minute fraction in the final price of any commodity. Employers could easily afford to grant higher wages to truck drivers without raising prices or hurting sales. Second, by organizing employers, he could assure that no employer in any market area would have an advantage over the others in trucking costs which made it attractive for employers to reach agreement with the Teamsters. Third, by refusing to indulge in political or ideological campaigns for general social goals, Beck made himself far more attractive to employers than the radical, Communist, Socialist, or other left wing union leaders in the labor movement who argued for revolutionary change, and the nemesis of Harry Bridges.

Beck was as non-ideological and apolitical a union leader as has ever existed. He believed that labor was a simply a commodity that workers had, and all that they had to sell. They should try to get the best price they could for it. Unions should not disperse their efforts in obtaining social, economic, or ideological goals. Beck was also among the most energetic and aggressive leaders ever to hold a union position. A no-holds-barred competitor, Beck announced that he would fight all comers by any rules or none to attain the Teamsters' goals.

Beck in essence used the Teamsters' over-the-road jurisdiction to pressure on employers to hire teamsters and recognize other unions. Employers had a choice: either recognize the Teamsters union, or not receive deliveries by truck. In smaller communities, Beck even offered to organize employers into associations so that he could better negotiate with them. He provided offices in Teamster buildings to the employers associations. Employers usually succumbed to Beck without a fight. Beck then demanded that the employers also recognize other unions for their workers. He was, for example, responsible for the establishment of the Retail Clerks Union in Seattle. For many years, the Seattle Retail Clerks' office was located in the Teamsters' office building, where the employers association also had their offices.

In the early 1930s, Beck's statewide over-the-road Teamsters jurisdiction developed into the Western Conference of Teamsters, which covered 11 western states, Alaska and Hawaii. By the late 1930s, he had organized virtually every teamster in the West and destroyed the Open Shop in Los Angeles, which had kept that city union-free for generations. By refusing to allow truck shipments into the city Beck quickly forced the employers to recognize the unions where generations of organizing had failed. Beck also became a power within the national teamster organization.

As much as Beck disdained political campaigns for progressive social policies, the election of Franklin Roosevelt to the presidency in 1932 greatly benefited the Teamsters along with other labor organizations. The election of pro-labor, usually Democratic politicians throughout the West also helped Beck and other labor leaders and buttressed labor's position generally. Franklin Roosevelt supported labor legislatively and administratively. It created a Labor Relations Board to rule in cases of disputes over the law. The Wagner Act of 1935, for example, required employers to allow unions to organize and workers to bargain collectively; it required them to recognize unions following successful elections. Under Roosevelt, the federal government abandoned high tariff policies of the past and began to negotiate fair trade agreements with other nations. This did not immediately result in any significant lowering of trade barriers, but set the stage for the rapid reductions in tariffs and other barriers to trade that began following World War II and that have continued into the 21st century. These reductions allowed for a vast expansion in the available markets for Washington's products including wheat, apples, airplanes, and later computer software and coffee franchises. The wholesale migration of Progressive Republicans, into the New Deal coalition helped secure Roosevelt's victory. Their price for their political support was a massive public power program that included the Tennessee Valley Authority in the East and the Bonneville Power Administration in the Columbia River region. Vast public works projects such as these led to the expenditures of huge sums of money in the Pacific Northwest propping up employment in the region. The dams built as a result allowed increased navigation of the Columbia and its tributaries and created a huge surplus of cheap electricity, which allowed the creation of a large aluminum industry in Washington State and greatly promoted the Boeing Company's manufacture of aluminum-skinned airplanes. The economic collapse of the Great Depression coupled with the rise of totalitarian regimes of the left and right in the Soviet Union, Italy, and then, most menacingly, Germany and Japan, sent a chill through the American establishment in the 1930s. Under Roosevelt however, this chill proved invigorating. Rather than retreating into a conservative shell, Roosevelt determined to restore capitalism. Challenged on both the Left and the Right Roosevelt continued to asset the superiority of American capitalism. Under Roosevelt, the federal government actively aligned in favor of labor's right to organize and bargain collectively. By pressing for federal programs to support workers and their families – by not being merely neutral or actively opposed to labor – Roosevelt kept the vast majority of American workers committed to democratic institutions and was able to resist voices calling for radical, non-democratic solutions. Neither fascist nor Communist ideologies were able to make significant inroads either in Washington State or elsewhere.

The Great Depression revived the fortunes of the radical industrial unionists, virtually expelled from the labor movement after the General Strike of 1919. They took advantage of the pro-labor policies of the New Deal to organize actively in the longshore, logging, lumber, and brewery industries among others, in the Pacific Northwest and in Washington and won remarkable gains very quickly. By 1938, they had organized approximately 65,000 workers in Washington State alone at a time when the AFL-affiliated unions in the State boasted only 46,000 members. Harry Bridges of the International Longshoremen's and Warehousemen's Union, energetically competed with existing craft unions across the gamut of the union movement. The CIO succeeded beyond their wildest dreams elsewhere in the United States, especially in the coal, steel, automobile, and rubber industries. However, their victory in Washington State was limited to the ILWU, the International Woodworkers of America Union (IWA), and a few smaller unions. Their success was limited because Dave Beck and the WSFL led a ferocious counterattack that quickly repelled the CIO's efforts to organize other workers. Except for the Teamsters, the AFL and the WSFL, its Washington State affiliate, were slower to respond to the organizing opportunities available under the New Deal, but when they did, it was on a much broader scale.

The industrial union resurgence in Washington inspired an even more vehement response from the AFL and WSFL beginning in 1937. As de facto leader of the AFL and WSFL in their campaign against the CIO, Dave Beck sent in his Teamsters organizers to compete for the workers in virtually every plant and industry targeted by Bridges and his men. When the industrial union organization – the Committee of Industrial Organizations (CIO) – was expelled from the AFL in 1937 and reorganized as the Congress of Industrial Organizations (CIO) Beck redoubled his efforts. The WSFL expelled the CIO and all their affiliated unions.

Schism or conflict within an organization is normally a preface to decline and dissolution. Indeed, the labor movement had always stressed the great importance of unity, or "brotherhood" among unions and union members. Despite this the fear that the civil war between AFL and CIO, represented in Washington by the conflict between Dave Beck's Teamsters and Harry Bridges' Longshoremen, never became a reality. Indeed, it was a very short civil war. In Washington, the CIO never surpassed its initial membership claims in 1938, then declined steadily, to 45,000 in 1945, and 24,000 in 1956. Meanwhile, energized by the conflict and Beck's vigorous leadership, the WSFL grew from 46,000 in 1938, to 88,000 in 1945. By 1956, when the AFL and CIO reunited to create the AFL-CIO, the WSFL, with 129,000 members, dwarfed the sagging CIO.

It may be that the reunification of the two union federations might have occurred much earlier than it did but for the outbreak of World War II. During the war, both federations faithfully adhered to an inter-labor truce, effectively preserving the status quo ante until the end of the war. This effectively brought to an end the WSFL's increasingly effective State CIO unions and slowed the erosion in CIO membership. In practical terms, it hurt the CIO in Washington far more than the WSFL. This was due, primarily, to the ideological affiliations of the CIO. The heavily ideological CIO found itself deeply split over the issue of communism.

At the fourth annual Washington State CIO convention in Olympia, in 1942, Adolph Germer, president of the International Woodworkers Union, the largest CIO union in Washington addressed these divisions:

We are facing a new order of things. The world is being remade and reshaped. I heard one of the speakers refer to Communist and Socialist economy. Personally, I am not a prophet[,] and I don't know that anyone else can prophesy with accuracy just what is going to take place and how the world will look when the war is over. That will depend in large measure upon the extent to which workers are organized, and what voice they will have in determining an economic program and policy and political and social conditions, after the war. ... And above all, our sacred duty to ourselves, ... and to this country is to maintain our democratic institutions and our democratic processes. [It] is to guard against moments of hysteria and allow no man on horseback in the role of Hitler, a Mussolini or other dictator to take the powers that dictators always take in the guise of saviors of their country.[13]

Part 2: Labor Rules

The mutually agreed on labor peace in effect during World War II solidified Labor's gains won during the thirties. Federal policies supported labor's right to organize and bargain collectively, and for conditions and benefits continued into the postwar era. But the war and the overriding need to sustain production had the untoward effect of undermining the federal government's support for labor. Victory and the return of prosperity had reinforced the credibility of the federal government and democratic ideas, while defeat and the collapse of Germany, Italy, and Japan diminished the appeal to workers of fascist solutions. The need for national unity in the face of external danger seemed to diminish. The internecine divisions over Communism, and public disgust with its sympathizers further undermined labor's public support. The rise of the Soviet Union to world power, the onset of the Cold War and the threat of nuclear war, coupled with the spread of Communism to Eastern Europe and China through coups and civil wars greatly eroded the appeal of socialist and communist solutions. Before World War II, CIO union members from Eastern and Southern European immigrant groups, including Finns, Norwegians, Lithuanians, Poles, and Swedes, had sympathized with the anti-fascist struggle in Europe and allied themselves with Communist and "Popular Front" organizations to oppose Hitler and Mussolini. They had formed the backbone of CIO membership in the logging camps and mill towns of Washington. In the postwar era, they now found themselves opposed to Soviet occupation of, or threats against, their homelands. Thus, as the postwar era dawned labor had reduced political importance. With the United States rising to become the dominant world power, the federal government saw less and less reason to accommodate labor.

Few Washington labor leaders understood or anticipated the changes. Rising prices after the War caused a number of unions to strike for and win higher wages. Their success led to a backlash against unions, nationally. The public felt the balance between labor and management had swung too far toward labor, and Congress began to explore ways to limit labor's power, climaxing in the Taft-Hartley Act of 1947. A few "corrupt labor leaders and the control of some unions by communists" increased the pressure for reform.[14] The AFL had long fought Communist influence in its member unions and was largely insulated from the rising tide of anti-Communist feeling.

But the CIO was not so lucky. In the postwar era, the ideological conflicts within the CIO spread across a wide spectrum of issues but the issue of communism remained at the center. The bulk of the CIO leadership, for example, wanted to support the Democratic Party in the 1948; however, the Communists wanted to support the Progressive Party. In 1949 when the CIO withdrew from the World Federation of Trade Unions, charging that it was under Communist influence the Communist CIO leaders bitterly objected. Communists used CIO publications like the CIO News to attack US foreign and other policies; non-communists in the CIO strongly objected to this use of the CIO's publications. The upshot was that a number of CIO unions began expelling communist members and officials, including the United Automobile Workers, the National Maritime Union, and the Transport Workers Union. AFL and Non-communist CIO unions freely "raided" the membership of Communist CIO unions, hurting Communist unions financially. The United Farm Equipment and Metal Workers and the United Electrical, Radio, and Machine Workers took the heaviest attacks. In response, between 1949 and 1950, the CIO expelled these, and eight other member unions for refusing to rid themselves of Communist, or Communist-influenced leaders.

As the international threat from the Soviet Union and, later, Communist China grew worldwide, and especially after the Soviet Union exploded an atomic bomb, the domestic fear of Communist infiltration of American institutions became pervasive. The trend against labor was strong in both national parties and began even before the war started. The trend began with the creation of the House Un-American Activities Committee, in 1937. During and after the war, Congress strengthened HUAC and passed a series of increasingly stringent measures to control the activities of "Un-Americans."[15] The passage of federal anti-Communist legislation, and continued after the war into the era of the Cold War with the passage of the Taft-Hartley Act (1947), the Communist Control Act of 1954 (Butler Act)[16] and the Landrum Griffin Act (1959)[17] among many others. Section 9h of the Taft Hartley Act, in particular, had a significant negative impact on labor. This provision required every union officer to sign an affidavit certifying that he is not a member of the Communist Party or affiliated with such party, and that he does not believe in, and is not a member of or supports any organization that believes in or teaches the overthrow of the United States government by force or any illegal or unconstitutional methods.[18]

In Washington, the legislature reflected this sentiment when it appointed the Canwell Committee (1947-1949) to investigate the activities of communists in Washington institutions and passed a statute requiring teachers to sign a loyalty oath.[19] In the 1952 gubernatorial election liberal, former U.S. Senator Hugh Mitchell lost. His opponent accused him of being too 'pink.'[20]

While basic federal government support for labor continued to be strong even under Republican administrations, these measures also sharply limited its ability to grow by imposing more stringent regulations on unions, limiting the kinds of strikes and boycotts unions could employ and increasing the ways employers and government could combat unions. Republican administrations further restricted labor by placing critics of organized labor on the National Labor Relations Board, the Department of Labor, and similar bodies on a state and local level where they could affect the direction of labor relations.

Nationally, the decline in federal support for Labor and the rise in anti-communist efforts hurt the CIO much more than the AFL. In Washington, the impact was greatest on the International Union of Fishermen and Allied Workers (IUFAW), the National Union of Marine Cooks and Stewards (NUMCS) the International Union of Mine, Mill and Smelter Workers (IUMMSW), and to a lesser extent on the Internal Longshoremen's and Warehousemen's Union (ILWU). In the postwar era, membership in the IUFAW collapsed from a peak of 25,000 in 1947-1948, to a "negligible" figure by 1970. The MUMCS disappeared entirely by 1956. The IUMMSW, a descendant of the Western Federation of Miners fell from approximately 100,000 in 1946-1947 to approximately 60,000 in the US and Canada by 1970. Few of the remaining members were in Washington State.

Perhaps the one who most correctly understood the choices was Harry Bridges, the radical and possibly Communist head of the International Longshoremen's and Warehousemen's Union, the dominant longshore union on the West Coast. Bridges had led the union since its formation in the early 1930s, and out of the AFL and into the CIO in 1937. He had then led the CIO's bitter struggle with the AFL for dominance on the West Coast. Unlike the other Communist union leaders and their sympathizers in the CIO, Bridges was able to separate his ideological affinities from his practical responsibilities as a union leader and the higher wages in the longshore industry affected domestic and international shipping companies equally. Whereas the others sacrificed their practical responsibilities in order to maintain their ideological loyalties, Bridges adhered to his responsibilities to his members. In 1949, Bridges reversed course, ideologically, and negotiated a trend-setting contract with the longshore employers' organizations on the West Coast that allowed the employers to replace workers with new, more efficient, technology, so long as they employed ILWU members to operate the new equipment and passed on the savings in the form of higher wages. The agreement made possible the dramatic improvements in port operations throughout the West Coast and the rise of the longshoremen from among the poorest paid American workers to the elite class. At the same time, the number of longshore jobs has dropped dramatically as employers found that they could operate with fewer and fewer workers. In microcosm, this is the story of all of the great manufacturing and extractive industries in Washington since the end of World War II. Labor has exchanged better pay for a smaller workforce. As a result, membership in the ILWU remained stable in the postwar period from 1949 to 1970 at about 60,000.[21]

By the mid-1950s, as the CIO eliminated the Communists among its membership and the AFL unions found it increasingly difficult to organize, both found that they had a strong incentive to reestablish labor peace. As result, a strong movement arose on both state and national levels to reunify. In 1956, both organizations voted to merge, and by 1957, they had completed negotiations to form a single organization. At their 1957 convention, the WSFL and the Washington State CIO Council met together as the Washington State Labor Council (WSLC). The WSLC remains today the most significant statewide labor organization in Washington State.

Communists were not the only labor leaders to feel the effects of the anti-labor backlash during the 1950s. Federal and state prosecutors honed in on union corruption of various kinds. They singled out the International Longshoremen's Association on the East Coast and the International Brotherhood of Teamsters. By then, Dave Beck had risen to become President of the national Teamsters Union. Hemmed in by increasing regulations and legislation, the Teamsters had continued to grow and expand into non-traditional sectors. Beck faced investigations by Congress and the Eisenhower Administration in the 1950s. After a federal trial and conviction on tax evasion charges, Beck served several years at McNeil's Island Federal prison. The federal government also investigated and convicted Beck's replacement as Teamster President Jimmy Hoffa. Hoffa's replacement suffered a similar fate. With its leadership diminished and disrupted, the Teamsters' rate of growth has slowly declined.

HL

Dave Beck and Jimmy Hoffa, rulers of the Teamsters. (About 1949).

Ideological conflicts and legislative changes also weakened labor internally, as Washington State labor struggled against a changing economic environment after World War II. Labor found it increasingly difficult to retain the percentage of the work force that it had organized in 1937-1945. Labor union membership continued to grow but not as fast as the labor force, or the population as a whole. After reaching a peak in the 1950s when it represented over 50% of the state's non-farm labor force, the labor movement found it increasingly difficult to maintain its rate of growth.[22] The percentage of the labor force organized in unions began to decline steadily from the mid-1960s onwards. This trend has continued down to the present day. In part due to the long-term decline in manufacturing, the rapidly growing productivity of Washington labor, which allows ever-fewer workers to produce an ever-growing volume of goods, has also played a part. In part, the rise of the service industries, including restaurants, hotels, governments, and entertainment industries, which are notoriously difficult to organize, has also contributed to this decline. Finally, Washington's most profitable and rapidly growing new manufacturers, the electronic software industry, led by giant Microsoft, have proved impossible to organize. Their highly paid, professional and part-time employees have failed to identify with the cause of labor to date.

Stagnation and decline in union membership was also due to the rise of foreign competition. From the mid-1960s and especially since the late 1970s, foreign competition has achieved an ever-bigger percentage of American markets. Large American producers, protected from foreign competition for nearly a century and half by tariffs, Depression, world wars and cold wars, faced rapidly mounting competition in the latter third of the 20th century. The continuous fall of tariffs after the 1930s, the end of World War II in 1945, the economic recovery of Europe and Japan between 1950 and 1970, the collapse of Communism in the 1990s, and the rise of a new "global" economic system, increasingly exposed American and Washington to increasingly intense foreign competition.

The crises faced by bell-weather Washington industrial giants as the Boeing reflect these challenges. The great Boeing collapse of the 1960s, when the federal government cut back on military contracts after the Vietnam War, caused employment at the company to fall from nearly 120,000 to under 60,000. The collapse devastated both the International Association of Machinists (IAM) and the state's economy as a whole and made it increasingly difficult for the labor movement to grow. From 1963, when the WSLC represented 44.5% of the state's non-farm labor force there began a steady decline that lasted at least until 2000, when the WSLC represented only 17.51% of the state's non-farm labor force.[23] By strenuous organizing efforts, labor was able to maintain its membership, but in a growing labor force, it represented an ever-smaller percentage of that labor force.

As the 21st century dawned, Boeing, like Washington's largest businesses faced unprecedented competition, both domestic and foreign. With practically all trade restrictions eliminated by international agreement, they can only continue to exist by strictly controlling their costs – especially labor costs, and intensive efforts to improve productivity and the quality of their products and marketing. Each of these trends reduced further the ability of labor to bargain with their employers, or at least required them to make unheard of concessions. The International Association of Machinists has agreed to a long-term contract with Boeing – hailing it as a great victory – although it provides for no wage increases over the term of the contract.[24]

The economic policies of the federal government have also crimped labor's bargaining power. From the 1930s through the 1970s, the Federal Reserve Board controlled interest rates but allowed

A rally between capitol and Supreme Court, in 1982 against unemployment compensation "reforms."

the money supply to fluctuate freely, assuring that manufacturers a steady supply of buyers despite steadily rising prices. In the late 1970s, the combination of low interest rates and rising labor costs produced a soaring rate of inflation. As the price of American-made products rose, free trade allowed a flood of imported goods in to take their place. This forced a rising tide of layoffs and bankruptcies across the nation. It was quickly apparent that the influx of imported goods from the economically reviving nations of Europe and Asia would force a change in American economic policy. Simply to cut interest rates and allow the money supply to expand, would only encourage more inflation, which would encourage even more imports. To force American manufacturers to rise to the challenge of foreign competition, the Federal Reserve Board, therefore, switched policies to allow interest rates to float freely while strictly controlling the money supply. Firms that could not control their prices found they could not borrow money and faced bankruptcies. Many did not survive, leaving their employees unemployed. Those that survived became ever more resistant to labor organizers and ever more resistant to making concessions in negotiations. The Reagan Administration's successful destruction of the Air Traffic Controllers Union symbolized the decisive switch in the role of the federal government and gave encouragement to employers.

The growth of the service economy and especially of public employees unions, also presented labor with organizing opportunities. Manufacturing industries were a declining percentage of the economy and were becoming more resistant to organizing. Pressed ever harder by foreign competitors, they became harder for unions to deal with. Public employees, on the other hand, were an ever-larger portion of the work force, and subject to pressure from voters, governments were becoming easier to organize. Since the 1950s, Washington public employee unions have grown far more rapidly than other unions and have become an ever-larger percentage of both the work force and the unionized work force. Governments employ tens of thousands. With a single paid organizer, a union might organize a hundred thousand government workers. Other service workers are not so easy to organize. Service industries, including restaurants, hotel, retail stores, especially franchises, individually employ only small numbers of workers. It might take several hundred to organize that many restaurant workers. So it is, therefore, much more cost-effective for a union to organize and then provide services for a government union than to organize and provide services to their members working for a firm in the service industry. Since the 1950s, government unions have dominated Washington's labor movement, as in many other states; on the other hand, they have failed to make inroads in many service industries. With the continuing decline in manufacturing, Washington unions have been hard-pressed to maintain their numbers. Since the population and work force have continued to grow rapidly through births, extended working lives, immigration, and the entry of women into the work force, union members have represented a constantly declining percentage of the population and work force in the last years of the 20th century.

Since the Depression Washington labor has been allied informally with the Democratic Party and liberal political groups. It has won increasing support from the minorities, immigrants, and women who formed an increasing percentage of labor's membership. Before 1930, native born, White Anglo Saxon Protestants, and immigrants from Western and Northern Europe dominated organized labor in Washington. During the Depression and World War II, Scandinavians, Southern and Eastern Europeans, of employees to join unions, the means to organize them do not yet exist. Jewish, Catholic, and Orthodox faiths, working in the great mass production industries, entered the labor movement in large numbers. Since 1945, unions have increasingly recruited its new members from the ranks of women, African Americans, Hispanics, and immigrants from Asia and Latin America, and from non-Judeo-Christian faiths, increasing replaced the previous groups. These workers have tended to work in the service industries and governments.

This political transformation of the labor movement has mirrored a generational shift. During the 1970s, the generation that organized and built the labor movement in the 1930s and 1940s

In the spring of 2011, state employees flooded the Capitol to protest budget cuts and any threat to collective bargaining.

passed from the scene. It fought for the right to organize and bargain collectively and developed personal ties and commitments to their union leaders. The new generation beginning in the 1970s inherited the gains of their predecessors, but had no personal connection to it. Some began to resent the fact that they had to pay union dues or to see their union dues used to support political campaigns and issues that they opposed. Others began to see the unions as simply another bureaucracy governing their lives and to resent the labor leadership as they might resent a government bureaucracy. This trend is likely to continue.

Even as traditional unions lost economic influence, public employee unions have gained politically. Today, Washington public employees have never been more powerful than in 2005, based largely on government decisions. Recent legislation requiring public employees to pay dues to public employee unions whether or not they favor the union or its political goals and bargaining policies is a good case in point. They have made it easier for unions to organize but made it harder for them to mobilize their members. It is difficult to see how this trend can continue for long, especially when workers in other industries are unable to share in the benefits.

As public employees capitalize on their political influence to win benefits for government workers, they may cause workers in private industry to resent their success. Eventually voters may come to resist calls for pro-labor measures if they believe they will primarily benefit government workers.

It is difficult to see how the labor movement can sustain its present direction. By far the majority of Washington public employees are already union members. The potential for growth in this economic sector is, therefore, relatively small. The great bulk of the remaining unorganized workers, especially those in the service sector, are inherently difficult to organize since they are small units. Unions must make very heavy investments in organizing manpower to organize such workers. Service sector units tend to be ephemeral and poorly capitalized, and wages low, as are union dues. This means highly paid workers must subsidize organizing efforts. Barring legislation to require employees to join unions, the means to organize them do not yet exist.[25]

Table: Washington State Employment & Union Membership Statistics, 1900-2005

Year	Washington State Non Farm Labor Force (000)	Washington State Union Members (000)	Union Members as % of Non-Farm Labor-Force	WSFL / WSLC as % of Non-Farm Labor Force	WSFL / WSLC Member Bodies	WSFL / WSLC Members (000)	WSFL / WSLC Per Capita Tax Receipts ($000)
1900	224	-	-	-	-	-	-
1901	255	-	-	-	-	-	-
1902	286	7.20	2.52	2.01	132	5.76	1.38
1903	316	7.16	2.23	1.81	143	5.73	1.85
1904	341	10.04	2.94	2.35	106	8.03	1.93
1905	375	9.04	2.41	1.92	151	7.23	1.72
1906	407	9.98	2.45	1.96	130	7.98	1.92
1907	439	12.23	2.78	2.22	143	9.78	2.93
1908	470	13.56	2.89	2.3	188	10.85	3.24
1909	498	15.33	3.08	2.3	214	12.26	3.68
1910	520	20.82	4.00	3.07	232	15.42	5.55
1911	528	23.77	4.50	3.33	254	17.61	6.11
1912	535	25.25	4.72	3.49	257	18.71	6.73
1913	541	25.81	4.77	3.34	254	19.12	6.88
1914	545	26.88	4.93	3.65	277	19.91	7.07
1915	550	21.78	3.96	2.93	232	16.13	6.29
1916	553	20.37	3.68	2.72	224	15.09	6.04
1917-18	565	31.51	5.58	4.13	243	23.34	11.67
1918-19	566	70.93	12.53	9.28	243	52.54	21.10
1919-20	578	80.13	13.86	9.56	263	55.26	27.24
1920-21	584	48.23	8.26	6.83	334	33.26	19.96
1921-22	591	35.70	6.04	3.91	284	24.62	14.17
1922-23	600	29.67	4.94	3.87	261	20.46	11.38
1923-24	610	29.38	4.82	3.32	240	20.26	12.16
1924-25	615	31.02	5.04	3.47	250	21.39	12.82
1925-26	627	33.00	5.26	3.63	238	22.76	13.66
1926-27	639	39.27	6.14	4.23	274	27.08	18.45
1927-28	651	36.58	5.62	3.87	272	25.23	18.16
1928-29	656	36.76	5.60	3.86	272	25.35	18.25

Year	Washington State Non Farm Labor Force (000)	Washington State Union Members (000)	Union Members as % of Non-Farm Labor-Force	WSFL / WSLC as % of Non-Farm Labor Force	WSFL / WSLC Member Bodies	WSFL / WSLC Members (000)	WSFL / WSLC Per Capita Tax Receipts ($000)
1929-30	664	40.38	6.08	4.05	274	26.92	19.38
1930-31	670	37.22	5.55	3.70	279	24.81	17.86
1931-32	675	28.76	4.26	2.84	272	19.17	13.80
1932-33	681	20.70	3.04	2.02	245	13.80	9.93
1933-34	686	20.66	2.95	1.96	200	13.51	9.72
1934-35	691	26.73	3.87	2.76	214	19.09	13.74
1935-36	696	30.23	4.34	3.10	259	21.59	15.55
1936-37	701	47.46	6.77	4.83	265	33.90	24.41
1937-38	706	64.44	9.13	6.52	340	46.03	33.14
1938-39	431	175.00	41.3	11.23	396	48.39	34.84
1939-40	465	187.26	40.27	11.12	407	51.73	37.25
1940-41	540	211.23	39.12	10.81	432	58.35	42.02
1941-42	660	206.30	31.26	8.63	419	56.99	41.04
1942-43	735	229.04	31.16	8.61	480	63.27	45.55
1943-44	772	286.60	37.12	10.26	440	79.17	57.00
1944-45	706	320.04	45.61	12.60	565	88.96	57.69
1945-46	649	320.04	49.31	13.71	565	88.96	57.69
1946-47	671	320.04	48.79	13.48	640	90.43	63.60
1947-48	685	360.41	52.61	14.53	685	99.56	65.30
1948-49	671	359.83	53.63	14.81	710	99.40	70.26
1949-50	684	349.29	51.07	14.11	752	96.49	70.11
1950-51	735	370.15	50.36	13.91	770	102.25	71.67
1951-52	746	407.43	54.62	15.09	780	112.55	78.08
1952-53	749	394.00	53.3	16.90	781	126.60	88.43
1953-54	741	401.00	54.12	17.37	782	128.74	91.62
1954-55	768	404.80	52.71	16.85	774	130.16	93.85
1955-56	785	402.25	51.24	16.48	792	129.34	94.30
1956-57	803	391.05	48.70	15.66	-	125.74	93.45
1957-58	790	297.70	37.68	19.63	749	155.05	95.07
1958-59	813	341.61	42.02	21.88	781	177.92	136.51
1959-60	813	350.00	43.1	22.39	772	182.05	166.85
1960-61	819	-	-	21.63	761	177.14	156.54
1961-62	857	-	-	19.12	764	163.86	158.28

Year	Washington State Non Farm Labor Force (000)	Washington State Union Members (000)	Union Members as % of Non-Farm Labor-Force	WSFL/WSLC as % of Non-Farm Labor Force	WSFL/WSLC Member Bodies	WSFL/WSLC Members (000)	WSFL/WSLC Per Capita Tax Receipts ($000)
1962-63	851	-	-	21.14	764	182.18	174.78
1963-64	854	367.00	44.5	21.56	785	184.12	201.58
1964-65	896	-	-	19.72	762	176.71	206.22
1965-66	988	398.00	40.3	18.20	658	179.86	212.23
1966-67	1,045	-	-	18.47	658	193.01	301.32
1967-68	1,099	454.00	41.3	18.74	662	205.96	370.65
1968-69	1,120	-	-	19.48	691	218.17	386.02
1969-70	1,079	434.00	40.2	20.41	698	220.25	384.83
1970-71	1,064	-	39.7	17.94	718	190.91	281.21
1971-72	1,100	421.00	38.3	16.63	686	182.97	347.19
1972-73	1,152	-	35.6	14.63	660	168.55	389.55
1973-74	1,199	438.00	36.7	14.56	633	174.55	408.06
1974-75	1,226	540.00	36.5	14.11	601	173.01	451.67
1975-76	1,283	453.00	35.6	13.10	611	168.10	492.76
1976-77	1,367	-	31.7	13.09	571	178.95	524.91
1977-78	1,485	496.00	33.1	11.26	678	167.16	635.76
1978-79	1,581	-	34.7	10.42	560	164.81	726.32
1979-80	1,608	543.00	32.9	10.05	548	161.54	815.19
1980-81	1,612	-	31.5	-	-	-	910.22
1981-82	1,569	517.00	29.8	-	-	-	867.83
1982-83	1,586	420.00	28.1	-	599	-	870.40
1983-84	1,660	437.00	26.3	8.84	629	146.76	854.56
1984-85	1,710	405.00	25.6	-	-	-	-
1985-86	1,770	478.00	27	-	-	-	-
1986-87	1,852	443.00	23.9	7.51	-	139.00	1,025.30
1987-88	1,941	428.00	24.6	7.57	456	147.00	1,044.94
1988-89	2,047	479.00	23.4	-	-	-	1,146.55
1989-90	2,143	495.03	23.1	7.14	557	153.00	1,146.61
1990-91	2,177	505.06	23.2	-	-	-	1,201.89
1991-92	2,222	526.61	23.7	6.73	557	149.65	1,179.89
1992-93	2,253	545.23	24.2	-	-	-	-
1993-94	2,304	487.00	21.14	-	-	-	1,400.88
1994-95	2,347	477.00	20.32	-	-	-	-

Year	Washington State Non Farm Labor Force (000)	Washington State Union Members (000)	Union Members as % of Non-Farm Labor-Force	WSFL / WSLC as % of Non-Farm Labor Force	WSFL / WSLC Member Bodies	WSFL / WSLC Members (000)	WSFL / WSLC Per Capita Tax Receipts ($000)
1995-96	2,416	464.00	19.20	6.45	609	155.74	1,367.44
1996-97	2,514	508.00	20.20	7.52	-	189.00	1,535.98
1997-98	2,595	537.00	20.30	7.73	629	200.57	1,715.85
1998-99	2,643	535.00	20.20	-	-	-	-
1999-00	2,690	471.00	17.51	-	-	-	-
2000-01	2,722	-	-	23.74	536	646.32	292,907.20
2001-02	2,656	472.00	18.6	22.14	549	588.04	300,284.51
2002-03	2,659	-	-	21.12	540	561.71	310,341.17
2003-04	2,665	-	-	20.40	531	543.63	305,708.52
2004-05	2,724	-	-	10.40	230	283.17	194,317.97
2005-06	-	-	-	-	617	540.51	-
2000-01	2,722	-	-	23.74	536	646.32	292,907.20
2001-02	2,656	472.00	18.6	22.14	549	588.04	300,284.51
2002-03	2,659	-	-	21.12	540	561.71	310,341.17
2003-04	2,665	-	-	20.40	531	543.63	305,708.52
2004-05	2,724	-	-	10.40	230	283.17	194,317.97
2005-06	-	-	-	-	617	540.51	-

SOURCES: STATISTICAL ABSTRACT OF THE UNITED STATES, 1959-1965, 1969, 1973, 1975, 1978, 1979, 1980, 1984, 1988, 1996-2003; JOHN P. HERING, LABOR FORCE, EMPLOYMENT, AND UNEMPLOYMENT ANNUAL ESTIMATES BY STATES: 1900-1940, (SEATTLE: UNIVERSITY OF WASHINGTON PRESS, 1951), P. 41; "EMPLOYMENT AND EARNINGS, STATES AND AREAS, 1939-78," U. S. DEPT. OF LABOR, BUREAU OF LABOR STATISTICS BULLETIN NO. 13370-13, (1979), PP. 669; "TOTAL NON-FARM LABOR FORCE: WASHINGTON STATE, IN JANUARY, SEASONALLY ADJUSTED, 1990-2005" (HTTP://DATA.BLS.GOV/PDQ/SERVLET/SURVEYOUTPUTSERVLET); PROCEEDINGS OF THE WASHINGTON STATE FEDERATION OF LABOR, 1905-1957 (N 979.706 / WFL 1905-57); PROCEEDINGS OF THE ANNUAL CONVENTION OF THE WASHINGTON STATE INDUSTRIAL UNION COUNCIL, 1938-57 (UWAS SP PNW PAMPHLET FILE #N979.7 LABOR AND LABORING CLASSES);

Chapter 5

A Progressive State
with Regressive Taxes

Donald R. Burrows

Introduction

In November of 2010, Washington voters will once again have an opportunity to vote on whether the state's tax structure should include a personal income tax. The measure, Initiative 1098, would impose a statutory income tax on high-income taxpayers.[1]

With the exception of the personal and corporate income taxes approved by 70 percent of Washington's voters in 1932, numerous other attempts to add an income tax to the state's tax structure have failed. The State Supreme Court rejected some of the measures; the voters rejected others.

This chapter describes the important changes in the state's tax structure since statehood. Moreover, it carefully examines the previous failed attempts to add income taxes to the state's taxes and addresses the following questions:

- What has caused the changes in the Washington's tax structure since statehood?
- Is Washington's current tax structure fair?
- How does the State's tax structure compare with the tax structures of the other 49 states?
- Why have the state's voters consistently rejected income taxes since 1932?
- What is the outlook for the adoption of an income tax in Washington?

Overview

Washington's tax structure has changed from a "one tax" (i.e., the property tax) structure at statehood in 1889 to a structure that currently has more than 60 taxes and hundreds of state and local license taxes. It has gone from a system that mandated uniformity and equality of taxation, which only permitted tax exemptions for public and quasi-public property, to a system that contains over 500 statutory tax exemptions and other tax preferences for business, agriculture, individuals and other groups.

It is no secret that Washington is one of the more progressive states in the nation in terms of its people, its government and its laws.[2] On the other hand, it might be a secret to most Washingtonians that the state has one of the most regressive tax structures in the nation.[3]

Numerous state and national studies have shown that Washington's tax structure is regressive and places a disproportionate burden on low and moderate-income families. Since 1921, there have been eight citizens' committees in Washington that have each spent a year or more studying the state/local tax structure.[4] They all concluded that Washington's tax structure is unfair. Seven of the eight tax study committees proposed the addition of income taxes as the best way to make it fair.[5]

Part I:
The Move Toward and Away From Income Taxes

By far the strongest support for a broadening of the state's tax structure during the first 40 plus years of statehood came from the growing demand for property tax relief. The property tax provided the vast majority of state and local tax revenues during the early years.[6] The 40-mill limit initiative in 1932 reduced property taxes substantially and resulted in the broadening of the state's tax structure with the addition of the B&O, retail sales and several other taxes in the mid-1930s. It also diminished the need and desirability of adding an income tax to the tax structure in the minds of the majority of voters.

More importantly, changes in the Constitution and property tax laws made during the past 45 years have further reduced the level of property taxes. Those changes, together with the increasing affluence of the state's residents, have further reduced the support for an income tax.[7]

The Rise and Fall of Property Tax Levels

Washington's tax structure during the early years was essentially a one-tax system, the general property tax. As government programs and services expanded, so did the tax on property owners. The increasing level of property taxes was not the only concern. There was concern with the non-uniformity of property assessments and the fact that some property was escaping taxes altogether.

Chart 1: Effective Rates of Washington's Property Tax, 1890 to 2009

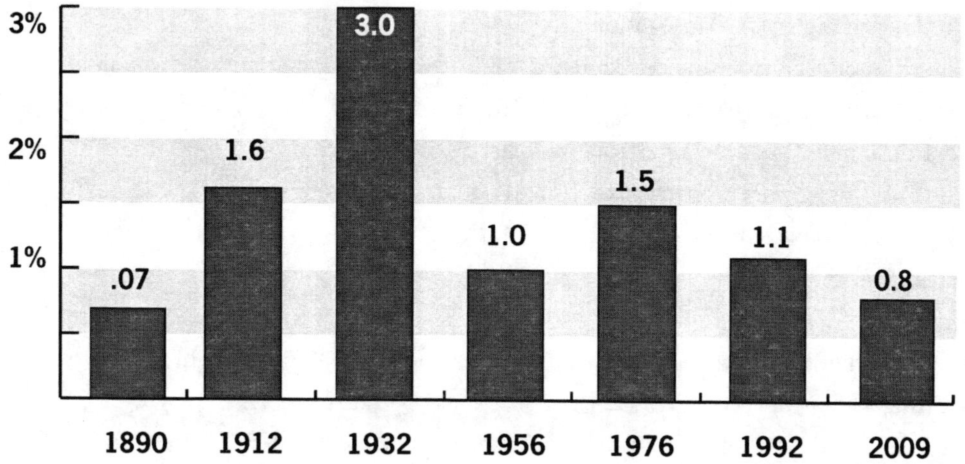

SOURCE: REPORTS OF STATE REVENUE AGENCIES.

In reality, the tax was not imposed "uniformly and equally" on all property as prescribed by the Constitution and state law. Large amounts of property were escaping taxes and other properties taxed at only a fraction of their value. Public officials were well aware of these inequities and the increasing taxpayers' demands for property tax relief.[8]

Washington's early governors all expressed concern about the fairness of the tax structure. In his first inaugural address in January 1897, Governor John Rodgers said that Washington's tax laws "throw the burden of government almost entirely upon property owners of small means, while wealthy corporations escape with nominal contributions to the public treasury." Rodgers wanted the legislature to enact new taxes to allow a reduction in property taxes. His suggestions of possible new tax sources included taxes on "corporation stock, limited partnerships, foreign insurance companies, incomes, collateral inheritances and liquor." (Underscore added)[9]

Despite the enactment of a few new taxes, property taxes continued to provide the state and local governments with over 90 percent of their revenues for the first forty years of statehood. As state and local expenditures increased, the effective rate of the property tax moved steadily upward from 0.7 percent in 1890 to a peak of 3.0 percent in 1932.[10] In 2009, the effective property tax was at its lowest level in hundred years. (See Chart 1).

Attempts to provide property tax relief prior to the 1930s either failed or provided only a minimal amount of relief. Those efforts included:

• Adding new taxes
• Attempting to tax intangibles

- Attempting to equalize property assessments
- Creating committees to study ways of providing property tax relief
- Amending the state's Constitution

The legislature added the insurance premiums tax in 1890. In 1897, it imposed corporation license taxes and it enacted the inheritance tax in 1901. The three taxes failed to produce enough revenues to allow a meaningful reduction in property taxes. A gasoline tax added in 1921 did allow the elimination of two highway property tax levies, which provided a temporary respite from property tax increases. It also enacted a state poll tax in 1921. However, it was so unpopular voters repealed it the following year.[11]

Attempts to effectively tax intangible properties, which taken together had a greater value than taxable tangible real and personal property, failed because of the difficulty of locating and assessing such property.

The legislature's next attempt to improve the fairness of the tax structure was to create tax study committees.[12] The first tax study committee was the 1921 Tax Investigation Committee. The second was the 1929 Tax Investigation Commission. The two groups conducted extensive studies of the state's tax structure and held public meetings throughout the state. Both concluded that Washington needed to add income taxes to provide property tax relief and improve the fairness of the state's taxes.[13]

Constitutional Amendments

The legislature approved several proposed constitutional amendments in an attempt to reduce the property tax burden on homes, farms and other real properties during the early years. The voters approved some and rejected others.[14] The legislature passed proposed constitutional amendments in 1907 and 1927 that gave it the power to classify property for property tax purposes. There was considerable opposition to the two proposed amendments. Businesses feared that the proposed classification amendments would result in a substantial shift in the tax burden from residential to business properties and they, along with some other groups, fought the measures. Moreover, many citizens believed the proposed amendments would have permitted the legislature to enact personal and corporate income taxes. The voters rejected both the 1907 and 1927 proposed amendments.

In 1929, the Legislature submitted yet another proposed property classification constitutional amendment to the voters. This time the voters approved it at the 1930 election as Amendment 14 to the state's Constitution. Two of the features in the failed 1927 amendment were included in the latest version: (1) allowing the legislature to classify property for tax purposes; and, (2) allowing the legislature to exempt private property.[15]

There was one important difference, however. Amendment 14 required that all real property be taxed uniformly with the exception of "mines, mineral resources, and lands devoted to reforestation". This meant that all other taxable real property, such as residential, farm, commercial and industrial properties had to be valued and taxed uniformly and equally.

Among the strongest supporters of Amendment 14 were groups that favored income taxes, particularly income taxes on the income from intangible properties. However, several subsequently Court decisions have indicated that the Amendment did not allow the legislature to impose an income tax. Thus, the pursuit of property tax relief continued as property taxes remained high.

Major Property Tax Relief in the 1930s

In the meantime, on October 29, 1929, the bottom fell out of the New York stock market. It precipitated a long and deep business recession - the Great Depression. Within months, Washington's economy began to suffer. Personal incomes plummeted and unemployment levels eventually reached 25 percent. The total personal income of the state's residents dropped from $1,152,755,000 in 1929 to $636,859,000 in 1932, a 45 percent decrease.

Many taxpayers were unable to pay their property taxes, property values were decreasing and property tax revenues fell sharply. Large numbers of Washington's citizens were in desperate need of food and other necessities. The state needed new sources of tax revenues to keep the public schools open and to provide assistance to unemployed and needy.

The 1931 legislature responded to the situation by enacting personal and corporate income taxes as recommended by the 1929 Tax Investigation Commission. The revenues from the new taxes were to be used to provide property tax relief and to provide the revenues needed for other essential government programs. However, Governor Roland Hartley (R) vetoed the income tax measures and refused to call a special legislative session in 1932 to deal with the economic and tax problems resulting from the depression.[16]

The 1932 Income Tax and Property: Tax Initiatives

At that point, the state's citizens took the matter in their own hands. They approved two initiatives aimed at providing property tax relief and broadening the tax structure. Although property tax relief happened when the voters approved the first 40-mill property tax limit law (Initiative 64) in 1932, the state Supreme Court rejected the voter approved income tax initiative (Initiative 69).[17]

The 40-mill initiative reduced the property tax revenues of both the state and local governments. It limited regular state and local property taxes to 40 mills on a 50 percent

Table 1: The 1935 Revenue Act Taxes

New Taxes Still in Use	New Taxes Not in Use	Re-imposed Taxes
Retail Sales	Admissions (E)	Business & Occupation
Compensating (Use Tax)	Stock Transfers (V)	Public Utility
Liquor	Radio (U)	Inheritance (E)
Cigarettes	Fuel Oil (E)	
	Medicines & Toiletries (V)	
	Chain Store Tax (V)	
	Gift (V)	
	Corporation Net Income (U)	
	Conveyance (E)	

E = eliminated in later years   V= vetoed by governor
U = held unconstitutional

SOURCE: REPORTS OF STATE REVENUE AGENCIES.

valuation, a 2.0 percent effective rate limit. State government suffered the largest percentage loss of tax revenues from I-64. Its property tax revenues dropped from $11.9 million in 1932 to $6.5 million in 1934, a 43 percent drop.

In rejecting the voter approved income tax initiative, the state Supreme Court ruled that the income taxes were non-uniform property taxes and, therefore, unconstitutional.[18] The Court's rejection of the income tax in 1933 was a major turning point in the evolution of Washington's tax structure.

Part II:
A New Tax Structure – Two Cents For the Governor

A second 40-mill property tax limit, approved by the voters in 1934 (Initiative 94), took effect in 1935 and further reduced the state's share of property taxes. At the same election, the voters defeated a proposed constitutional amendment that would have allowed the legislature to impose graduated income taxes. In effect, the voters, with a 57% margin, rejected the 1934 income tax proposal two years after they had approved income taxes with a 70 percent majority vote. The support for an income tax had diminished substantially. Many of the groups that had previously supported the income tax were content with the reductions in property taxes resulting from the 40-mill limit law and were no longer concerned with providing replacement revenues.

In the meantime, the state and numerous local governments were in danger of going bankrupt. The dire fiscal conditions of state and local governments set the stage for three of the most difficult legislative sessions in the state's history, the 1933, 1934 and 1935 sessions. However, conditions for dealing with the state's tax and expenditure problems had changed with the new makeup of the state's elected public officials. The voters elected Clarence Martin, a Democrat at the 1932 election. The legislature changed from an overwhelming majority of Republicans in both the Senate and House in 1931 to a majority of Democrats in both Houses in 1933. It was the first legislative session in the state's history that the Democrats had majorities in either house.

Chart 2: State Government's Retail Sales Tax Rates, 1935-2009

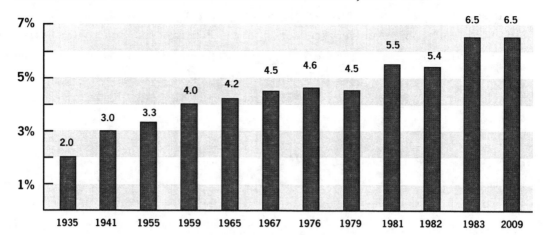

The 1933 legislature took action almost immediately to provide assistance for the unemployed and needy and, at the same time, to increase the state's financial support of the public schools, which had lost a large amount of their property tax revenues. Many school districts were on the brink of closing their doors.[19]

To provide the needed revenues, the 1933 Washington Legislature issued bonds and enacted the Business Activities Tax. The new gross income/gross receipts business tax applied to most "business" type activities. It applied to corporations, partnerships, sole proprietors, nonprofit organizations and the business type activities of government (e.g., utilities, etc.). The state Supreme Court approved the Business Activities Tax as an excise tax. It was, therefore, not in violation of the constitutional uniformity provisions that applied to property taxes.[20]

The bonds and the Business Activities Tax proved to be only stopgap measures. In 1935, the Governor and legislature turned to the retail sales tax and other excise taxes for additional revenues when it passed the Revenue Act of 1935. It also enacted personal and corporate income taxes but the Court ruled both taxes unconstitutional.

There were sixteen different taxes in the Revenue Act of 1935. The Act was 143 pages long. Although there have been numerous changes and increases in state taxes since 1935, the basic tax structure remains essentially the same. Table 1 lists the taxes included in the Revenue Act of 1935 and indicates the taxes that are still a part of the state's tax structure.

By far the most important of the Revenue Act taxes were the retail sales tax and its companion, the compensating (use) tax. The initial rate of the retail sales tax was 2.0 percent. In a few years, the sales tax would become the most important tax in the state's tax structure.

The additional revenue produced by the 1935 Revenue Act reduced the need and desire for an income tax in the minds of the voters. The revenue from the retail sales and other excise taxes has resulted in a substantial reduction in importance of the property tax in the tax structure. The property tax has gone from providing 90 percent of state/local tax revenues in 1930 to 27 percent in 2008. It presently accounts for only 10 percent of state government's tax revenues but still provides 65 percent of the tax revenues for the state's 1,721 local governments (e.g., schools, cities, counties and a host of junior taxing districts).

Changes in Excise Taxes since the 1930s

The excise taxes of today are not a great deal different from those of the mid 1930s. There have been a few new taxes added but the taxes enacted in the 1930s continue to provide the great majority of tax revenues for state government. The most important changes in the 1930s excise taxes have been the numerous rate increases and large number of tax exemptions and other tax preferences added to the laws.[21]

Chart 2 shows the rate changes in the state government's retail sales tax since 1935. The rates of other taxes, including the B&O, public utility, gasoline, cigarette, liquor, etc. have also been increased several times since the 1935.

The state government's sales tax rate has gone from 2 percent in 1935 to its current level in 6.5 percent. In addition, the legislature gave cities and counties authority to impose retail sales taxes in 1970. The general purposes city/county sales tax rate is currently 1.0 percent with additional sales tax authority for specific programs. Moreover, several other local government jurisdictions (e.g., transit districts, regional transportation districts) are now imposing sales tax. The combined state-local retail sales tax rates in Washington currently range from 7.0 percent to 9.5 percent, with rates of 9.0 percent or more in the most populous areas of the state.

Changes Since 1960 that have reduced Support for Income taxes

During the past 45 years, changes in the Constitution and state tax laws, along with the state Supreme Court's decision on the state's responsibilities for the funding of education, have significantly reduced the support for income taxes. The more important of these changes are:

- A change in the state's Constitution that allows the legislature to provide property tax relief to retired homeowners (1966)
- A constitutional amendment allowing agriculture, timber and open space property to be assessed and taxed at less than true and fair value (1968)
- The lowering of the constitutional regular property tax limit from a 2.0 percent effective rate limit to a 1.0 percent limit (1972)

- Court decisions disallowing the schools' use of voter approved special levies for "basic education" programs and requiring the state legislature to provide for the funding of those programs (1976)
- Exemption of prescription drugs (1974) and groceries (1983) from the retail sales tax
- Numerous new business tax preferences, including rate reductions, exemptions and
- A 1.0 percent limit on the annual increase in the property tax revenues of taxing districts tax credits (1965 -2010) (1999)[22]

Regardless of the benefits provided by the above changes, they have reduced the support for income taxes form many groups.

Part III:

A Closer Look at Attempts to Enact Income Taxes

From 1929 to 1982, the legislature enacted fourteen proposed income tax measures. (See Table 4). The voters rejected all but one. The only income tax proposal approved by voters was in 1932. In eight subsequent statewide elections beginning in 1934 through 1982, large majorities of Washington voters have rejected income taxes. In six of those elections – 1934, 1936, 1938, 1942, 1969 and 1973 – both personal and corporate net income taxes were included in the ballot proposals. In the other two elections –1975 and 1982 – only corporate net income taxes were on the ballot.

The 1929 National Bank Income Tax

The first state net income tax passed by the Washington legislature was in 1929.[23] It was imposed on national banks in response to the U.S. Supreme Court's rejection of Washington's property tax on bank shares. The bank income tax was quickly subject to legal challenge. In a 1930 case, the Washington State Supreme Court ruled that it was unconstitutional.[24]

The 1932 Income Tax Initiative

Governor Roland Hartley (R) vetoed the 1931 income taxes enacted by the legislature. In 1932, thousands of the state's citizens marched on Olympia requesting assistance for the needy and relief from the high property taxes on homeowners, farmers and others. They wanted Hartley to call a special session in 1932, but he refused. He believed that it was not the government's responsibility, but the responsibility of private charities, to provide assistance for the unemployed and other citizens in need.

Hartley's refusal to deal with tax or other problems provided the impetus for the launching of two tax initiatives by the state's citizens in 1932. The first measure placed a new limit on property tax rates, which resulted in a lowering of property tax burdens and a reduction in the property tax revenues of state and the local governments. The second initiative imposed personal and corporate income taxes. The voters approved both measures with 70 percent majorities in November 1932.

Initiative 69, the income tax measure, imposed graduated personal and corporate income taxes. The rates of the income taxes ranged from 1 percent to 7 percent. The law allowed taxpayers to take a credit of up to 50 percent of their property taxes payments against any income tax liability.

The income tax initiative had strong support from taxpayers and many organizations, including farm groups, labor groups, real estate associations and education groups. No one submitted an opposition statement to the initiative for inclusion in the voters' pamphlet.

Following the voters' approval of the income taxes, the state Tax Commission blanketed the state with income tax forms so that the taxpayers could begin preparing their tax returns. A Seattle Times editorial noted that:

"One glance at the dreadful blanks mailed out by the State Tax Commission was sufficient to convince them (the taxpayers) they did not want the new system nearly so much as they previously had assumed they did."

The Times editorial implied that the voters favored the income tax until they discovered they might have to pay it. Not knowing who might be liable for the tax, the Commission sent tax returns to all residents with postal addresses. Only a portion of those residents would have owed income taxes after taking the allowable exemptions and the 50 percent property tax credit. Nevertheless, the average taxpayer did not understand this.

Court Rules Income Tax Unconstitutional

Whether this apparent change of heart on the part of taxpayers had any influence on the state Supreme Court's income tax decision is debatable. The first vote taken by the Court on the 1932 income taxes resulted in a tie, four to four. The ninth justice, Kenneth N. Parker, was absent because of illness. Parker eventually resigned and Governor Clarence Martin, who became Governor in January of 1933, appointed his executive assistant, James M. Geraghty, to replace Parker. Since Geraghty favored the income tax, it appeared that the Court ruling would be 5 to 4 in favor of the tax. It did not work out that way. One of the judges who originally supported the income taxes changed his position between the first and second vote of the Court.[25]

In a 5 to 4 decision (Culliton v. Chase, 174 Wash. 363, 25 P. 82 (1933)) the Court ruled that an income tax was in violation of the "uniformity clause" in the state's Constitution. In reaching its decision, the Court ruled that the income tax was actually a property tax.

The Court said that the graduated income tax violated the uniformity requirement for property taxes. In effect, the court ruled that all income is one class of property and that a small amount of income must be taxed at the same rate as a large amount of income.

In his comprehensive analysis of the history of state income tax litigation in Washington, Professor Hugh Spitzer noted that:

> *"the majority opinions in Culliton and Jensen were founded on the mistaken, or perhaps disingenuous, proposition that the Aberdeen Court (in the 1929 bank tax decision) had considered and settled the question of whether income constituted a form of property under Article VII of the Washington State Constitution."*[26]

Spitzer noted that the 1929 Court decision had not addressed the question of whether income was property under the state Constitution in the Aberdeen decision. Spitzer further indicates that the majority of court decisions throughout the nation have held that income is not property and that Justice Holcomb's majority opinion in Culliton was clearly wrong when he represented that the "overwhelming weight of judicial authority (throughout the nation)" supported the view that income is property. Nevertheless, in several subsequent decisions, the Court has not reversed its position that income is property under the Constitution.

1935 Legislative Privilege Taxes

The 1935 legislature decided to enact statutory personal and corporate income taxes. The legislature labeled the two taxes "privilege taxes" in an attempt to avoid the Court declaring them to be property taxes.

The 1935 personal income tax applied to "every resident for the privilege of receiving income while enjoying the protection of state laws." However, the Court did not recede from its former opinion that income is property, and that an income tax is a property tax (Jensen v. Henneford, 185 Wash. 209, 53 P 2nd 607 (1936)). The Court ruled that it was in violation of the constitutional uniformity provision and that by calling the tax a privilege or excise tax did not change the real nature and purpose of the tax.

The Court also rejected the 4 percent corporation net income. The Court said that it was also a property tax and, therefore, it was in violation of the constitutional uniformity requirement because it did not apply to non-corporate businesses. (Petroleum Navigation Co. v. Henneford, 185 Wash. 495 (1936)).

Proposed Constitutional Amendments, 1934-1942

With the Court's ruling that the 1932 income taxes were unconstitutional, the 1933 legislature passed a proposed constitutional amendment, House Joint Resolution 12, which would authorize the legislature to impose a graduated net income tax. There were no rate limits in the proposed income tax amendment. Moreover, the legislature did not enact an implementing income tax law. The voters rejected the 1934 proposed amendment by a vote of 134,908 in favor and 176,154 opposed. Although the measure gained the support of only 43 percent of the voters, it is a greater percentage of support from the state's voters than received for subsequent income tax proposals.

Because the legislature had concerns that the Court might reject its 1935 statutory personal and corporate taxes on the "privilege of receiving income", it submitted another proposed constitutional amendment to the voters in 1936 that would have allowed graduated income taxes. However, the voters rejected it along with similar proposals in 1938 and 1942. There were no strong campaigns in support of the three proposed amendments.

However, the legislature provided one incentive to the voters for the proposed 1942 income tax amendment. The law that increased the retail sales tax from 2 percent to 3 percent in 1941. It contained a provision that the sales tax rate would revert to 2 percent should a graduated income tax be enacted. This incentive did little, if anything, to change the voters mind. The voters rejected the 1942 proposed income tax amendment with 66.3 percent voting against it.

The 1951 Corporation Income Tax

In the early 1950s, the legislature approved another income tax.[27] The state's general fund surplus accumulated during WW II turned into a deficit in February 1950 following the voters' 1948 approval of an initiative that provided a large increase in public assistance grants. With the 1949 legislature's failure to agree on tax increases needed to pay for the increased welfare costs, the general fund deficit continued to grow.[28] At the 1951 session, Governor Arthur Langlie (R) proposed balancing the budget by imposing a 4 percent net income tax on corporations.[29] The legislature approved the tax, as part of budget bill, at the first 1951 special session.

The legislature labeled the corporate income tax an excise tax in the hope that the Court would not rule it a property tax, which would make it subject to the constitutional uniformity requirements applicable to that tax. Nevertheless, the Court said it was not an excise tax but that it was, in fact, a property tax. The Court ruled the tax was not uniform on the same class of property (i.e., income) because individuals and partnerships in competition with corporations were not subject to the tax.[30]

Recent Income Tax Proposals

Legislators introduced several proposed constitutional amendments, which would have permitted income taxes, from the early 1950s to 1967. However, the bill sponsors were never able to obtain the two-thirds majority of the two houses needed to refer the measure to the voters. That all changed during the 1969 session. The impetus for the 1969 income tax proposal came from a three-year study by the Tax Advisory Council, which Governor Daniel J. Evans appointed in 1965.[31]

Governor Evans, more than any governor in the state's history, worked harder to achieve tax reform and add net income taxes to Washington's tax structure. Largely through his efforts, two proposed constitutional amendments that would have allowed income taxes passed the legislature. However, the voters rejected both of them, one in 1970 and the other in 1973. The major differences between the two 1970s measures and the earlier proposed income tax amendments was that the 1970s measure included constitutional limits and implementing laws detailing the specific changes in the taxes that would become effective if the amendments passed. The sponsors and supporters of the two proposals wanted to achieve four major goals:

- Increase the fairness of the state/local tax burden by lowering sales and property taxes, two regressive taxes
- Reduce the incentive for tax evasion resulting from the high rates of the sales and other excise taxes
- Reduce property tax levels by reducing special M&O school levies
- Increase the elasticity (i.e., normal growth without rate increases) of the state's tax structure, which lowers the need for periodic tax rate increases[32]
- The 1970 Proposed Income Tax Amendment (House Joint Resolution 42)

House Joint Resolution 42, approved by the legislature in 1969, would have allowed the state to impose net income taxes. It also would have lowered the constitutional limit on regular property taxes from 2 percent to 1 percent.

The income tax part of the amendment permitted the legislature to impose a single rate income tax for the first five years. At the end of that period, the voters were to be presented with a referendum to see if they wanted to allow a graduated rate or stay with the single rate tax.[33]

The implementing law included the personal and corporation taxes, along with reductions in other taxes. The major components of the bill were.

- A 3.5 percent single rate income taxes on individuals and corporations
- Sales tax rate reduced from 4.5 percent to 3.5 percent
- Exemption of prescription drugs from sales tax

- A sales tax credit/refund in-lieu of the exemption of food from sales tax
- Reduction in B & O tax rates of at least 50 percent, larger for services
- A phase-out of the personal property tax on business inventories
- Additional property tax credits to retired citizens with low incomes, and
- Shifting of 2 mills of the state's property tax levy to local governments

The proposed change in the state's tax structure would have changed the distribution of taxes from very regressive to slightly progressive.

The total reform package was designed to produce more revenue than the existing state tax structure. The additional revenue was to be used to increase the state's support of local schools to allow reductions in local school district special M & O property tax levies. This, in turn, could have reduced total property taxes by about 25 percent.

A major incentive for taxpayer support of HJR 42 was the proposed reduction in the regular property tax limit from a 2.0 effective rate (i.e., 40 mills at a 50 percent assessment level) to a 1.0 percent effective rate limit. However, the support for property tax relief was not as strong as it was two years earlier. The voters in 1968 approved a constitutional amendment allowing the current use taxation of agriculture, timber and open space properties. That measure, which provided substantial relief to the timber and agriculture industries, diminished the support for an income tax from those industries. The voters rejected HJR 42 in November 1970 by a 2 to 1 margin.

The 1973 Proposed Income Tax Amendment: House Joint Resolution 37

Undaunted by the failure of HJR 42, Governor Evans appointed a new and larger citizens tax committee and asked the committee, the Committee for a New Tax Policy, to develop a tax reform proposal that would have broad support.[34] That committee's proposal was introduced in the 1971 session but the legislature could not agree on the details. An ad hoc legislative committee finally agreed to some changes in the proposals submitted by the citizens' Committee and referred it to the voters in 1973.

The measure, House Joint Resolution 37, differed from HJR 42 in several ways. The major tax incentive that was included in HJR 42, cutting the constitutional limit on regular property taxes in half, was already in the Constitution when HJR 37 came before the voters. The voters approved reducing the constitutional limit on property taxes a year earlier when they approved Senate Joint Resolution 1. The major constitutional provisions in HJR 37 were:

- Allow the state to impose graduated personal and single rate corporate net income Taxes.
- Constitutional maximum rate limits on income, sales and B & O taxes.
- Elimination of voter-approved M&O property tax levies for schools.

- Require state full funding of K-12 basic education.
- Sales tax exemption of prescription drugs and food.
- Exemption of business inventories from property taxes.

The vote on the HJR 37 was 228,823 yes and 770,033 no. In percentage terms, it was 22.9 percent yes and 77.1 percent no. The 22.9 percent favorable vote compares to the 33.7 percent favorable vote for HJR 42. There were several reasons why the support for an income tax declined from three years earlier. The most important was that the 50 percent reduction in the constitutional limit on regular property levies that was part of the HJR 42 proposal was no longer available. Secondly, the adding of constitutional limits on the sales and B&O tax rates and the proposed income taxes worried some supporters of government programs.

Moreover, many K-12 education supporters, who had always supported income taxes in the past, were concerned about loosing the ability to use voter approved special levies for their local schools. In their minds, it was a question of maintaining local control, and they wanted the ability to have programs over and above those funded by the state.

Although HJR 37 had the official support of important groups, including some labor groups, farm groups, church groups, various education organizations, real estate organizations, the League of Women Voters, and others, there appeared to be little grass roots support from the members of those organizations. The level of support for HJR 37 was less than the organized support enjoyed by HJR 42. The campaign committee supporting the measure was only able to raise only a small amount of funds and did virtually no media advertising.[35]

1975 and 1982 Corporate Tax Initiatives

Subsequent to the defeat of the 1970 and 1973 proposed constitutional amendments, the sponsors of two initiatives were successful in placing corporate income tax proposals on the ballot, in 1975 and 1982.[36]

Initiative 314 in 1975 would have imposed a 12 percent privilege/excise (net income) tax on all corporations. The revenues from the tax would go toward the support of the K-12 schools. The additional revenues were to be used to reduce special school M&O property taxes. The opponents argued that approval of the initiative, if ruled constitutional by the Court, would open the door for a personal income tax. Although the measure was supported by the Washington Education Association, the Washington State Labor Council, the AFL-CIO, the Leaguer of Women Voters and other groups, it was rejected by a 323,832 yes vote to 672,178 no vote.

Initiative 435 in 1982 provided for a 10 percent corporation franchise (net income) tax, the elimination of the B&O tax on corporations and the exemption of food from a sales tax. The

1982 legislature had reinstated the sales taxation of food for a fourteen-month period from May 1, 1982 to July 1, 1983 to replace part of the large revenues loss during the period's severe economic recession. Although the initiative's sponsors acknowledge the taxation of food was to expire under the current law, they argued in the voters' pamphlet no replacement revenue was available and the legislature might have to extend the food sales tax again. The voters defeated I-435 by a vote of 453,221 to 889,091. Although sales tax on food exemption expired on July 1, 1983, there was a need for replacement revenues. The 1983 legislature had to increase the sales tax from 5.4 to 6.5 percent to balance the 1983-1985 biennial budget.

No income tax proposal has passed the legislature in the past 37 years. The last time the citizens voted on an income tax was 27 years ago. In 2010, the voters will again have the opportunity to decide if they want to add income taxes to the tax structure when they cast their votes for or against Initiative 1098 at the November general election.

Part IV::
Why Income Taxes Have Failed

For many years, the income tax had strong support from many important groups in our state, including farm organizations, labor organizations, the real estate industry, the Democratic Party, supporters of education programs and others.[37] However, that support has declined precipitously during the past 40 years. A major reason for supporting previous income tax proposals, to provide property tax relief, is no longer a factor, at least at the present time. A secondary reason for the reduced support for an income tax is the Court's 1976 ruling that the state government must provide for the full funding of basic education costs instead of forcing school districts to rely on special M&O levies for basic school programs. The full funding law and other property tax limit measures have lowered effective rates of property taxes from 1.5 percent in 1977 to 0.83 percent in 2009.[38]

Representative Mary Ellen McCaffree, Chair of the House Revenue Committee, nurtured two failed attempts at comprehensive reform in 1971 and 1973.

Not only are most interest groups and most state elected officials no longer advocating an income tax, but also the state's voters have shown their disdain toward an income tax in numerous elections following their approval of an initiative imposing personal and corporate income taxes in 1932. Since that time, the voters have rejected amendments to the state's Constitution six times. The last time was in 1973.

Why have the voters rejected all of the income tax proposals for the past seventy-five years? No one knows for sure. We know the need for property tax relief is no longer as important as it was in 1932. Apparently, the regressive impact of the current tax structure is not a good enough reason for the voters to support an income tax.[39] The simple answer is that the majority of voters are opposed to a state income tax.

What are the Voters' Objections to a State Income Tax?

Although each voter has his own reasons, some of the most common reasons given by voters for their opposition to the two most recent constitutional income tax proposals, HJR 42 and HJR 37, were:

- It is simply a tax increase"
- "We cannot trust the legislature"
- "It adds a tax without eliminating a tax"
- "We need spending reform"
- "Taxes are already too high in Washington"

These are not easy statements to refute, especially when individuals have a deep dislike of taxes. Moreover, these have become "sound bite comments" by the opponents of income taxes, which are often taken at face value by the average voter. I believe it is important for the voter to have the other side of these arguments before making up their minds on the income tax issue. Here are some answers to the objections to a state income tax.

It is simply a tax increase. It certainly would be for the wealthy. One of the major reasons why committee after committee has recommended an income tax is to eliminate the extremely heavy tax burden on lower income families. If we are to lower the tax on the $20,000 family now paying about 15 percent of its income in state and local taxes, then we will have to increase taxes on the those in the higher income brackets now paying 4 percent or less of their income in state and local taxes.

We cannot trust the legislature. There is a feeling that the legislators would increase taxes at greater rates than in the past with the availability of a new tax source. Although most legislators will often vote for new and expanded government programs that will benefit their constituents, most hate to vote for tax increases necessary to fund those programs. Getting a majority of the legislators to vote a tax increase needed to balance the budget has always been a difficult task. It usually requires an extra legislative session, and much pressure by party leaders, to obtain enough votes to pass the tax increase. It would be no easier to obtain legislative votes for increases in an income tax than for other taxes. Moreover, most recent income tax proposals have included constitutional limits on tax rates, which would make it more difficult for the legislature to increase taxes. There are no constitutional limits on sales and other excise tax rates.

It adds a tax without eliminating any taxes. This argument is generally true if we are talking about eliminating either the property and/or retail sales tax. It is possible to substantially reduce the sales tax rate and eliminate the state government's property tax levy. Previous tax reform proposals for adding income taxes have included reductions and placed new limits on the existing "big three" taxes (i.e., property, B&O, and retail sales). Some proposals would have eliminated the B&O tax altogether.

One of the major reasons for adding an income tax is to bring amount a more balanced and fair tax structure. To eliminate the retail sales tax, for example, would require a state personal income tax with higher rates than used by any of the 43 states currently using that tax.[40] A state income tax that high would not result in a balanced tax structure.

Experience of other states indicates that imposing both a retail sales and a personal income tax does not necessarily equate to higher total taxes.[41]

We need spending reform. Most of the citizens that call for spending reform believe that there is a great amount of waste and inefficiency in government. Those that criticize the level of state and local spending, more often than not, never identify the programs that they would cut. There is undoubtedly some waste and inefficiency in state and local government but the amount is small, probably less than in many large private corporations. Eliminating waste and efficiency should be a constant goal but it will only have a marginal affect on the level of taxes. It is necessary to make real cuts in programs before it is possible to significant reduce taxes.[42]

Taxes are already too high in Washington. Waste and efficiency notwithstanding, most people calling for expenditure reform believe that the Washington's tax levels are among the highest in the nation. This is true with some of the state's taxes, such as the retail sales tax, but it is not true with regard to the total Washington state/local taxes.

Part V:
State/Local Tax Levels in Washington and How They Compare

One of the most important reasons for adding an income tax to the state's tax structure is to improve the fairness of the tax burden. However, many people, perhaps the majority of the state's citizens, are more concerned with the total level of state/local taxes and not so much on how the tax burden is distributed. Much of the opposition to income taxes comes from the mistaken belief that Washington's taxes are among the highest in the nation.

The following discussion addresses three questions that are of concern to citizens and public officials alike:

Chart 3: Washington State and Local Taxes as Percent of Sales Personal Income, 1933-2008

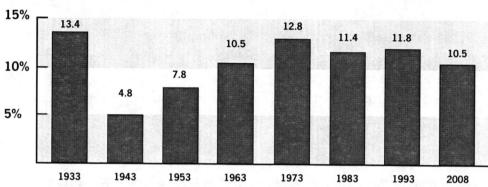

SOURCE: REPORTS OF THE U.S. BUREAU OF THE CENSUS, GOVERNMENTS DIVISION.

- How does the level of Washington's taxes compare with those of other states?
- How high are Washington's state/local taxes in relation to the citizens' incomes?
- Are Washington's taxes distributed fairly among families of different income levels? incomes?

State and Local Tax Levels in Washington

There are at least two approaches to measure the level of state/local taxes. One is to look at the dollar amount of taxes collected and compare those collections with earlier years. The problem with that comparison is that changes in tax collections results from many factors, including changes in population, the level of economic activity, inflation, etc.

A better way to evaluate tax levels is compare the dollar amounts of taxes collected to the citizens' incomes. This tells us how much of our income goes to support state and local governments. It will also tells us whether this percentage is higher or lower as compared to earlier years.

In Washington, taxes collected by the state and local governments amounted to 10.9 percent of the total personal income of all the state's residents in fiscal year 2007 (the latest year that interstate comparisons are available from the U. S. Census Bureau).

Chart 3 shows the percentage of Washington's total state personal incomes paid in state and local taxes during different periods of our state's history.

State/local Taxes took 13.4 percent of personal income in the 1933, mainly because income levels had declined steeply during the depression. The low level (4.8 percent) of taxes during 1943 was due to higher incomes of that period and lower spending by state and local governments because of the large amount of resources devoted to WW II.

During the past 35 years, the percentage of personal income taken in state and local taxes has ranged from a high of 12.8 percent in 1973 to a low 10.1 percent in 2002. The major causes of the reduction in state and local tax levels during the past few years have been:

- The I-601 expenditure and tax limit initiative approved in 1995.[43]
- The elimination of the motor vehicle excise tax in January 2000 by Initiative 695 and subsequent legislative action.[44]
- The one percent limit (I-747) on the annual increase in state and local government regular property tax revenues approved by the voters in 2001.[45]

State and Local Tax Burdens: Washington Versus Other States

Another criterion for evaluating Washington's taxes is to compare Washington's taxes with the taxes collected in the other 49 states. The average percentage of income taken in state and local taxes for all 50 states in 2008 was 11.2 percent, compared to 10.5 percent in Washington. (See Table 3) Twenty-nine of the other 49 states collected a larger percentage of their citizens' incomes in taxes than Washington did that year.

Although the average tax burden in Washington, as measured by the percentage of state and local taxes to personal income, is slightly below the average for all states, averages can be deceiving. For example, the average depth of a river may be one foot but many people have drowned in spots where the depth is 10 feet. The average percentage of taxes to the state's total personal income tells us nothing about how much taxpayers with different incomes are paying. That is, how is the tax burden distributed among low, middle and high income taxpayers? A closer look at a state's tax structure and the types of taxes it imposes is necessary to determine this.

The types (and tax rates) of taxes, such as income, retail sales, property, gasoline, etc., is the primary determinant of how the tax burden is spread amongst a state's taxpayers. For example, sales taxes are regressive and net income taxes are progressive in their distribution of tax burdens among taxpayers. Washington, with its heavy reliance on sales taxes and no income tax, has one of the most regressive among the fifty states.

As indicated in Chart 4, Washington relies on general sales taxes for 48 percent of its total state and local tax revenues. This compares to the average for all 50 states of 23 percent. Washington also relies more on selective sales (i.e., cigarette, liquor, gasoline) than the average of all states, 15 percent for Washington and 11 percent for all states.

Washington's relies on property taxes for 27 percent of its taxes compared to 31 percent all states combined. The largest discrepancy between Washington and the all-state average is in the net income tax category. Net income taxes provide 27 percent of the tax revenues for all 50 states and zero percent of Washington's tax revenues.

The general sales, income and property taxes are the most important taxes used by the states. Table 2 shows the number of states using one or more of these three taxes. Washington is one of seven states that do not impose a personal income tax. Only five of the 50 states do not impose a corporation income tax. How Regressive is Washington's Tax Structure Compared to Other States?

Table 4 shows how Washington's state and local taxes are distributed among families with different levels of personal income. The percentage of income paid in state/local taxes by lower income families in Washington is greater than the percentage paid by higher income families. Lower income families (i.e., up to $20,000 annual income) pay 15.7 percent of their income in state and local taxes and the higher income families (i.e., incomes of $130,000 or more) are paying only 4.4 percent of their incomes in state and local taxes.

The table shows that moderate-income families with incomes between $30,000 and $40,000 are required to pay twice the percentage of their incomes in taxes as families with incomes of $130,000 or more. The distribution of Washington's taxes among the state's citizens is regressive and not fair unless one believes that lower and moderate-income families should pay higher percentages of their incomes in taxes than wealthy families.

Table 2: Use of the Major Tax Sources by the Fifty States

Type of Tax	Number of States	Washington
Retail Sales	45[1]	Yes
Personal Income	43[2]	No
Retail Sales & Personal Income	40	No
Corporate Income Tax	44[3]	No
Property	50	Yes

[1] ALASKA'S RETAIL SALES TAX IMPOSED LOCAL GOVERNMENTS ONLY
[2] TWO STATES, NEW HAMPSHIRE AND TENNESSEE, TAX DIVIDENDS AND INTEREST ONLY
[3] SOME OF THE NON-CORPORATE INCOME STATES IMPOSE GROSS RECEIPTS BUSINESS TAXES SOMEWHAT SIMILAR TO WASHINGTON'S B&O TAX

The regressive impact of Washington's taxes on families of various incomes is no surprise in view of the state's heavy reliance on the retail sales tax and the fact that Washington imposes no income tax. The distribution of the tax burden in the 43 states with personal income taxes is considerably different from the distribution of tax burden in Washington. Most income tax states use graduated income taxes, which results in a progressive distribution of taxes.

A recent study of the tax burdens in the fifty states from 1980 to 2000 indicates that Washington's tax structure, along with Nevada and South Dakota, are tied with having the third most regressive tax structure in the nation. The study determined that Wyoming has the distinction of having the most regressive tax structure, followed closely by Tennessee.[46]

Indeed, Washington can lay claim to one of the best states in the country for the wealthiest folks to reside. As long as the state does not have an income tax, this distinction will continue.

Chart 4: Percentage Reliance on Taxes Sources Washington vs. U.S. Average, 2008

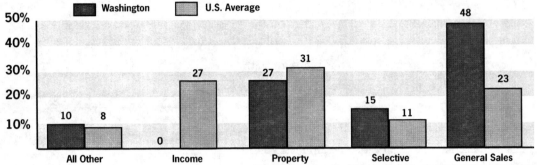

*SOURCE: U. S. CENSUS BUREAU (REPORT RELEASED JULY 2010)

Part VI:

The Outlook for Adding a State Income Tax

The outlook for adding an income tax to Washington's tax structure is not particularly good at the present time. There are no longer as many incentives for voters to want to approve income taxes. Many of the proposed tax reductions and tax limits contained in last two proposed constitutional income tax amendments, HJR 42 and HJR 37, are now in the Constitution and tax laws. These include:

- The lowering of the constitutional limit on regular property taxes from 2.0 percent to 1.0 percent
- The state's full funding of basic K-12 education and subsequent reduction in the M&O school levies for basic school programs
- The exemption of groceries from the sales tax
- The elimination of the inventory tax

Not having those "incentives" to include in future tax reform proposals will make it even more difficult to sell tax reform to the taxpayers.

In the past few years, the businesses received the greatest share of tax preferences and the need to change from the B&O tax (a gross receipts tax) to a business net income tax from that sector of our economy is seldom heard.[47] The business community historically has opposed a personal and corporate income tax.

There is little grass roots support for income taxes from the average taxpayer. One reason is the state's residents have become more affluent during the past 60+ years. They are much more concerned on how a state income tax might affect them. They appear to be satisfied with the present tax structure because they have lived with it a long time and there is a fear of the unknown.[48]

Table 3: State and Local Taxes as Percentage of State Personal Income, Washington versus Other States, 2008*

State	Amount	Rank	State	Amount	Rank
Alaska	34.7%	1	Kentucky	10.7%	27
Wyoming	15.1%	2	Mississippi	10.7%	28
New York	14.9%	3	Montana	10.6%	29
North Dakota	13.6%	4	**WASHINGTON**	**10.5%**	**30**
Hawaii	12.9%	5	Massachusetts	10.5%	31
Maine	12.9%	6	Arizona	10.5%	32
Vermont	12.5%	7	North Carolina	10.5%	33
New Jersey	12.4%	8	Arkansas	10.5%	34
New Mexico	12.3%	9	Maryland	10.5%	35
Connecticut	11.9%	10	Florida	10.3%	36
California	11.8%	11	Georgia	10.2%	37
West Virginia	11.8%	12	Nevada	10.1%	38
Wisconsin	11.8%	13	Idaho	10.0%	39
Louisiana	11.6%	14	Oklahoma	9.9%	40
Ohio	11.5%	15	Texas	9.8%	41
Rhode Island	11.5%	16	Virginia	9.8%	42
Kansas	11.4%	17	Missouri	9.6%	43
Minnesota	11.4%	18	Colorado	9.6%	44
Nebraska	11.2%	19	Oregon	9.4%	45
Pennsylvania	11.2%	20	South Carolina	9.3%	46
Utah	11.1%	21	Alabama	9.2%	47
Michigan	11.0%	22	Tennessee	9.0%	48
Illinois	10.8%	23	New Hampshire	8.8%	49
Iowa	10.8%	24	South Dakota	8.6%	50
Delaware	10.7%	25	**U.S. AVERAGE**	**11.2%**	
Indiana	10.7%	26			

SOURCE: U. S. CENSUS BUREAU (REPORT RELEASED JULY 2010). THE NUMERICAL RANKINGS OF THE STATES ARE CORRECT BASED ON CARRYING OUT THE FIGURES ONE ADDITIONAL DECIMAL POINT. FOR EXAMPLE, PRIOR TO ROUNDING TO ONE DECIMAL POINT, WASHINGTON'S PERCENTAGE IS SLIGHTLY HIGHER THAN THE OTHER FIVE STATES THAT SHOW 10.5% PERCENTAGES

There is little interest in the legislature to add an income tax. In recent years, the "I" word is seldom mentioned in the legislative chambers. Legislators have learned that proposing an income tax is not a good strategy in an election campaign.

Table 4: Annual Average State and Local Taxes Paid by Washington Households

Income Group	Average State-Local Taxs	Taxes as Percent of Personal Income
Up to $20,000	$1,837	15.7%
$20,000 to $30,000	$2,402	9.8%
$30,000 to $40,000	$3,217	9.4%
$40,000 to $50,000	$3,700	8.3%
$50,000 to $60,000	$4,393	8.2%
$60,000 to $70,000	$4,936	7.7%
$70,000 to $80,000	$5,477	7.4%
$80,000 to $100,000	$5,947	6.8%
$100,000 to $130,000	$6,769	6.0%
Over $130,000	$9,198	4.4%

SOURCE: "TAX ALTERNATIVES FOR WASHINGTON STATE", WASHINGTON STATE TAX STRUCTURE COMMITTEE, NOVEMBER, 2002.

The state's two most recent governors, Gary Locke and incumbent Christine Gregoire, both Democrats, mostly avoided even discussing the income tax issue. Likewise, there is currently little support in the legislature to pass a proposed income tax constitutional amendment to allow the voters to decide. The two governors before Locke, Mike Lowry (D) and Booth Gardner (D), proposed income taxes but were unable to obtain sufficient legislative support to allow the citizens to vote on the issue.

What could bring support for an Income Tax?

The continuation of large budget cuts in important state programs made during the 2009 and 2010 legislative sessions[49] will cause many groups and individuals to rethink their position on taxes. Those budget cuts will likely become greater in the future unless taxes are increased. A recent projection by the Governor's budget agency (Office of Financial Management) indicates that the state will face a revenue shortfall of $3 billion during the 2011-2013 biennium and a possible shortfall of $8.8 billion during the 2013-2015 biennium unless taxes are increased. Budget cuts of that magnitude will have a devastating impact on many state programs and do further harm to the state's economy.[50]

Tax increases under the present tax structure will be hard to come by

Increasing existing taxes, such as the retail sales and other excise taxes (cigarette, liquor, etc.), will move tax rates toward their practical maximum. Inequities will increase and incentives to evade taxes will climb to new heights. The higher rates will also encourage businesses and other groups to seek additional exemptions, further narrowing and eroding the tax base.

Table 5: Annual Average State and Local Taxes Paid by Washington Households

Year	Type of Measure	Measure Number	Type of Tax Authorized	Outcome
1929	Legislative Bill	Ch. 151	National Banks	Unconstitutional
1930	Constitutional Adm. Ra	14th Amend-ment	Allows Differential Property Taxes (1)	Voter Approved 322,919 to 136,983
1931	Legislative Bill	SB 26, SB 27	Personal & Corporate	Vetoed
1932	Citizens' Initiative	I-69	Personal & Corporate	Unconstitutional
1934	Constitutional Adm.	HJR 12	Allow Graduated Income Tax	Voters Reject 134,908 to 176,154
1935	Legislative Bill	Ch. 178	Personal Graduated	Unconstitutional
1936	Constitutional Adm.	SJR 7	Allow Graduated Income Tax	Voters Reject 93,598 to 328,675
1938	Constitutional Adm.	SJR 5	Allow Graduated Income Tax	Voters Reject 141,375 to 285,946
1942	Constitutional Adm.	HJR 4	Allow Graduated Income Tax	Voters Reject 89,453 to 176,332
1951	Legislative Bill	Ch. 5	Corporate	Unconstitutional
1959	Legislative bill	Ch. 5	Real Property Gross Rental Income	Unconstitutional
1970	Constitutional Adm.	HJR 42	See Text	Voters Reject 309,882 to 672,446
1973	Constitutional Adm.	HJR 37	See Text	Voters Reject 228,823 to 770,033
1975	Citizens' Initiative	I-314	12% Corporate	Voters Reject 323,831 to 672,178
1982	Citizens' Initiative	I-435	10% Corporate (2)	Voters Reject 453,221 to 889,091

AMENDMENT 14 ALLOWS PROPERTY IN DIFFERENT CLASSES TO BE TAXED DIFFERENTLY BUT ALL REAL PROPERTY IS IN ONE CLASS AND MUST BE TAXED UNIFORMLY WITH EXCEPTION OF MINES AND TIMBERLAND. I-435 INCLUDED A JANUARY 1, 1983 REPEAL OF THE SALES TAX ON GROCERIES THAT WAS IN EFFECT FOR 14 MONTHS FROM MAY 1, 1982 TO JULY 1, 1983.

Federal court decision and laws that currently allow thousands of out-of-state sellers to sell sales tax free to Washington residents is costing the state treasury hundreds of millions of tax dollars a biennium.[51] This tax lost means a higher tax burden on those Washingtonians who do not evade the tax.[52] Further increases in the high rates of sales, B&O and excise taxes will increase the tax evasion problem.

With an income tax, the legislature could not only decrease the high rates of the current regressive taxes but also target any need for additional revenue to those with greater ability to pay taxes.

The bottom line, however, is that a majority of the citizens are opposed to a state income tax. Either the majority of the state's citizens are not aware of the unfairness of the present tax structure, or they do not care. I believe it is the former.

The problem, I believe, is that citizens do not fully understand the importance of state and local taxes in supporting the government programs that are vital to their individual welfare and to the state's economy. The first step toward genuine tax reform is education programs, reinforced by the return of high school "civics" classes. State and local government officials must do more to inform taxpayers on where the taxes are going, how the tax burden is currently distributed among the citizens and how state and local governmental programs affect the state's economy and the quality of life of its citizens. This may also help to close the everlasting gap between what we expect from our governments and what we are willing to pay for it.

Chapter 6

Boldt From the Blue: Struggles over Salmon

Mason Morriset

On January 31, 1855, at the close of the treaty negotiations, Issac Stevens, Governor of the Territory of Washington, met with the chiefs and headmen of the Makah Tribe at Neah Bay. The signing ceremony is recorded as follows:

Tse-Kaw-Wootl (a chief of the Makahs) brought up a white flag and presented it saying "look at this flag, see if there are any spots on it. There are none, and there are non on our hearts."

Kalchote (another chief) presented another flag. "What you have said was good, and what you have written is good."

The Indians gave three cheers or shouts as each concluded. The Governor then signed the treaty, and was followed by the Indian chiefs and principle men.

In similar scenes repeated throughout Western Washington, the Indian tribes and bands ceded title to vast areas of land and reserved for themselves in turn certain rights, including "the right of taking fish at usual and accustomed places in common with the citizens of the Territory." The presentation of white flags symbolized to the tribes their feeling that the United States had dealt fairly with them and that their right to fish, the nucleus of their culture, had been reserved.

The actual realization of that guarantee, however, proved difficult.

The Role of Fish in the Pre-Treaty Economy

It would be difficult to overemphasize the importance of anadromous fish to large and complex native culture of the eighteenth century European explorers discovered in the Pacific Northwest. The Indian population density was higher than almost anywhere else in native North America, north of Mexico.[1] The salient feature of the native economy was an abundance of anadromous fish which were available for harvest at predictable times and could be preserved for later use.[2] Although various cultural and political differences existed, a common cultural characteristic of all the Indian groups was the paramount dependence on the products of an aquatic environment, especially anadromous fish.[3]

Species of Pacific salmon and the steelhead trout are indigenous to the Pacific Northwest. These anadromous fish are borne in fresh water, spend their adult lives in the Pacific Ocean, then return to the precise location of their nativity to reproduce and die.[3] The Indians' lives in general were tied to this migratory cycle, and each tribe was tied to the distinct spawning units which invariably returned to its traditional harvest areas.[4]

Anadromous fish were revered and respected by the tribes. Nearly all of the tries performed a First Salmon Ceremony, designed to insure that the fish would perpetually return.[5] Other procedures insured that salmon were not wasted and that water pollution was not permitted. Refuse was never deposited in streams during the salmon season and the Skokomish even beached their canoes to bail them.[6] So central to the Indian culture were these fish that the Nisqually, for example, projected their preoccupation with fisheries in their perception of the stars. The constellation Orion was identified as three Indians catching small fish in schools. The Pleiades were described as a species of fish with large heads and small tails. The northern lights were viewed as schools of herring turning up the whites of their bellies.[7]

Fish were vital to the Indian diet. They were also a major element of Indian trade and economies.[8] Indian harvest and use of salmon and steelhead therefore required not only sophisticated fishing equipment, food preservative techniques and storage facilities, but also exchange system.[9] Through trade, surplus fish could be converted into wealth. As Dr. Lane reported:

Extensive trade was carried on among Indian groups in western Washington in order to acquire food stuffs, raw materials, and manufactured goods not available locally. The trade involved both basic necessities and luxuries of native life. The trade existed because different localities had different resources. The variation in local habitats is an important factor in understanding the native economy.[10]

Tribes in Eastern Washington traded across the mountains with tribes on Puget Sound.[11] The Makah Tribe, at the mouth of the Strait of Juan de Fuca, acted as middleman in the trade from the west coast of Vancouver Island down to the trading posts on the Columbia River. They traded ocean-going canoes, lumber, ceremonial masks, vermilion, slaves, blankets, and other items with tribes up and down the coast. The imported blankets, guns and kettles from the Europeans which the paid for with dried halibut, smoked salmon, processed oil and other items.[12]

For trade over long distances, the salmon were preserved by sun drying, wind drying, or smoking. The Indians also found markets for fresh fish among other tribal groups who desired fish of different runs (or fish from the same run caught in a different location), for variety in diet or for differences in keeping qualities.[13]

By treaty times, the growing number of white settlers created s substantial market for fish. Salmon were exported as well as traded for local consumption. All of these fish markets were supplied by tribal fisheries. In fact, the trade of salmon had wide geographic distribution and high volume. Indians captured millions of pounds of salmon annually.[14] Commerce in salmon was "the crux of the Indian economy in Western Washington."[15]

The Stevens' Treaties Protect Indian Fisheries

1. The Europeans' Arrival Increased Demands for Indian-Caught Fish.

In 1790, Manuel Quimper commanded the first European expedition to venture into and explore the inland salt waters of Western Washington. Vancouver, sailing for Great Britain, conducted further exploration of the Strait of Juan de Fuca and Puget Sound in 1792. Both Quimper and Vancouver reported trade with the Indians for fish.[16]

By treaty with Spain in 1819, the United States began the process of extinguishing the claims of other sovereigns to the wealth of the Pacific Northwest. An agreement was reached with Russia in 1824, followed by a treaty with Great Britain in 1846 under which these nations essentially quit– claimed the region to the United States. By United States law, the United States Government alone could obtain clear title from the Indian tribes[17] and this the United States was anxious to do. The Federal Government, anticipating settlement of the area by white settlers, wished to avoid friction between Indians and settlers over use of property rights.

White settlers began to reach the Western Washington area by land in the 1840's. In 1848 the United States created the Oregon Territory, of which the Puget Sound country was a part.[18] The Territorial Act explicitly preserved "rights of person or property now pertaining to the Indians,"[19] and extended the application of the Northwest Ordinance provisions calling for "good faith" dealings with the Indians.[20] However, the influx of white settlers brought strong demands for prime agricultural lands. Congress and the Executive, therefore, authorized Isaac Stevens to negotiate treaties with the tribes in order to avoid hostilities and the possibility of a prolonged and distant war.[21] The Federal government hoped to thereby consolidate and protect

Indians and their canoes on Elliott Bay in the 1880s.

the Indians on residential reservations, thus freeing land for settlement and enclosure by the white settlers.[22]

The treaty negotiators did not wish to interfere with Indian commercial fishing; to do so would have been highly inconvenient since Indian fishermen caught most of the fish used by whites.[23] Early non-Indian commercial fishing enterprises were rudimentary and largely unsuccessful so the settlers relied on Indians for fish.[24] In addition to their traditional trade with other Indian groups, the Puget Sound tribes supplied the growing market for fresh fish, and sold large quantities of salted salmon to the Hudson Bay Company for shipping to markets in New York, San Francisco, China, South America, Hawaii, and Great Britain.[25]

Non Indians did not engage in fishing as competitors on any scale until the late 1870s.[26] Instead the settlers concentrated on agriculture, mining and logging. Thus, for many reasons, by the time the Stevens treaties were negotiated, Indians were deeply engaged with non-Indians in commerce in fish. When the United States asked the tribes to cede their land, therefore, the tribes asked for guaranteed right to their fisheries.

The Intent of the Treaty Negotiators.

The treaties negotiated by Governor Stevens and the Indian tribes were clearly designed to protect both Indians and settlers.[28] They extinguished tribal title to the lands so that the settlers could obtain United States land patents for their claims, and the tribes received assurance of federal protection of their reserved lands and fisheries.

Communications between the parties during the negotiations was obstructed by both language and cultural barriers. The vast majority of Indians at the treaty councils did not speak or understand English so the treaty provisions and the remarks of the commissioners were interpreted by Colonel Shaw in Chinook jargon. Chinook was then translated into native language by Indian interpreters, since many of those present did not understand Chinook jargon.[29] The evidence indicates that there were no words in the Chinook jargon for "common", "usual", "accustomed", "citizens", "steelhead", and other phrases which have become controversial in interpretation of the treaties.[30] The treaties themselves are written in English; the clauses were essentially drafted before any formal meeting at a treaty ground.[31] With some exceptions the treaty signatories representing the tribal units were important men of the winter villages who had some prior contact with non-Indians or spoke some Chinook jargon.[32]

Dr. Lane's conclusion regarding the parties intent was not "controverted by any credible evidence." In addition, the concept of relinquishing one-half their rights was not unknown to the tribal negotiators. This notion was espoused at the treaty of Neah Bay:

Ka-bach-sat of Tso-yess – My heart is not bad but I do not wish to leave all my land. I am willing you should have half, but I want the other half for myself. You know my country, I want part for my village. It is very good. I want the place where the stream comes in.

In-an-da-ha of Waatch – My Father! My Father. I now give you my heart … My wish is like the rest. I do not wish to leave the salt water. I want to fish in common with the whites. I don't want to sell all the land. I want a part in common with the whites to plant potatoes on. I want the place where my house is. We do not want to say much, we are all of one mind.[33]

To these tribal negotiators using the fisheries and the lands "in common with" the whites was consistent with the idea that each could take up to one-half.[34] The bountiful fish resources of the era implied that there would be no limitation of the tribes' existing uses of the fisheries, particularly since the Indians did not expect non-Indians to use the tribal fishing locations at the same time.[35]

Anthropologists testified that the treaty negotiators sought to protect continued Indian fish harvests from possible future r estriction.

Preemption of Indian Fisheries and Over fishing by Settlers

Initially, at least, the intent of the treaty parties was generally followed. During the 1850's, 1860's and 1870's Indian fishing and Indian trade in fish was integral part of the pioneer economy.[36] Before Washington was admitted to the Union in 1889, most interference with treaty

By the 1910s, the 'Iron Chink' (background), gutted salmon faster than they could reproduce.

Indian fishing stemmed not from acts of the legislature but from settler's attempts to monopolize traditional Indian fishing spots. Such interference gave rise to the first reported litigation regarding the treaties' effect. In United States v. Taylor, 3 Wash. Terr. 88 (1887), the United States and Yakima Indians complained that they were prevented from reaching a traditional site on the Columbia River by a land owner's fences. The Supreme Court of the Territory construed the treaty in favor of the Indians:

[I]t seems to us the Indians in making the treaty would have been more likely to have intended to grant only such rights as they were to part with, rather than to have conveyed all, with the understanding that certain rights were to be at once reconveyed to them ...

It will be seen by the statement of facts above set out that at the time this treaty was made there existed within the territory which was the subject-matter of the treaty, certain ancient fisheries which had for generations been used as such by said Indians, who had certain well-defined habits and methods connected with such use.[37]

Preemption of Western Washington Indian fisheries by non-Indians was infrequent during the two decades following the treaties. Heavy white settlement came later to that region and early settlers in the Puget Sound area concentrated on agriculture.[38] Development of the canning process, however, greatly increased the interest of investors and non-Indian fishermen in the commercial potential of Washington's anadromous fish runs. The first cannery was built on Puget Sound in 1887 although production was minimal until the middle 1890's.[39]

Responding to the new market created by the canneries, settlers adopted a traditional efficient Indian fishing technique, the fish trap;[40] and non-Indian commercial fisheries grew by leaps and bounds. From three canneries in 1894, the Puget Sound industry expanded to 24 canneries in 1905. Investment syndicates formed companies to operate both canneries and huge new traps.[41] Efficient trap fishing requires that the trap be located so as to intercept salmon traveling along the shoreline toward their natal rivers. Because some locations were better than others, conflicts developed between Indians and settlers.[42] In 1898 settlers frustrated the Lummi Indian's traditional use of Semiahmoo Spit and their practice of going to Point Roberts to catch and dry fish during the bountiful runs of Frasier River salmon. Settlers claimed the shores beside the Indian fishing site and drove away at gun-point native reef netters who tried to erect temporary fish-drying houses on the shore.[43] The tribes' fear that they would be pushed out of their usual and accustomed sites, voiced in the treaty negotiations[44] had been realized.

Heavy harvests by non-Indian trap and cannery crews also brought about the need to restrict fishing for conservation's sake.[45] As Dr. Lane testified, it is likely that the United States treaty commissioners foresaw the need for such restrictions, although they did not contemplate that the Indian fisheries would be restricted.[46] Forty years later, the consequences of an unrestricted non-treaty fishery were clear. "In the history of the salmon fisheries of the Atlantic Coast", said one Washington Fish Commissioner, "there is a warning against the extravagant manner in which our Pacific Coast salmon fisheries have been carried on for many years past."[47]

In the 1890 session, all salmon fishing was outlawed for three months each year.[48] In the early 1890's, the State began licensing and prescribing permissible types of fish traps and times of operation.[49] Later, the legislature specifically prohibited spearing, gaffing snagging and snaring fish.[50] Each of these enactments effectively curtailed treaty Indian fishing.[51]

Restriction of treaty Indian commercial fishing resulted also from the non-Indian view that conservation required curtailment of fishing in rivers and streams but no in the salt water areas of Puget Sound.[52] In 1897 and 1899 the legislature halted fishing in all Puget Sound tributaries and nearby bays.[53] Such freshwater closures varying in extent, have been enacted repeatedly by nearly every Washington State Legislature since1897.[54] They have drastically curtailed fishing at the most lucrative Indian fishing places-forks in rivers, outlets of rivers into lakes, and saltwater estuaries.[55] Each of the areas closed was a usual and accustomed fishing place of one or more tribes.[56]

In later years, the Department of Fisheries expanded the freshwater closures to saltwater areas of Puget Sound it called "salmon preserves." The effect was to outlaw fishing in most of the remaining usual and accustomed grounds of the Makah, Lower Elwha, Skokomish, Squaxin Island, Nisqually, Puyallup, Tulalip, Stillaquamish, Swinomish, Upper Skagit and Sauk-Suiattle Indian Tribes.[57] This effect is graphically illustrated by a map in the Joint Appendix.[58] Most importantly, harvest of the same anadromous fish runs elsewhere on their migration route was not restricted. Non-treaty fishermen could and often did capture the entire harvest before the fish returned to tribal fisheries near their natal streams.[59]

Over the years, before 1974, State regulations designed to restrict the harvest of anadromous fish were "apparently based more on political realities than on economic considerations."[60] As another economist has said, the "distribution of the salmon [harvest] is best understood as the product of a balance of power."[61] The treaty tribes, of course, had little role in this political process since their members were not made United States citizens until 1924.[62]

Post Decision Remedies of the District Court

For a number of reasons, vindicating the tribal right to take a fair share of the fish has not been a simple task. Both the District Court and Court of Appeals found that Washington's regulations typically permit most, or all, available salmon to be harvested by non-treaty fishermen prior to their return to tribal fishing places, which are near the end of the salmon migration paths. Thus, a crucial part of the District Court's apportionment was the requirement that the State of Washington:

Make significant reductions in the non-Indian fishery, as are necessary to achieve the ultimate objectives of the Court's decision without requiring mathematical precision, but ... consistent with the concept of permitting the full harvest of fish.[63]

Tribes have no opportunity to catch on-half of the salmon runs which normally return to them unless one-half of the fish escape "downstream" fisheries. Or, as the Court of Appeals said, "preserving the tribal opportunity requires limiting the non-tribal opportunity.[64]

Within a few months of the District Court's decision, several non-Indian fishing associations attempted to intervene or brought lawsuits directly against the federal court.[65]

Washington and its non-treaty fishermen have adamantly resisted making reductions in non-treaty fishing. Washington itself stimulated this resistance in 1974 by decreasing the sport salmon catch limit from three to two fish, over the opposition of Indian tribes who pointed out that the change would not make more fish available to tribal fisheries.[66] The State's action led to Commercial Passenger Fishing Vessel Association. v. State. In the state court litigation, Washington officials publicly described their "distasteful" duty of complying with the federal court decisions.[67]

At approximately the same time the Puget Sound Gill-netters Association obtained a state court injunction which interfered directly with the federal court's orders. Washington could offer no alternative means of complying with the federal decision.[68] Upon motion of the United States, the District Court then enjoined the execution of the state court order.[69]

In early 1975 Washington unilaterally revised the steelhead run size available to Indian fisheries on the theory that some fish were hatchery propagated. In regard of applicable federal procedural orders, the Game Department seized Muckleshoot Indian nets and fish.[70] Again the District Court was forced to intervene.[71]

A few months later the Purse Seine Vessel Association sued Washington to prevent compliance with certain District Court orders relating to the sockeye and pink salmon fishery.[72] On the motion of the United States, the District Court stayed the state's proceedings.[73] This time the state superior court held that it had not been properly enjoined and proceeded to judgment against the Department of Fisheries.[74] The judgment was affirmed by the Washington Supreme Court, Purse Seine Vessel Owners Association v. Moos, 88 Wn.2d 799, 567 P.2d 205 (1977).

On June 4, 1975, the Court of Appeals affirmed the District Court's 1974 opinion and order in a thorough opinion. A concurring opinion decried the need for the District Court to retain continuing jurisdiction but added:

The record in this case, and the history set forth in the Puyallup and Antoine cases, among others, make it crystal clear that it has been recalcitrance of Washington State officials (and their vocal non-Indian commercial and sports fishing allies) which produced the denial of Indian rights requiring intervention by the District Court. This responsibility should neither escape notice nor be forgotten.[75]

In the fall of 1975, Washington's reluctant compliance forced the District Court to enter a series of further remedial orders designed to give the treaty tribes a realistic opportunity to share in the Coho and chum salmon runs.[76] In response, many of Washington's non-treaty fishermen engaged "in a substantial fishery on the 1975 Coho salmon run in direct violation of regulations issued by the State of Washington and order of [the] court."[77] The State of Washington did little to prevent these recurring violations. Citations were ordered thrown out by county prosecutors and local judges[78] and out of 300 citations issued to non-treaty fishermen, only one led to a penalty.[79]

The 1976 fishing season was similar. In April the Department of Game abruptly terminated a co-management agreement with the Quinault Tribe and threatened to arrest tribal employees moving steelhead smolts from the tribal hatchery to the river.[80] The Department's action was based on its interpretation of the state court decision in Department of Game v. Puyallup Tribe, 86 Wn.2d 665, 548 P.2d 1058 (1976).[81] It apparently determined that the treaty right did not even extend to tribally reared hatchery fish.

During the fall salmon runs, Washington authorized non-treaty fishermen to take much of the catch prior to the fish reaching the major tribal areas.[82] Hen the State announced additional non-treaty fisheries, the District Court again had to intervene.[83] Undaunted, the Puget Sound Gill-netters Association publicly encouraged non-treaty fishermen to disregard the court-ordered closures.[84] Within four nights some 247 non-treaty vessels were observed illegally fishing.[85] Washington announced that it was unable to control the illegal fishing, although the Assistant Fisheries Director admitted that in some areas state policy was to make no arrests.[86]

Alison Bridges Gottfriedson being arrested in the 1970's

Washington's position throughout the litigation had been that the Department of Fisheries had no authority to limit non-treaty fishing so as to increase the number of fish available for harvest at usual and accustomed places.[87] Accordingly, until 1977 the District Court relied on Washington to promulgate regulations appropriate to that purpose. In 1977, however, a successful state court collateral attack foreclosed that remedial tool

In June 1977, the Washington Supreme Court decided Puget Sound Gill-netters Association v. Moos,[88] an original action filed directly with the Supreme Court. In this, and subsequent rulings,[89] the state court opined that neither state statutes nor the Equal Protection Clause permitted Washington to restrict non-treaty fishing in order to make fish available at "usual and accustomed grounds and stations." The State Supreme Court decisions effectively required Washington to disregard the Interim Plan, 384 F. Supp. At 420, Joint App. 230.[90]

In advance of the 1977 fishing season, Washington adopted regulations which "made no allowance [and] no exceptions for the Indian opportunity to harvest."[91] When harvestable fish reached Lake Washington, the Department of Fisheries authorized sports harvesting but refused to allow treaty Indian net fishing.[92] The Director of Fisheries admitted that no conservation needs justified the restriction of the Indian fishery.[93]

The new circumstances compelled the District Court to directly allocate the opportunity to take fish.[94] The court accepted the unanimous report of a joint technical committee listing the harvestable numbers of fish for each 1977 run and the number of fish which had already been caught by Washington troll and sport fishermen.[95] Since both the treaty and non-treaty fleets possessed the ability to harvest a full 50 percent of the Chinook, Coho and chum salmon runs expected to return to usual and accustomed fishing grounds in Puget Sound, [96] the allocation order simply expressed the fishing opportunity to be accorded to each side in terms of the number of fish of each species in each region.[97] On the basis of the order, fisheries biologists of the treaty tribes and the State of Washington could, and did, design fishing regulations so that neither fishery would preempt the others fishing opportunities.

In the 1977 salmon season illegal non-treaty fishing reached unprecedented heights. Washington informed the District Court that there was little possibility of obtaining state prosecutions or convictions for offenders, [98] and the Department of Fisheries said it would issue no State or federal citations designed to stop incursions into the treaty share.[99] A state fishery biologist observed nearly 200 non-treaty gillnet boats fishing in a closed area.[100] The situation, the District Court found if permitted to continue, will lead to a breakdown of law and order, ... the substantial denial of federally guaranteed treaty fishing rights and will endanger the preservation of the fishery resource.[101]

Accordingly, the court enjoined the state-licensed fishermen from violating the state regulations which implemented the allocation order.[102]

A highly organized campaign to violate the court's injunction ensued. The National Marine Fisheries Service reported that about one-fourth of the non-Indian fishermen contacted indicated that they planned to violate the court's orders.[103] Non-treaty fishermen unloaded tons of illegally caught fish in "a carnival atmosphere, laughing and joking."[104] Shooting threats were reported.[105] Non-treaty fishermen extensively used citizens band radio equipment to report contacts with federal enforcement officers. A shore based transmitter also warned illegal fishermen of the Coast Guards' approach.[106] Consequently, when enforcement vessels stopped to issue a citation most of the violators would escape.[107] After the season, the State's technicians reported that over 183,000 salmon had been taken illegally by the state licensees.[108]

In early 1978 the court heard testimony and argument from the parties and many non-treaty fishermen, regarding whether an injunction should restrain illegal non-treaty fishing for an additional season. Counsel for the Puget Seine Vessel Owners participated[109] in the hearings although they entered appearances on behalf of individual fishermen, not the trade associations. Washington indicated that its policy of not enforcing restrictions on the non-treaty fleet would continue.[110] Accordingly, the court issued the injunction of June 6, 1978 which is before this court on certiorari before judgment of the Court of Appeals.

At least twice during the 1978 fishing season, Washington adopted regulations, not required for conservation, curtailing treaty Indian fisheries. In the Strait of Juan de Fuca, the state adopted emergency regulations forbidding treaty fisheries on the grounds that the tribes might intercept a few fish from runs needing protection. However, the state simultaneously authorized non-treaty harvest in nearby areas, which had a much larger effect on the same weak fish runs.[111] Again, the District Court was forced to intervene. The court found to evidence showing that a total closure of treaty fishing was reasonable or necessary for conservation.[112]

Washington also exercised its emergency conservation authority[113] to close Indian fisheries in the wake of a dispute over the way a telephone hotline message announced openings and

SEATTLE TIMES

Judge George Boldt.

closing of non-treaty fishing.[114] It was undisputed that there was no conservation need for terminating Indian fishing; the matter was resolved in the Fisheries Advisory Board.[115]

Illegal non-treaty fishing raged in 1978. The Coast Guard Commander testified:

[T]he fishermen are better organized this year. They have tailed our boats, reported our positions from the shore, from the water, from bridges … We find … one boat … the rest of them, of course, scatter. They are warned that we are coming.[116]

A National Marine Fisheries Service officer recounted hearing non-treaty fishermen joking as they were being arraigned for federal contempt of court, discussing when they would fish again in violation of the orders and speculating on the amount of fines they would have to pay.[117] By November 3, 1978, 177 citations had been issued ordering fishermen to appear and show cause why they should not be held in contempt.[118] Non-treaty fishermen took 95.3% of the 1978 illegal catch.[119]

Despite the illegal fishing the treaty tribes have obtained increasingly significant opportunities to take fish at usual and accustomed areas. In 1977 treaty fisheries harvested nearly 43% of the Puget Sound origin runs combined.[120] Of course, in the areas most heavily impacted by illegal non-treaty fishing the tribes took far less than their share. In 1977 at least, the District Courts' accommodation to the rights of the parties was largely successful, in spite of "the most concerted official and private efforts to frustrate a decree of a federal court witnessed in this century."[121]

Chapter 7

The Greening of the Evergreen State

Daniel Jack Chasan

We can't claim it was a big surprise. When the National Marine Fisheries Service listed Puget Sound chinook salmon as a threatened species in 1999, the listing made front page headlines in the Puget Sound area and drew major coverage from the national press. Nevertheless, anyone who paid attention had realized for many years that the fish and their habitat were in trouble. NMFS merely recognized the obvious.

People who lived in Washington had always known that the salmon runs and the other natural resources at which they marveled were basically fragile, and that to preserve them, human society had to act with a certain restraint. This has been a hard principle for European-American society to follow.

At first, many of the European Americans who came to Washington – and to other parts of the West – may truly have been naive. James Willard Hurst wrote in Law and the Conditions of Freedom in the Nineteenth-Century United States that "[f]or most of the nineteenth century ... [l]ooking upon our [natural] wealth, we found it obviously 'inexhaustible' – the adjective appears ritually in public and private documents – and drew the conclusion that we should press our present ambitions by whatever seemed the quickest route."

In Washington, almost from the start, some people realized that resources weren't really inexhaustible. The Indians had known that they shouldn't block salmon streams, and early non-Indian inhabitants – at least the more thoughtful ones – knew it, too. The first legislature that met in the Oregon country and the first legislature that met in the new territory of Washington

Skid Road, logging down Seattle's hills in the 1870s.

both passed laws against blocking streams. "Salmon protection has been part of [the political landscape] since the first [Oregon] territorial legislature of 1848," the fisheries biologist James Lichatowich has written in Salmon Without Rivers. "We knew since 1875 ... what was going to cause the collapse. We put in all these things to prevent it." Obviously, we failed – but not through ignorance. Society did not obey or enforce its own laws against catching too many fish or blocking streams.

Virtually everyone's perspective was short-term.

Early loggers approached Washington forests much as early sport and commercial hunters approached the buffalo on the Great Plains: take only the very best parts, and leave the rest to rot on the ground. But even late-19th- and early-20th-century timber barons knew that the forests were not "inexhaustible."

They had seen the great pine forests of the upper Midwest largely destroyed. Indeed, they had helped to destroy them – which is why they had invested in mills and timber farther west. From a very early stage, they could see that in the forests of western Washington, virtually everywhere an ox team could haul old-growth logs to salt water, the best trees were already gone. In January 1884, the acting manager of Bainbridge Island's huge Port Blakely mill, C.W. Young, wrote to his home office in San Francisco: "The timber contiguous to [Puget] Sound is nearly exhausted. The part remaining is such as was passed by in past years." Young was talking about straight-grained timber that was considered good enough for flooring, but at that point in Washington history, five years before statehood, it was remarkable for a lumberman to realize that even the finest grade of timber was already "nearly exhausted."

The largest fish runs were already diminished, if not exhausted, too. The development of salmon canning, which provided a way to preserve fish indefinitely and sell them all around the world, had created an economic incentive to catch too many of them.

The first salmon cannery on the Pacific coast began processing fish on the Sacramento River in 1866. Six years later, in 1872, the first cannery opened on the Columbia River. Five years later, in 1877, the industry reached Puget Sound.

The effects were hard to miss, although people tried hard to ignore them. In the lower Columbia River, fishing from row boats, fishermen were obviously catching too many salmon by the late 1880s. A regional magazine observed that "[t]he large pack and the fact that the run of fish in July was very great are pointed to as evidences that the supply of salmon in the river is not becoming exhausted. To achieve this result a greater number of boats, larger nets and more assiduous fishing were necessary, and it is pretty certain that the proportion of salmon running in April, May and June, the ones which go to the headwaters and become the chief propagators, that escaped the miles of meshes spread for them, was very small ....[I]n spite of the increase in the size of nets, the number of boats and the skill of the fishermen, the average caught by each boat has largely decreased."

But people didn't want to believe the evidence of their own eyes and statistics. The 19th-century magazine writer who cast a skeptical eye on claims that over fishing had not diminished the Columbia River's salmon runs concluded, "All these things point to the necessity of a propagating establishment" – which is to say, people had better build fish hatcheries, but they did not have to stop fishing. Hatcheries saved society from making hard choices.

Canning gave wealthy corporations an incentive to invest in salmon fishing. The early 1880s saw the establishment of the first fish traps, funnels of nets supported by wooden pilings into which salmon on their way to spawning streams would swim. Traps were a very efficient way to catch salmon. Anyone with a leaky rowboat could still go out and catch salmon, but a corporation with enough money to erect a trap could catch many more. The big canning companies soon relied primarily on traps. Before the end of the decade, traps were taking the lion's share of the salmon caught in Puget Sound.

Concentrations of capital were taking the lion's share of the best timber, too. The Northern Pacific Act, which President Abraham Lincoln signed in 1864, put vast tracts of Washington timber into private hands. In exchange for building a railroad from St. Paul to Puget Sound, it offered the builder all odd-numbered sections of land for twenty miles on either side of the track through states, and for forty miles on either side of the trace in territories. When the Northern Pacific Railroad Company laid the rails, it got the land. It chose its route with care. "In locating an exact route from the Columbia to Puget Sound, [Northern Pacific] engineers tried to lay track through the most heavily timbered areas, so that valuable timberland would be included in the land grant," Robert E. Ficken writes in The Forested Land.

Railroad construction on a smaller scale also enabled forest products companies to profitably log trees that grew far from salt water. In the early 1880s, companies started to build logging railroads into the woods. For the first time, the big trees did not have to be moved to tidewater by the muscle power of man or beast. As the old-growth forests receded, loggers could follow them farther and farther from salt water. The construction of logging railroads meant that except in the high mountains, where grades were too steep for locomotives, virtually any forest could be cut at a profit.

In those high mountains, no one objected to saving scenic but apparently worthless rock and ice – which was one of the reasons why, before the 19th century ended, Mt. Rainier became the nation's third national park.

Everyone valued Mt. Rainier as a scenic icon. The railroads thought they could make money by hauling tourists to the mountain. (A quarter century earlier, the Northern Pacific had pushed for creation of Yellowstone National Park.) They also thought they could make money by swapping high-altitude scenery for prime timber land at lower elevations that had somehow been left in the public domain. Alfred Runte has written that "only where scenic nationalism did not conflict with materialism could the national park idea further expand. First to exemplify the interplay of both forces after 1890 was Washington State's Mount Rainier." An "obvious concession to economic interests ... [took] the form of a land exchange between the government and the Northern Pacific Railroad. In return for the company's claim to portions of the mountain, the government allowed the line to select compensation from federal property in any other state served by its tracks. ... [T]he Northern Pacific ... divested itself of rugged, marginally-productive land at the expense of the nation at large. ... Mount Rainier National Park ... can be interpreted as an example of scenic preservation designed to the specifications of big business and frontier individualism."

In contrast, no one stood to profit from preserving the core of what would become Olympic National Park. A million and a half acres of the Olympic Peninsula were designated a national forest reserve in 1897. Within a few years, hunters started slaughtering the huge Olympic elk primarily for their teeth – just the incisors, two teeth per elk – which fashion-conscious turn-of-the-century men wore on their watch chains. The 1905 state legislature made it illegal to kill an

Clear cutting in the Olympics went on for 50 years.

elk in Washington. Four years later, largely to protect what would become known as "Roosevelt elk," President Theodore Roosevelt set aside more than 615,000 acres of the forest reserve as a national monument.

By that time, all over the west, city governments had started looking up into the hills and mountains for new sources of water and power. In 1901, the city of Seattle dammed the Cedar River and diverted water through wooden pipes to supply its growing population. Other dams soon blocked salmon spawning runs in clear violation of the law. James Lichatowich has written, "even before the 1930s [when the first big federal dams were built on the Columbia River], hundreds of smaller dams were built for municipal water supplies, stock watering, irrigation, placer mining and power generation. Like their large counterparts, these small dams also prevented salmon from reaching spawning areas, flooded upstream habitat and degraded salmon habitat downstream by altering flow patterns."

Despite the laws against blocking fish passage, timber companies in the late 19th and early 20th centuries routinely built destructive "splash dams" that stored water to float logs down small streams. The water "would be released suddenly to 'flash-float' logs down the river," according to one description. "The sudden wall of water and logs crashing downstream was like a spring freshet occurring several times during the spawning and incubation periods. The salmon didn't stand a chance of spawning effectively, for they were carried downstream with the flood each time it was released. In between floods the stream bed was nearly dry and in the winter the eggs were exposed and frozen."

Some changes in the natural environment were inadvertent. Others were deliberate. The Black River, which drained Lake Washington into the Duwamish River and ultimately into Puget Sound, vanished abruptly in 1916, when the U.S. Army Corps of Engineers completed a ship canal between the northern part of Lake Washington and salt water. As soon as the canal locks opened, the lake level dropped nine feet. Lake water stopped flowing into the old shallow river channel.

By that time, Seattle had started working to change the Duwamish itself. Ports all along the west coast expected a flood of new shipping when the Panama Canal opened, and they wanted to be ready to grab their shares. In Seattle, the port dredged a deep ship canal straight through the river's old meanders. Dredge spoils were dumped on salt marshes beside the new channel to create industrial land. At the river mouth, more dredge spoils formed Harbor Island, one of the largest man-made islands in the world.. An estimated 80 percent of the estuary's tidal swamps and marshes, its original shallows and flats, vanished when the channel was dredged and the dredge spoils dumped in the name of progress. By the end of the century, less than two percent of that habitat remained.

No one campaigned to save the Duwamish or the rivers that were altered by early dams, but some people already saw clearly that hatcheries could not overcome the effects of simultaneously catching too many salmon and destroying their natural habitat. In 1917, John N. Cobb, who would soon become the first director of the University of Washington's college of fisheries, described "an almost idolatrous faith in the efficacy of artificial culture of fish for replenishing the ravages of man," and warned that "nothing has done more harm than the prevalence of such an idea." But most decision makers chose to ignore this inconvenient reality.

Despite all evidence to the contrary, the atmosphere was one of self-congratulation. Most of the salmon caught in Puget Sound spawned in Canada's Fraser River. Nineteen-thirteen was a record year for Fraser River salmon. "Extensive as are the operations of the industry, they do not necessitate the annihilation or reduction of the great wealth which the waters hold," the 1914 Pacific Fisherman Yearbook proclaimed. Right after the record season of 1913, though, when the Canadian Pacific was building a railroad through Hell's Gate, northeast of Vancouver, a dynamite blast touched off a huge rockslide that tumbled down into the Fraser River, blocking most of the channel. Fraser River salmon were clearly in trouble.

Soon after World War One, the quality of water in parts of Puget Sound, which everyone had taken for granted, was clearly in trouble, too. The first sulphite pulp mills were erected in the 1920s. The hanging sulfurous stench of the pulp mills, which as late as the early 70s would enable even small children to recognize mill towns with their eyes closed, was something new. Equally new was the sight of pulp liquor flowing out into the water of the Sound.

Water pollution had arrived. People had already observed elsewhere in the country that aquatic life did not benefit from the presence of sulfite pulp mills. When a state Investigation Committee on Pollution Problems met in January 1927, "one of the Fisheries Inspectors handed the Supervisor a report that in the bay at Port Angeles, boatmen claim they keep the hulls of their boats clean if they can be moored opposite the pulp mill which discharges its waste water into the head of the bay. Likewise, shingle mill men advised him that they moor their bolts [of cedar] in that end of the bay if possible to keep the bolts free of marine growth."

When a pulp mill started up at Shelton, oysters in southern Puget Sound took a turn for the worse. Oyster spawn did not survive. The yield of commercial oyster beds declined. The oystermen saw their living and their way of life going down the drain.

The facts of the situation have never been totally beyond dispute. The number of oysters harvested behind dikes had never approached the number harvested from wild beds early in the century. As the wild populations were depleted, though, dike culture became the industry's only hope for survival. The dikes did not protect oysters from climatic conditions, silt deposits or non-native predators. The mill companies attributed the decline of oyster populations to those natural causes and the imprudence of individual oystermen. The oystermen, in turn, were sure that pollution from the mills was decisive.

Fishing played a much greater role in Washington's economy than shellfish culture, but projects that would destroy salmon habitat attracted little attention – except as welcome signs of the region's material progress. The culprits weren't just greedy Eastern entrepreneurs. They were also the municipal utilities that many citizens saw as salvation from the greedy entrepreneurs who owned private utility holding companies. Seattle City Light completed its first big dam on the Skagit River in the 1920s, and without even a gesture toward the law, the city of Tacoma's Cushman power dams blocked the north fork of the Skokomish River. By the end of 1930, 90 percent of the North Fork's flow was diverted from the Skokomish River system.

Fish hatcheries encouraged people to ignore the brazen destruction of salmon streams, but it didn't take a John Muir to recognize that western Washington's forests were becoming battlefield landscapes of tall stumps and combustible slash. And things were getting worse, not better; the internal combustion engine enabled loggers to move higher and higher into the hills.

The business was, truly, timber mining. Just as the forest products companies had cut their way through the forests of the Midwest in the late 19th century, they were cutting their way through the readily accessible forest of the Northwest. Once the trees had been cut, there was no market for most of the land. Big companies mostly hung onto the land. Smaller entrepreneurs didn't want to pay the taxes. When the timber was gone, they simply abandoned the property. They did nothing about the piles of combustible slash. They did not pay taxes.

Fires roared through the slash. Washington counties took over miles of charred stumps for back taxes. Clarence Bagley, who had come to Washington in 1864, wrote that "[o]ur boasted heritage of inexhaustible forests is nearly dissipated." State Land Commissioner Clark Savidge called the problem of logged-off land "the largest unsettled one that our state has before it today." As steps toward reforestation, the Washington legislature passed statutes that enabled the state to buy and manage cutover private land and to acquire cutover land from the counties.

The potential markets for timber were obvious, although, during the Great Depression of the 1930s, they were severely limited. When the federal government started building dams on the Columbia River – Bonneville Dam was completed in 1938, Grand Coulee in 1941 – and created a Bonneville Power Administration to transmit and market the power, no one had a clue where all that electricity would go.

Nevertheless, the region was willing to pay the environmental price. When Grand Coulee was completed without fish ladders in 1941, everyone knew that 1,100 miles of spawning streams would be sealed off forever, and that a stock of huge chinook, some weighing close to 100 pounds and known colloquially as June hogs, would pass into oblivion. Even at Bonneville, past which virtually all the river's salmon had to swim, no one knew how well or even whether the new fish ladders would work.

A year before Bonneville was completed, Jim Marshall wrote in Collier's: 'There is real fear that the [Bonneville] dam will just about abolish the $10,000,000-a-year Columbia River salmon industry.' But as Marshall paraphrased the prevailing attitude: "If the salmon cease to run – well, that'll be just too bad, but, after, all, it's only $10,000,000 a year. What's that trifle in these days of billions?"

Most people who cared about salmon fishing worried less about saving fish stocks than about getting more fish than their competitors. In 1934, sport fishermen and purse seiners pushed Initiative 77 to outlaw the cannery-owned fish traps that still took most of the salmon caught in Puget Sound. The initiative would also ban both traps and fish wheels on the Washington side of the Columbia River. A pro-initiative brochure claimed that banning the traps would be "the absolute saving of Washington's third-largest industry." Initiative backers also claimed that banning the traps would strike a blow for conservation. This was nonsense. Fish traps were no worse – and could have been much better – much better for the wild salmon runs that disappeared or joined the endangered species list by the end of the century than a labyrinth of nets set from hundreds of small boats. A House Merchant Marine and Fisheries Committee staff member who was intimately familiar with the old politics of Pacific salmon observed--decades later but before the Endangered Species Act became a factor – "'conservation' means that you want the fish."

Initiative 77 passed in a landslide. Washington's big canneries had harvested most of the Fraser River fish for generations. With fish traps banned from Washington waters, Canadians started catching most of the depleted Fraser River salmon runs. The canneries had either opposed a treaty with Canada or had held out for a treaty that would leave their share of the fish intact. Now, a treaty that would guarantee the United States half the catch looked pretty good.

The Senate ratified a treaty the following year. Under its terms, the US and Canada would jointly manage the fishery through the International Pacific Salmon Fisheries Commission. Beginning in 1944, fish ladders would be built around the Hells Gate rockslide. The Fraser River runs –which provided most of the salmon caught in Puget Sound – would be at least partially restored.

Banning the traps may also have had less positive, long-term political consequences. Arguably, forcing the canneries out of the fishery eliminated the one concentration of money and political influence that in later years might have weighed in on the side of preserving salmon habitat.

At around the same time purse seiners and sport fishermen started campaigning to ban fish traps, conservationists started pressing for the creation of a national park on the Olympic Peninsula. But local entrepreneurs wanted access to public forests there, and in 1935, the first bill to create an Olympic National Park went nowhere. Two years later, President Franklin Delano Roosevelt visited the peninsula, where he was shocked by what he later called the "criminal devastation" of the forests. Finally, in 1938, Congress created a 648,000-acre national park. The original boundaries did not include the rain forests that now form the park's main attraction and were largely responsible for the park's designation as an international biosphere reserve. The bill allowed the president to expand the boundaries, though, and at the beginning of 1940, Roosevelt added the upper Hoh, Bogachiel, Calawah, Quinault, Queets and Elwha valleys. (The park started managing most of the wilderness beaches that same year, although it didn't formally take them over until 1953; the northern beaches weren't added until 1976.)

By that time, privately owned and state-owned timber in accessible lowlands was largely gone. When World War Two pushed up demand, big forests products companies – which were major landowners – began planting trees. The World War Two years saw Weyerhaeuser and its competitors start the first tree farms. After the war, loggers started going up into the national forests. (At that time, the state's vast timber holdings were mostly too fragmented and isolated to be managed, in any modern sense of the term, and the state did not even know what it owned.)

No one had built logging roads up into the national forests of the Olympics or the Cascades before. The companies that cleared and graded the first ones weren't building for the ages; in fact, they were barely building for the coming year. Sloppy road construction led to decades of road failures and erosion that washed tons of soil down clear cut slopes into salmon spawning streams.

The politics of natural resources were shifting. The federal government now owned a lot of the timber that everyone wanted. And the federal government was building the big dams, with their associated shipping locks and irrigation projects. Under

WSHS

State Tree Farm 1 at Montesano planted in 1942.

the New Deal, the Columbia River became a cornucopia of subsidized power and water. The state faced a surplus of electric power. It therefore welcomed the aluminum plants that soaked up all the otherwise-unmarketable electricity from the new federal dams.

The huge dams drew international attention, but historically, their significance paled beside that of a project that initially drew virtually no attention at all. In 1944, in the desert of central Washington, the Hanford Atomic Works became the first plutonium factory in human history. Hanford started turning out plutonium in late 1944. By mid-1945, it had turned out enough for the bomb that exploded at the Trinity test site and for the bomb that incinerated 70,000 people at Nagasaki.

It had also started creating the world's first large quantities of long-lived radioactive waste. Almost no one paid the problems of waste disposal much attention. Low-level waste was dumped into trenches. More dangerous substances were buried in single-walled steel tanks. And there they stayed, largely unremarked, until the 1970s

If no one confronted the future of that radioactive waste seething in the tanks at Hanford, the state did, for the first time, confront the growing problem of water pollution. Buoyed by a wartime budget surplus, in the wake of a tank-car oil spill that nearly wiped out the Soos

Creek fish hatchery, and faced with recurrent worries about drinking water supplies, the 1945 legislature passed the state's first water pollution control law almost unanimously. .

After World War II, the gap between urban economies and rural, resource-based economies grew wider. Increasingly, an urban population did not have to ignore its own economic interests to advocate the preservation of land or resources. One could fight to save forests or stop pollution more easily if one's own income did not depend on logging or milling, or the economy of a small town dependent on the local mill.

The years after World War II brought other changes, too, including a rapid increase in the number of automobiles and a blossoming of new suburbs, accessible only by automobile. The electric power surplus didn't last long.

In the Seattle metropolitan area, even before sprawl took hold, people who lived in communities all around Lake Washington had come to realize that piping raw sewage into Lake Washington was not a good idea. As early as the 1930s, communities around the lake had started treating their sewage. Treatment broke down the wastes, eliminating the threat of disease to people who drank or swam in lake water, but making nutrients more readily available to algae in the water. Algae populations boomed. Then the algae died, sank, and rotted. The decay process used up much of the dissolved oxygen in the water, making it harder and harder for salmon and other fish to live there. As population increased, so did the supply of nutrients. The water of the deep lake, grew murky. And because all those algae were rotting in the sunlight, the lake started to stink.

In the mid-1950s, a young Seattle attorney named James Ellis came up with a plan for saving the lake: build a big sewer line all around the lake and run the sewage first through a treatment plants and then out into Puget Sound; form a quasi-governmental organization that could oversee construction and operation of the system; issue bonds to pay for construction; levy service charges to pay off the bonds and cover operating costs. (The new organization would be known as the Municipality of Metropolitan Seattle or Metro.) Ellis and his colleagues lobbied a bill through the state legislature of 1957. The legislation put the Metro plan up to a vote of the people in the area within which the new organization would function.

There was still time to put a mass transportation system into place before the population sprawled incoherently toward the mountains. And there was time to make decisions about where and how the region should grow. The initial Metro proposal would have empowered the new agency to do land-use planning and run a transportation system. In March 1958, the measure won a majority but lost under a complicated geographical balancing system of weighting votes. Metro's backers dropped transportation and planning from the proposal, and ran it again in September. This time, it passed. By the mid-1960s, the lake was clear again.

In Puget Sound, pulp mill pollution was still an issue. The harvest of Olympia oysters dropped from 319,000 pounds in 1936 to 31,884 pounds in 1956. In 1956, the Pollution Control Commission gave the pulp mills exactly one year to submit plans for evaporating their pulp liquor. The Pollution Control Commission's time limit was extended, renewed in 1961, and never enforced. On January 1, 1961, the Pollution Control Commission gave the seven most polluting mills exactly one year to propose alternatives to their current means of waste disposal and three months beyond that in which to submit engineering plans. The dates were soon extended, and the mills kept on as before.

Even in the 1960s, people weren't willing to confront the problems of increasing population and population density. In 1968, with metropolitan population still relatively concentrated in the city of Seattle and the federal government ready to pay 90 percent, people in the Seattle metropolitan area voted down a mass transportation system that could channel growth along rail corridors before it had a chance to sprawl wholesale beyond Lake Washington. (Actually, the measure won a majority, but not the 60 percent the law required.) Automobile companies covertly poured money into the fight against it. Two years later, the citizens turned down a mass transit proposal again. The chance to let transportation and meaningful land-use planning get ahead of the region's growth had come and gone.

Energy planners weren't willing to confront a changing reality, either. They still assumed an uninterrupted growth of demand. The commitment to damming the rivers of the Columbia Basin continued for more than 30 years after the Depression ended, for increasingly marginal benefits. The dams on the lower Snake River were just the caboose on the Columbia River gravy train. Ice Harbor Dam, the lower end of the gauntlet that fish subsequently had to run on the Snake, was finished in 1961. The upper end of the gauntlet, Lower Granite Dam, wasn't completed until 1975. (However marginal the benefits, subsidized barging and irrigation water boosted local economies, and veterans of the pre-World-War-Two crusade for publicly owned utilities considered the expansion of power generation by public entities an inherently good thing.)

But virtually all dam sites for generating truly significant amounts of electricity were already taken. In the late 1960s, the Bonneville Power Administration and regional utilities put together a "Hydro Thermal Power Program," under which the region would build seven new nuclear and coal-fired generating plants. A consortium of public utilities called the Washington Public Power Supply System (WPPSS) would build three nuclear plants. Private utilities would build nuclear plants of their own. The Bonneville Power Administration – which had no legal authority to build generating plants itself--would basically guarantee the WPPSS bonds.

Energy development and its implications became a hot topic. The North Slope oil discovery, announced in 1968, soon made people think about tanker traffic into Puget Sound. The oil lay beneath the Alaskan tundra at Prudhoe Bay, near the edge of the Arctic Ocean. The oil companies decided to transport it nearly 800 miles south from Prudhoe Bay to the ice-free port of Valdez through a huge pipeline, load it onto tankers, and send it south. No one knew where the tankers would go. The closest harbors in the lower 48 states lay in Puget Sound. The oil might all go to a new oil port in Puget Sound, then through a pipeline to the Midwest. Nineteen sixty-nine had begun with the Santa Barbara oil spill; images of dead or dying seabirds, coated with thick black oil, had appeared in newspapers, magazines, and television news broadcasts across the country. It didn't take much imagination to envision the same kind of scenario in Puget Sound. By early 1970, a hand-lettered sign over the doorway to the Seattle office of the Sierra Club proclaimed, "If the Puget Sound – Chicago oil pipeline is built, we will have to start measuring our tides with a dipstick."

WSA

During the 1971 environmental wave, the legislature passed six major ecology bills in 33 days, including siting nuclear plants, restoration after surface mining, oil spills cleanup, the shorelines act and double bottoms for tankers entering Puget Sound. Pictured: An installation on the lower Columbia River in Southwest Washington.

The 1971 state legislature passed a law imposing unlimited liability for oil-spill damage on whoever was responsible. Nevertheless, on environmental issues, the public seemed to be way ahead of its elected representatives. The Washington Environmental Council tried and failed three times to lobby a shoreline-protection law through the state legislature. In 1970, the group announced that it was going to launch an initiative campaign. "We are appalled by what is being done on the shorelines," said the WEC's president, Jack Robertson. "The last three legislatures tried to come to grips with it but the special interests wouldn't let them come up with anything meaningful."

A campaign led by ex-WEC president Tom Wimmer collected enough signatures to put a shoreline management initiative on the ballot in 1972. The bill would require a permit for any significant development on and state shoreline. Suddenly, the legislature sprang into action, quickly passing a bill that differed from the WEC's largely in that it gave much greater discretion to county and city governments. Both measures went on the November ballot. The legislature's initiative passed.

Passage of the Shorelines Management Act gave environmentalists an implicit club to hold over the legislature for many years: if the legislators didn't act, the people would.

A low snow pack in the mountains during the winter of 1972-73 had aluminum companies shutting down plotlines that spring. The region lived through most of the year with a consciousness of low water behind the dams. Then, in the fall, after the Yom Kippur war in the Middle east, the Arab nations slowed the flow of oil to the United States and Western Europe, and energy supplies became an obsession: speed limits were lowered, thermostats were turned down, and people started lining up before dawn to buy gas ...

It would have been hard to create a better atmosphere for a decision to build more nuclear plants – or, if anyone were interested, for a commitment to conservation. Utilities had signed up for the first WPPSS nuclear plant in 1971. Two years later, they signed up for two additional plants, and agreed with the BPA to launch a second phase of the Hydro Thermal program, which would include WPPSS' fourth and fifth nuclear plants. The BPA pressured utilities into signing contracts for WPPSS 4 and 5. When environmental groups began questioning the demand forecasts on which the utilities' construction plans were based, BPA Administrator Don Hodel struck back at the environmentalists, inveighing against them, somewhat illogically, as "prophets of shortage."

In 1975, Seattle City Light began to talk about buying a 10-percent share of WPPSS 4 and 5. The Washington Environmental Council sued the city to force it to prepare an environmental impact statement on the decision. WEC dropped the suit in exchange for City Light's commitment to set up a citizens' advisory committee that would examine the need for power and the most desirable way of meeting it. The citizens committee decided that the City Light demand forecast was too high, and that any gap between supply and demand could be met by a 230-megawatt conservation program.

The Seattle City Council voted to stay out of WPPSS 4 and 5. This was a historic decision. No major city had staked its future on conservation before.

Energy policy stirred less discussion than the prospect of an oil spill in Puget Sound. When it became clear that the Coast Guard had neither the will nor, in some cases, the authority to force extra safety features on tankers, the 1975 legislature passed what was known as the "tanker" or "tug escort" law, under which no tanker of more than 125,000 deadweight tons was permitted to enter the Sound, and any tanker of more than 50,000 deadweight tons either had to be equipped with a double bottom, twin screws, and collision-avoidance radar or be accompanied by a tug at all times. The next year, the anti-tanker lobby slipped language into a coastal zone management statute that explicitly forbade an oil port on the inner Sound.

Meanwhile, ARCO had gone to court to challenge the constitutionality of the tug escort law. In 1976, the 9th U.S. Circuit Court ruled against the state. The next year, the U.S. Supreme Court upheld that ruling.

But protection of the Sound had become a motherhood issues, and in early 1977, the legislators passed a law that would have confirmed the ban on supertankers in the inner Sound. Governor Dixie Lee Ray vetoed it.

Members of Washington's congressional delegation felt that something had to be done, and done quickly. In October, 1977, Senator Warren Magnuson introduced an amendment to the Marine Mammal Protection Act that forbade any expansion of oil port capacity on the inner Sound. Magnuson twisted enough arms and enlisted enough allies to move it through both houses without objection.

When President Jimmy Carter signed the Magnuson legislation, the issue of a major oil port in or near Puget Sound was finally settled, at least for a while. The idea of a Northern Tier Pipeline from Port Angeles, which the initial backers of anti-tanker legislation had advocated as a less dangerous alternative, had evolved from a pipeline around the southern end of the Sound to a pipeline under the Sound. The old anti-tanker position largely dropped from public view. By 1980, most environmentalists opposed Northern Tier. They didn't want an oil port in the Strait of Juan de Fuca any more than they wanted one inside the Sound. When the pipeline permit application reached the desk of Washington's staid Republican governor, John Spellman, in 1982, Spellman turned it down.

During the energy-conscious 1970s, while pro- and anti-tanker forces battled about an oil port on Puget Sound, the Northwest's congressional delegation wanted to make sure that everyone would continue to get a share of the Columbia River's subsidized power. The aluminum industry, which was taking some 40 percent of the power marketed by BPA, wanted new, long-term contracts. The private utilities wanted access to some of the same cheap hydropower to which the original Bonneville legislation gave the public utilities preferential access. The public utilities naturally wanted to make sure their good thing lasted. The Northwestern delegation wanted to prevent an unseemly scramble for kilowatts that would leave the aluminum industry and perhaps some utilities out in the cold. Senator Henry M. Jackson and regional utility and aluminum executives began developing legislation that would allocate the region's cheap hydropower in a time of scarcity. Their vehicle was the 1980 Pacific Northwest Electric Power Planning and Conservation Act, which set up a Northwest Power and Conservation Council to create power plans for the entire region.

The region would have formal, centralized energy planning. The aluminum companies would get new long-term contracts. The private utilities' residential and agricultural customers would get Columbia River kilowatts at the same low rates enjoyed by customers of public utilities. The public utilities would not have to fight for their shares of the power. As the legislation evolved, conservation became the preferred alternative, the development of renewable resources became a goal, and the preservation of fish and wildlife gained – in theory – equal status with power production.

The price of passing the Power Act, as it is generally called, was a promise to do something for the fish. In the late 70s, NMFS had already starting looking at the possibility of listing Columbia River salmon runs. Most regional politicians wanted very much to avoid a listing. The Power Act offered a way out. The region would commit itself to saving the salmon, and NMFS would put listing on the back burner. That's exactly what happened. The act gave the council the task of making sure the salmon got "equitable" treatment. However, the legislation did not spell out or even suggest how power production would be balanced with the preservation of wild salmon or other environmental goals.

Assumptions about energy started to change. The Iranian revolution in 1979 drove up energy prices, the recession of the early 1980s drove Northwestern sawmills and aluminum smelters temporarily or permanently out of business, and the region's energy use actually declined. At the same time, WPPSS' construction cost estimates had risen exponentially. Originally, all five nuclear plants were supposed to cost $4.075 billion. By the end of 1981, the figure reached $23.8 billion. (As construction, energy, and regulatory costs rose, nuclear construction projects all over the country left their budgets far behind, but WPPSS compounded its problems with hubris, bad planning, lax oversight, and a lack of accountability.)

Not surprisingly, Wall Street was losing its appetite for WPPSS bonds.

When the Northwest Electric Power and Conservation Council started meeting in 1981, representatives of Washington utilities lobbied it heavily to get 4 and 5 included, at least as options, in the first regional energy plan. Council members realized from the start, though, that the old demand forecasts were way off, that the power from 4 and 5 wasn't likely to be needed any time soon, and that even if the kilowatts should be needed someplace far down the road, there would be cheaper ways of getting them.

The Council did not pull WPPSS' fat out of the fire.

The following year, the WPPSS board voted to terminate the projects. In 1983, WPPSS declared itself in default on $2.25 billion worth of bonds. It was the largest municipal bond default in American financial history.

The WPPSS disaster drove home the point that rising demand wasn't a fact of nature, and undermined the belief – a kind of civic religion among public power advocates – that by building more and more generating capacity, one was doing the people a favor.

These were revolutionary concepts.

It emerged just as much of the public was discovering water quality problems in Puget Sound. Until then, most people had assumed that wastes dumped into the Sound more-or-less magically disappeared. But new information that came to light in the 1980s helped create an unprecedented level of public concern. The really critical new information was the presence of toxic wastes in the sediment. Tacoma's Commencement Bay made the EPA Superfund list in 1981. In 1980, an interdisciplinary NOAA research group headed by Donald Malins announced that the sediments in industrial urban areas – primarily Commencement Bay and the mouth of the Duwamish River – were heavily contaminated with PCBs, chlorinated hydrocarbons, heavy metals, and other highly toxic materials. Fish taken in those areas displayed unnatural percentages of liver abnormalities, including tumors. And while Malins' discovery of toxic hot spots got most of the attention, the startling part of his first-year report was that his group had also found heavy metals in non-urban, non-industrialized areas.

Still, research was not the main thing that drove public consciousness. The keys were two other events: The Seattle Times ran a front-page series on "The Imperiled Sound," leading off with high PCB levels in harbor seals. A dead gray whale turned up near Port Angeles with apparently high levels of PCBs, pesticides, and heavy metals in its body, and a Seattle veterinarian announced that the chemicals had done it in. Other people, including Malins and the toxics coordinator for Greenpeace, quickly pointed out there was no evidence whatsoever that pollution had killed the whale, but the incident certainly got people's attention.

This was not an ideal environment in which to get waivers from federal water pollution laws that required secondary treatment of municipal sewage.

And yet, that was exactly what Metro and other municipal sewage utilities were trying to do. In the United States as a whole, secondary treatment was an idea whose time seemed to have come nearly 15 years earlier. In 1972, the federal Clean Water Act required secondary treatment of all municipal wastes. Almost immediately, Metro and the sewage utilities of other coastal cities started lobbying for an exemption. When the Act was amended in 1977, the utilities got their wish. If a municipality on salt water could prove that its sewage discharges wouldn't hurt a minnow without secondary treatment and if the relevant state government concurred, the EPA could grant it a waiver for a period of five years. Metro and virtually every other coastal city applied for waivers in the late 1970s.

But the EPA could grant waivers only if state government concurred. And the state was operating under statutory language that required the use of "all known, available and reasonable methods of treatment." Unlike the federal standard, state law did not permit waivers if one could show that water quality wouldn't be affected. The legal language that proved so inconvenient in the mid-1980s had been written into Washington's very first water pollution statute in 1945. The language was unequivocal. Secondary treatment technology was clearly "known" and "available;" was it also "reasonable?" The DOE had found it reasonable in the past. During the early and mid-1970s, going to court against pulp mills, lawyers representing the agency had argued that secondary treatment was indeed reasonable – and they had won. Now, the DOE wasn't sure.

Things had come full circle. The treatment plants that Metro would have to bring up to higher standards were the same plants that had played a key role in cleaning up Lake Washington two decades before. In the 1950s, when the Metro system was conceived, there was no known good reason not to dump treated sewage into the deep waters of the Sound, just as in the 1970s, there was no known good reason why Metro and other municipalities on Puget Sound shouldn't get waivers. The pollutants people worried about at those times were biological oxygen demand and solids, and so far as anyone knew, the Sound shuffled them through 100 fathoms or so of salt water and washed them out to sea.

By the early 1980s, though, scientists and some bureaucrats knew perfectly well that when water flowing northward toward the Strait of Juan de Fuca reached an underwater sill some 60 meters down in Admiralty Inlet, much of the water was just pulled down to lower depths and recirculated. Another underwater sill, at the Tacoma Narrows, bottled up a lot of the water farther south.

By the middle of 1984, some people also realized that sewage was inextricably tangled up with the toxics problem. To be sure, not all the toxic substances in Puget Sound came from municipal sewage. Most did not. The Hooper Chemical Company had dumped an estimated 245,000 tons of chemical waste into Commencement Bay between 1945 and 1972, when it was still perfectly legal. Lead and PCBs had made their way into the Duwamish River and then into Elliott Bay from well-established industries. Chemicals in the sediment at Mukilteo had come from military fuel tanks. Still, municipal sewage plants clearly did deposit some toxic substances into the Sound, and Metro's West Point treatment plant dumped a greater volume of toxins than any other single source – some 900 pounds a day. Metro's own water quality study – undertaken to support its waiver applications – made the connection between sewage and toxics perfectly clear. Metro staffers had, in fact, begun to wonder how the study could be used to justify Metro's request.

Ultimately, it couldn't. In August 1984, regional EPA director Ernesta Barnes and Department of Ecology director Don Moos jointly announced that there would be no waiver for Metro or any other large municipality on the Sound. Not everyone jumped on the secondary bandwagon. A group of oceanographers and other scientists said publicly that the benefits of secondary treatment wouldn't be worth the cost. They were largely ignored. The city of Bellingham, denied a waiver from the requirement to install secondary treatment, appealed to the state Pollution Control Hearings Board but lost. After the hearing, a state Hearings Board member said that if water quality had been relevant, Bellingham would have gotten the waiver. But it wasn't relevant – the law specified a means, not an end.)

The mid-80s also saw a growing recognition of the problems of non-point-source or "lifestyle" pollution, the cumulative effect of pollutants running off lawns and driveways and roads and parking lots, washing into streams from dairy farms and horse pastures, leaching from septic systems all around the Sound.

In the late 1960s and early 1970s, when oil spills seemed an imminent threat, people worried about what we might do to the Sound. By the mid-1980s, they were worrying about what we had already done.

At Hanford, people may have worried about what had already been done, but the federal government hadn't made much progress in dealing with it. That seemed about to change. In 1989, more than a decade after radioactive leaks from Hanford's old, cheap, single-walled waste tanks hit the press, the federal Department of Energy, the Washington Department of Ecology, and the federal EPA signed a Tri-Party Agreement that gave Ecology authority to oversee a Hanford cleanup and established schedules for cleaning up a large number of sites and substances within Hanford's borders. Those old, leaky, single-walled tanks were covered specifically. The first step was "interim stabilization" of the waste stored in them. That meant pumping out most of the liquid and storing it temporarily in newer, double-walled tanks. (The DOE would fail repeatedly to meet its deadlines for interim stabilization. The state would threaten to sue the DOE, and in 1999 would obtain a consent decree under which DOE would move toward interim stabilization of the waste in 29 tanks under a fixed schedule that could be enforced by the United States District Court for Eastern Washington. By the autumn of 2004, DOE seemed to have pumped virtually all of the liquid waste into safer tanks. But – as cost estimates rose for the vitrification plant, which would embed high-level waste in glass-it had no chance of meeting the deadlines specified in the Tri Party Agreement.)

At the end of the 1980s, alarmed by years of rapid economic growth that had transformed the skyline of downtown Seattle and brought suburban sprawl to many formerly-rural areas, Seattle voters passed a "CAP" initiative to limit the heights of downtown buildings and the annual growth of downtown office space. Responding to the same burst of development and encouraged by the success of the CAP initiative, environmentalists prepared a growth management initiative for the 1990 statewide ballot. To head off the initiative, the 1990 legislature passed its own landmark Growth Management Act, which allowed local government more discretion than the environmental groups' version.

The main environmental battles, however, focused not in urban growth areas but in the federal forests and the isolated mill towns that had never had to deal with years of rapid economic growth.

The late 1980s and early 1990s were above all the years in which the region battled over the fate of the northern spotted owl and the old-growth forests in which it lived. This was arguably the most significant American environmental battle of the 20th century's closing decade, and while it had fewer economic ramifications than the subsequent battles over threatened and endangered salmon runs, it drew more national attention.

In 1987, a long-since-defunct Cambridge environmental group petitioned the U.S. Fish and Wildlife Service to list the Northern Spotted Owl as a threatened or endangered species. At the end of the year the Fish and Wildlife Service decided against a listing.

The next year, United States District Court Judge Thomas Zilly ruled that the Fish and Wildlife Service's refusal to list the owl was arbitrary and capricious and violated the Endangered Species Act. Zilly said that the Service had "disregarded all the expert opinion on population viability, including that of its own expert, that the owl is facing extinction."

After that, listing was a foregone conclusion, although two administrations and three Congresses tried to delay the inevitable or avoid its effects.

Later in 1988, the Forest Service released a spotted owl plan but by that time, scientific estimates of the territory occupied by a pair of spotted owls had increased dramatically, and scientists both inside and outside the government criticized the plan as scientifically insupportable.

In March 1989, environmental groups argued in federal court that the plan and its environmental impact statement violated both the National Environmental Policy Act and the National Forest Management Act. United States District Court Judge William Dwyer issued a preliminary injunction against imminent Forest Service timber sales in spotted owl habitat.

Congress directed the Forest Service to prepare a new spotted owl management plan and an environmental impact statement by October 1990. It told the agency to consider the recommendations of an Interagency Scientific Committee, which had been formed to devise a scientifically credible conservation strategy for the spotted owl. The committee was chaired by the Forest Service's senior wildlife biologist, Jack Ward Thomas, and was universally known as the Thomas Committee.

In 1989 the Fish and Wildlife Service proposed listing the owl as threatened. The listing became final in June 1990. The Thomas Committee had already issued its report. Unlike the widely-anticipated listing, it was a bombshell: Thomas and his colleagues concluded that the Forest Service's 1988 plan was unlikely to save the spotted owl from extinction, and they recommended the preservation of much more habitat than had been reserved in any previous owl plan. The committee's numbers went far beyond the federal government's worst nightmares – or most environmentalists' wildest dreams.

In May 1991 Dwyer permanently enjoined the Forest Service from selling additional timber in spotted owl habitat until it complied with the National Forest Management Act and the National Environmental Policy Act. In issuing the injunction, Dwyer observed that "more is involved here than a simple failure by an agency to comply with its governing statute. The most recent violation of the NFMA exemplifies a deliberate and systematic refusal by the Forest Service ... to comply with the laws protecting wildlife. This is not the doing of scientists, foresters, rangers and others at the working levels of these agencies. It reflects decisions made by higher authorities in the executive branch of government."

WSHS

Federal Judge William Dwyer stopped the cutting of what remained of old growth timber in the Olympics to save the Spotted Owl.

On April 2 1993, soon after President Bill Clinton took office, he kept a campaign promise by holding an all-day Forest Conference in Portland to hear from a wide variety of experts and citizens about the ancient forest controversy and what could be done to resolve it. In 1994, the Clinton administration came out with a Northwest Forest Plan designed to preserve habitat for the owl and other species while permitting a predictable level of logging. The plan withstood a court challenge. And it to some extent governed management of federal forests in western Washington, western Oregon and northern California into the new century.

It never delivered the billion board feet of timber per year that Clinton – in a pie-in-the-sky promise to logging communities – once claimed it would. At the same time, the plan did not prevent the continued decline of the Northern Spotted Owl. "Populations of northern spotted owls continue to decline across the range of the species," the U.S. Fish and Wildlife Service concluded in a status review ten years after the plan went into effect, "with the most severe declines occurring in the northern portion of the range (Washington and British Columbia)." (No one knew exactly why. Competition from the larger, non-native barred owls and lingering effects of past habitat loss seemed likely reasons.)

Just about a century after statehood, a lot of environmental bills were coming due. In the midst of the spotted owl battles, the federal government started listing populations of wild salmon. It started in April, 1991, when the National Marine Fisheries Service proposed listing Snake River sockeye as a threatened species. If any fish run deserved federal protection it was the Snake River sockeye – assuming it wasn't already two late: in 1989, just two mature sockeye had returned to Idaho's Redfish Lake; in 1990, none had.

The Power Planning Council had used BPA revenues to launch what has been described as "the largest biological restoration project on the planet." Hatcheries were built, streamside habitat restored, dams equipped with screens to keep young fish from getting ground up in the turbines. Juvenile salmon were trapped and carried downstream in barges or trucks. Forty-four thousand miles of streams were declared off-limits to small hydro development. A "water budget" – water to be released from the dams whether or not it could be used for power generation – was set aside to meet the needs of fish.

And yet, by the end of the century, the fish had not recovered. The causes of their decline were well known and widely acknowledged. People had caught too many of them. People had destroyed their habitat by cutting forests, building erosion-prone logging roads, letting cattle graze along streams in arid lands, paving and building in flood plains, dredging and filling estuaries and wetlands, blocking streams, removing logjams from rivers, building dikes to keep rivers from spilling into their natural flood plains, flooding spawning streams with hatchery fish, and building dams. On the Columbia River, the dams were the most obvious, although not the only, salmon killers. Even a dam with fish ladders does not support salmon as well as an undammed river. If the turbines are not screened – as those on the Columbia originally were not--young fish traveling downstream can be chopped to pieces. Water in the pools behind the dams may become too warm for salmon, although just right for salmon predators. And the water inevitably flows more slowly through the broad, deep lakes behind dams than it did through the original riverbed. Young salmon, borne downstream by the current, have been equipped by evolution for a relatively quick trip to the sea. When they are forced to travel slowly, they change to saltwater fish too soon, and their chances of survival plummet.

The Columbia River was not, of course, the only Northwestern river system in which salmon had found it increasingly difficult to survive. In 1990, a widely-quoted article by members of the American Fisheries Society's Endangered Species Committee, identified "214 native naturally-spawning Pacific salmon and steelhead stocks in California, Oregon, Washington, and Idaho that appear to be facing a high or moderate risk of extinction, or are of special concern."

As the listings of Northwestern salmon stocks began, the political and legal focus shifted to preserving the gene pool of wild fish runs. Once that became the goal, hatcheries were clearly part of the problem, rather than the solution. Released into a stream with naturally spawning wild fish, hatchery fish can compete with the wild fish for a limited food supply. They may also compete for food in the ocean. If the hatchery fish are significantly larger than wild salmon fry when they are released, they may actually devour the wild fish. They can spread disease to the wild population. They can interbreed with wild fish and alter the natural gene pool.

Finally, they put pressure on fishery managers to let fishers deplete wild salmon runs. If a relatively large hatchery run mingles with a relatively small wild run and people are allowed to catch a reasonable percentage of the hatchery fish, they will probably catch an unreasonable percentage of the wild fish. In 1997, the Washington Department of Fish and Wildlife identified 89 wild stocks in such mixed-stock fisheries that had deliberately been left unprotected. Perhaps nowhere had society thrown more good money after bad in an attempt to avoid dealing with habitat decline and over fishing than in the state of Washington. "The extreme example of a recently expanded [hatchery] program may be Washington State," Ray J. White and colleagues wrote for an American Fisheries Society symposium in 1995.

To save salmon stocks that nature had equipped to migrate far up into the Idaho wilderness, environmental, fishing and tribal groups advocated breaching the lower Snake River dams. The dams generated some power for the entire region, but they had become sacred cows largely because they were vital to a system of barge transportation that enabled farmers to ship grain down the river at subsidized rates. Several different Presidential administrations avoided confronting the issue. (At the same time, most mainstream environmental groups avoided confronting the fact that commercial harvesting was a significant part of the problem. Environmentalists had made common cause with commercial fishermen in a way they never had with loggers, and did not point accusing fingers at them. Some environmentalists also joined with commercial fishermen in arguing against salmon farming, which had become a huge industry in Canada, Chile, and Norway, and had driven down salmon prices worldwide.)

By the mid-1990s, while the federal government and its critics sparred over the dams on the lower Snake, a political consensus favored removal of two tall concrete dams on the Elwha River, just west of Port Angeles. The 108-foot Glines Canyon Dam and the 210-foot Elwha Dam had been completed there in 1913 and 1927. Neither included a fish ladder. The two dams kept six different species of Pacific salmon from swimming to their historic spawning beds in what by then was Olympic National Park. In 1992, Congress authorized dam removal, contingent on environmental reviews. The Interior Department bought the dams in 2000. No one had ever taken out dams of that size before, and at this writing, the project still represents a significant leap into the unknown..

A statewide poll taken in 1998 indicated that some 70 percent of the people in Washington thought restoring wild salmon was important. People often overestimated the value of commercial fishing to the region's economy but perhaps not the value of fish. In the 1980s, economists and business leaders had started acknowledging that a key to attracting the people who started and ran companies in computer software, biotechnology, and other lucrative high-tech fields – companies that could operate virtually anywhere – was providing a natural environment in which they wanted to live. "A healthy environment is a major stimulus for a healthy economy," a large group of Northwestern economists proclaimed in December, 1995.

The perceived value of healthy salmon runs and intact forests went far beyond their attractiveness to tourists or entrepreneurs. "Wild salmon's existence value"– the value people placed on simply knowing the fish were there – remained "very important in the Pacific Northwest," the National Research Council's Committee on Protection and Management of Pacific Northwest Anadromous Salmonids noted in 1996.

The region's sense of identity – and its self-congratulation about the biological health of Puget Sound – received a major blow when the National Marine Fisheries Service listed Puget Sound chinook salmon as a threatened species.

So did the region's century-old illusion that it could avoid making difficult choices.

"The announcement ... marked the first time the 26-year-old Endangered Species Act ... has been imposed across such large metropolitan areas," Tim Kenworthy reported in The Washington Post. "The decision to list seven salmon and two steelhead populations is expected ... to have a broad impact across a wide swath of the booming Northwest, on everything from home construction to agriculture to logging, even on such mundane tasks as washing cars and fertilizing lawns. ... 'We are fond of saying around here that without salmon, there's not much difference between us and Los Angeles,' added Tim Ceis, the Endangered Species Act coordinator for the Seattle area's King County. 'We just got a wake-up call.'"

Chapter 8

The Rise of Women in Washington's Politics

George W. Scott

"Distaff Democracy"

Mankind's greatest travesty has been unwillingness to fully employ the talents of half the race. Washington State has led the nation in realizing political equality with a host of "firsts." In 1910, Washington women got suffrage. Two were elected to the House in 1912, one as Senator in 1922, the first acquired real power there in 1937, and another became an executive insider and sponsor of the governor's prime policies in 1962. Senator Jeannette Hayner holds the record tenure record as Minority, and Majority Leader (1979-1993). By then, the State had the most women legislators (43 percent). In 2004, five women and four men were Supreme Court justices. In the 2005 legislature, all four of the Senate's majority leadership were women. Our sketch must be limited to paradigm leaders in elective office, centering on the legislature, the proving ground for would-be professionals. Honoring charitable, educational, environmental and philanthropic volunteers, and the public servants who sustain the state would bring on a cast of hundreds of thousands."[1]

Halted Steps

At the first Territorial Legislature, in 1854, Arthur Denny's amendment to grant white women suffrage failed by a vote. At least one of the legislators voting "nay" was married

Proposed Bill

HAT PIN DANGER

HOUSE . . . . No. 1847

House No. 1815 as passed to be engrossed.

The Commonwealth of Massachusetts.

In the Year One Thousand Nine Hundred and Thirteen.

AN ACT

To regulate the Use of Hat Pins

*Be it enacted by the Senate and House of Representatives
in General Court assembled, and by the authority of the same,
as follows:*

1   SECTION 1. It shall be unlawful for any person to wear
2 in public a hat pin unless the point of the hat pin is pro-
3 tected in such manner as to prevent the injury of persons
4 coming in contact therewith.
1   SECTION 2. Violation of the provisions of this act
2 shall be punished by a fine of not more than one hundred
3 dollars for each offence.

HOUSE OF REPRESENTATIVES, Feb. 3, 1913.
Passed to be engrossed.
Sent up for concurrence.
JAMES W. KIMBALL, *Clerk.*

AMENDMENT

An amendment has been introduced by Mr. Hilton.
394. Bill (H.) to regulate the use of hat pins (House,
No. 1847). [Question on engrossment.]

[Mr. Hilton moves that the bill be amended by striking
out section 1 and inserting in place thereof the following
new section: "SECTION 1. It shall be unlawful for any
person to wear in public a hat pin which protrudes more
than one half inch beyond the crown of the hat, unless the
point thereof is protected in such a manner as to be incapable of causing injury to others."]

WSA

The Hat Pin Danger. Circa 1905 WSA

to an Indian. Seven years later Governor Elisha Ferry promoted but Congress ignored the legislature's petition, rendering it "useful only as a document of history." By then, Abigail Scott Duniway, a pioneer Oregon farm wife who had lost her sweat equity in a ranch to her husband's misjudgments had taken up the cudgel as editor of The New Northwest. In 1871, she was joined in Olympia by the indefatigable Susan B. Anthony, Vice President of the National Woman's Suffrage Movement, the first female to address the legislators. Governor Edward Solomon evaded the suffrage issue, saying Congress must act first. Women got marital rights, but not the vote. The two crusaders went on a grinding 2,000 mile lecture tour of the two states. Their struggle to form a state association was all up hill. The first women's club began at the capitol in 1883. A second at Walla Walla in 1886 was only for "self improvement" and "a mutual interchange of ideas."[2] The vote was proffered and pulled away three times in three years. Bills signed in 1883 and 1886 were declared unconstitutional: the first on a technicality, the second because "Congress had not intended for the territories to enfranchise women." The State Constitutional Convention 1889 offered a separate referendum, defeated with the argument it would delay statehood, and tavern owners who saw the risk of prohibition. The Washington Women Suffrage Association was down to five members by 1904.[3]

The "turning point" came in 1900, when Carrie Chapman Catt replaced Anthony as President of the National Association for Woman Suffrage, and made it into "one the first and most effective pressure groups." Trade union organizing tactics, and seeking the help of prestigious women who had shunned the movement were part her "Society Plan" to educate males to the virtues of "distaff democracy." By 1910, the "suffrage gospel" reached middle class club meetings, and finally, in 1912, the General Federation of Women's Clubs joined in. The chief obstacles were "the widespread belief" women were not inclined by nature to engage in politics, would be compromised, or harsh and unlovable, were paired with paternalism: their place in the partnership of genders was with the family – at home. Sexism was the core of "debate over Democracy itself."[4] Woman suffrage was a concrete if secondary interest of Washington's Republican Progressives – behind the initiative, referendum, recall, governmental efficiency, and ethics. Marion Hay was governor as the movement peaked (1909-1913), and both suffered.

His equivocations and tiffs with suffragettes, revealed "a lack of firm convictions on the issue."[5] In October, 1909 he was "not a supporter of woman suffrage…. Neither am I sufficiently opposed to it to oppose… in any way… I do not believe it will do any good." A year later, after a referendum was approved, he found "every reason to believe the voters acted wisely…." At a mass meeting of suffragists in New York City, he lauded the decorum of Washington women, and excoriated militants. Emmaline Parkhurst, a famed English suffragette, scourged him as she lectured in Seattle that fall, as Washington's Emma Smith DeVoe was complimenting Hay, and wondering why Eastern women were looking to England when one victory followed another in the West.[6]

SEATTLE PUBLICS SCHOOLS ARCHIVES
Former teacher Carrie Shumway was elected to the Kirkland City Council in 1911, the first femaile to hold this office in the state.

The question, "Would women vote?" was answered in 1912. Ernest Lister became the first governor likely owing his election to them, in 1914, despite his lingering doubts as to whether it was a good thing. In1908, the vote for the office was 176,141; in 1912, 315,359, striding far ahead of the state's robust population growth. Queries to peers in suffrage states got responses like Arthur Capper's of Kansas: "Many of those opposed the amendment before its adoption supporters of the… cause and none of those who favor it are now opposed." Lister concluded "Good results have certainly be attained…."[7] World War I was the proscenium for "The Suffrage Machine's" final thrust. Here was a chance to do war work and demonstrate patriotism, (something radicals and Pacifists in women's ranks despaired of). June 4, 1919, the U.S. Senate referred suffrage to the states by a vote of 56-25. In 1920, the nation's women went to the polls, voting for Warren Harding and "normalcy" – and prohibition – which detractors of "distaff democracy" groused we should have expected. As importantly, NAWSA was reborn in Seattle as the League of Women Voters, a finishing school and springboard for most of the women who shattered the last barriers.[8]

The Shame of the Cities

The Gold Rush turned Seattle into Alaska's entrepot – and downtown into a tenderloin for lonely miners, loggers, and farmers from the hinterlands. The struggle to keep a "wide open town" businesses and their customers liked, or a sober, orderly, quiet, "Queen City of the Northwest" lasted 40 years. Bertha Landes, was elected to the city council in 1922, "by a small group of women" who were novices in politics "but strong in the faith," she had met as president of the Century Club, and the Seattle Federation of Women's Clubs. Twenty candidates split the votes for three places in the general election, where she won 80 percent of the vote, stressing the "right of women to be represented in government."[9] Her credo was, "Above all, be a good

SED
Seattle's Mayor Bertha Landes in 1927.

sport, able to take the hard knocks ... no tears, and no showing of the white feather ... women must be able to work with men on an equal basis." As City council president and Acting Mayor in 1926, she fired the Chief of Police, and backed a city manager system. When it failed at the polls, she ran, and became the nation's first female big city mayor. The WASPs of the burgeoning residential north end and women had sided with her stand for "civic decency and law enforcement."

Landes found the work of the Council "more concrete." "The mayor, if wise, stays within his own domain." She began a "municipal house cleaning," and appointed women to the Park and Civil Service boards. She fought bootleggers, reckless drivers and for regulating dance halls and cabarets, to make Seattle "cleaner and more law abiding." Her advocacy of City Light, and financing of the ailing Street Railway also reverberated for 20 years. Bertha's legacy was a recreation program, and the Civic Auditorium (later the Opera House.) The city reverted to form in 1928. One man wrote: "I voted for you as Mayor, but never again You said you would clear out the booze joints, but no mayor had ever kept his ... promises and I did not think you would, but, darn you, you have, and you won't get my vote again." Bertha was beaten by an unknown – with downtown dollars.[10]

Mildred Powell, daughter of a high school principal in New London Connecticut, and a Smith College graduate, was emblematic of the burgeoning residential north end. She remained "Mrs. F.F. Powell" after her husband died, and "had to do something" to keep herself and three children. Being President of the Parent-Teacher Association in (1933-35), Vice President of the YWCA (1933-39), and the Council of Churches (1940-50) were the bases of her 15 year tenure on the Council (1935-1950).[11] Her victory over five men was "a refutation to the accepted theory a woman cannot became a candidate for public office without soiling her womanhood in the dirt of politics." "This is not a question a sex, but a question of honesty and loyalty ... sound homes and the old pioneer teamwork. I cannot ask for you to vote for me because I am a woman."

The "independent," claimed "no alliance" with any individual or group on the council, but she quickly fell in with the three eager young reformers of the New Order of Cincinnatus, Arthur B. Langlie, David Lockwood, and Frederick Hamley, also elected in 1934, in a reaction to "circus politics."[12]

She too believed "the people of this city desire clean, honest government…" and seconded the Cincinnatan's inspections of the city's morals, "vigilance" on gambling, and moves to prohibit movies and cabarets near schools: "We, of the city, are doing our best to improve moral conditions through legislation." She chaired a panel to examine the impact of the 40 mill property tax limit voted in 1932, was on the Transportation Committee, had a hand in restoring the Ballard Bridge, raising City Light's Ross Dam on the Upper Skagit, and "tried hard to fill [a] woman's traditional role…as a force for peace and cooperation." "Up" in 1938, she spoke with rectitude for her end of Seattle: "When political expediency meant compromising the standards of Christianity, purity unselfishness and love… I refused to go along. …Because I was following God's guidance there were no compromises, and no fear of not being [re]elected." Powell's record vote against State Representative Jeannette Testu (D), underlined the difference between partisan state, and "non-partisan" local politics. Mayor Bill Devin and the downtown establishment considered her one of their own.[13] Powell chaired the Harbor, Police and Grounds Committee 13 years. "Many have never had contact with the sordid and degrading side of the city's life I do…" There had "never been anything to compare" with the cooperation of the Mayor and Chief of Police, but she again chastised him in 1948: "Our goals are in jeopardy…." She had sponsored him to keep gambling suppressed, but in the last 18 months it was back In fact, it never left.[14] Powell again garnered the largest city vote, without campaigning.

Now Governor Langlie urged Powell to run for Congress from the first District in 1944, and belatedly in 1950, at age 54, she did. The state and county GOP sent $5,000, and 15,000 individuals contributed, but four easy wins had taken their toll. Powell took just one day off to campaign in the primary, and got just 4,987 of the 20,000 votes cast. Some realized she would never have seniority. Others identified her as a Republican for the first time, or disagreed with her strident anti-Communism. ("We too must send out thousands of ideological fighters.") Seattle's riotous politics were now placid, its "Day of the Mugwump" done, and Powell's popularity was not transferable to the new rings of suburbs. The amateur lost to a professional politician.[15]

Ahead of the Curve: "The Woman from Wall Street"

The might have beens, the legion of qualified and committed candidates the tides of politics wash away, deserve their due. Phyllis Lamphere made the only other serious female run for Seattle executive, in 1977. Her "earthy sophistication and humor … [and] mastery of words" in

10 years on the council may have too much for a city still not fully metropolitan.[16] The Barnard graduate, erstwhile ballet dancer and Wall Street "Systems Service Analyst" was chronically overcommitted, but a remarkable number of her ideas for upgrading the city's management came to be. In the 50's Lamphere drafted charter changes. As a councilman by the late 60's, she utilized the expert staff now available for large projects across the administrative spectrum, like "two tier" regional government. She won the Municipal League to an overdue "systems" approach, and chair the implementing it.

What is still Seattle's only freeway ("I-5"), was slashed through downtown in 1962. Environmentalist outrage erupted over a proposed second proposal, the "R.H. Thompson," included a tunnel under Capitol Hill, bifurcation of the Arboretum, and another crossing of the Ship Canal. As Chair of the Planning Committee after 1968, Phyllis arbited a no-win situation and lost cause. She devised the city's responses to the six major environmental laws passed by the 1971 legislature. Knowing the "rationale" behind some of the council's decisions was" frequently not evident," Phyllis piloted a "Storefront City Hall" in the Central Area for closer contact with Seattle's only multicultural neighborhood, facilities now in every sector of the city. If there was a "lack of communication between the city and its institutions," it was not her fault.[17]

Her ambitions were as well defined. She meticulously replied to constituents, even writing appreciations for each invitation to an event she could not attend, or in declining honorary memberships. In 1977, she was active in a dozen major civic organizations, while President of the National League of Cities. "I try to do too much," she confessed. In the seven way mayoral race, her fund raising fell behind Wes Uhlman, the city's first fully professional politician. Phyllis Lamphere a paradigm of intelligence, commitment, and expertise for a new generation of women, also left a transparent lesson: energy needs discipline.

Yakima: Who's in Charge Here?

The two largest cities East of the Cascades elected women of the next generation. Keeping house without electric appliances, rural life of tending a farm without outside activities, and social conservatism were cloistering. Yakima, incorporated in 1895, got its first female councilman in 1964, and its first mayor in 1976. Lenore Lambert observed the Council for the LWV, served seven years, (1964-71), and was the first female County Commissioner (1973-77). She insisted women needed self-education, and go from being passive to participative: "You have to actually work on committees not just sit on them." Good government "should be a leader, not a follower." "Professional management of personnel," training programs, job descriptions and salary classifications," and a "business manager" were just as foreign. Things like zoning unincorporated areas were ignored. Lenore preferred developing rough land to encroaching on prime agricultural fields. Her proposals came to pass, and the city and county started interacting.

She started as a Red Cross volunteer. Then came the Yakima Symphony Orchestra, Central Washington University, the Girl Scouts and Planned Parenthood. "I was always involved in organizations…chairing committees…it's been a lifelong pattern." Now she led to the Downtown Coalition in urban restoration.[18] LaFitte, Auslese, and Perrier Jouex were unheard of in Yakima before Lenore opened her Wine Cellar in the basement of the Greystone. The longtime member of the National Committee on Alcoholism, and the Governor's State Council acknowledged, "I worked to help the 1 in 13 persons who have a problem with alcohol. Now I am working to please the 12!" She predicted Yakima, was on the cusp of growing world class varietal wines. Viniculture is now the valley's cash cow and prime attraction.[19]

Betty Edmondson took Lenore's seat on the Council – on recommendation of the LWV. In the 50's, she as Yakima's "Television Homemaker" on KIMA TV, patterning on Congressman Catherine May, whom she helped reelect in 1958, enroute to becoming chair of the county GOP, and Secretary of the Republican State Central Committee "There's always been a place for me or a need" Betty believed, in women's networks – the Agenda Club, Woman's Century Club, the Hospital Guild, YWCA Board, March of Dimes, Good Neighbors and the LWV. " The more I learned as a volunteer, the more I was stimulated to know." In 1960, Betty became Yakima's first female mayor on a 4-2 vote. Parochialism was the perennial opponent. She was careful " not speak for the council[men]," who tried to reduce the mayor's limited power as they jockeyed for her chair, keeping city government split into blocs. Motions were made to cut the Mayor's salary from $750 to $400 a month, and to limit her to 20 hours a week. The office had "grown larger than called for in the charter"! This under the city manager form of government, where the mayor's role was welcoming, presiding over the Council, pacifying the irate or confused on the telephone, sitting on the police and fire pension boards, the Clean Air Authority and attending intergovernmental conferences, things her businessmen-competitors could not afford to do, were it not for the glory of the thing.

The Nixon administration's revenue sharing made the Yakima Convention Center possible; the state reconstructed the Capitol Theater. "The good times were handled responsibly." In Betty's sixth year, the Council limited the mayor to a two year term, presumably to offer ample rotation. She retired, and spoke out: the mayor should be popularly elected, without term limits and for public accessibility, be full time. If not, "being executive was limiting." Her enforced and real modesty cut both ways. She still denied her status: "I do not think of myself as a politician, but as a volunteer." One persistent council motion maker later credited her with " a beautiful job in the community in the last years."[20] The next mayor, Lynn Carmichael, had her salary reduced by $200 a month, but the gate had been crashed. By 1981, three other women had been on the council, Pat Berndt was the third woman in four mayors, and 35 of Washington's 265 were women.[21]

Spokane Shakes Off Its Lethargy

Spokane still is the Indianapolis of the West, but not without sophistication. A lagging economy froze the population at under 200,000 until the 70's. The Cowles family still owns a third of downtown, the premier television station, and both newspapers. And until recently, legislators of both parties, be they from South Hill aeries, working people in the Valley to the East, or the heavily Catholic neighborhoods north of the Spokane River straddling Gonzaga University, have been hard to tell apart. The coterie of "movers" who staged "Expo '74," a cameo World's Fair, realized things had to change. They left an Opera House, and an elegant River Front Park. The city's traditional civility was knotted to an incipient urbanism.[22] Mayors Vicki McNeill, a committed conservative, and liberal activist Sherry Bernard frame the transition.

McNeill, a Simmons College graduate, left an editorial job at Boston's Allyn and Bacon to marry Dr. Jim McNeill. Arriving in Spokane in 1962, she plunged into civics from the Symphony to the PTA, and raised $750,000 for the Washington Pavilion surrounding the Opera House. Mayor David Rogers appointed the born organizer to the Spokane Sports, Entertainment, Arts and Convention Advisory Board overseeing the facilities. Here, in 1981, Vicki met Councilman James E. Chase, Spokane's first black mayor, who asked her to take his place on the council. She took the chair in 1985, as the city's protracted era of municipal peace was waning. A bond issue to upgrade the original civic Coliseum fell decisively at the same election. Undeterred as Mayor, the "relentlessly upbeat" McNeill talked the council into bonding an Agricultural Trade Center adjacent to the Opera House, and River Front Park. She helped form a consortium of four colleges and WSU on 49 acres of reclaimed land across the river from Gonzaga University. The biomedical-technical-educational campus attracted Boeing, Seafirst Bank, and the Marriott Hotel to Spokane. The city and its suburbs are now the same size, and the temperament of both changed. Tenacious Vicki McNeill, the woman who called herself a "lightning rod – one who can take the heat" – shaped Spokane's new face more than anyone.[23]

McNeill's waste-to-energy plant in the Valley turned into a furor, and half of Sheri Stovin Barnard's "Stop the plant, and save the Davenport [Hotel]" themes when she announced for mayor in 1989. Linking the recycling plant as environmentalism gone awry, and resuscitating the city's crown jewel, long vacant because of industrial seepage, was characteristic of the activist's aligned targets-of-opportunity approach. The active Democrat and neo-Populist's childhood outrage at racism in Florida, was a reason her father, an MIT and Harvard Business graduate came to Spokane as a minister at the Unity Church of Truth. (1955-64). Sheri was Sunday School Superintendent, and President of the Unity Church board (1973-76), and absorbed as her mother in the LWV. She became President, chaired the school district's Affirmative Action Council, the Citizens' Coalition for Schools, and presided over the Inland Empire Girl Scout Council. As a City Councilman (1983-89), she was on the Long Range Planning Committee for the new Public Library (completed in 1994).[24] Sheri Bernard took Spokane to the next level: taking social services seriously. She also provoked the contentiousness still plaguing the once homogenous business community that had retrieved Spokane from insularity.[25]

The Mid-Sized Cities Clean Up Their Acts

One can build a dossier in the smaller cities and not face the bashing campaigns of larger venues. Amanda Smith was the first female mayor of Olympia, and of a capitol city (1953-60). Government is the business of the elongate town of 40,000 at the southern tip of Puget Sound. Eldon Marshall, hired by her as Clerk-Treasurer, and later a successor, remembers "She was not very stoppable."[26] Amanda arrived in Olympia in 1922, and armed with business college education, worked for Thurston County, and ran a credit bureau with her husband. Disgusted by discarded whiskey bottles on the front yard of her parent's home on East Bay Drive, close by shacks used by bootleggers and prostitutes since the Depression, Amanda campaigned for a man who promised a clean-up, and did nothing. She ran for mayor when offered $2,000 not to run. Unlike her predecessors, she was at City Hall every day, "poking my nose where it wasn't wanted." The new mayor was one of three commissioners, and in charge of sanitation, the fire and the police departments. She found "The jail was a disaster. You wouldn't keep pigs in a place like that." She ordered it cleaned and painted flamingo rose, emerald green and camellia pink. Pornographic magazines disappeared from downtown too, as did the city dump. A Golden Age Club for seniors was started. Amanda's best idea was taking the dirt dug for the state's new General Administration Building to make Capitol Lake Park, Olympia's axis. "Little things" for the "little people"? Perhaps. But tending the store and incremental progress is what local government is about.[27]

Olympia's executive Amanda Smith put a fresh face on the jail in the 1950s.

Pullman, the largest city in Whitman County and home to Washington State University, was perfect for Karen Kiessling, wife of an English professor. At 35, in 1975, she became its youngest, and first woman mayor. Karen had no prior public service other than as an observer of the Council for the LWV. Asked by a councilman who also found the incumbent 'rude,' she filed on the last day. She "door belled" with her five year old son, along for a penny a door, advocating public transit, low cost housing for low income seniors, downtown enhancement, televising council meetings, and a voice for small rural towns at the Association of Washington Cities in Olympia. All five were reality when she voluntarily left office in four years. In the 70's boards and commissions were looking for female members, and by 1980 she was on or chairing 30, including the Association of Washington Cities and agencies of the National League of Cities. How was it done, when you have to be home by three to welcome you grade school sons from school? Her prescription fits any public office: a supportive spouse, a sense of humor ("She who laughs lasts'), "a sense of proportion", (she kept literary club meetings "because it reminded me that citizens lived happy productive lives without ever thinking of city hall),"a large helping of common sense," and "impartial treatment … the same courtesy to all." "The amazing thing is that in a small town you can make a real difference, and you should be willing to try." Remarkably, the political 'medicine' did not take. Both parties asked Karen to run for the legislature. Family came first.[28]

The Indispensables

The versatility and staying power of those in the smallest cites is wondrous. Barbara Harrer, Mayor or Harah in the central Yakima Valley was in her 27th year in office in 2004. Cook, parade organizer, mediator, dogcatcher, park custodian, waster-water treatment operator, she was paid $250 a month, and had three employees to keep the town of 620 in order. It was shrinking, and initiatives had choked off state dollars – but there was still a five year reserve, something no big city can conceive of. At 72, she was undecided about running again in 2007. And as Clerk-Treasurer Pat Morell said, "Somebody else would have a hard time knowing what to do."[29]

Country Mice: The Counties

Until the New Deal, counties were most citizens' original and primary government. Then the State began to fund and manage schools and social services. By the '70's growth forced most counties to hire professional managers. Their commissioners are now as much functionaries as policy makers, validating expenses, vacating roads, and hearing land use applications, on rules laid out in Olympia.[30] The expansion was in the Public Utility Districts ("PUDs") that mushroomed in the 1930's to meet rural needs for cheap power and electrification, and later "ports." The PUD's 30 years' war with private power was state's hardest fought of a generation. Women engaged as speakers for the Grange, "the backbone of the [public] power movement," an unofficially "politicized" arm of the New Deal.[31] Grant County built the Priest Rapids Dam in the 1950's, one of the Columbia's largest non-federal projects. It is now part of the PUDs'

Washington Public Power Supply System, builder of enormously expensive nuclear reactors abandoned in Mason County in the '70's. WPPSS, (pronounced "WHOOPS"), the largest default in government in the nation's history, suggests local agencies run by amateurs do well to stay within their capabilities.

Sexism lingers in the "commissioner" counties, where the focus is still on "men's jobs," roads, utilities, law enforcement, and the "ports." Almost all women in county office have, by "necessity or chance," been county Clerks, Auditors, or Treasurers, and kept there, even if these "understudies actually ran the show." In 1977, the Democratic fathers of Kittitas County (Ellensburg, and environs), couldn't find " a woman improvement [on the incumbent,] or one that wasn't to radical." They settled on Beverly Allenbaugh, newly widowed with five children, who served as Auditor for 20 years. " It takes a certain [kind of female] personality to serve … and stubbornness … " she confirmed. " If you don't want to be at the back end of the big dog you have to … want to do it better." "The janitors made more than I did." The Commissioners gave her male successor a $650 a month raise.[32]

Democrat Donna Karvia's tenure as Auditor of conservative Lewis County along the Chehalis River shows respect can be individually earned in rural communities, and the ability rise to the national level, if one is willing to 'work up.' She started in the Clerk's office in 1967, and was appointed Clerk 1983. Entries were still made in large bound volumes with fountain pens; when she left they were optically scanned. Donna helped make Washington the first state to have work training for local prisoners. Her biggest disappointment was the reluctant cooperation of small businesses. The stress was in dividing time between mandatory tasks, while serving at the state and national levels, an "imperative for me to be the best government and community representative I could be."[33] Karvia refused to be partisan, and "never felt any discrimination or reduced recognition" as a woman. Her philosophy that "we are all the government at all levels … credibility in one area is carried to work and achievement … [in] the others" is the common denominator of the successful public servant.

Four of the largest counties adopted "home rule" in the 70's and 80's for more freedom from the state, as their social portfolios ballooned from subsidized housing, to the arts, and education. Bernice Stern's years on the Jewish community's front lines led her to the new King County Council in 1968. Chairing the Land Use Task Force was most wearying, drafting the raft of environmental regulations to implement laws cascading out of Olympia after 1971. Bernice's approach was fiercely independent, moderate and bipartisan. She told the Municipal League's Candidate Evaluation Committee that not only King County's METRO, now its sewer and transportation utility, had to integrate, but the three Puget Sound counties must take a "regional approach." "Being responsible cannot always mean agreement," but she and

Republican Councilman Bob Dunn ("The Bernice and Bob Show"), were the anchors in the coalition that sorted out civil service, and provided indigents legal defenses. Stern modeled pragmatism's value in public life.[34]

Lois North, a Berkeley Phi Bete, modeled the upward mobility of women into professional politics. Elected the King County Charter Review Committee in 1967 for $121 (the cost of penny post cards to other LWVers), she was in the House from Northeast Seattle's 44th District in a year. One of six women Representatives in the GOP Caucus 1969, she got the only feminine "leadership" job – Secretary. A major-issue person, Lois prime-sponsored the abortion bill approved in November, 1970, the Equal Rights Amendment (1972), and "living Museums," – " Natural Area Preserves" in important ecosystems. Three other women sat in the 49 seat Senate when she arrived in 1975. Though in the Minority for the next four years, North succeeded in reforming the law on prosecuting rape. Victims can now complain knowing their characters will not be "put on trial."

Legislators were paid $7600 a year, and divorce drove a tearing campaign to move to the full time and well-salaried King County Council in 1980. There were "huge public turnouts" at the hearings on her ordinance ending sexual discrimination in personnel practices – "and ugly threats and telephone calls." North found adjusting from the excitement of philosophic and statewide issues in Olympia to dickering with communities over land use tedious. "It amounted to endless small amendments and struggles to line up the votes for sensible curbs on unbridled growth." But when Governor Locke needed a Republican woman with expertise in local government to balance the new Puget Sound Growth Management [Appeals] Hearing Board in 2000, the chair of the Council was the obvious choice. If Bernice Stern proved a citizen-activist can still gain office in a metropolitan county, Lois North's graceful transition from citizen-legislator to professional politician opened what is now well worn path.[35]

Delayed Destinies: Legislative Leaders

Republican Frances Axtell of Bellingham, the wife of a doctor, and Progressive Nena Croake a Tacoma an osteopath, took seats in the 1913 legislature. They spoke a femimine voice, one typically more moderate, or liberal, than male peers. Axtell was one of the few, with Governor Lister, to press for overlooked sources of revenue, and relief of the small home owner. Why not tax exploiters of natural resources, timber, coal and fish? Croake had been President of the Washington Equal Suffrage Society, leaguing with Emma Smith DeVoe in 1910 to secure the vote for women. Her issues were firmed in the homes of women in that campaign: opposition to child labor and capital punishment, vocational training, juvenile courts, and a teacher's retirement fund. "Consideration for Women is the Measure of a Nation's Progress" was her theme. "Now that woman is enfranchised," she argued, "it is only just and fair that she be given a trial ... we know that men have not always made a success of lawmaking."[36]

Reba Hurn, the first woman admitted to State Bar, and the only female lawyer or

JEFFERSON STUDIO, OLYMPIA
Reba Hurn of Spokane, an attorney and the first female State Senator (1923-1931).

elected official in the city or county of Spokane, became the first female State Senator in 1922. The question of whether a woman should be in politics still hovered. None of the five women elected to the House had survived for a second term; she reasoned that in four years the novelty might wear off.[37] Governor Louis Hart's Administrative Code of 1921 had sifted and recombined the new agencies, but the wheat economy East of the Cascades was already in free fall, and the public mood was to "hold the line." All but three of the 42 senators were Republicans; fights were more geographic than philosophic. Reba wanted to be thought of as a senator, not as a woman. She put up with cigar smoking with politesse, entertained wives, and at least once the entire senate for breakfast. Women were saddled with the Public Morals, Libraries, or Education Committees until the 1930's. Senator Hurn was the

first not made to carry 'female' portfolio, unless it was prohibition, a residue of the wreckage she had seen in the small town in the mid west in her childhood. Washington had passed it in 1916; the need was to sustain a law honored in the breach by most colleagues. In 1923 her Public Morals panel favored a "Temperance Day" in the public schools that was not signed by the governor.[38] A never anticipated "Cloak Room" had to be carved into the senate side of the new capitol. (A complete bathroom for women waited until the 70's.) Assignment to Education, and Parks, and heading the Library Committee and Educational Institutions in her second term were predictable. Two years later she broke precedent in being on Judiciary, and Appropriations, which had not been 'women's' work.'[39] It was a chance to show her conservative colors. Reba was one of four members (of) 13 who voted against the UW's budget, a teachers' retirement fund, and even against reopening the Women's Industrial Home, a correctional facility at Medical Lake: economy took priority over a cause local women had worked on two years. Buying seeds for drought stricken farmers, and turning idleness into education at the Penitentiary were worth it.[40]

Senator Hurn's first speech in 1925 was in support of a memorial to Congress to regulate the workplaces of those under 18. True to the times, it was badly defeated, as was a substitute referendum in 1926. She was tactfully neutral in legislators' struggle with the incorrigible Governor Roland Hartley, although one of his 59 vetoes in 1927 excised the help for farms.[41] Reba was not at odds with the strongest lobbies of the time, business, tax hawks, or the farmers and "drys" at home, and cast a flinty eye on their "fluid" tactics the liquor lobby. Her bill regulating and registering the "Third House" is earliest attempt at public disclosure. Senator Hurn's fall can ironically laid to a stroke for efficiency, a 1929 bill to end her county's superfluous townships, whose paid officials rose up in 1930. Reba endured in a man's world for eight years on because she fit her times, was talented demure, feminine, and diplomatic, a charactered "woman in full." And "After all, there are no women's issues."[42] She was accepted, but could not avoid what she most feared, a unique, a minority of one.[43]

Mary Farquharson: The Socialist Who Was Senator

The coming of the New Deal opened almost every partisan office in the state. Democratic women took advantage of their party's deep schisms, and the multitudes of candidates. Mary U. Farquharson entered the State Senate from the 46th District at 32, in 1934, a prototype of an idealistic but pragmatic liberal, one burdened by both the ideologues of the Left, and still viable Republicans on the Right. Formed in 1895, the district stretched Seattle's University District to the Snohomish County line, and down the eastside of Lake Washington to the village of Bellevue. The proudly bourgeois new northeast of the city and its sparse suburbs elected only two other Democrats in 85 years. But the class war was real for her: "Every single inch of 'progress' in working conditions for children … has been bitterly contested by those who own as opposed to those who produce …. Ninety-five percent of the consuming public … are misled into opposing

State Senator Mary Farquharson (1933-1941) an antiwar, social justice advocate.

their own interests …. " Capitalism," she reminded Presbyterian pastor Dr. Wendell Fifield, was "the antithesis of Jesus' religion … in crude language it means fight and grab …." This theme coexisted with an idealist's belief in "strong side" to human nature, "the desire for community, friendship and cooperation."[44] [Mary and husband Burt, an engineering professor, were early principals in the Washington Commonwealth Federation, a coalition of leftist groups that emerged out of the Seattle Unemployed Citizens League in 1935. Overproduction had been solved by "an economy of scarcity." Distribution needed to be "production for use," by turning idle businesses into state run cooperatives. "We do not seek the collapse of the capitalist system," the WCF asserted. "We are building a road from its present collapse to a NEW WAY OF LIFE," by melding individualism and collectivism. The Farquharsons soon sensed the WCF's leadership was Communist influenced. They agreed on ends, but felt the WCF was acting deceitfully as a stalking horse of Democracy. "Totalitarian" methods meant breaching civil rights. They resigned.[45]

Tze staunch defender of civil liberties and ACLU member was put to the test in January 1941, when she and the Senate voted not to seat Linus Westman, who admitted being in the CP for 18 months. "I am one of the reprobates who helped push Westman out of his senate seat," she wrote Roger Baldwin. "The sooner CP tactics are clarified the better off is the cause of civil liberties, and all other liberal or radical issues.... If Westman had been elected on the Communist ticket or any other ... I should have voted for him," she told another liberal questioner. "It is the organized policy of deceit ... [that] is the worst obstacle to advocating the public toward a more liberal viewpoint ... " The Cold War pushed her further. The CP was a "Soviet fifth column," and should be outlawed." I have never felt that 'free speech" included unlimited lying."[46]

Mary seconded Governor Clarence Martin's efforts to implement the New Deal in 1935, but was "restlessly dissatisfied with the mediocrity of our achievement." "I have been fired with an overwhelming sense of my own guilt.... The system was so "feeble." The "stalling, delaying, trading, bargaining – a road here for a vote there – all elements of machine politics ... [found] perfect expression through our outdated two-house system." Meeting 60 days biennially was not enough for the "business of a modern state." A unicameral professional body was overdue. If legislature had more women there would likely be less drinking, fewer "sell outs," and special interests. "I was a little embarrassed at first being one of two women [in the Senate]. I thought they looked askance because I had been publicized as a Communist ... but I soon found out they are all friendly."[47]

Governor Martin was reelected in the 1936 primary by cross-over Republicans. Mary's liberal faction of the senate "majority" was in an increasingly tentative position, as conservative Eastern Washington Democrats joined Republicans on the governor's behalf to foil many of their initiatives. In the shaken culture of the Depression, she did not feel "discriminated against" in committee assignments, and penetrated the corridors of power denied Maude Sweetman and Reba Hurn. Farquharson was on Appropriations, Judiciary, and Constitutional Review by her third session in 1937. The "business-like senator" tapped her foot impatiently, and threatened a filibuster (by moving to have the Clerk read the 601 page budget), if some of her bills did not emerge from Rules Committee.[48] She wanted a mental institution on the west side, board certification of the heads of institutions, the "Community Property bill of 1937," a "secured place" for a Division of Children in the Department of Institutions, all "women's issues," and passed teacher's civil service unanimously. Mary and the senate's other formidable female, Island County's Pearl Wanamaker, staged " a sudden invasion of the appropriations Committee considering the Supplemental Budget...." on public, and higher education, and took their the "biggest defeat" in failing to up Governor Martin. They did prove "women in politics can take it as well as dish it out."[49]

A rationalist more than an ideologue, Mary had matured as a legislator. "As to my work with the 'Martin Democrats,' I have come to realize unless I am willing to work with people who disagree with me on many major issues, I might just as well get out of politics entirely."[50] The left wing had little to show for its filibusters, refusals to answer roll calls, and outspoken criticism of the governor. Her apex was repealing the World War I law on syndicalism, (An undefined term which meant anything the State – or Federal Government determined was against them). By "skillful attention," she cajoled enough conservatives to join in 'pulling' it from Rules – and do the speaking on the floor. "More can be accomplished by negotiation and compromise than by attempted force and intimidation. The appeal to intelligence and to reason is stronger than to fancied fear, Mary had learned. " I disagree with the senators on most questions, but I think I am good friends with all of them personally."[51] Her diligence was being rewarded.

Senator Farquharson was shelled from both sides in seeking reelection as an "independent liberal" in 1938. Bertha Landes weighed into the strenuous race against former Senator Frank "40 mill" Jackson, the father of the property tax limitation initiative of 1932. She had tried to amend the Unemployment Relief Bill to establish cooperatives, backed $30 pensions (raised from $22 a month, but never funded), a graduated net income tax (overturned by the Supreme Court), was for larger inheritance and gift taxes, and changing the Business and Occupations Tax to include real estate rentals over $200 a month. Centering any campaign on "the tax problem" is perilous. Her "whole record" would have to be "sufficient evidence."[52] The Seattle Argus bombarded Senator Farquharson on behalf of the enlightened establishment: "The Common Weathers, the share-the-wealthers, the Howard Costigans [Executive Secretary of the WCF, and later an admitted Communist], and Mary Farquharsons are due to take over the city of Seattle lock, stock and barrel..." The "Democratic Party in this state is still [the Communists' [preferred] vehicle "to get into power as quickly as possible." Mary privately conceded the WCF dominated it in the 46th District. The Progressive Democratic Club was run by Dorothy Butterworth, and Farquharson observers saw Democrats voting for Jackson in the primary. "The Communist Party would rather crucify a liberal who does not join them than unseat a conservative" she fumed. "I still think I'll have it in a walk away." But the glory days of the of the New Deal were over. She got 3,159 of the 7,657 votes in the primary. "The only reason I made it" was "a young lawyer … [on the East Side who] filed as a Cincinnatus … splitting the Republican vote."[53]

In 1939, Senator Farquharson found herself in the minority of the non "majority." Coalition Democrats from East of the Cascades and the resurgent Republicans controlled the Senate for most of the next 18 years. The new Women's Legislative Council was not "thinking in terms of women … [but] "The basic so-called liberal issues … ." It was stronger than she realized, but hardly offsetting. "The big question," Mary mused "is why anybody in his right mind ever wanted the job anyhow! … ."With no income tax possible and the 40 mill limit and legitimate demands … greater than ever … it looks like a desperately bad situation to me … . If people were only educated as to … their own interests"[54] Mary's "independence," and conflict between her beliefs and loyalties boiled over with the coming of World War II. She was "well pleased" with Republican Governor Arthur Langlie's 1941 inaugural address. "I think some of us Democrats liked it better than some of the Republicans." She was "skeptical" as to whether enough money could be raised, a doubt World War II's boom dimmed in the eyes of most. She was engrossed in the "under yielding" leases of the University's downtown Metropolitan Tract, arrangements beyond generations of part-time legislators. "As usual, I have so many irons in the fire that some of them are apt to get cold before we start ironing with them." In contrast, Farquarharson fulminated at U.S. Senator Mon Wallgren, the century's second bonafide liberal governor, who defeated Langlie in 1944. "Wallgren's determination to pay off a load of political debts a one fall swoop … .is probably the most flagrant example of pure(or impure) politics that I have ever seen."[55]

Mary had refused to be a delegate to the Democratic national convention in 1940, with a "feeling of nausea at the idea of helping to reelect Roosevelt … no one could be quite as dangerous a menace as he is … "[in leading the country into war]. "If I had run [in 1942] I would have been completely trounced because the Communists … would have … got me. I would have admitted … I was opposed to the war." (She conceded in1945 that America could not have stood "aloof," but insisted "We were largely the cause of and effect which we feared and abhorred."[56] The conscientious Quaker-Socialist-humanist saw her role, in and out of office, "as helping to educate the public … .and continued to, with extraordinary effort. After a 1947 trip to Europe, which was "depressing beyond words," she gave "dozens" of speeches opposing the military government in Germany, and Stalinism with equal vigor. Over the next 30 years 2,000 articulate letters flowed s to local editors, The Progressive, the New York Times, presidents, members of Congress, and as the Vietnam quagmire deepened in the late 60's, to the state's leading hawk, Senator Henry Jackson . "The moral universe is as real as the law of gravity … which is genuine community, " she wrote President Kennedy.

The idealist with the faith of a believer persisted in her convictions, because and despite the lessons of two world wars.[57]

Senator Lady Willie Forbus: Steel Magnolia

As World War II unfolded women lost critical mass in the Senate for three decades. The army took the younger men, the women were at Boeing, the shipyards or being single parents; priorities were foreign not domestic. Pearl Wanamaker became Superintendent of Public Instruction in 1941, leaving four female senators in 1943, and one in 1945. "Majority Leader"Albert Rosellini (1939-56), and his protégé R.R. "Bob" Grieve (1957-74), practiced the arts of personal agenda that drug the body to a hiatus by 1973, when there were no women.[58] Lady Willie Forbus, the most potent feminine force, was a burr under the saddles of what became an old boys' club.

Into the 20th century, Mississippi girls named after their fathers had surnames preceded by "Lady." In Seattle, despite her Southern drawl and manners, Lady Willie had to explain she was not European royalty. Her crisp, quick, self-certain assertiveness was impossible to ignore. Forced to be mother to younger siblings while in high school, Lady Willie opted for an early 'liberation.' She taught kindergarten in Laurel on graduation in 1910, studied shorthand and typing nights and worked for a Superior Court judge for a year, and graduated from the University of Mississippi in three years, in 1915. Told by the Harvard Law School it did not take women, she went to Michigan, and was the only female in a class of 50 in 1918. Leaving without her diploma, she got off a day coach in Seattle with $10 in her pocket, and went to the YWCA. Brilliance, extraordinary ambition and the handicaps of being female lawyer, compounded by desire for public career led to self-defeating criticisms of the establishment. Lady Willy Forbus was the most controversial woman in Seattle since Anna Louise Strong.[59]

"A lawyer must be a business go-getter ... " she advised a woman inquirer two decades later, "else her legal qualifications will become stultified for lack of clients. Some lawyers, like myself, have to go out into the community and create a demand.... She still wanted to believe "the opportunities for women are just exactly the same as men, but business is harder to get ... there is still some sex discrimination, and men lawyers ... are given to the false notion that they are the chosen people. "I was a curiosity," she finally admitted in 1983, "but when I began dealing with them, they discovered I was tough and hard ... so that I had to build my way."[60]

In 1922, she convinced a grand jury a Seattle policeman was murdered – with pistols of two different calibers – contrary to the County Prosecutor's perfunctory ruling of suicide. Challenging him brought visibility, a chance for a public career, and a way to prove her premise: "In brains there is no sex, in achievement not private hunting grounds." Reality drew out vitriol: "The 'gang' was with him ... The bank wreckers, ferry grabbers, the bootleggers and 'respectable thieves.'"[61] She lost to Malcolm Douglas, "because of last minute lies," but ran 12,000 votes ahead of the county Democratic ticket.

In three years Lady Willie was "one of the best known and most capable attorneys in Seattle,"[62] but the combination of courage and corrosiveness recurred in her campaigns for the superior court in 1932 and 1934, blunting her political aspirations for a decade. She kept a pall mall speaking schedule, testifying for a child labor amendment at the legislature (1925), an illegitimacy law, a home for the feeble minded, teachers' retirement, a cabinet department of education. If 1 of 13 marriages ended in divorce in King county, she reasoned, 1 of 13 judges should be in special "Family Relations Court. Lady Willie applied to Governor Hartley for an opening on the bench. When "The plum ... [fell] to a Lithuanian lumber jack-lawyer" [Kazis Kay], she announced, "The time has come when we should have a women's viewpoint in our judicial system.[63]

On running third in the 1932 Bar poll she excoriated it as "reactionary and prejudiced. ... Nobody knows better than I how little ability counts in this matter of a lawyer's choice of a judge." She lost in the primary. "Brains," She admitted, "played a great part in my likes and dislikes for all people."[64]

In 1934, Lady Willie, down to 14 of the 825 votes in the Bar's poll, railed at "the leeches who fasten themselves on dead men's estates, upon bankrupts, upon receiverships ... " in vowing to "expose the lawyer's recommendation racket. "Many" women's organizations had approached her, and although "women may reasonably insist upon greater representation " she "preferred to base my claim ... solely on my ability as a lawyer." On surviving the primary, her tune changed. "A Woman for Judge ... It will be pioneering ... for the Bar is opposed ... and ... will do everything in its power to prevent her election." Women did not turn out in equal numbers, and Forbus lost to an "old line" Democrat."[65]

Referrals were few, but Lady Willie could not divorce herself from politics. Known across the state after stumping 40 towns in three weeks as part of the Roosevelt Caravan in 1936, and as chair of the DNC's Speaker's Bureau, and at county conventions, she was dogged by controversy.[66] Her main chance lay in a smaller venue, the 36th District, the State Senate seat for Magnolia and Queen Anne hills in 1942, where Community work and intense campaigning had maximum impact. Elected, She boldly asked for Appropriations, and got the chair of First Class Cities, and was on Judiciary, and Revenue, all a novice could hope for. One of the "18," the minority of the "majority," she failed to get the 40 mill limit restricted to homes valued under $5,000, or amend the bills by the Business and Professional Woman's Club and Labor to broaden equal wages to all women.[67]

Lady Willie was intensely partisan. There were not "moderates in those days like you have today … [and] I don't think you can say that there was much difference between men and women in politics." She fought Governor Langlie's attempt to merge natural resources agencies, including forestry, the prized possession of the Democratic Commissioner of Public Lands, whose office would be abolished, and the state officials threatened wider reorganization He counted on the nine Democrats who Senator Forbus felt "deserted their party," but was upended by GOP dissenters. On the losing side of another 'split' decision, to investigate Langlie's release of prisoners for 1943 harvests, she begged off an ad hoc committee to confer with him in the 1944 on the "soldier vote" bill, then damned his veto of extending polling hours to 10 P.M. Forbus favored a one-time exception to the blanket primary in favor of partisan ballots.[68] His veto would shut out the swing shift voters at war plants.

Senator Forbus' greatest impact was negative, when the governor and the Liquor Board obtained scarce whiskey from Tennessee's Waterfill and Frasier Distillery. She sensed the 'tea-totaler' was vulnerable in rural counties. She stormed through them, asserting he had personally profited. "Effective word-of-mouth lies," mourned Fred Baker, Langlie's consultant, after the Governor unexpectedly lost by 26,000 votes. Charlie Hodde, a former Democratic House member from Stevens County then lobbying for the Grange, was blunter: "[Mon] Wallgren beat Langlie on liquor."[69]

Lady Willie reached her apex in 1945 as chair of the Judiciary Committee, one of the four "majors." She sided with Governor Mon Wallgren's liberal-labor administration to disburse all of the $172 million reserve built by the war. The Seattle Municipal League conceded she had a "good legislative Record," and was a "hard worker." In 1949, as President of the Magnolia Community Club, she fought conspicuously for 4,000 neighbors agitated at the prospect of the Seattle School and Park Boards taking of 60 homes separating a new field house from the junior high school. A "holdover," she escaped the Republican upswing that switched the House to the GOP in 1947, but could not avoid the drift of Magnolia and Queen Anne Hills to the GOP in 1948, or identification with the Progressives who were sundering her party. Her opponent, Hal Kimball, the community minded publisher the Ballard News, negated the Democratic advantage at the center of the District, and took the north end two to one.[70]

Lady Willie is a study in chiaroscuro: a driving intellect, with ambition to "rise above one's class," unwillingness to admit professional limitations, vehement frustrations, harboring contrasts between traditional marital views and modernist social stances.[71] Women's drudgery was over, she proclaimed, but the efficiencies of the industrial age had led men to take what should be women's work. Excluding married women from the workplace was "economically unsound." "Good family incomes make business good." In time, she was more jaundiced: once at home with nothing to do, "he arrogated to himself the dominant position in the clan … leaving … work for women to do." "She asks only to be reevaluated as his intellectual equal." "We must urn his mental shirt inside out."[72]

The woman who castigated the Unemployed Citizens League in 1933 for "the idea … the taxpayer is a big capitalist … who should be made to pay. … " adding, "The unemployed are willing to bring others down to their condition, instead of trying to raise their own condition up," was driven steadily Left by her frustrations. She drafted the planks in the 1962 King County Democratic platform demanding total nuclear disarmament and universal health insurance. " The contrast between Mary Farquharson' accommodations to the 'system' and her successes was all too transparent.[73] Woman suffrage, Lady Willie thought, obligation them to enter the "New Frontier" of public life. If it was " highly unsportsmanlike and unbecoming for a woman to attack her own kind ….." If this did not apply to the men she contested, no one could accuse Senator Forbus of not being "a willing soldier in the field."

Representative Mary Ellen McCaffree: The First Insider

Mary Ellen McCaffree represented District 32A, Seattle's University District and East to Laurelhurst on Lake Washington, for four terms (1963-1971).[74] It was so closely balanced and small she won each time by several hundred votes in a Democratic backyard. Like the most capable of leaders of her generation entered she entered politics through the LWV, urging civil rights in 1948, School, College and Institution Bonds (Referenda 7,8,9) in 1950, and presided over the LWV in Seattle in 1959-60. If "Women, as a voting power and as candidates … COULD be a major influence in politics but they do not choose to use the prerogative won fifty years ago … Men would be out of luck if women took the initiative."[75]

Mary Ellen was the first woman gubernatorial insider, policy formulator and promoter. The 1956 election had swept a "New Breed" of talented professionals into the GOP, able enough to make up their minds to either get into the majority, or get out. Mary Ellen McCaffree had "a very, very, very good experience in the legislature. The men with whom I was most closely associated … became very, very good friends, and we worked very closely together … I always felt very accepted."[76] In 1963, the 'Dan Evans Cohort,' with Joel Pritchard, Slade Gorton and freshman McCaffree as lead actors, cobbled together a coalition with eight conservative Democrats that felled five term House Speaker John O'Brien. The new Speaker, Democrat Bill Day, ruled Governor Al Rosellini's eight last-minute executive requests could not be heard in the Special Session, opening the 1964 gubernatorial contest, which Evans won.[77]

McCaffree had co-authored the LWV's I-211, neutered by legislators, to force the redistricting rural areas had delayed decades. In March, 1962. The U.S. Supreme Court, in Baker v. Carr, ruled for 'one man, one vote.' In 1965, she and soon Majority Leader Gorton bargained and deliberately stalled the matter in court, to get a better deal than they could make with the Democratic senate. The court-appointed "master," a University of Washington geographer (and Democrat) dutifully drew new districts on fresh criteria. More were competitive, and two years later the first of successive GOP majorities was seated in the House, the first since 1933.[78] Rising resistance to the Vietnamese war let loose a surge against the status quo, and Dan Evans, metamorphosed by circumstances and a statewide perspective, turned into the legislature's demanding reformist taskmaster, giving the GOP and agenda, and moderate caucus cast to enact it. Finally, wartime prosperity and inflation gave the state the "matching" dollars needed for Lyndon Johnson's "Great Society" programs,

There were few women legislators, none in "leadership." As Chair of the House Revenue Committee in 1969, Mary Ellen's monumental task was to be point woman for the governor's prime issues, the tax reforms of 1971 and 1973. The wife of a University of Washington economics professor and mother of five was relatively conservative on money. "Fair taxation," she argued, was a " three legged stool." The sales and property taxes were "archaic" as the major sources of revenue … " Instead of taxing wealth as it is earned" the state taxed "that part which is spent."[79] Her package had a 3.5 percent single rate income tax with a $1,000 exemption (based on Adjusted Gross Income). The real rate for a family of four making $12,000 a year be 2.62 percent. The referenda were "revenue neutral." The sales tax would drop from 4.5 to 3.5 percent, (with a $15 rebate against the sales tax on food), and the 2 mill property levy for public assistance the state had levied since the 30's. Seeing the constitutional limits on the three major taxes, all but 9 of the 55 member GOP House caucus, and a third of the Democrats gave Mary Ellen the two-thirds vote needed for a constitutional amendment, and everyone a standing round of applause. The Democratic Senate could not appear obstructionist. Senator Mike McCormick, McCaffree's counterpart, covered for the majority Democratic Caucus. The bills were "regressive" for lack of an graduated net income tax, and having constitutional limits. "Passage of comprehensive tax reform is its (the 41st Legislature's) claim to lasting fame" the Post-Intelligencer wrote, "although many taxpayer may see it as infamy."[80]

"Women's organizations," the PTA, LWV, and AAUW, the counties, and the Association of Washington Business had met with a statewide tax reform committee formed in summer of '69. The enemies were the public's unwillingness to read what was put before them, hypocrisy in indicating they were for reform, and voting against it, and the legacy of five previous "defeats" (two in the Supreme Court), the active opposition of retrograde GOP chairs in the counties on Puget Sound, and foremost, and chronic distrust of the legislature. Governor Evans hoped Washingtonians "will not look back in anger" after two-thirds of them voted no.[81]

The phrase "A woman's place not only is in the House, but in the Senate" was in vogue, and the Evans team's last hurdle was the crusty 48 man, one woman senate. It already had 18 lawyers, Mary Ellen reminded her constituents as she ran against the other Representative, Pete Francis, in 1970. Each got "outstanding" ratings from the Municipal League, but the western half of the 32nd (Wallingford and Ballard), was as Democratic as any place in the state, something doorbelling by Evans, his Chief of Staff Jim Dolliver, and Gorton could not overcome. Its voters knew not of the effects ending the seniority system, choosing chairs on ability, or speeding procedures with an electric roll call.[82] I am afraid your excellent work in helping guide tax reform ... and your courage and fine leadership in promoting it may have lead to your defeat .... The governor wrote. "You were so willing to put everything on the line ...." "Damn, damn, damn," Majority Leader Stu Beldsoe groaned, "Often the best people get the worst shots.... I'm having a hell of a time writing this Mother. Baby." Her loss had the reverse of the desired effect, removing the last mainstay of the Evans House leadership cadre. "Mother" McCaffree's remarkable cohort lost its majority in 1972, having restored two party competition in the House for the first time in 30 years.[83]

Mary Ellen McCaffree was the best profile of the now diminished League of Women Voters, which did more to prepare women for office than any other vehicle. She arrived in Olympia a fully armed reformer, able to address core issues. McCaffree shattered the "glass ceiling" that kept women from being legislative leaders. Her finest attribute was the courage of the few. The ultimate risk taker from the most perilous of districts also took on the Law Officers and Firefighters' overgenerous and under funded pension system, and at the peak of Vietnam protests, when older constituents judged students by the rioting on University Way, the 18 year old vote. "It took men to give the suffragettes votes .... Now it will take adults to give their right to vote." It was the right thing to do.[84]

Senator Jeannette Hayner: Washington's 'Iron Lady'

It took nearly half century after the coming of the New Deal for Republicans in the state senate to overcame their minority status – and mentality.[85] Jeannette Hayner (House 1973-77; Senate 1977-95), and the women who joined her in the Senate in the 70's did for it what McCaffree had done for the House – restore two party politics. The most skillful leader of her era was one of the first women graduates of the University of Oregon Law School in 1947 Jeannette's entered politics on the Walla Walla school board (1956-

Representative Jeannette Hayner was elected to the State Senate in 1972, a year before the State's Equal Rights Amendment to the Constitution passed.

Jeannette Hayner was Senate Minority or Majority Leader from 1981 to 1995. The Senate was no longer a "man's world."

63), serving community services from Meals on Wheels to the Mental Health Board, and as a Republican State Committeewoman.

A traditional Republican uncomfortable with Dan Evans' liberalism, she evolved into an unflappable Minority Leader in 1979, as adaptable as Speaker Bill Polk was fixated, in a dramatically more difficult situation. Hayner was installed in a 10-9 caucus coup over a well-liked Wenatchee apple grower and "old boy" whose allies dropped out, and played golf with business lobbyists as the 1980 campaign got underway. The "team effort" the new leaders had long called for was just six senators, three of them women. The Caucus' new "Executive Chairman," Spokane's Bob Lewis, was preoccupied with a losing effort to keep his seat, leaving the GOP with a gain of five, one short of a majority, in November. The 1981 session was a month old, when petulant Democratic Senator Peter Von Reichbauer, provoked by now Congressman Jim McDermott, switched sides. The "Saint Valentine's Day massacre" embittered Democrats, none of whom had ever been in the Minority in the Senate, and jolted the GOP senators, none of whom had served in the majority there. Overnight the senate changed from what was a men's club in 1973, into a strident a partisan battlefield, with a woman in charge. Hayner had to mediate between equivocal Governor John Spellman who had bashed his erstwhile opponent, McDermott, as taxing "Seattle liberal psychiatrist" and now swung to them as the solution, and Polk, whose "troglodytes" promised none and meant it. Jeannette never had a working majority. Three senators, as confused as conservative, tried to wag the dog. Evans era prosperity turned into a $1.2 billion deficit, in the worst meltdown since 1933. For five sessions over the next 20 months, Hayner patiently led her caucus through grinding five hour sessions. Votes were found for 9 taxes totaling $750 million, matched by cuts, with Spellman fighting one, and the Speaker the other. By January 1983, the "majorities" were gone, and the governor mortally wounded.[86]

Her caucus' survival hinged on two traits, the ability to bring, and keep people together. It obeyed her infamous "Rule of 13:" all did whatever a majority decided, inconceivable in the "Old" senate. And she had no personal agenda: if no bill could be taken "hostage" it was impossible for House Democrats to play trading game. To get his landmark environmental bill, surely on of the highest impact bills of the 90's passed, Speaker Joe King acceded to Hayner's term and had her help. Managing one vote majorities for 14 years as Minority or Majority Leader is both remarkable, and a record. Proving women could survive and succeed, be tough and ladylike erased the vestiges of sexism. In 2005, all four of the Senate's majority party leaders were women.[87]

The Superintendent of Public Instruction: A Woman's Place?

Women have been Superintendent of Public Instruction, all but eight 09-13/years since 1909, than in the eight other statewide offices.[88] Belle Reeves Secretary of State (1937-1948); Jennifer Belcher Lands Commissioner, Debra Senn Insurance Commissioner (1993-2001), and Christine Gregoire Attorney General (1993-2005); Governor since 2005. Josephine Corliss Preston (1913-29), and Pearl Anderson Wanamaker, (1941-57), two of the state's ablest administrators, represent the juxtaposed philosophies of their eras.

The 1909 Code of Public Instruction specified all instruction be in English, and American history, "and such other studies as may be prescribed," along with "attention" to "honesty, honor, industry and economy." Josephine Corliss Preston Preston effected 55 other new laws in 16 years with alacrity, clarity, and confidence. Consolidation and classification of school districts, a survey of conditions and needs, and vocational education were in place by 1917. Until then, World War I was thought to be the business of the "Old World." Legislators were deluged with protests against any kind of military preparedness for public school children. "Submarine frightfulness" soon turned America from a "peace-loving and strictly neutral nation … to one demanding world-wide democracy … determined to crush … the evil attempt at world-wide autocracy." In six months in "patriotic teaching" was mandatory, and the SPI's Bulletin filled with patriotic songs, quotations, prayers, and "The mystic Meaning of the Flag" was in every child's hands. Physical education, equalization of property assessments, teacher's retirement, and a minimum state payment of $20 for each child were law by 1921; "Eighth Grade Examinations" (the normal termination point), certification standards for teachers, and liability insurance for school busses by 1926.[89]

Urbanization exacerbated the plight of small school districts mostly east of the Cascades, whose Assessors' rates only half those of Westside counties in 1920. Preston got a minimum district levy enacted, as a requisite to getting the State's 2 mills of support. The other major vexation was hiring and retaining talented teachers. Preston improvised: "teacher's cottages" (as of 1915), often canvass-covered shanties were rolled up next to the schoolhouse once the season for feeding harvesters in the wheat fields was over. Her arguments were always practical, and insistent on local control: "The modern theory of the State" assumed "government not only can levy taxes for the establishment and maintenance of schools, but is just as much its duty ... to protect itself against ... paupers ... or ... criminals. An educated citizen is a more valuable asset to the state ... He will produce more revenue and be less likely to become a liability. It is only [italics mine] on the ground of an investment – an economic necessity – that the State can justify the imposition of taxes for public education .....A school system ... is a great social agent of the State ...." In 1935-36, their salaries were where they had been two decades earlier, ranging from $1740 a year in Clallam County to $3,034 in King.[90]

Pearl Wanamaker, the daughter of a Fin and a Swede, began teaching in a one room school at 18 (1917-21), graduated from the "Normal School" in Bellingham(1922), and elected to her first office, Island County Superintendent of Schools, at 24 (1923-27). She was also in the House, (1929-31, 1933-35), and quickly became one of the state's most proficient – and insistent politicians. Pearl pressed for the Deception Pass Bridge. In 1934, Governor Martin suggested she consider an "indefinite holiday" to come to the capitol to "help stand guard over some of these situations." He soon had second thoughts, but its priority moved up, and the bridge passed at the next session. In 1937, Pearl was appointed to the Senate, and Mary Farquharson as chair of Education Committee and to Appropriations, and the two mounted a full assault on Martin's budget.[91]

Pearl's claim to a "part in drafting "every school support law under which schools now operate" when she ran for her fourth office, S.P.I., in 1940, was exaggeration. It did apply to her time as a legislator: the "Showalter Bill (1933), guaranteeing $25 a day per student, co-authoring equalization (1937), and the regrowing trees on logged off lands to sustain the Permanent School Fund. Incumbent Stanley Atwood's awkward scuffles in court over who would govern vocational education gave Pearl her opportunity. Wanamaker got – and kept – the allegiance of principals as well as superintendents, a statewide grass roots network, and 59 percent of the votes in November.[92]

Governor Langlie's "accounting approach"[93] upset Pearl, as well as his bills to relieve the Land Commission she was on of forestry, but like Mary Farquharson, Wanamaker was entirely put off by Mon Wallgren's partisan maneuvers. Jerry O'Connell his ubiquitous Democratic State Chairman denied they wanted to capture the schools: her policy was "to tell the biggest lie you She was relieved to be invited to Japan in 1946 by General MacArthur to restructure militarism and nationalism out of education. The next year the landmark "Strayer Report" Pearl had planned to document her demands was ready, but the House went Republican, and viewed a 25 percent increase in teacher salaries with disbelief. Nine of her 28 "personal request" bills did pass, after "extreme pressure" on her part.[94] But she was falling behind teacher sentiment in two arenas. In her exiting presidential address to the NEA's First General Assembly, She came out against federal aid to education, and declared "the best interests of public education are not served" by unionizing. Stating "For immediate gain … the entire profession loses stature" was unpopular, if prophetic. By 1952, "attacks on public schools" were treated proprietarily, and her resistance to state dollars for parochial schools was circulated in "in every [Catholic]church in the State." The huge majorities of 1944 and 1948, evaporated: she survived with 54 percent of the vote. The Republican was former Senator Agnes Gehrman, whose late entry was likely at Langlie's urging.[95] Democratic gubernatorial candidate Albert Rosellini tried to exploit Catholic voters by endorsing Republican Henry W. Turner in the primary.

An astute admirer knew Pearl "could not help arousing the enmity of a number of people." Her speech files show she was working harder. Although she raised $77,740 to lightly qualified and very conservative Spokane Senator Lloyd Andrews' $13,150 in the 1956 primary, "the most adroit political battler for education Washington has ever known," lost her 11th campaign. The voters had wearied of the "fighting lady," but her record is prodigious: 1600 school districts had fallen to 400, and state support of public schools peaked at 56.4 percent. The "local control" myth lives on, but the State was paying most of the bills and calling the tunes.[96]

The Accidental Incumbent: The Governorship of Dixy Lee Ray

Nineteen seventy-six was the year of the outsider. Georgia's Governor Jimmy Carter came to the nation's capitol in the wake of Watergate. A 62-year-old marine biology professor whose managerial limitations were evident as chair of President Ford's Atomic Energy Commission decided "the real action" was in the states. Dixy had been a fascinating teacher never advanced to full professor in Marine Biology for 20 years at the University of Washington, presumably for failing to publish. Then she ran the Pacific Science Center for 9 years, making it Seattle Center's anchor attraction. The lady with the classic jaguar convertible and the hand-honked rubber horn was assured, impressive, informal, "The faculty club version of the bionic woman."[97] The bachelor who had controlled her three work forums was completely misplaced in an arena where compromise and criticism are the order of every day.

"The professional politicians who are my primary opponents so others can step in," said she with customary aplomb and innocence. Dixy likely ran as a Democrat thinking she could not beat King County Executive John Spellman in the Republican primary, certainly not because of her approach to government.[98] Her campaign was amateur until professional consultant Blair Butterworth came on after the primary. Ray's bright-eyed charisma and practiced speaking style continued to mesmerize the voters. Hello Dolly" became "Hello Dixy," as she quashed Spellman November 2. From there it was all down hill. "We've shown that you the people are electing your representatives" she told 500 at he victory party, "They are not being elected by the publishers and editors of the daily papers." Lou Guzzo, former Arts Editor of the PI and her staff director in D.C. soon proved inept, and a retired army colonel who kept a red light when his door closed made Chief of Staff. The Governor-elect was sensitive to invidious comparisons to Dan Evans, pulling back his bills and appointments, and installing over-age-in-grade bureaucrats as directors. Budget director Orin Smith from Touche Ross as was her only superior choice. At year's end, the cabinet had one Mexican-American not women, and six vacancies. "With every pink slip we're going to send some Kleenex." She spouted.[99] Dixy turned a deaf ear to liberals, and to the brightest man in the senate and a natural ally, Majority Leader August Mardesich.

Ray confirmed no one can be a good governor who does not know the capitol. "Welcome to controlled chaos," she greeted the media in January. Her inaugural speech was suitably modest: she did not "know all the answers" but wanted to share my views" with the legislators. Dixy's agenda was to limit the size of government, simplify regulations and create a "balance between economic growth and environment," a euphemism for subordinating ecology and touting her unqualified enthusiasm for atomic energy. The core thrust was allowing the executive to "reorganize " state government subject to legislative veto, within 60 days unless the legislature forbid it, something even Evans could not bring off. The idea of redoing 20 agencies in 36 months was naïve in the extreme. Inflation was in double digits. By 1978, and as revenue poured, Ray reversed herself to sign a biennial budget increase of 36 percent. Tax reform was doused: taxes might be made less regressive in "small but significant ways."[100] Four task groups named to develop executive request for the session came up with nothing new. She restarted them in 1980, blaming a lack of staff support and facilities, and grossly underestimating the task. Orders went to agencies consulting their managers. "About the only way I can get in to see her is to do something that makes her mad," one complained.[101] The veto pen was wielded erratically. An act "sun setting" agencies not specifically reapproved was axed as "lacking in executive participation," then an identical one signed as repassed. The state was being set up for a shortfall of $1.3 billion two years hence, when the governor simultaneously reversed her fiscal policies, and erased revenues like the inheritance tax unaware she had lost the game in the first half.

Dixy's press relations sealed her fate. Ray never learned, and could not adhere to the politician's rule: "Never argue with a man with a barrel of ink at his back." The vindictive Post-Intelligencer led the charge. She cancelled press conferences, and turned to favored reporters, one hour telecasts, and "Town Hall Meetings" in the hustings. The torment continued, and Ray butchered piglets on her Fox Island farm named after the press, and tossed them to the gaping reporters. In 1980, only business was in her camp. She had tangled with Senator Magnuson over double-bottom hulls on the Sound, and her manager had called Scoop Jackson "the most dangerous man in the United States."[102] Montgomery (Gummie} Johnson, former Republican State Chairman. The Democratic leaders of the House and Senate suspected she instigated an FBI "sting" operation that put both to prison. Intelligent, articulate, self assured, and unexpurgated, Dixy Lee Ray was impolitic enough to take on all parties at once. She was defeated for the same reason she was elected. It takes, as she said, "a politician to deal with politicians."[103]

Congress: The Final Forum

Washington has sent eight women to Congress. Catherine May (Bedell),(R), served in the Minority in the House for twelve years (1959-71), tending agricultural communities at the state's center. Jolene Unsoeld (D), (State Representative 1985-89), and painstaking defender of Public Disclosure Law, won three terms in Congress from Olympia base (1989-95), from Southwestern Washington's swing Third District. The liberal's contortions to accommodate her constituency were exposed by conservative-Populist-initiative guru State Senator Linda Smith, who won an unprecedented nomination as a write-in candidate, and in turn lost the 1998 U.S. Senate race to Patty Murray. Cathy McMorris (R) 35, took the GOP dominated Eastern-most Fifth District in 2004, after a term as House Minority Leader in Olympia, where she was long on strategy and campaigning, and short on substance.[104]

Julia Butler Hansen, (1907-1988) the formidable chair of the House Highways Committee in Olympia came within a vote of being Speaker. She served 20 years in Congress.

Julia Butler Hansen (1907-88), from the hamlet of Cathlamet was the state's most capable, formidable, and outspoken woman official, winning 23 elections, over 37 years. "She would drive a hundred miles to meet a dozen people … ." a friend recalled, "She'd see a farmer out in his field …. stop the car, pull on some overshoes, and climb right through the barbed wire … or blackberry vines."[105] "Every day" [was treated] as "election day." Asked to be a Precinct Committeeman, Julia was Democratic Chair of tiny Wakiakum County, the first woman elected to the Town Council, and in the secretarial pool at the legislature, in 1937. Elected State representative in 1939, she was not to be trifled with. When a male peer dismissed another female colleague as "just a woman," Hansen decked him. She introduced the "50-50 bill" requiring the parties to give women organizational quality. "Some of you dandies have always claimed you had the women's vote in your pocket," Julia told men in the House, "Now's your chance to prove your earnestness."[106]

Julia was just married and intending to quit Olympia, but her husband prevailed on her to keep up the fight. A close ally of Pearl Wanamaker's, Julia tried to overturn Governor Mon Wallgren's veto of a teachers' pension bill in 1945. His henchman threw her out as County Chair, refused to let her run as a Democrat, and endorsed an opponent. She ran as an Independent Democrat, and in two years. The employee of the County [Road] Engineer soon was the unchallengeable chair of the 30 member Highways Committee, when roads and bridges were not allocated by formulas. She knew who needed what, and was relentless once her mind was made up.[107] When the GOP took over in 1953-55, she beat autocratic parliamentarian John O'Brien for Minority Leader, only to lose the contest for Speaker to him in two years, by one vote.[108] The upshot was the creation of a Committee on Committees: appointments no longer fulfilled promises. "I had the [most] votes [on it] and he had the speaker ship," she remembered.[109]

Unlike most women in Congress in 1961, Julia was fully armed, and robustly backed Lyndon Johnson's "Great Society."[109] Catherine May and Julia, who had shared an apartment in Olympia as state representatives, were now in the only state delegation with two women. The 1964 election reversed its partisan balance, and Hansen set about "organizing" the new House Democrats so that Senators Magnuson and Jackson were not its leaders by default. She was the first woman to chair an Appropriations Subcommittee. Julia might be put upon, but never run over. Both Interior and Related Agencies, and the Public Works subcommittees. Seattle Congressman Tom Pelly (R) said, "Mrs. Hansen is probably more forceful than I've ever known any man to be …. If you opposed anything she was for, you did so at your own peril … ."[110]

Jennifer Dunn (1941-2007), the svelte, stylish, Stanford alumna was first female chair of the State Republican Party, in 1981. She sustained its technological and fiscal lead a decade.[111] From being deep in and devoted to the "unifying" Reagan campaign of 1980, Jennifer moved to

National Committeewoman, gathering votes on the State Central Committee to become party chair. Elected in 1992, "the year of the woman," she moderated in office. "My inspiration comes from a very broad base ... " she insisted, "from a lot of people who had been left on the outside" [of the Party]. Her legislation over 12 years in Congress (1993-2005) was drawn from home. The [Federal] Open Meetings Act, and "Meagan's Law" are near replicates of the State's Public Disclosure Initiative, and State Representative Ida Ballisote's bill registering sex offenders, the "Amber Alert" coordinating police searches for abductors.[112] The expansion of Mt. Rainier for conservation; leading roles in welfare reform, free trade with Australia, (temporary) reduction of corporate taxes, and ending the Estate Tax were orthodox conservatism. The "woman soldier in the field" who had raised money for foundations, now did it for colleagues, and between 1998 and 2001, another $500,000 for conferences touting the benefits of being a woman Republican. This, and Vice Chairmanship of the Republican Leadership Conference were her bases as the first woman to run for Majority Leader, against Dick Armey of Texas. The other votes split three ways, between former Seattle Seahawks end Steve Largent, and last minute entry (and now Speaker) Dennis Hastert.

Dunn, sought to "soften the party's image," "always wanted more responsibility," and did not want to leave Congress in 2005. The leadership defeat, and the ascension of another Texan, Tom Delay, blocked the way up. Congress demands "consolidated" (deny all else) service, and in 2004 "circumstances," notably her remarriage to a Washington D.C. business man, made that impossible. "Carrying the banner" for abortion may have had something to do with her never being a sub-committee chair. Jennifer Dunn gave more than she got, but exited on her own terms, as a firm partisan "respectful of other people's points of view," and a "person of integrity and respect."[113]

"Nine and Counting": Women in the U.S. Senate

Washington is one of three states where the both U.S. senators are females. Patty Murray lobbied the legislature to stop cuts in pre-school programs in 1972, but her sense of timing was more impressive than her first term State Senator in 1992, when she ran against a gray-haired Congressman, one of the men in "dark suits and red ties." She was everywoman, a "mom in tennis shoes," who carefully nurtured a "unique voice" for "working families." "I am the only senator in the history of this country to be a pre-school teacher before I became a United States Senator," she told an amused audience in 1998, battling a newspaper endorsement that she was "much improved, but had "a slow learning curve." Fortunately, Congresswoman Linda Smith had a slower one, refusing PAC dollars while Murray laid on $1 million of "issue ads" paid by the DNC. Before being unseated as chair of the Transportation Sub Committee in 2003,

Govenor-elect Christine Gregoire, center, joined by U.S. Senators Maria Cantwell, left, and Patty Murray in 2004.

she advertised $130 million more for state systems, and two pieces of pork, $3 million for a maritime museum in Seattle, $4.7 million for a Coast Guard patrol boat, small slices by Senate standards. Her only visibility came as head of the Democratic Senatorial campaign committee in 2002.[114] Murray is now at the end of her third term, and although she is on the Appropriations and Budget panels, she has claimed only to have secured $1.2 billion to hire and train more by teachers in 1998, and to have been the "architect" of a just settled decade long struggle between Airbus and Boeing, who will convert 100 747's as refuelers.

Murray is "used to being underestimated." Standing in the shadow of four giants, Warren Magnuson, Scoop Jackson, Dan Evans and Slade Gorton is hard. But six things suggest a forth term: incumbency, Washington's increasingly Democratic lean, generous liberalism (Murray opposed Bush I's tax cuts), seniority, the women's vote (Emily's List was her largest contributor), and reputation for 'delivering the bacon.[115]

Maria Cantwell, a talented if not charismatic as a State Representative (1986-92), and defeated for reelection as to U.S. House (First District) in 1996, turned out three term U.S. Senator

Slade Gorton in 2002 by investing $10 million of the dollars she had earned in the interim as a Real Networks executive, made her the state's first self-financing U.S. senator.[116] Her nose for being on the 'right side' of appealing issues, like making the state sales tax deductible from one's federal return, and a parallel 'below the radar' stance give her long odds for a third term in 2012.

Women were "pampered, patronized, and their power frequently neutralized" until the 1930's. Their lack of 'critical mass' in the next 40 years was due to the residual idea and practical constraints of being

WSBN

Left to right: Justice Mary Fairhurst, Chief Justice Barbara Madsen and Justice Debra L. Stephens at their alma mater, Gonzaga University in Spokane in 2010.

"homemakers, and return of cultural calm. Since 1976, gender differences, at least in Olympia, have evaporated. Women are now the Majority Leaders in both houses of the legislature.[117] The Bar is nearing parity, and the judiciary is more of a meritocracy. Carolyn Dimick became the first Justice in 1982. Twenty years later, Washington was the first state to have more female justices (5 of 9, in 2002)."In the State of Washington, the election of women is just the way we do business," as Justice Barbara Madsen said in swearing in Mary Fairhurst.[118]

Chapter 9

Ultimate Democracy:
Initiatives and Referenda

Daniel Jack Chasan

At the turn of the 21st century, high-minded editorial writers and good government advocates fretted publicly that Washington's initiative process had gotten out of hand. A string of tax-cutting initiatives pushed by a conservative souvenir watch salesman named Tim Eyman had squeezed state budgets and had many legislators looking over their shoulders, afraid that anything they did to raise revenue would quickly be undone by the budget-cutting hordes.

Some critics thought that the people should not routinely take law-making into their own hands; they should leave that to the professionals. They should act themselves only in extraordinary circumstances. That was not the original theory. And it has never been the practice.

The Washington residents who originally advocated and voted for the initiative and referendum in the early 20th century did not trust legislatures or legislators. The initiative and referendum institutionalized that popular mistrust – not of government per se, but of the venal individuals who actually made the laws. (Legislators probably weren't any more venal than their fellow citizens, but they weren't any less venal, and they had different opportunities.) Populist farmers and organized labor did not believe that legislatures or legislators represented their interests or values. Direct Democracy: The Initiative and Referendum Process in Washington, published by the League of Women Voters of Washington Education Fund in 2002, explains: "Many western voters believed that their legislators were only representing railroad, bank and timber interests."

The Washington Supreme Court observed in 1919: "It is well known that the power of the referendum was asserted ... because [the people] had become impressed with a profound conviction that the legislature had ceased to be responsive to the popular will."

This conviction extended beyond the borders of Washington. "[Theodore] Roosevelt, [William Jennings] Bryan, and [Woodrow] Wilson ... represented ... a common political mood, a mood that arose in America during the nineties and continued, with some changes of objective, into the present century, until displaced by the coming of the Great War in 1914," Mark Sullivan wrote in a 1926 social history entitled Our Times, "a mood in which the common man regarded himself as oppressed, as in danger of becoming stratified economically; a mood of revolt against organized wealth, of resentment against the union of 'big business' and the boss system in politics."

"During the last forty years of the Nineteenth Century there arose and grew in democratic republics and commonwealths a popular distrust and dislike of their parliaments," the Washington Supreme Court explained in its 1916 Berry opinion. "They became tired of the representative system. In the latter part of that period the people of the democracies submitted to their representative legislatures only under the pressure of stern necessity. The growing distrust and contempt for legislative bodies – municipal, state, and federal, and the tendency to restrict them culminated with the beginning of this century, in numerous returns by states to the primitive systems of direct legislation, modified by modern systems of election."

Washington's "primitive system" enables the people to draft and pass their own legislation. If enough registered voters (8 percent of those who voted for governor at the last regular gubernatorial election) sign petitions for an initiative to the people, it goes before the voters at the next general election. If enough registered voters (also 8 percent) sign petitions for an initiative to the legislature, it goes before the next session of the state legislature; if legislators do not pass it, it goes before the voters at the next general election. The referendum enables the people to vote on legislation that their elected representatives have already passed.If enough registered voters (4 percent of those who voted for governor at the last regular gubernatorial election) sign petitions for a referendum, it goes before the voters at the next general election. The constitution shields legislation that is "necessary for the immediate preservation of the public peace, health or safety" or "support of the state government and its existing public institutions" from the referendum.

The initiative process rests on the concept that legislation by the people is no less legitimat e than legislation by their elected representatives. "We now have a dual system of legislation," the

Berry court observed: "one by a delegated, bi-cameral legislature, deliberative, maker of its own rules of procedure in general; the other by the legal voters of the state in mass."

Inevitably, some things have changed since the initiative and referendum process became part of the Washington constitution. By the late 20th century, when the legislature employed a small army of staff members and met annually, most legislators clearly knew more – or had ready access to more information – than the average citizen. But in 1912, when the constitution was amended to allow the initiative and referendum, and for many years afterward, there was less of an imbalance between the legislature and the people. Legislators had no staff to research issues. They met for only 60 days, every other year. There was no reason to believe that the average legislator knew more – or had ready access to more information--about any given subject than a well-informed private citizen.

South Dakota became the first state to adopt the initiative and referendum in 1898. Oregon followed three years later. People south of the Columbia River took to the initiative and referendum so enthusiastically that the tools of popular democracy had become known as the "Oregon system."

At around that time, Washington's Grange and labor unions campaigned for a constitutional amendment that would give them the initiative and referendum in Washington. In September 1910, Governor M.E. Hay wrote to Grange Master C.B. Kegley that "in traveling around the state, I am now satisfied that this coming session of the legislature will prepare a bill submitting a constitutional amendment to be voted on in 1912. … There is a great unrest or feeling among the people that our form of government can be materially changed for the benefit of all."

The governor and the grange master disagreed about whether or not the people knew what they wanted. The governor wrote: "The people are reaching out, grasping for something, not knowing just what is best but feel that a change will improve matters."

The grange master replied: "It is a mistake to suppose that the people do not know what they want. They do know what they want – it is the elimination of the party boss and legislation for special privilege interests … . The people want a square deal, and want the legislative machinery perfected so that they can hereafter be absolutely sure of getting it."

The people may or may not have gotten a square deal, but they did get their hands on the legislative machinery. In 1912, after 10 years of lobbying and campaigning, the Grange and its allies persuaded the legislature to put a constitutional amendment enshrining the people's right to legislate on the ballot, and persuaded the voters to pass it. Arizona, Arkansas, California, Kentucky, Maine, Michigan, Missouri, Montana, Nevada, New Mexico, Oklahoma, and Utah, as well as South Dakota and Oregon, already had the initiative process. Colorado, Idaho, Ohio, and Nebraska adopted it that same year. (By now, 24 states have it.) The first seven initiatives went before the people in 1914, just a few months after the start of World War One. Proposals to ban the sale of alcohol and to give workers an 8-hour day drew most of the attention.

Ernest P. Marsh, the relatively moderate leader of the State Federation of Labor, pushed the eight-hour-day initiative as an alternative to the more radical approach advocated by the International Workers of the World. "In his pledge to achieve the eight-hour day without a strike, Marsh had staked the future of the federation on his faith in direct legislation," Norman Clark wrote in Mill Town. "Marsh … and his friends … worked against the opposition of employer groups that were quite willing to drown the initiative measure with their money, and against the opposition of almost all the important newspapers in the state." Voters passed the Prohibition initiative. They rejected the 8-hour day. "Within the ranks of the timber workers, the moderates had clearly seen their day," Clark wrote. "November, for the radicals, had exposed the polite dream of education and political action as a fraud."

The very next year, the legislature tried to abuse the constitutional provision that shielded laws "necessary for the immediate preservation of the public peace, health or safety" from the referendum. The legislators tried to cast a 1915 law that changed the makeup of the state board of land commissioners as emergency legislation. The Supreme Court didn't buy it. "The real question," the Court wrote, "is: Can the people, as distinguished from a representative legislative body, indulge in constructive legislation and reserve that right without interference by the Legislature or the courts, except where, in certain enumerated instances, they have waived the right in order that the immediate necessities of health, peace and safety and our public institutions may be met by their representatives duly convened in legislative session?" The Court's answer was yes. It ruled that the emergency clause violated the state constitution. In the future, legislators would try many times to invoke the "peace, health or safety" language. Sometimes the courts let them; other times the courts did not.

The initiative power played a fairly minor role until the Great Depression. Then, in 1930, a public power bill pushed by the Grange significantly altered Washington's politics and economy. Seattle and other city governments already operated electric utilities. The Grange initiative would permit the citizens of any county to form a public utility district, and permit a public utility district to take over any privately owned power system within its boundaries.

Washington's private power systems belonged to Eastern holding companies, which were easy to resent. By the middle of the Depression, utility companies were "perhaps the least popular of business groups," writes Robert S. McElvaine in The Great Depression. "The worst abuse in the power industry was the pyramiding of holding companies on top of the operating utility firms… By 1932 thirteen such companies controlled 75 percent of the nation's private power interests. The results were huge profits for speculators and grossly overpriced electricity for consumers." Whoever owned them, private power companies wouldn't string wires long distances through sparsely-settled countryside to isolated farms. It made no economic sense. Farmers would have to keep milking by hand and lighting their houses with kerosene lamps until the decision to serve them became political, rather than economic.

The Grange collected signatures for an initiative to the legislature in 1928. After the 1929 legislature rejected it, the measure went automatically to the people the following year. That fall, the Seattle Times argued that the public power bill represented a huge step in the wrong direction. "Anyone who has read the text of the district power bill … or who has followed any of the arguments … cannot have failed to see how it would open the way to an increase of taxes and of public debt," the Times warned.

The Grange viewed the power bill differently. "Who are the people who support the District Power Bill?" State Grange master A.S. Goss asked. " They are the organized farmers, the organized workers and the common people of the state who are paying the light bills or who want electric power." The Grange passed its public power initiative. But its rural constituents lost their battle against Initiative 37, which required redistricting. Ever since the turn of the century, as population flowed to Washington's cities, rural areas had been increasingly over-represented. The legislature was constitutionally obligated to redistrict every 10 years, but re-drawing political boundaries was a task that lay beyond its institutional abilities. Obviously, the legislature's self-interest trumped its obligations to the people. This was by and large, just fine with the portion of the people who happened to live in the over-represented rural areas. And it was just fine with legislators who had secure seats in established electoral districts. Inevitably, the initiative had to survive a court challenge to even reach the ballot. But the state supreme court, in an 8 to 1 decision, ordered the Secretary of State to put it before the people. "It is common knowledge," the majority said, "that the State Legislature has ignored the mandate of our Constitution requiring reapportionment of the State Legislature since 1901."

Washington, like most other states, had relied for its revenue on property taxes. In 1932, hammered by the Depression, Washington's farmers found themselves with lots of land and no cash to pay the taxes on it. Charles Hodde, a Missouri-born farmer in his mid-20s living on rented acreage in Colville who had helped the Grange to pass the public power initiative in 1930, recalled years later that "in Chelan County where they had all the orchards and everything … less than fifty percent of the taxes were being paid … . You could let them go delinquent for five years before they could start foreclosing on your farm, so you just didn't pay them, see. Well," Hodde said, "we had to do something about it." The Grange did do something about it. The organization sponsored initiatives to limit the tax on property and replace the revenue with a graduated tax on net corporate and personal income.

The Grange had been pushing for years to shift the tax burden from farmers to somebody else. A Grange News cartoon from 1928 showed three men carrying a log: a poorly dressed man labeled "The Homeowner" was struggling with bent knees under the thick end of the log; "The Farm Owner," dressed in overalls, is struggling along with him; a third man, "The Bond Owner," dressed in a plutocrat's top hat and spats, strolls along resting a hand casually on the small end of the log.

The idea that income and other forms of wealth should be taxed was not new. People had been trying to push tax reforms through the state legislature for years. Before the Depression, attempts to shift the tax burden through a 40-mill property tax limit had failed in the state legislature. When the lumberman Mark Reed was speaker of the house in 1923, writes Robert Ficken in Lumber and Politics: the Career of Mark E. Reed, he "engineered the defeat of [the Washington Tax Limit League's] pet measure, the so-called forty mill bill … . The bill also provided for a state income tax to make up for much of the lost revenue, a factor that aroused opposition to the bill among some businessmen."

Some businessmen might still oppose a tax on income, but many other people had a different perspective. For most citizens, in the context of the early 1930s, voting for a graduated net income tax meant voting to tax someone else: the rich. Even in 1939, before the United States entered World War Two, only about 4 million Americans paid federal income tax. At the start of the Depression, therefore, the majority of Washington citizens chose what seemed a tax reduction pure and simple.A campaign led partly by Charles Hodde easily collected enough signatures to put tax reform initiatives on the ballot.

The people approved both a 40 mill limit on property taxes and a graduated tax on net personal and corporate income. To plug the revenue gap until the income tax went into effect, the 1933 legislature imposed a business and occupation tax – taxing the total amount a business took in, whether it was making a profit or not. Then the Supreme Court ruled that a graduated income tax was unconstitutional. The court reasoned that income was a form of property and the state constitution required all property in a certain category to be taxed equally. Therefore, the state could not have a graduated tax that forced some people to pay higher rates than others. The legislators could have come back with a flat-rate income tax, but they didn't. The Seattle Times noted that "the Legislature now has authority to enact a flat-rate income tax but apparently the Tax Commission does not favor it."

The legislature waited the constitutionally-mandated two years then exceeded the 40-mill limit on property taxes. The people wouldn't stand for it. Most voters didn't seem to care how the legislature paid the costs of government. That wasn't their problem. In 1934, the people passed another 40 mill limit on property taxes but turned down a constitutional amendment that would have authorized a graduated net income tax. That was evidently an idea whose time had already passed. "There is abundant evidence that [voters] knew what they were doing," J.W. Gilbert wrote in the Times. Nevertheless, the voters' choices on election day "complicate the problem of providing funds for the support of the state government and the schools, which the Legislature must solve. "The next session of the Legislature … must devise new sources of revenue."

The next session of the legislature did exactly that: it imposed a two-percent tax on retail sales. It exempted sales of bread, milk, butter, eggs and produce. These exemptions lasted only until 1939, when the legislature extended the sales tax to groceries. The people renewed the 40-mill property tax limit by initiative again in 1936 and 1938, until the limit was finally written into the state constitution. The business and occupation tax became permanent.

Two years after the income tax initiative passed, Hodde--who would later become Speaker of the state House of Representatives – organized and led a Grange campaign for an initiative to the legislature that would establish an open "blanket" primary. The campaign invited voters to reject traditional party discipline and cross party lines when they choose candidates for the general election. In a blanket primary, a voter could pick among either Democrats or Republicans for any given position. Party leaders hated the idea of a "blanket" primary because it would undermine party discipline – and the incumbent party's control of patronage. "At present a voter must ask either for a Republican or a Democratic ballot, and the record thus made is preserved for all time," J.W. Gilbert wrote in the Seattle Times. "It is used to determine the party regularity of the voter and his eligibility for holding a political job. It is the one test now made by the Democratic administration in the nation, the state or the county to ascertain the worthiness of a political job seeker. No primary vote, no job, is the inflexible rule." The people didn't seem to like that rule. "Notwithstanding the opposition of the leaders of both major political parties, the movement to permit voters to participate in primary elections without disclosing their party affiliation is steadily gaining ground," Gilbert wrote. "Whether the party leaders like the plan or not … there is every prospect that the blanket primary … will have the approval of the rank and file."

The initiative passed handily, and the legislature passed a blanket primary law the next year.

Inevitably, the blanket primary was challenged as unconstitutional. When the case reached the state supreme court, the justices gave short shrift to the interests of political parties. In 1936, ruling in Anderson v. Millikin, the court noted the argument "that the law tends to destroy political parties. Counsel [for the opponents] confess that they can find no specific provision of the constitution on which to base the contention, but they assert the general utility and necessity of parties, and argue there from that legislation tending to destroy them must receive the condemnation of the courts. It has seemed to us, however, that this is a political rather than a judicial question, and that an appeal from the legislative decision must be made to the people rather than to the courts." The supreme court said it was "undisputed" that "the constitution takes no concern of political parties." Therefore, "a law will not be held to be unconstitutional [just because] its may destroy these organizations."

In the depths of the Depression, populist sentiment ran not only against private utility companies and political parties, but also against the canning companies that dominated the salmon fishing industry. Initiative 77, on the ballot for the 1934 general election, set out to ban the fish traps that had caught the lion's share of salmon in Puget Sound since the 1880s. Wealthy canning companies owned the traps. Sport fishermen and purse seiners had always resented them. The seiners put up most of the money for the anti-fish-trap initiative. The sportsmen did most of the work. The campaign was ambiguous, combining but never fully reconciling appeals to conservation and to populism. The main pro-initiative brochure claimed it would "give this great natural resource back to the people instead of leaving it in the hands of a powerful financial minority."

Trap owners replied that abolishing traps would just leave most of the huge Fraser River sockeye salmon run to the Canadians, that the initiative was not really a conservation measure, and that it represented "the effort of the purse seiners to wrest from the pioneers of Washington their means of livelihood." This was a barely-guarded way of referring to the fact that most trap owners were Anglo-Saxon businessmen and most purse seiners were Slavic, Norwegian or other immigrants. Ken McLeod, the sport fisherman who helped lead the initiative drive, later recalled being offered $5,000 by a Seattle fish packer to abandon the campaign.

The conservation argument was phony. But that didn't matter to either the people or the courts. Before the election, the initiative faced a challenge that made its way to the state supreme court. The challengers argued that paid workers had been used to gather signatures in violation of state law, and that the voters had been deceived. As the majority put it in Edwards v Hutchinson, the court had been asked to intervene so that "popular government [could] be rescued from the slough into which it has fallen through the machinations of selfish interest." The court was not unsympathetic; but "much as we sympathize with that viewpoint and deprecate the use of methods such as are here charged" the majority believed it was being asked to exceed its authority.

The question wasn't whether or not the signature gathering was illegal but whether the signatures should be counted. "The law … makes it a criminal offense to hire or be hired for that purpose, but nowhere in the statute do we find a word or a line which invalidates the signature of a legal voter because it was obtained by the solicitation of a paid worker." As for the allegation that the initiative campaign had deceived voters, "[e]ver since popular elections were instituted, in every one held, some one, perhaps many voters, have been deceived, and so long as the political field remains free and open ... there is no way to prevent prejudices being appealed to; and voters to a greater or lesser degree will always be deceived." The anti-fish-trap initiative passed with 70 percent of the vote.

Just as the backers of Initiative 77 argued that salmon belonged to everyone, advocates of public power argued that falling water belonged in the public domain. Battles over public power would play a central part in Washington politics for the next 30 years. Public power crusaders tried to gain through the initiative process what the legislature would not give them: power to condemn utility properties across county lines, so that PUDs could take over the multi-county systems of Puget Power, in and around Seattle, and Washington Water Power, in and around Spokane. Private power interests tried to limit PUDs' power to condemn their property.

The battle over Initiative 139, which appeared on the 1940 ballot, may have been the most acrimonious of all. I-139 would have forbidden a PUD to issue bonds without a local referendum. It was couched in terms of the people's right to choose, but it was seen as an attempt to hamstring the PUDs by putting their vital functions at the mercy of elections that could be controlled by the wealth and manpower of their arch rivals, the private utilities.

The initiative may have been doomed when--right before the election – the Federal Trade Commission investigated private utility holding companies' involvement in the pro-139 campaign. The timing of the federal investigation was no coincidence. "By the way," Jack Cluck, attorney for the PUDs, wrote to Senator Homer Bone seven months before the election, "would it be possible to induce the Federal Trade Commission or other public agency to conduct an investigation concerning the sponsors of Initiative 139?" Cluck wrote that "the campaign is apparently well-financed, as a large quantity of literature is being circulated through the mails and a state-wide campaign is being conducted." A week later, Cluck telegraphed Bone: "Confidential suggestion received that we request you to ask [for an] investigation of utility financing of [the] 'Let the People Vote League.'" Bone came through. In November, I-139 met defeat, with people in rural areas voting heavily against it.

At the same election, the Washington Pension Union persuaded the people to establish the most generous old-age pensions and medical benefits in the nation. The Pension Union represented a wide spectrum of left-of-center political sentiment, but its initiative campaign was led by 25-year-old William Pennock, who – the world learned years later – had begun working for the communist party when he was still an English major at the University of Washington. Other Pension Union leaders were covert communists, too.

The federal government was not picking up much of the tab for the elderly yet, and pensions were a widespread concern. Initiative 141 would guarantee every old-age pensioner a minimum of $40 a month. It would guarantee everyone on public assistance free medical, dental, hospital or nursing care and let the recipient choose his own doctor. (The initiative would also get rid of the old requirement for proving need. The next year, N.P. Atkinson, president of the Washington Old Age Pension Union, told a radio audience that under the old law, "when the prospective pensioner wanted a pension, he practically had to sign his life away. He had to declare he was a pauper and that none of his relatives were willing to put up with him.") The initiative would not create a new source of revenue. If it passed, its financial impact would clearly be enormous.

UWA

The Washington Public Pension's Union's Representative William Pennock promoted Initiative 176, an expansion of welfare that kept State finances unbalanced in the 1950s.

Initiative 141 won by a margin of three to two. Writing in The New York Times, Oregon's future United States Senator Richard L. Neuberger called the new Washington pension statute "[o]ne of the most sweeping old-age pension laws ever proposed in this country." The initiative began decades of conflict between progressive social legislation and a regressive revenue system. "All over the Far West," Neuberger wrote, "people are watching intently to see if Washington can foot the bill." He explained that "Washington will pay the largest old-age pensions in the United States … . If the Washington measure proves successful, Social Security enthusiasts in other Western States announce, they will back similar bills." People were watching intently in Washington, too.

"The bill was unusual in that it specified no means of raising the money required," Neuberger observed. That was no accident. The Pension Union had deliberately left vague the source of funding. During the campaign, some of its backers had explained that "four years ago, a pension initiative was defeated because the people, although favoring the pension increase, nevertheless disapproved of the specific tax." They did not repeat that mistake. Unofficially, they did talk about a new tax on stocks, bonds, mortgages, and other "intangibles." They claimed it would tap the "56 percent of Washington wealth now untaxed." There was no precedent for a tax on intangibles, though, and no precedent for imposing one. Washington was, by and large, stuck with the tax system it already had.

The legislators of 1941 faced what seemed to be a clear choice: they could persuade the voters to pass a constitutional amendment permitting a graduated income tax, or they could increase the sales tax. Raising the sales tax was a much surer bet. Langlie proposed an increase from two to three percent. The legislature voted to do it, pending a vote on a constitutional amendment to permit an income tax. The Grange promptly threatened a referendum. The House promptly passed a constitutional amendment that could be submitted to the voters. But the voters never said yes. In the real world of Washington politics, a larger pension meant a larger sales tax.

The Pension Union kept pushing. Pension initiatives failed in 1942 and 1944, but in 1945, flush with a wartime budget surplus, the legislature increased the monthly pension to $50. Then the extremely conservative legislature elected in 1946 virtually did away with the pension law. Two years later, the Pension Union, still headed by Pennock, led a political crusade to restore and even expand it. A lot of political groundwork had already been laid. As the conservative 1947 legislature neared adjournment, the capitol was besieged by around 1,000 members of a "people's march" demanding a pension of $60 a month, a veterans' bonus, increased aid to public schools, and a fair employment practices act. Chartered buses from all over western Washington disgorged people carrying banners and placards. Communist banners were visible, but clearly, not all the demonstrators were communists. A dozen veterans, demonstrating for the bonus, pitched pup tents on the capitol lawn. Twenty-five demonstrators were thrown out of the Senate gallery after one had shouted that the senators were giving the veterans' bonus issue "a run-around." Another group tried to get into the House gallery but found the doors locked. The demonstrators banged on the doors and yelled, in the words of a popular novelty song, "Open the door, Richard." Both houses quickly recessed, after passing resolutions that no one should be let in for another two hours.

The next year, backers of the pension initiative dismissed concerns about the state's ability to pay. "Don't be misled by claims that '172 will bankrupt the state,'" they argued in the voters' pamphlet. "Washington is the fourth-wealthiest state in the United States, and as of September 1, 1948 had a surplus of over $60,000,000 in the general fund." They also tried to place the initiative campaign in a broader political context, shaped in part by the new Cold War and their own allegiance to the Soviet political line. "Friends," Pennock told a radio audience, "the campaign for Initiative 172 has become much more than just an old age pension measure … Since the ending of the war, the group of small but wealthy individuals and corporations which own nearly two-thirds of all corporate assets in America have set out to reverse the progressive policies of Franklin Roosevelt… . When you vote for 172 … you'll be helping say: 'no more billions for atomic bombs, for destruction, but America's resources shall be used for peace and for construction.'"

Seduced in part by the budget surplus–a carry-over from the war years--people voted to increase the old-age pension and to pay veterans a bonus. A number of other states voted for veterans' bonuses. No other state had a pension plan to equal Washington's. By 1950, the state's budget surplus was only a memory, and some people had second thoughts about the pension.

That spring, when the Pension Union was planning an initiative campaign to expand the pension program further and a group backed by Governor Arthur Langlie was preparing one to pare it back, Lawrence E. Davies reported in the New York Times that "Washington State's 'cradle to grave' public welfare program, which in its health-system aspect is unique in America and is contributing to a precarious financial situation in the state, will be subject to overhaul by the people next November." Actually, he wrote, it might be subject to overhaul by the legislature sooner than that: "Governor Langlie said [on May 13 that] a special session of the legislature this summer was 'inevitable' as a means of meeting the fiscal problems developing under the welfare program."

Clearly, the state was spending beyond its means. "Washington traditionally has been among the leaders in providing aid for the aged, the blind and the needy. Today, although it is in twentieth place in the country in per capital earned income, it ranks first in per capita assistance payments."

"Roughly a third of all those receiving any form of assistance are the 'reliefers,' and the stories of what some of them obtain … even in a legal way without the 'chiseling' that officials say is all too prevalent, are becoming legendary… . "The state pays for movies, newspapers, club dues, transportation and permanent waves for the needy citizens … "The Washington law is unique in this country in its medical aspect. Not only are old-age pensioners … entitled to all forms of health care … but the same privilege is extended to recipients of all forms of public assistance ….

"Free Choice of Physicians Prevails."

This was the height of the Cold War – and also of the very hot war in Korea – and the Pension Union's communist leaders did not confine themselves to pushing for increased old-age pensions. In 1950, following the Soviet Union's political line of the time, they also tried to pass Initiative 183, which would have required the state to petition Congress for a policy of "peaceful coexistence."

That failed miserably, as did the Pension Union's 1952 attempt to place a $75 floor under pensions. Pennock had already outlived his time. The Depression was over. He could not persuade voters to pass another pension initiative. He could not force a referendum on the legislation that soon gutted the initiative of 1948; the courts ruled against his challenges to the "emergency" clauses in anti-pension statutes. The federal government prosecuted him, along with six other defendants, for conspiring to advocate the overthrow the government of the United States by force. In the spring of 1953, shortly before the trial started, Pennock admitted that he had been working for the Communist Party all along. At the beginning of August, three-and-one-half months after the trial started, he appeared on the witness stand. According to his friends and family, he was too nervous to sleep. His doctor prescribed sleeping pills. Pennock brought home his own little bottle of chloroform. The pressure was about to increase. Some time in the next week, his own lawyer would finish direct questioning and the prosecution would start to cross-examine him. Pennock went to bed early in his West Seattle house. Later that night, his wife, Louise, found him dead. He had evidently committed suicide.

In the face of gaping budget deficits and a wave of right-wing political sentiment, the old radical consensus had faded; people would not vote to raise pensions again. But some things had not changed: the legislature still could not or would not tackle reapportionment. In 1956, the public, led by the League of Women Voters, forced the issue once again. The League had found that as the population of Washington grew more urban in the years after World War II, the political imbalance between rural and urban areas had increased dramatically. The League calculated that, according to the 1950 census, an eastern Washington legislator might represent anywhere from 18,000 to 80,000 people; a King County legislator, anywhere from 35,000 to 130,000. The League had to fight off a court challenge to even put a redistricting initiative on the ballot. In November, the initiative won by a landslide. The measure called for re-drawing the state's legislative districts on the basis of census tracts. It totally ignored the boundaries of established legislative districts, and the demographics and patterns of political loyalty that the existing districts reflected. Legislators feared for their seats. The Grange, with its base in the over-represented rural areas, feared for its influence.

Faced with the prospect of new districts that would turn many of its members back into private citizens, the legislature sprang into action. The legislature was bitterly divided on many issues, but it had no trouble mustering two-thirds majorities in both houses to gut the reapportionment initiative and maintain, as much as possible, the political status quo. The legislature's statute drew the new districts on the basis of existing precinct boundaries. The state supreme court allowed the legislature's version of redistricting to trump the initiative. Legislators could not bring themselves to commit political suicide. Once again, they had placed their own vested interests above the perceived interests of the people.

The new statute was nevertheless a landmark, the first time the legislature had tackled re-districting on any basis since 1901. As Justice Weaver's dissent to the Washington Supreme Court opinion observed, the "legislative history of reapportionment and redistricting in Washington is short, as it is in most states…. For fifty-six years – from 1901 to 1957 … our successive legislatures ignored" the clear constitutional requirement to re-district. "Lest this be interpreted as a criticism of our past legislatures, I hasten to point out that the experience of this state parallels the experience of most states. In varying degrees, they have all been affected by this system of 'silent gerrymandering.'"

The legislature's passage of its own redistricting law was not the end of the story. In 1963, a three-judge federal panel ruled that the law was "invidiously discriminatory" in its under-representation of urban areas and was therefore unconstitutional. The next year, the United States Supreme Court issued its "one-man-one-vote" ruling that required representation in direct proportion to population, killing any slight hope the state might have had of a successful appeal. A lower federal court subsequently ordered the 1965 legislature to pass a redistricting law before it did anything else. The House debate over redistricting dragged on for 47 days. Finally, a few Democrats sided with the House Republicans to pass a bill that most Democrats opposed. The next year's election gave Republicans control of the House for the first time since 1953.)

Initiatives played a limited role in the turbulent 1960s, but the people did use an initiative to repeal the old blue laws that had banned alcohol sales on Sundays.

By the late 1960s, Seattle's Pike Place Market had become run-down, home to a large low-income population, and definitely not modern. The city government wanted to replace it with a large urban renewal project that would have kept a cleaned-up fragment of the market for cosmetic effect but would have destroyed the look and character of the place. Led by a single-minded architect named Victor Steinbrueck, Seattle's citizens dug in their heels. The market was preserved by a city initiative in 1971. Early the next year, Seattle voters passed another initiative to block construction of two planned freeways that would have cut through city neighborhoods.

Many elected representatives lagged far behind public sentiment on urban-preservation and environmental issues. The shoreline management initiative showed just how far behind.

The Washington Environmental Council had tried and failed three times to lobby a law that would restrict development of the state's salt water and fresh water shorelines through the legislature. "We are appalled by what is being done on the shorelines," said WEC president Jack Robertson. "The last three legislatures tried to come to grips with it but the special interests wouldn't let them come up with anything meaningful." In 1970, the group announced that it was going to launch an initiative campaign.

The campaign easily collected enough signatures to put a shoreline management initiative on the ballot in 1972. The legislature quickly passed an alternative bill that differed from the WEC's largely in that it gave much greater discretion to county and city governments. Both versions went before the people, who chose the legislature's.

Before the shoreline initiative qualified for the ballot, a shopping mall owner tried to prevent people from collecting signatures on initiative petitions inside the mall. The state supreme court ruled that the owner could not constitutionally keep them out. The court reasoned that the constitutional right to initiative and referendum implied a right to gather signatures, and a private mall that functioned as a traditional public space could not prevent it. A mall owner could restrict signature gathering to certain areas but could not ban the activity.

Later, the court would decide that the right did not apply to signature gathering in a store that did not function as a traditional public space, and that signature gatherers had no right to wander freely through the Puyallup fairgrounds, which people perceived as a public space but was in fact operated by a private corporation. (No one had tried to keep people from gathering signatures within the fairgrounds, but the petitions had been restricted to certain areas.) Despite these subsequent limitations, the basic right to gather signatures had been established.

Passage of the Shorelines Management Act not only protected shorelines directly; it also gave environmentalists an implicit club to hold over the legislature for many years: if legislators didn't protect the environment. Another initiative passed in 1972 addressed the relationship between the people and their elected officials more directly. Shortly before the Watergate scandal made government lying and secrecy national concerns, Washington citizens voted to make their own government and political campaigns more transparent.

The new law gave every Washington citizen access to: all records kept by government agencies that did not include confidential information about other individuals or investigations by law enforcement officers; virtually all government records about themselves; financial disclosure forms that all elected office holders, candidates for elected office, political campaign organizations, and political action committees had to file; meetings held by elected public officials for the purpose of making decisions. Some sensitive issues could be discussed in executive session, but the final decisions had to be made in public.

People had already lost trust in their elected leaders. The Watergate scandal that erupted in 1973 only deepened their mistrust. Voters didn't turn against their own long-term incumbents, but the public mood had soured, and in 1976, the first major election year after Watergate, they elected "non-politicians" Jimmy Carter as President and Dixie Lee Ray, a cranky former zoology professor, as Governor of Washington.

The wave of initiatives in the 1970s seemed to reflect that same national mood. "Some political observers saw the increased use of direct democracy [in the 1970s] as a result of distrust of politicians and the legislative process," Les Ledbetter wrote in a 1977 New York Times article on Americans' increasing use of the initiative process. "Others interviewed said the growing number of issues on the ballot resulted from questions that legislators would not address or could not decide."

The time was ripe for conservatives – who had been battling the New Deal unsuccessfully for 40 years – to start making government itself the enemy. For the most part, they did so in the context of anti-tax initiatives. It all started in 1978, with the passage of California's Proposition

13. The state's property taxes were running 50 percent above the national average and the state's budget surplus had grown to almost $6 billion. Right before the election, the Los Angeles County assessor made it known that property taxes would increase by an average of 125 percent. The measure passed overwhelmingly. "[P]ollsters and pundits immediately interpreted Proposition 13 as the opening salvo in a national tax revolt," Bruce J. Shulman wrote in The Seventies. "Taxation had always been unpopular, of course," Shulman observed, "but it had long remained a weapon of class warfare–a way ordinary Americans could limit the power and influence of the nation's wealthiest citizens... . [President Ronald] Reagan transformed taxation: it ceased to be an issue of equity, and it became a matter of tyranny or freedom. Instead of dividing rich and poor, business and labor, the tax issue united them against big government and elitist bureaucrats."

Increasingly, it also united them against institutional liberalism. In 1978, after Seattle became the first city in the United States to bus students between schools for racial balance without a court order, the people of Washington passed an initiative that made busing programs illegal. The majority's ideas probably paralleled those of most Americans. "Legal segregation and denying blacks the vote–these were repugnant," Shulman wrote. "But few white Americans approved of busing and other forms of mandatory integration." The triumph of Washington's anti-busing sentiment proved short-lived. In 1982, the United States Supreme Court ruled that the anti-busing initiative was unconstitutional. At the same time, the Court upheld a California initiative with similar motivation and effect. The court voted 8-1 to uphold the California law, 5-4 to declare the Washington law unconstitutional.In the Washington case, Justice Harry Blackmun wrote: "The initiative removes the [local] authority to address a racial problem – and only a racial problem – from the existing decision-making body in such a way as to burden minority interests." Blackmun said the initiative "burdens all future attempts to integrate Washington schools ... by lodging decision-making authority ... at a new and remote level of government [i.e., the people]."

By the early 1980s, public utilities were no longer populist icons. The Washington Public Power Supply System, a consortium of public utilities in Washington and elsewhere, had set out to build five big nuclear plants. The project was coordinated and partially backed by the Bonneville Power Administration, which prodded utilities into signing up. Originally, all five nuclear plants were supposed to cost $4.075 billion. By the end of 1980, the figure had soared to $15.948 billion. (As construction, energy, and regulatory costs rose, nuclear construction projects all over the country left their budgets far behind, but WPPSS compounded its problems with hubris, bad planning, lax oversight, and a lack of accountability.) The state Senate Energy Committee held hearings on the projects' astounding cost overruns. A petition drive for Initiative 394 – which would require a vote of the people in every service area affected before bonds could be sold for any new power project of more than 250 megawatts or any project under construction whose official budget had doubled – started in 1981, just as the energy committee issued a devastating report. The final cost estimate of $23.8 billion would not surface until the following year, but with the region mired in a deep recession, the petition qualified easily for the November ballot. "Do we want our children to inherit WPPSS' debt?" asked a pro-394 flyer. "It's now $30,000 per household and rising. And we never even got a chance to vote on it."

Shortly before the election, Wallace Turner reported in The New York Times that "[c]onstruction companies, banks, brokerage houses, electrical manufacturers and power companies are contributing heavily [to defeat I 394] in the most expensive initiative campaign the state of Washington has ever seen." The Times reported that "[m]ore than $1 million from about 500 contributors is being used by Citizens Against Unfair Taxes to try to defeat Initiative 394… .In support of the initiative, a group called Don't Bankrupt Washington has raised $163,000 from 2,300 contributors." The initiative passed overwhelmingly.

Continental Illinois, Seafirst, and Morgan Guaranty Trust, acting as trustees for the bondholders, immediately challenged it in court. In April 1982, federal judge Jack Tanner ruled the initiative unconstitutional. His ruling was upheld on appeal. But the initiative had an effect. The threat and then the reality of its passage contributed to Wall Street's uneasiness about, and ultimately to the financial collapse of, projects 4 and 5, which led WPPSS into the largest municipal default in American financial history.

Just as people in Washington and elsewhere were turning more frequently to "popular democracy," the United States Supreme Court changed the rules of the initiative game. Paying people to gather signatures on initiative petitions had always been illegal in Washington. In 1988, though, the Court ruled unanimously that a Colorado law which barred paid signature gatherers violated initiative backers' First Amendment rights to free expression. The justices reasoned that a ban on paid signature gathering limited the number of voices that could express an initiative sponsor's point of view and reduced the chance that an initiative would reach the ballot, where it could become the subject of statewide discussion. They also reasoned that the grass-roots character of the initiative process would be protected adequately by the requirement that a certain percentage of voters sign petitions, and that paid signature gatherers would be no more likely than amateurs to falsify signatures.

By that time, the deep recession of the early 80s had given way to an economic boom. At the end of the 1980s, alarmed by years of rapid growth that had transformed the skyline of downtown Seattle and brought suburban sprawl to many formerly-rural areas, Seattle voters passed a "CAP" initiative to limit the heights of downtown buildings and the annual growth of downtown office space. Responding to the same burst of development and encouraged by the success of the CAP initiative, environmentalists prepared a growth management initiative for the 1990 statewide ballot. To head off the initiative, which would have limited local governments' discretion, he 1990 legislature passed its own landmark Growth Management Act.

Increasingly, Washington voters both elected liberals to top offices and passed socially conservative initiatives. In 1992, when Washington voters elected a liberal Democratic governor, Mike Lowry and helped elect a Democratic president, Bill Clinton, they also tried to limit the terms of their elected officials. A term limits initiative had failed the year before. This time, it passed, with 53 percent of the vote.

Under the terms of Initiative 573, a Representative could serve only six years in Congress. A number of groups, including the League of Women Voters and the ACLU, quickly challenged the new law on constitutional grounds. The case acquired its most symbolic plaintiff when the Representative from eastern Washington's Fifth Congressional District, Tom Foley, entered the suit. Foley had represented eastern Washington in Congress since 1964. By 1992, he had become Speaker of the United States House of Representatives. Foley and his co-plaintiffs triumphed in the federal courts, which ruled the term limits initiative unconstitutional.

Foley did not get the last laugh. Two years later, his Republican opponent, George Nethercutt, made the Speaker's opposition to term limits a major election issue. It wasn't the only issue but it was crucial. Foley became the first Speaker to lose an election in 134 years. (Nethercutt pledged that he himself would never try to hang on for more than six years. When his six years were almost up, he alienated hard-core term limits advocates by reconsidering. But term limits had become yesterday's issue. Nethercutt won fourth and fifth terms.)

In 1993, Washington voters passed Initiative 593, a "3 strikes you're out" law that imposed a mandatory lifetime prison term on anyone convicted a third time of any felony classified by the initiative as a "most serious offense." There was a growing sentiment in favor of such laws, and by 2004, 25 other states had passed similar legislation, but Washington's was the first. At the same election, the voters also approved the most draconian state spending limit so far. Initiative 601 limited the annual increase in state spending to an expansion factor that considered inflation and population growth. The state could exceed that limit only if the governor declared an emergency. Government could no longer grow faster than the state's population or economy.

Even when professional sports were involved, people were slow to open their wallets. The Seattle Mariners baseball team had known virtually nothing but failure since it came to Seattle in 1977. The team had enjoyed only two winning seasons. Not surprisingly, fans did not flock to Seattle's ugly concrete Kingdome, completed with public money in 1976, to watch baseball played indoors on artificial turf by a losing team. In the summer of 1995, with the baseball season in full swing, the people of King County were asked to pay for a new stadium. They voted – albeit narrowly – against it. But just about the time the people were saying no, the Mariners took off. Starting thirteen games behind the division-leading California Angels, they finished the season tied for first. They won a one-game playoff against the Angels, then faced the New York Yankees. Improbably, the Mariners won again. The Cleveland Indians beat them for the American League championship, but that hardly mattered. Much of the Seattle area had been captivated by the team's late-season heroics. People listened to the games all over the Seattle area. Total strangers would ask each other the score.

No politician wanted to be responsible for "losing" the Mariners. And yet, Mariners president John Ellis said that unless the public committed itself to a new stadium the team would go up for sale. Business and political leaders, including Governor Mike Lowry, King County executive –and soon-to-be governor – Gary Locke, and county councilman – soon-to-be county executive – Ron Sims, wanted very much to keep the Mariners in town. "No less magical than the way the Mariners are performing on the field is the epiphany that has seized Washington's elected officials since the [stadium ballot measure's] apparent light loss at the polls," the Seattle Times editorialized in late September. "Predictions that voters are in no mood for tax increases proved accurate. But voters are in the mood for winning baseball." Clearly, they were, but the people evidently remained less enthusiastic than their elected representatives about paying for a stadium. The Times reported in early October that a poll it had commissioned showed that a majority of voters "said they oppose using state money to build a new baseball stadium."

That didn't stop the legislature. Legislators didn't want to be responsible for losing the Mariners, either. And they didn't want their decision second-guessed by the people. They passed a stadium financing bill with an emergency clause that shielded it from referendum.Opponents sued. The state supreme court upheld the emergency clause. Basically the justices decided that if the legislature said the prospect of losing the Mariners constituted an emergency, that was good enough for them.

A similar "emergency" soon arose when an out-of-state owner threatened to move Seattle's professional football team, the Seahawks, to California. The chronically mediocre Seahawks had been sold by their original local owners to an unpopular California real estate developer named Ken Behring. Behring announced that King County, which owned the Kingdome, had violated its contractual obligation to provide him with a first-class facility. He had team equipment trucked to California, and announced that he was moving the team. King County got a court to halt the move, but the region still faced the loss of its team. The same political leaders who had fought to avoid losing the Mariners wanted to keep the Seahawks in town. Microsoft billionaire

ST

The Washington Education Association staged a week-long demonstration on the capitol campus in 1987.
The state's most powerful interest group also uses court injunctions and initiatives to pressure the legislature.

Paul Allen agreed to buy the team and keep it in Seattle – but only if the state would help pay for a new $425-million stadium, and only if voters would support it voluntarily.

The legislature passed a suitable law. Allen then used his own money to place a referendum on the ballot, hold a special election, and run a massive public relations campaign – the highest-spending such campaign in state history--to gain what turned out to be only 51 percent of the vote. It was an unprecedented use of the initiative process: a billionaire, wanting a demonstration of public support, pays to gather the signatures, pays to convince a majority of the voters, and even pays for the election. A process conceived and begun as a way to circumvent the political power of concentrated capital became a tool of concentrated capital. Allen's next venture into popular democracy fared less well. In 2000, he backed and financed I-729, which would have permitted charter schools in Washington. It was the second time in four years that charter schools had come before the people.

All over the United States, a strange alliance between conservatives who disliked teachers' unions, the predominantly liberal cast of public school culture, and, in some cases, state requirements to teach pernicious doctrines such as evolution, and inner-city parents concerned about their kids' ability to get educated in urban schools pushed for legislation that would make it possible to create charter schools – to all intents and purposes private schools, free from some of the legislative restrictions and union contracts that hamstrung traditional public schools, but supported by public education dollars. In 1996, Dick Spady, heir to Seattle's Dick's Drive-in restaurant business, and his wife, Fawn, gathered enough signatures to put a charter school initiative on Washington's ballot. The voters rejected it, nearly two to one. Allen's initiative did better, but it still lost. (Ignoring the two popular votes, the legislature passed a charter school statute in 2004, but it was quickly undone by a referendum.)

At the same election, public school supporters sponsored two initiatives that would funnel more state money to the conventional public schools. I-732 required cost-of-living increases for school employees. I-728 channeled extra money to schools for reducing class sizes, giving teachers paid time to work on curriculum, and other possible programs to be designated locally. Both passed. Neither created a new source of revenue. Neither directed the legislature to spend less money for anything else. Neither dealt with the effects of the tax-cutting initiatives that the same electorate had passed. Like the Washington Pension Union in the 1940s, the state teachers' union had deliberately created unfunded mandates. Faced with an extremely tight budget, the 2003 legislature suspended 732 and reduced the rate at which funding for 728 would increase. Public school advocates subsequently came up with Initiative 884, which would generate an additional billion dollars a year for public schools and colleges by increasing the state sales tax from 6.5 to 7.5 percent. In 2004, I-884 lost overwhelmingly. People were all for public education as long as they didn't have to pay for it.

They evidently felt the same way about road improvements. In 1998, they approved Referendum 49, which authorized a package of transportation improvements that depended on money from both bonds and license tab fees. The local economy was booming, but people resented the fees they paid to renew their vehicle licenses every year. In 1999, Tim Eyman sponsored Initiative 695, which would cut everyone's fee to $30. The years before, Steven Hayward had written .in the Washington Times that "[l]iberals have been hoping for years that the tax revolt would slowly fade away, but in fact, the conditions are building for another taxpayer blow-up." He was certainly right about conditions in Washington state. Thirty dollar license tabs became a new kind of inalienable right, something to which every Washington citizen was somehow entitled. And unlike most initiatives of the past, I-695 operated on a reverse Robin Hood logic. It had little in common with attempts to shift tax burdens during the Great Depression. People weren't trying to lower taxes on their heavily mortgaged homes or unprofitable wheat fields; they were trying to lower taxes on their expensive cars. This was not taking from the rich and giving to the poor. On the contrary, the bigger and more expensive your vehicle, the more you saved.

Eyman's initiative passed overwhelmingly. However, it ran afoul of the requirement – established by the state constitution and long enforced by the courts – that a single piece of legislation could address only a single subject. Opponents sued, and King County Superior Court Judge Robert Alsdorf ruled that the initiative violated the single-subject rule. "Poor Tim Eyman threw a tantrum on Tuesday, tearing up a campaign sign and flinging the shreds around a King County courtroom," wrote John Webster in a Spokane Spokesman-Review editorial. "The fast-talking souvenir watch salesman had just been forced to sit in silence while a judge shredded his attempt to pose as a maker of laws." But Eyman and his supporters had the last laugh. Elected officials scurried to legislate the fee reduction that the people had approved unconstitutionally.

On the same day Alsdorf ruled against the initiative, "Gov. Gary Locke and many legislative leaders wasted no time … assuring voters the $30 license tabs they approved in November are here to stay – regardless of what a King County judge says," Joseph Turner reported in the Tacoma News Tribune. "'Vehicle license fees were one of the most hated taxes in Washington,' the Democratic governor said. 'Despite the court's ruling today, we have no intention of returning to the old system of high license tab fees. The $30 fees are here to stay.'" Even many of the writers who deplored Eyman's initiative conceded that the license tab fee had grown excessive and unfair. The legislature quickly enacted a law to accomplish what Eyman had tried to do through I-695.

Suddenly, Eyman was regarded as a political power. I-695 wasn't his first venture into initiative politics. Two years before, he had launched I-200 which prevented state or local government from granting opportunities or benefits based on race. It was directed against most form of "affirmative action." State or local government could no longer make decisions based on an applicant's race, gender or ethnicity. The initiative came straight from California, where voters had passed an almost identical measure in 1997, but there was no reason to doubt that Washington voters meant what they said when they voted to end racial preferences. (In fact, there was no reason to believe that a majority of voters anywhere had ever favored affirmative action. The idea that preferential treatment was equality under the law had been accepted as an article of faith by many people in academia and government, but for the public at large, it had always been a hard sell.) Conservative talk show host John Carlson soon took over leadership of the initiative campaign, and voters passed I-200 in 1998.

However significant Eyman's role in launching I-200, tax-cuts made him a celebrity. The year after I-695 passed, his second tax-cut initiative, I-722, also won handily--and then, once again, was ruled unconstitutional because it dealt with more than one issue. The year after that, his I-747 limited property tax increases to one percent. (The state supreme court ultimately ruled it unconstitutional, too, on the grounds that voters' pamphlet language might have led voters to believe they were altering I-722, which was no longer on the books.) And Eyman himself survived a scandal. At the beginning of 2002, it turned out that he had been diverting initiative campaign money into his own pockets – which was legal – but not declaring it on public disclosure forms, which was not. The state sued him in Snohomish County Superior Court, alleging that a for-profit organization established by Eyman had billed his non-profit

political action committee, Permanent Offense, for campaign services. The state also alleged that Eyman had violated the law in a variety of other ways, including the use of Permanent Offense funds to reimburse him for campaign contributions. Eyman wound up settling the case by agreeing to pay a $42,000 fine plus $8,000 to reimburse the state for its legal expenses, and to never again serve as treasurer or exercise any control over

HL

Conservative serial initiative signature gatherer Tim Eyman (center) hobbles the legislature with his initiative requiring a two-thirds vote in each house of the legislature to increase taxes.

the finances of any political action committee. Some people thought Eyman was finished. Some certainly hoped so. But Eyman's tax-cut supporters didn't seem to care about his well-publicized brush with the law. Only three months after he agreed to the fine, his I-776 did away with licensing fees collected in four counties, an excise tax to finance mass transportation projects collected in three, and fees on light trucks, all of which had driven annual license payments above $30 despite the legislation inspired by I-695.

People still did not trust politicians. They had not tired of the perhaps illogical open primary that they had adopted by initiative in 1934. The major parties still hated it, and as the new century began, they went to court in an effort to get it declared unconstitutional. It wasn't their first attempt. But the legal landscape had changed significantly. This time, they won. The 9th U.S. Circuit Court ruled that Washington's blanket primary violated political party members' Constitutional right of free association. The 9th Circuit judges said that the United States Supreme Court's recent ruling in a similar California case left them no choice. "The Washington [primary] scheme is materially indistinguishable from the California scheme held to violate the constitutional right of free association in Jones," they explained. "The Washington scheme denies party adherents the opportunity to nominate their party's candidate free of the risk of being swamped by voters whose preference is for the other party."

The court had ruled that political activists have a perfect right to exclude outsiders. It said that "those who actively participate in partisan activities, including … holding precinct caucuses in their homes, serving on local and state party committees, contributing money to their parties, canvassing, and watching polls for their parties, have a First Amendment right to further their party's program for what they see as good governance. Their right to freely associate for this purpose is thwarted because the Washington statutory scheme prevents those voters who share their affiliation from selecting their party's nominees. The right of people adhering to a political party to freely associate is not limited to getting together for cocktails and canapes."

The legislature quickly passed – but Governor Gary Locke vetoed – a bill that would have established a "top two" primary in which the two candidates who received the most votes in the primary, regardless of party, would appear on the general election ballot. After Locke's veto, the Grange sponsored an initiative, I-872, to make the top-two primary into law. The people passed it overwhelmingly, but the parties challenged it and again, a federal court found that it violated the party members' right to freedom of association.

Exactly 90 years after initiatives first appeared on a Washington ballot, one could argue that the state's politicians and political parties had showed that their interests and the people's perceived interests still weren't the same. One could also argue that the assumptions of people who resorted to "direct democracy" had changed radically. The people who first advocated the initiative process, those who passed the early initiatives for public power and tax reform and old-age pensions, those who passed the later initiatives for open government and shoreline protection, may have given up on the legislators of their day, but all recognized a need for collective action. In contrast, the people who introduced and voted for tax-cutting initiatives at the turn of the 21st century seemed to deny or ignore any need for collective action.

In 2005, faced with predictions that the Alaskan Way viaduct along Seattle's waterfront–the second-busiest roadway in the state–would collapse in a major earthquake, and that the floating bridge that carried Interstate 520 across Lake Washington was likely to sink unless it underwent major repairs, and facing a long list of road projects that had been deferred for years, the legislature did manage to agree on a package of road improvements that would be financed in part by a phased 9.5-cent-per-gallon increase in the gasoline tax. To shield the tax measure from referendum, the legislature attached an "emergency" clause–as it had done to numerous other statutes in that session. It couldn't prevent an initiative, though, and predictably, an initiative to roll back the gas tax increase hit the streets almost immediately.

The seemingly-inevitable anti-tax sentiment was bolstered by a feeling east of the Cascades that the big-ticket items on the legislature's list were Seattle problems and by the fact that during the summer of 2005, gasoline prices reached record levels. The state's major newspapers and largest businesses opposed I-912. The state Republican Party endorsed it. Two conservative radio talk show hosts, John Carlson–who had not only led the I-200 campaign but had also run unsuccessfully for Governor as the Republican candidate in 2000–and Kirby Wilbur, promoted it on the air. The Public Disclosure Commission soon ruled that the two men had to list their broadcast promotion of the initiative as in-kind campaign contributions. (Carlson complained that the major newspapers, which editorialized relentlessly against the initiative, weren't held to the same standard.) Interviewed on the radio shortly before the election, Carlson said that the initiative would "send a message," letting legislators know that people were tired of paying more taxes for longer commutes. Some prominent initiative supporters argued that they wouldn't vote for any tax increase unless it promised to reduce peak hour congestion. Anyone who knew anything about the subject realized that reducing peak hour congestion wasn't an option. Perhaps because so much of the state's establishment opposed I-912, perhaps because gas prices had declined, voters defeated the measure, 53-47.

The 2005 legislature had managed to agree on a list of road projects and a funding mechanism. Caught between powerful interest groups, it had not managed to agree on tort reform. In the absence of legislation, the medical establishment and the insurance industry launched an initiative that would cap damages for non-economic loss–that is "pain and suffering"–at $350,000. Proponents argued that a cap on damage awards would cut doctors' medical malpractice insurance premiums, which would keep doctors from leaving the state, hold medical costs down and, in the long run, benefit everyone. Opponents argued that it would keep people who had been horribly injured by egregious medical errors from getting justice. And the initiative didn't stop with the cap, or even with a provision that would have allowed medical facilities to force their patients to accept binding arbitration. It was laden heavily with provisions that loaded the dice in the insurance industry's favor. The text in the official voters' pamphlet ran to more than 7 pages.

The trial lawyers launched a rival initiative that would require the state to revoke the license of any doctor who lost three malpractice suits in ten years, and would require disclosure to patients–and their lawyers–of settlement details and records. The lawyers' initiative embraced a long series of extra provisions, too; it covered more than 12 pages of the voters' pamphlet. Both measures had started out as initiatives to the legislature, which could have but did not come up with alternatives. The legislature simply passed both along to the voters.

Doctors, trial lawyers, and insurance companies all had a lot to win or lose. Not surprisingly, spending on I-330 set a new state record for initiative campaigns. However, record spending didn't translate into a majority vote. I-330 won only 46 percent. I-336 won only 41. (Spurned by the voters, the organized doctors and trial lawyers subsequently agreed on compromise legislation.) One could argue that the doctors and insurance companies had drafted I-330 (and the trial lawyers had drafted I-336) because the legislature hadn't done its job. But one could argue just as persuasively that I-912 was on the ballot because the legislature had done its job. With this damned-if-you-do-and-damned-if-you-don't response to legislative action, combined with the reflexive opposition to new taxes, the attempt at government by talk radio, the obvious vested interests masquerading as public interest, the record spending, and the extreme complexity of the ballot measures, the election of 2005 arguably pushed "popular democracy" to its reductio ad absurdum.

Ever since the Supreme Court ruled that paying people to collect signatures on initiative petitions was protected by the Constitution, the veneer of populism had worn thinner and thinner. The election of 2005, when competing initiatives were backed by organized doctors, lawyers, and insurance companies, showed just how thin.

One person's public interest has always been another person's special interest. Many initiatives have been special-interest legislation. Their advocates have never said so and have not always believed it, but the fact remains that measures advocated in the name of the people have often benefited only some of the people. When the Washington Grange intervened in the state's attempt to preserve the blanket primary, the 9th Circuit had little use for the Grange's argument that it represented a broad public interest. "As the State puts it," the court said, "the blanket primary 'recognizes the associational interests of groups other than political parties' by enabling voters to 'form ad hoc political associations which cross party lines to support a particular candidate or a particular cause.' The Grange argues that its members support water and public utilities for farms and that its members' rights to advance their rural agenda in both parties will suffer if each Granger is forced to choose a party ballot. The Grange says that it spearheaded the initiative in 1933 [sic] that led Washington to adopt the blanket primary, which has successfully prevented 'a politically corrupt nominating process controlled by political bosses or special interests.' "'Special interests' are evidently in the eye of the beholder. Some urban voters might think that special protection for rural water and electricity concerns serve a 'special interest' of farmers and that the Grange is a special interest group."

Mistrust of politicians has been a constant–although perceptions of their frailties have changed. Originally, populists feared that they had been corrupted by the money of railroad companies and other big economic interests. By the end of the 20th century, people who styled themselves as populists believed that legislators had simply bought into the values and viewpoints of big government. Corrupt government was no longer the perceived foe; government itself had become the problem.

There was a certain irony: initiative backers didn't trust legislators in general but did trust them to somehow find the money for programs that had passed without designated sources of funding or to somehow figure out which programs to cut in the aftermath of initiatives that reduced funding.

At the end of the 18th century, the Founders designed a system of representative government that would insulate political decision-making from the mob. The late-18th-century authors of the Federalist papers worried that the masses would make a mess of things if they got their hands directly on the machinery of government. Madison wrote in Federalist 63 that "there are particular moments in public affairs when the people, stimulated by some irregular passion or some illicit advantage, or misled by the artful misrepresentations of interested men, may call for measures which they themselves will afterwards be the most ready to lament and condemn."

Roughly a century later, populists and progressives designed an initiative and referendum process to give the mob a direct role in decision-making. Another century has almost passed since that process reached Washington State. We're still not sure where it will lead.

Chapter 10

Redistricting Wars

Howard E. McCurdy

During the Great Depression, in 1934, the Washington State Grange prepared an initiative to the Washington State Legislature for the purpose of creating a blanket primary for the nomination of candidates to elected offices. At the time, the state utilized a modified form of the direct primary. Upon arriving at the polls on primary election day, voters were required to declare their party affiliation and chose among those candidates seeking nomination within their declared political party. Fred W. Lewis, acting on behalf of the executive committee of the State Grange, proposed to change that procedure. Under the blanket primary, all candidates seeking nomination would appear on a single ballot. Citizens could vote for prospective nominees without reference to their political party. Without spoiling his or her ballot, a voter participating in the primary election could approve a Democrat seeking the party's nomination for governor and a Republican running for the state senate.

Members of the state legislature understood the intentions of Grange officials in proposing this electoral curiosity. John Wilson, a state representative from downtown Seattle, announced that he would vote against the initiative "because I believe that this will destroy parties and party responsibility."[1]

Writing in support of approval of the U.S. constitution many years earlier, before the creation of American political parties, James Madison had warned of the violent effects of faction. "Our governments are too unstable," he had argued, when "the public good is disregarded in the conflicts of rival parties." Where factions and parties appear, he said, "measures are too often decided, not according to the rules of justice and the rights of the minor party, but by the superior force of an interested and overbearing majority."[2]

Madison hoped that ratification of the U.S. constitution would lead to a polity free of parties and factions. By the time that he ran for president in 1808, however, political parties had appeared and Madison ran under the banner of what became the modern Democratic Party. Across the continent, some 150 years later, reformers in Washington State hoped to accomplish for their state what the proponents of the U.S. constitution had failed to install in the nation at large – a polity free of the "pernicious" effects of party and faction.[3]

The blanket primary was one of many reform measures designed by Washington voters to permit a purer, less factionalized form of democracy. The indirect initiative was another – the provision utilized by the State Grange to force members of the Washington state legislature to consider a blanket primary. Progressive reformers in 1912 had secured amendments to the state constitution permitting the initiative, referendum, and recall. The indirect initiative provided that a citizen-sponsored measure with sufficient signatures would go directly to state law-makers and "shall take precedence over all other measures…except appropriation bills and shall be either enacted or rejected without change … before the end of such regular session."[4]

Using this provision, members of the State Grange placed the blanket primary before the 1935 meeting of the Washington State Legislature. Initially, the State Senate rejected the initiative, the matter failing by a single vote. Hopeful of circumventing the intent of the initiative without voting against the Grange, the House leadership attempted to refer the initiative to the voters. That tactic failed as well. Sensing the public antipathy toward political parties, the legislators gave in and enacted the proposed measure.[5]

For many years, Washington was the only state in the union to utilize a blanket primary. To many in Washington State, the system represented the dream of a less partisan, factionalized state. Samuel B. Hill, an early representative to the U.S. Congress from Washington State, expressed these hopes when he explained to his colleagues in Washington, D.C.

In my district and in my state is developing an increasing body of citizenship, independent, thinking men and women upon whom the bonds of party regularity rest lightly. They no longer follow blindly in the path of partisan leadership.[6]

Few issues more severely strain the vision of non-partisanship than the matter of legislative redistricting. Through measures such as the blanket primary, public-spirited citizens in

Washington State worked to prevent the development of party machines as cankerous as those found in Eastern cities and states. Yet faced with the mandate to redistrict, state politicians split into factions and engaged in partisan battles as divisive as those the State Grange sought to moderate. The redistricting wars that engaged state politicians in the mid-twentieth century created the severest test between the vision of non-partisanship and the forces of faction and partisanship.

Citizens Act

For state representatives, legislative redistricting is a torturous, agonizing act. It requires representatives to sit in judgment over their colleagues, to decide who shall receive the opportunity to return to the assembly and who shall likely be expelled, consequences rarely made obvious by simple shifts in population. Legislative redistricting also invites partisanship of the most divisive sort, since the process provides bill drafters with the opportunity to manipulate district boundaries in such a manner as to produce significant electoral advantages for their own political party or faction.

In what was for them a perfectly sensible response, members of the Washington State Legislature refused to redraw their own legislative boundaries. The state constitution provided that legislators should redraw district boundaries every ten years, following each census.[7] Since the constitution provided no penalty for inaction, the legislators simply ignored this provision. They recast district lines in 1901, mitigating the pain inflicted upon displaced members by increasing the number of available seats, then in a voluntary fashion declined to do so again for sixty years, ignoring substantial population growth.[8]

What the elected members of the state legislature refused to do, citizens of the state attempted. Pursuing the concept of direct democracy, citizens groups utilized the constitutional provision permitting voter-initiated legislation by filing redistricting initiatives with the Washington Secretary of State. The initiatives redrew the legislative boundaries of the electoral districts from which state senators and representatives were elected.[9] The initiative process was first used in 1930. Friends of the legislature sued, insisting that redistricting was a legislative process not capable of delegation to the people. This was a somewhat disingenuous argument, inasmuch as the legislators had no desire to complete the act. The State Supreme Court upheld the use of the initiative process for redistricting and voters approved the citizen measure at the 1930 election.[10]

State legislators failed again to adjust district boundaries following the 1940 and 1950 census. To do so would have excited partisan battles and divisiveness, and the legislators graciously refused. Spurred by post-war population boom, however, the populations of existing districts shifted considerably. This created unequal representation, a situation as egregious to the advocates of good government as excessive partisanship. The population of existing districts ranged from less than 19,000 in rural southeast Washington to nearly 152,000 in the Seattle suburbs. In response, the State League of Women Voters attempted to repeat the 1930 citizen-led redistricting process. Its leaders, with the help of some legislators, drafted a redistricting bill that adjusted the boundaries of the state's legislative districts and secured a sufficient number of signatures to place the measure before the voters at the 1956 general election.

The State League of Women Voters was a non-partisan group of citizens organized "to promote political responsibility through informed and active participation of citizens in government."[11] They disseminated information on ballot issues and worked to protect the right to vote. They did not endorse candidates for public office. To their supporters, they represented the type of public-spirited association around which the state's reputation for nonpartisanship had formed. To their critics, they were a politically naive, "essentially upper-middle-class" group of do-gooders.[12]

WSA

Senate Majority Leader R.R. "Bob" Grieve spent nights in a locked 'Map Room' devising ways to protect his flock.

"Make Washington's Legislature truly representative of all the people," League members urged in presenting their initiative.[13] League leaders hoped to enlist the cooperation of labor, business, farm interests, and both political parties. They received little direct support; members of the State Grange and Farm Bureau Federation objected to the concentration of representatives in urban Seattle and Tacoma. No groups formally opposed the initiative in the official Voter's Pamphlet, and the measure passed by a vote of 488,121 to 406, 287.

Legislators elected from the old districts assembled in Olympia in January. "They all were afraid of what would happen to them if they had to run in these new districts," observed State Senator R. R. "Bob" Greive. Senate Democrats had selected Greive as their Majority Leader, succeeding Senate Majority Leader Albert D. Rosellini, who had been elected governor in the November election. Greive had come into the state legislature in 1947, defeating an incumbent state senator in the 1946 election when only twenty-seven years old. He represented West Seattle, a working class district spreading to the south and west of downtown, full of pragmatic

Democrats who turned out a more ideological liberal in favor of what Greive called "the vigor and energy of youth."[12] Greive subsisted on little rest, prowling the state capitol from early morning toward midnight during legislative sessions. "Few legislators could match his capacity for work," wrote one observer, a trait that won him a succession of leadership posts.[13]

Greive loved politics. "I'm not saying that it's impossible for a person to be motivated just by public service," he reflected at the end of his career. "I think a person is motivated more by the love of battle, and the power and importance." He had little use for good government groups. "A pain in the neck," he said. "Those people pretend that they've got lofty motives that really don't exist."[14]

The legislature could amend a voter-approved initiative, and Grieve set out to do just that. Democrats controlled the state House and Senate, as well as the governorship, but the state constitution required a two-thirds majority to alter an initiative. He needed Republican votes to change the League's redistricting plan. "Nobody thought we could do it." Greive confessed.[15] He hired a staff to work out the details, met with legislators individually, and provided comfort by loosening the population standards. The League initiative had created districts whose populations from large to small varied by a ratio of about two-to-one. In an effort to lessen the pain of realignment, the League's initiative increased the number of districts from 46 to 49. Grieve retained the enlarged legislature and widened the population spread to more than four-to-one.[16] The courts had not yet imposed strict population standards on legislative redistricting. In the absence of specific standards, line-drawers could be as strict or lenient as they chose to be.

Greive's bill passed the Senate and House with the required majorities; the dissenters coming from urban areas due representation under the initiative. Democratic governor Albert Rosellini allowed the bill to become law without his signature. The leadership of the League of Women Voters appealed to the state courts, insisting that Greive's bill had effectively repealed their initiative. The state constitution allowed the legislature to amend a recently-passed initiative with a two-third's vote, but not repeal one. By a 5 to 4 vote, the justices of the State Supreme Court upheld Greive's approach.[17] His acumen in amending the League's initiative won him the title of "Mr. Redistricting" around the state capital, as well as the leading role as his party's principal representative in future redistricting battles.[18]

Following the 1960 census, the League of Women Voters prepared another redistricting initiative, which they placed on the 1962 general election ballot. While members of their redistricting committee drew the new districts with more care, their renewed effort encountered fresh complications. Rural interests, fearful of the transfer of legislative power to urban districts, openly opposed the initiative. They placed their objections in the state Voters Pamphlet. "One county already has 30% of both houses of the Legislature," they complained. The proposed initiative "would increase this lopsided representation. Historically, lopsided government has been bad government for all."[19]

Rural interests favored a "little federal plan," in which each county would be granted at least one state senator. To do this, they needed to amend the state constitution and expand the number of legislative districts, an act that required a two-thirds vote in both houses of the state legislature. Leaders of organizations like the Washington State Grange reasoned that a malapportioned legislature would be more likely to approve such an amendment than a reapportioned one dominated by urban representatives. They were not opposed to the "good government" impulse that motivated redistricting in general, so long as they were given time to revise the criteria under which it would occur. The open split among "good government" groups, joined with the memory of the overridden 1956 initiative, undercut voter support for the 1962 redistricting plan.

The second complication was more monumental. In March, 1962, the U.S. Supreme Court issued their decision in the redistricting case Baker v. Carr. Prior to that time, federal courts had refused to provide remedies for citizens seeking judicial involvement in legislative redistricting. Most previously in Colegrove v. Green (1946), the justices of the Supreme Court refused to breach the separation of powers between judicial and legislative branches and enter what they called "this political thicket," urging aggrieved voters to seek solutions through their state governments.[144] The court's suggested solution was clearly absurd, inasmuch as the injured parties were grossly underrepresented in local assemblies. Baker was a resident of Tennessee, where the legislature had not redrawn district lines since 1900. His vote was diluted by a factor of ten by comparison to the representation afforded voters in the smallest rural districts of Tennessee.

In Baker v. Carr, the Supreme Court reversed its previous stand.[20] It provided no guidelines for redistricting, but merely instructed the federal district court serving Tennessee to act on Baker's complaint. Within months, an attorney from an underrepresented district in Washington State filed a suit challenging that state's congressional and state legislative districts. Rather than name himself as the plaintiff in the suit, he enlisted a local justice of the peace, James Thigpen. The attorney, M. L. Borawick, was a graduate of Columbia Law School and president of the South King County Bar Association.[21] He filed the case before a three judge federal court under the title Thigpen v. Myers, the latter being the Washington Secretary of State in charge of elections.[22]

Borawick wanted the three judge panel to issue a restraining order preventing any further elections under the current electoral districts. This the justices refused to do. Noting that the League of Women Voters had prepared a redistricting initiative, which the voters would consider at the November 6, 1962, general election, the court postponed any action until the election was held.

Voters rejected the League's initiative by a margin of 441,085 to 396,419. This confounded observers who believed that the 1962 initiative would resolve the court case. As promised, the court reconvened. One member of the three-judge panel, William T. Beeks, heard the suit, issuing his opinion on December 13, 1962. Beeks ruled that the state legislative districts established by the 1957 redistricting act were invidiously discriminatory. (He dismissed that part of the suit dealing with the state's seven congressional districts.) He deferred any judicial remedy, however, pending the regular meeting of the state legislature due to commence less then one month later, on January 14, 1963. Significantly, Beeks did not instruct the legislature to achieve perfect equality in district populations, so long as discrepancies could be justified by objective criteria such as geography or group voting strength. "Redistricting should be accomplished by the body constitutionally responsible therefore," he said, but issued a warning designed to motivate the state legislature to fulfill its constitutional responsibilities.

If it fails, we, ever conscious of our oath to uphold the Constitution of the United States, will unhesitatingly take appropriate action to correct the inequity.[23]

Factions Emerge

If Washington had been a state with strong political parties, the task of legislative redistricting might have been relatively easy. Following the 1962 general election, Democrats controlled the state House of Representatives 51 to 48 and the state Senate 32 to 17. The incumbent governor, Democrat Albert Rosellini, was completing his second term. Bob Grieve, Democratic leader of the State Senate, had acquired considerable experience with redistricting. The exercise of party discipline in each House along with the governor's signature would have completed the process. But the state did not possess strong political parties. The impulse toward good government had produced citizen initiatives and weak political parties. Confronted by a judicial mandate to redistrict, the legislators splintered in one of the most dramatic displays of factionalism in the state's political history.

The factions emerged in the State House of Representatives. Republican leaders blamed their 48-member minority status on Greive's 1957 redistricting bill. "We got only forty-eight in '63 because of Greive's redistricting," Representative Joel Pritchard, the chief strategist for a group of young Republican legislators explained. Joel Pritchard, along with his brother Frank, were part of a politically active group of young Republicans known as the "new breed."[149] Both worked in a series of Seattle campaigns until Joel, at the age of thirty-three, had won election to the state House of Representatives from the Queen Anne-Magnolia district in which he had been raised.

In the state legislature, Pritchard teamed up with Daniel J. Evans, who had arrived as a first time legislator after the 1956 election, and Slade Gorton, who had arrived with Pritchard in 1958. Evans, with a degree in civil engineering from the University of Washington, was the charismatic leader of the group, elected as the House minority leader in 1960. The only non-Seattle native among the three, Gorton had grown up in Evanston, Illinois, and graduated from Dartmouth College and Columbia University Law School. He had moved to Seattle, become active in local politics, and was admitted to the state bar in 1953.

Gorton emerged as the group's leader for redistricting, the antithesis to Bob Greive. "Greive was the master of redistricting," Pritchard observed. "He was Machiavelli on redistricting. He was too smart for everybody in that respect, until he ran into Gorton. Gorton ran our redistricting and he knew every jot, diddle, corner, whatever it was."[24] Ironically, Gorton was elected to the state legislature as a result of a Republican district created in Greive's 1957 bill.

WSA

GOP House leaders Mary Ellen McCaffree, Governor Dan Evans, Speaker Pro Tem Tom Copeland and Majority Leader Slade Gorton study options. Gorton stalled the matter into the State Supreme Court so Republicans could get a fairer shake.

The triumvirate were part of a larger group of young Republicans anxious to capture control of the state government, beginning with the State House of Representatives. They included Charles P. Moriarty, state senator from Queen Anne and Magnolia; Mary Ellen McCaffree, state representative from Seattle's university district and a leader in the state League of Women Voters, and Thomas L. Copeland, state representative from the Walla Walla area in Eastern Washington. The group confronted a well-established majority Democratic Party and a relatively disorganized Republican old guard. Well-educated, civic-minded and highly competitive/ politically ambitious, many found themselves closer to the policies of the Democratic Party than those of the business-oriented conservatives in their own. Many won election from legislative districts in Seattle at a time when residents of that city – or at least the more affluent northern sections – were still willing to vote for progressive Republicans.

The new Republican leaders were convinced that redistricting had diluted their party's strength. In the 1962 election, Republican candidates for the state House of Representatives in the aggregative had outpolled Democratic candidates by a margin of 53 percent to 47 percent. Candidates do not run in the state at large, however; they run in districts. Republicans brandished this fact, along with their 48 to 51 member minority status in the House, as evidence that Greive's 1957 redistricting bill was biased in favor of Democratic candidates. The Republican "new breed" was deeply suspicious of what Greive had done in 1957 and fearful of what he might do to them again. "With a Democratic governor and a Democratic House and Senate, we'd be redistricted right out into the street," Pritchard predicted.[25]

Analysis of statewide election returns suggests some basis for Republican suspicions, at least in the state House of Representatives. Republican representation lagged 7 percent behind the party's cumulative statewide totals in the three elections since enactment of the Greive redistricting bill. Republicans had increased their numbers in the 99-member House from 33 to 40 to 48 members, but their actual numbers remained below the proportion of their cumulative statewide total.[26] Further analysis suggests, however, that a more perfect redistricting bill may not have helped the Republican party in that respect. In fact, population readjustments in legislative districts, to the effect that they had any effect at all, might have worked to the advantage of the Democratic members.

This was a strange phenomenon and one not much noticed by legislators at that time. Population inequities in legislative districts were extreme, especially after the 1960 census. Yet the inequities, where they did balance each other out, disenfranchised Democrats rather than Republicans. Were the votes of legislators weighted on the basis of their district populations, the party balance in the 1959 House and Senate would have changed not at all. In the 1961 session, Democrats would have gained two votes in the House and one vote in the Senate. In the 1963 session, where Republicans felt they should have controlled the House based on total votes cast, a rearrangement of members based solely on population would have decreased their numbers. Weighted populations in 1963 would have produced two additional Democrats in the House for a 53 to 46 split, while Senate Democrats would have gained one vote.[27]

Analysis additionally suggests that the misalignment of legislative districts based on population disparities had limited effect on the most controversial issues placed before the legislature. In the 1959 and 1961 sessions, legislators divided over public versus private electric power provision, the right of public employees to join labor unions and strike, and reform of the state's antiquated state liquor control board. The outcome of three contentious votes on these issues would not have changed significantly had the votes of members been weighted so as to account for the number of people they represented.[28]

In opposing the 1962 League of Women Voters redistricting initiative, rural interests argued that the plan would not improve the state's "comparative position on representation."[29] The statement, while self-serving, contains an element of truth. Part of the explanation for this strange result may have been due to the possibility that, when confronted with redistricting, legislators were as if not more interested in protecting incumbents than in advancing the position of the dominant political party.

This did not lessen Republican concern. As a growing minority, they felt disenfranchised by Greive's 1957 legislative redistricting act and extremely vulnerable by the prospect of a new one.

During the 1961 legislative session, conservative Democrats had joined with the Republican minority in an attempt to limit the authority of public electric power utilities. In a state containing numerous government-sponsored hydroelectric power facilities such as the massive Grand Coulee dam, electric power issues provided one of the most controversial issues afflicting state politics. Power issues divided the state along ideological, sectional, and party lines. The particular issue in this case concerned attempts by a Thurston County public electric utility to condemn facilities owned by Puget Sound Power and Light Company, a privately owned company. Using their governmental powers, managers of public utilities could seize the assets of private utilities and convert them to public ownership. Opponents of public ownership viewed seizures as rampant socialism and prepared legislation that granted local residents the "right to vote" on such actions.

Allied with the Republican minority, private power Democrats in the House Public Utility Committee approved "right to vote" legislation and sent it to the floor of the House of Representatives. Conservative Democrats believed that they had the votes, along with Republican help, to pass such the bill. The Democratic Speaker of the House, John L. O'Brien, was determined that they should not. O'Brien was a tough, hard-boiled Democrat who had served in the state House of Representatives since 1939, representing a working class district in southeast Seattle. His colleagues had selected him as Speaker of the House in 1955. With Bob Greive and Governor Albert Rosellini, he formed the triumvirate of Democratic power that dominated state politics in the late 1950s.

Relying upon his powers as Speaker, O'Brien utilized a number of rules to prevent consideration of the bill. So long as the proponents of the bill seemed to possess a majority, O'Brien alternatively entertained amendments and adjourned the House. The legislative battle lasted four days, until O'Brien and the Democratic leadership assembled the 50 votes necessary to refer the bill to the House Rules Committee from which it never emerged. The battle was divisive, reappearing at the 1962 state Democratic convention, which O'Brien chaired. Dissidents from O'Brien's Democratic party walked out of the convention and resolved to never support him for the Speaker's position again.[30]

Between the 1962 general election and the meeting of the legislature in January, the elected members of the House of Representatives met in party caucuses to select their leaders. The Republican legislators met and reelected Dan Evans as their minority leader. The Democrats met and reelected Speaker O'Brien. Without alerting O'Brien, a small group of dissident Democrats met with the Republican leadership and prepared a plan to depose the incumbent Speaker.

The most outspoken dissidents were William S. Day and Robert A. Perry. Day, a large man with a gregarious personality, was a two-term legislator from Spokane where he worked as a chiropractor. Perry, who like Day had served two terms in the state legislature, was charming and mysterious. Legislators knew little about his background. A product of various union battles, Perry had remained a Democrat but grown more conservative, leading the fight on behalf of private power in the 1961 session. The other dissidents included Margaret Hurley, a Spokane school teacher; Chet King, a Grays Harbor boom man and labor representative; Dick J. Kink, a Bellingham fisherman; and W.L. "Bill" McCormick, a Spokane labor union representative.

Meetings between the Democratic dissidents and Republican leadership were a closely-guarded secret. Most House Republicans were not told about the meetings until the morning that the legislature met. O'Brien failed to gauge the intent of the dissidents. Despite the divisions within the Democratic caucus, he fully expected to become Speaker and prepared his committee assignments.

The Speaker is elected by majority vote of the House members, generally along party lines, in the first few hours of the legislative session. The majority party votes for its nominee; the minority votes for its leader. Yet on the first ballot, six Democrats withheld their votes from O'Brien, voting instead for William Day. With the Republicans voting for Evans, this created a deadlock. O'Brien did not realize the extent of his situation until the third ballot, when he heard Evans vote for Day. All 48 Republicans joined nine dissident Democrats to elect Day as the House Speaker. The Democrats divided; a coalition government formed.

O'Brien and the regular Democratic leadership, reduced to a 42-member minority, fought to regain control for five days. They appealed to Evans; they appealed to Day. They obstructed the coalition's efforts to approve committee appointments. On Saturday, January 19, the coalition shouted down O'Brien's forces and completed the organization of the House. As compensation for Republican participation, Day appointed Slade Gorton as chair of the House committee in charge of redistricting.

The Legislature Deadlocks

By controlling the House redistricting machinery, the Republicans ensured that they would be a party to any redistricting bill to emerge from the legislature. "Our deal with the seven Democrats was that they could have their district pretty much the way they wanted it," explained Joel Pritchard. "Then we would go ahead and do the rest of the state."[31]

This created an extraordinary challenge for Bob Greive, operating the counterbalancing redistricting machinery from his position in the Senate. Senate Democrats were independent and difficult to lead. Before the 1963 legislative session, members of his Democratic caucus attempted to deny him the Majority Leader's post, failing by only a few votes. Wilbur Hallauer, an cerebral fruit farmer from rural Okanogan County, found Greive too political. Michael Gallagher, a stalwart Democrat from north Seattle with twenty years experience in the legislature, worked quietly with Governor Rosellini to make sure that Greive did not compromise too much. By dealing with the Republicans, Greive risked the possibility that he would lose control of his own caucus.

Legislative strategy played a substantial role in the redistricting efforts that followed. Whichever side moved its bill first incurred a substantial risk, a boomerang effect created by the legislative rules. An originating bill entering the opposite chamber could be stripped of all but its title, where the opposition could substitute its own plan. The opposing plan would return to the originating chamber, subject to a sudden up-or-down vote, without the opportunity for delay so often necessary to assemble one's forces. In a Gaston and Alphonse display, Grieve wanted Gorton to go first. Gorton insisted that Greive begin.

The dance of legislation was further complicated by the continuing desire of the State Grange to create a "little federal plan" for the Washington State Legislature. The principal advocate for this approach, Republican Representative Donald W. Moos, proposed an ingenious plan. Moos was well-liked wheat and cattle ranger from the small rural community of Edwall in Eastern Washington. Working with Gorton, Moos devised a constitutional amendment ensuring that the smallest districts in the state would be rural ones, set at the lowest permissible population. To pass, the amendment needed the support of two-thirds of the members of both Houses and approval by the voters at the 1964 general election. Although the amendment provided additional representation by allowing the number of legislative districts to grow from 49 to 52, it did not satisfy the State Grange, whose leaders continued to insist on a minimum of one Senator from each county.[32]

As a condition for his support, Greive inserted a clause tying the amendment to the fate of redistricting. If an implementing redistricting bill failed to pass, the amendment would die even if the legislators approved the Moos plan.

Substantial ambiguity affected expectations regarding the reaction of the courts should the legislature fail to redistrict. Some thought that the court might abolish the old legislative districts, thereby forcing all candidates for the state legislature to run in at-large statewide. To incumbent legislators, this was a nightmare scenario and one sure to produce calls for a special legislative session devoted to redistricting. Some, including Slade Gorton, believed that the court might appoint a Master to prepare its own redistricting plan. This appealed to Republican leaders, who thought they might get a better deal at the hands of a court Master affixed on population rather than from Bob Greive. A few suspected that the judges were bluffing.

Compounding these expectations was additional ambiguity regarding population standards. The courts had proclaimed their support for the "one person, one vote" standard, but provided no guidance as to what this meant in practice. Legislators commonly assumed that courts would approve districts that varied in population by as much as 1.5-to-one, but no one was sure. It could be more; it might be less.

All of these factors, joined with the traditional legislative distaste for redistricting, created a situation in which legislators remained reluctant to compromise. Circumstances favored no redistricting at all; which is was the state law-makers did during the 1963 legislative session.

Activity occurred, but it ultimately proved pointless. On March 6 and 25, the House coalition held as Representative Gorton presented redistricting bills and sent them to the State Senate with the help of Democratic dissidents. As expected, Greive stripped Gorton's bill of all but its title and inserted his own. Due to divisions within the Democratic caucus, Greive lost two floor votes before he ultimately prevailed. With more than fifty Representatives watching from the wings of the Senate floor, Greive sent his bill back to the House on March 30. The following evening, House members considered Greive's bill. Greive thought he had wooed a sufficient number of dissident Democrats and wavering Republicans to prevail. The Republican leadership believed that the coalition would hold, although they arranged with state party officials to barrage wavering Republicans with telegrams and telephone calls from supporters back home.

The coalition prevailed. Legislators from both parties had met with Greive and suggested alterations to their districts, implying that they could support such changes. Yet they were not always willing to vote for the whole bill that emerged. Later that night in the Speaker's office, Greive assailed the recalcitrant legislators. "I don't mind telling you, I've been double crossed. Some of the people I've been dealing with haven't kept their word." He said he was fed up with redistricting.[32]

Members of the Senate Democratic caucus met on Monday morning, April 1, where a majority decided to end the redistricting effort. "There have been too many concessions made already to allow us to reach a solution in a few days," said Senator Nat Washington, a Democrat from Grant and Kittitas counties. "Any plan would just be too political … my own district would be better served by sending it to the court."[33]

With help from Republicans and a few party defections, Greive secured sufficient support to launch conference committee negotiations between the House and Senate. While he possessed sufficient support to begin talks, however, he was powerless to conclude them. Greive and

Gorton negotiated for four days; Gallagher, Perry, and two other conferees watched over them. The group produced a patchwork compromise incapable of attracting a majority of Greive's own caucus. By a single vote, Senate Democrats meeting in caucus decided to reject the redistricting compromise that Greive brought them. Shortly thereafter, the regular House Democrats did the same by an equally-divided vote of 23 to 20.

Faced with a court mandate to redistrict, majority party Democrats splintered in the 1963 legislative session. House dissidents broke from old-line Democrats and formed a coalition government with Republicans. Anti-Greive Democrats in the Senate opposed pro-Greive Democrats. Anti-redistricting Democrats in the House opposed pro-redistricting Democrats. On the minority side, Senate Republicans splintered. Only the House minority, led by the "new breed" Republicans, remained cohesive.

Alone among the groups, the House Republicans alone possessed a substantial motive for redistricting. Their leaders believed that a fair redistricting bill would give them a chance to capture control of the House, where they were only two members short of a majority, and in turn, provide a launching platform from which they might win the governorship and other state offices. Democrats, on the other hand, had little motivation to redistrict. They confronted a vague court mandate, unspecific in its consequences. This situation was quite unlike the one in 1957, when failure to unify meant that legislators would have to run in the following election within the districts created by the League of Women Voters initiative.

In the final hours of the legislative session, Representative Moos brought his constitutional amendment to the floor of the state House of Representatives on behalf of the state Grange—the organization partially responsible for the system of weak political parties that characterized the state. In what was largely a tribute to the likable, soft-spoken Moos, the amendment received the necessary two-thirds majority. It received the vote of every Republican, all of the Democratic dissidents, and a sufficient number of rural Democrats. Coalition leader William S. Day, in one of his last acts as Speaker of the House, cast the decisive vote.

The vote was largely symbolic, since the compromise amendment, which the Senate had approved earlier, contained the conditional cause tying it to redistricting. To go before the people, the legislators needed to pass a redistricting bill.[34] In the interim, the U.S. Supreme Court would declare the concept of geographic representation in state legislatures to be unconstitutional.

The Moos amendment passed, nonetheless, a testimony to the very personal nature of redistricting legislation. People liked Moos; they voted for his bill. Conversely, they voted against redistricting bills that threatened to remove them or their friends from the legislature. "The Legislature's all shot through with friendships," Greive explained. "Even if I didn't happen to need it," he said, reflecting on the factors that prompted legislators to support or oppose various plans, "my seatmate or my best buddy might."[35] In Washington State politics, friendships and factions created stronger bonds of attraction than parties.

The Courts Pause

M. L. Borawick, acting on behalf of his client James Thigpen, asked the court to declare the existing Washington State legislative districts to be unconstitutional. Such a declaration, he reasoned, would force the state to confront the necessity of an at-large election for all members of the state legislature, which the suggested declaration would not preclude. This unpalatable possibility, he concluded, would force the governor to call a special legislative session and the legislators would complete the redistricting task. Both Borawick and Lyle Iverson, the attorney appearing on behalf of the state, agreed that the court should not take on the politically-charged assignment of drawing the districts itself. The court met to hear these arguments three weeks after the legislature adjourned and Judge Beeks issued his oral opinion on May 3, 1963.

Given his earlier mandate to the legislature, Judge Beeks had anticipated that the law-makers would complete the redistricting task during their regular legislative session. He and his law clerk apparently did not believe that they would need to fashion a post-session remedy.[163] "Redistricting is primarily a political act to be performed by the legislative branch of our government," Beeks affirmed in his oral opinion.[36] He declared the 1957 redistricting act to be unconstitutional and forbid the state from conducting any further elections under it. His declaration did not prohibit the state from conducting at-large elections for the House and Senate.

Governor Rosellini did not want to convene a special session of the state legislature. The legislative factions, he believed, were hopelessly deadlocked. "I have no indication at this time to believe," he stated in an affidavit to the court, "that another special session of the legislature called prior to the next general election would be able to enact a constitutionally valid redistricting statute."[37] A special session, moreover, would provide his opponents with an opportunity to investigate his administration and engage in legislative mischief. Rosellini was preparing to run for a third term. Dan Evans, the House Republican leader, was preparing to run against him. A special session would provide Republicans with a pulpit for their campaign. Rosellini could call the legislators to Olympia, but he could not send them home. Although Gorton and Greive prepared extensively for a special legislative session, the governor steadfastly refused to call one.

Rosellini and his Democratic supporters wanted to put one more election between themselves and redistricting. Senator Robert C. Bailey, head of the Senate Democratic caucus and not always a Greive supporter, told Judge Beeks in a court affidavit that "the failure of the Washington State Legislature to pass a legislative reapportionment act ... was the result of an unprecedented political deadlock."[38] A new election, he insisted, would change the composition of the legislature and permit the enactment of an appropriate bill.

State Attorney General John J. O'Connell, a Tacoma Democrat, along with the Seattle attorney appointed to argue the state's case, Lyle Iverson, devised a series of strategies that effectively delayed implementation of the judicial declaration. They appealed Thigpen v. Meyers to the U.S. Supreme Court. They sought an order staying the district court ruling. When the Supreme Court returned Thigpen v. Meyers to Washington State with a simple unsigned order, upholding the district court, O'Connell employed the customary 25 day waiting period before new orders became effective. When Supreme Court Justice William O. Douglas, who kept a home in Washington state, issued an order shortening the waiting period, O'Connell petitioned the district court to allow additional filings for elections under the old districts. Not until July 16, 1964, fifteen months after the legislature adjourned, did the three-judge panel reconvene. O'Connell personally appeared before the judges and pleaded for one more election under the old, unconstitutional districts. A short delay in due process, he insisted, would be preferable to the chaos created by any revision of the electoral process so close to the 1964 primary and general elections.

The federal judges were clearly frustrated by the inaction of the state government. Said Beeks:

> More than two years have now expired since the date of the original hearing without any accomplishment and the woes of reapportionment are now still upon us. Like an echo from the past, we are again assured that the 1965 Legislature will lawfully reapportion itself it we will stay the effect of our decree.[39]

The judges threatened to impose a system of weighted voting on the 1965 legislature, apportioning the votes of members on the basis of their district populations. O'Connell objected. On October 5, one month before the 1964 general election, the judges announced their remedy. They decreed that the state legislature scheduled to assemble in January of the following year make redistricting its first order of business. In other words, the legislators could pass no other bills until they completed the redistricting process.

Earlier that year, the U.S. Supreme Court had clarified the standards for redistricting by issuing its decision in Reynolds v Sims. The Supreme Court justices prescribed strict population standards for state legislative districts. "Legislators represent people," wrote Chief Justice Earl Warren, "not trees or acres."[40] State officials could not emulate the U.S. Senate by creating one house apportioned on some basis other than population – not without violating the equal protection clause of the U.S. constitution. The decision effectively sunk any hope among rural interests for a state constitutional amendment approving their "little federal plan." Any redistricting bill enacted in Washington would need to produce districts with relatively equal populations for both houses of the state legislature.

A Legislative Blitzkrieg

Democratic state leaders believed that they could pass a redistricting bill if they won large majorities in the Washington state legislature. The 1964 general election fulfilled their premise. Enthused by an election ballot headed by then-popular Lyndon B. Johnson running against conservative presidential candidate Barry Goldwater, Washington State Democrats acceded to a 60 to 39 vote majority in the state House of Representatives. Regular Democrats commanded a clear majority, even though all six of the original dissidents won reelection. In the State Senate, Democrats retained their 32 to 17 member margin of control.

One great exception to the nation-wide Republican debacle was the state's new governor elect, Daniel J. Evans. Running 17 points ahead of the Goldwater ticket, Evans defeated incumbent Albert Rosellini. Evans' first legislative priority was redistricting. Yet he might never see a redistricting bill. The state constitution provided that the outgoing governor serve during the first three days of the new legislative session. If the Democrat-dominated legislature, which convened on Monday, January 11, could pass a redistricting bill before noon Wednesday, January 13, outgoing governor Rosellini would sign it. Rejecting requests for compromise, Greive prepared to do just that.

Greive arrived in Olympia with a new redistricting bill and moved it through the Senate in a session that lasted past midnight on the first day. In the pre-legislative Senate caucus, his Democratic opponents had made a serious bid to deny him the post of Majority Leader. They had failed by four votes, leaving him at least temporarily without a working majority. When the legislature convened, he reassembled the Senators and produced a 28 vote majority for the redistricting bill.

Attention turned now to the House. So as to prevent further division, Representative John O'Brien had declined to seek the speaker ship. Day, Perry and the other dissidents were welcomed back into the House Democratic caucus. Members of the caucus calmly chose Robert M. Schaefer, a three-term legislator and Vancouver attorney, as the Speaker. Without a working majority in the House of Representatives, Republicans could do little but wait and hope that the Democrats would divide. Talk of compromise was useless while what they called the legislative blitz was on.

Representative Gorton examined the Senate bill and predicted that it would make Republican control of the legislature impossible even in landslide years. In Tacoma, for example, where Republicans commonly controlled two of the five districts and 40 percent of the vote, Greive had drawn the district lines so adroitly that Democrats were likely to win all five. Gorton's aide analyzed the bill and announced that it would probably meet the constitutional requirements of the courts. Greive and his aides had carefully distributed the districts so as to meet the population standards thought to be in effect. "The Democrats usually come up with the votes when they are needed," Representative Pritchard added glumly.[41]

In extreme secrecy, Republicans prepared their final defense, to be used if all else failed. They would inaugurate Evans prematurely. The statute providing for gubernatorial succession provided that the governor be sworn in on Wednesday, in the legislative chambers. It did not specific a time. Democrats expected the succession to occur at noon.

Republicans devised a strategy for delaying a final vote on the redistricting bill until late Tuesday night. They were confident they could execute such a delay. At one minute past midnight, governor-elect Evans would step into the gallery of whichever House was considering the redistricting bill and be sworn in as governor. Evans and his advisers had contacted a sympathetic State Supreme Court Justice who was prepared to perform the ceremony. The minority leader of that House would then read a prepared statement, advising the legislators of Evan's presence and asking the Democrats to forget their redistricting bill and adjourn. The Democrats might balk at this, and Washington State would have two governors for twelve hours, likely one with a redistricting bill and the other in the state courts trying to take it away from him.

It would have been an exciting event, but it never occurred. Meeting in caucus, House Democrats could not produce the 50 votes needed to pass Greive's bill. At best, the leadership counted 47 or 48 votes within their 60 vote majority. Sometimes they counted as few as 45. The dissident Democrats, remembering the commitment they had made to the Republican minority two years earlier, continued to press for a negotiated compromise. Some representatives genuinely suffered under the new plan. One had personal issues with Senator Greive. Others felt intense pressure from rural and industrial interests. Democratic leaders called in union lobbyists to counter that influence, without effect. At 10 pm on Tuesday evening, House Democrats went into caucus for the third and final time. They were still at least two votes short. Democrats broke through the caucus doors, through the crowd of Republican legislators waiting outside, and voted to adjourn for the night. Republicans cheerfully concurred.

Confrontation and Compromise

With Dan Evans in the governor's chair, the Democratic majorities in the state legislature could not enact a redistricting bill of their own choosing. If they did, the governor would veto it, which the Republican minorities could sustain. Logically, the leaders of both parties would have met, formulated a compromise and fulfilled the judicial mandate. Politics, nonetheless, has its own logic and this did not occur. Legislative factions drafted bills that could not command majorities and confronted other factions with them. When this strategy failed, legislators sought to create simple majorities by combining factions in creative ways.

A broad compromise, involving all parties and most factions, would have commanded a large majority. As many political scientists have noted, however, large majorities are more unstable than small ones.[42] The simple explanation for this phenomenon can be found in the observation that the spoils of victory are more easily divided among a small group of winners than one consisting of many participants. In a small majority, just large enough to prevail, each individual receives the largest possible share. As a consequence, the legislative majorities for redistricting created in the Washington State House and Senate were small, producing deep divides and substantial bitterness.

At first, the factions refused to compromise. Speaker Schaeffer appointed a youthful second-term Democrat to head the House redistricting committee. Representative Gary Grant, a Boeing Aircraft Company supervisor from south Bellevue, proceeded with the help of other young Democrats to draft a House redistricting bill. The normally soft-spoken Republican Representative Donald Moos lost his temper and bluntly told Grant:

Talk all you want, but don't kid yourself that you are writing the redistricting bill. The subject is too important to waste on a bunch of freshman and third-stringers. When this bill finally is written it's going to be written by a lot of wheeling-dealing senators – not you. And they don't know you either, so guess whose blood is going to come rolling out from under the conference door.[43]

Working with the House Democratic leadership, Senator Greive revived the bill that he had presented at the opening of the legislature. It passed the House and Senate. When Governor Evans vetoed it, the Democrats sent him another. The bill did not satisfy all of the Democrats and one adroitly observed that the Senate leadership would not have enough votes to pass it "if we didn't know he was going to veto it."[44]

Greive proposed that the legislature adopt a redistricting act through use of the referendum provision of the state constitution. A referendum passed by the legislature and referred to the people for approval did not require the signature of the governor. In that manner, Greive explained, his party could avoid a veto. Such an act would not appear before the voters until

1966, however, necessitating another legislative election under the old districts. The court would never allow another such an event, the legislators surmised, discouraging support for that strategy.[45]

Governor Evans, utilizing a plan prepared by Representatives Gorton and Mary Ellen McCaffree, proposed his own redistricting bill. Evans and Gorton sought votes from dissuaded Democrats, without success.

In one amusing incident, newly-elected Senator Robert Charette of Aberdeen, a Democrat whose district essentially disappeared under a redistricting plan being considered in the Senate, produced a copy of the Republican Governor's plan and proposed to substitute it for the current bill. He accused fellow Democrats of placing self-interest above party loyalty. Since that was how the game was played, he said, he was presenting the bill that "best takes care of me." Accusations normally confined to the Democratic caucus spilled onto the Senate floor. "As long as the Democratic party has been sold a bill of goods," Charette continued, "we might as well go all the way with Dan." Senator John T. McCutcheon, a long-term representative from Pierce County and head of the Senate redistricting committee, turned to the back of the chamber and told the rebellious Senators that he "wasn't going to take that from you back there."[46] When McCutcheon moved to table the governor's bill, angry Democrats broke with their Senate leadership and voted to keep the measure alive. With the help of all of the Republicans, the governor's bill remained before the Senate until the Democratic leadership managed to restore order and calm the rebellious crew.

Even the Republican House minority splintered. In early February, Republican Representative Thomas Copeland began secret negotiations with Senator Greive and ex-Speaker Day in a downtown Olympia hotel room. Ostensibly a member of the "new breed," Copeland undercut his party leadership by conducting negotiations. Representative Moos and three other House leaders sternly confronted Copeland and told him that he faced a caucus revolt if he continued the talks. Copeland reluctantly withdrew.

Clearly, some sort of a compromise was needed to pass a redistricting bill. But between whom and how? House Democrats wanted to form a conference committee, a formal procedure utilized to resolve differences between House and Senate bills. Being a legislative minority, Republicans would hold only two seats on a six-person conference. They naturally objected, instead favoring negotiations between an equal number of Republicans and Democrats in the governor's office.

To many legislators, redistricting provided an opportunity to improve their chances for reelection, by adding favorable precincts or at least not making their districts worse. This approach worked well for majority party Democrats. By protecting incumbents – including Republicans – they solidified their opportunity to remain in the majority. The Republican leadership faced a very different challenge. As the leaders of a legislative minority, Gorton and Evans needed to create a larger number of competitive districts in which Republican challengers had an opportunity to win. That required the creation of swing districts with no party possessing a clear advantage, the antithesis of incumbent protection.

Disputes accorded Seattle's 32nd district provide a good illustration of the challenges involved. The district, which ran from the Scandinavian community of Ballard through the Freemont neighborhood to the University of Washington, was represented by Mary Ellen McCaffree, a Republican, and Wesley Ullman, a Democrat. Prior to her election, McCaffree had helped draft the League of Women Voters' redistricting initiative; her basement served as the drafting room for the Republican redistricting work between the 1963 and 1965 legislative sessions. Ullman would later become the Mayor of Seattle. The district was too small – only 45,000 residents according to the 1960 census, 12,000 residents short of the target size.[47]

Adding people to the east side of the district, from the areas near Lake Washington, made the district more Republican. More people from the west favored the Democratic party. As few as three precincts one way or the other could prove decisive in a close election. Gorton wanted to maintain a swing district that could produce Republicans; Greive wanted to protect Ullman's opportunities for reelection. (The Senate seat flipped back and forth between the parties and was then held by a one-term Republican, Seattle attorney Jack England.) On such issues redistricting negotiations floundered, compounded by the manner in which changes in one district affected the make-up of adjacent ones.

On February 16, five weeks into the legislative session, seven Democratic leaders including Greive, Schaefer, and O'Brien marched out of the Speaker's chambers to the governor's office to demand conference negotiations. Waiting for them in the governor's office were Evans and Gorton and five Republican legislative leaders. Negotiations commenced and continued for three days. Schaefer and O'Brien became increasingly convinced that Greive was sacrificing House seats in order to protect Democratic Senators. Greive dismissed the allegations. House members and Senators ran in the same districts, he said, so "this is your own senator you are protecting."[44] House leaders were unconvinced and withdrew from the negotiations.

Negotiations moved to the Senate, where Greive announced that he was prepared to resolve the remaining issues. In one crucial area, he would allow Republicans to add three favorable precincts to the 32nd district. In exchange, he wanted to add a few more Democratic precincts to the 31st. The latter, a district south of Seattle, was represented by Democratic Senator Gordon Herr and two Democratic representatives, C. G. Witherbee and Georgette Valle. Greive also asked that the 32nd be divided into sub districts for the purpose of electing its two representatives, a western half that would protect Wes Ullman and and Gorton was furious when he learned of these demands.

The 31st district included suburban areas whose population growth promised to make the district more competitive with time; division of the 32nd removed the Republican opportunity to unseat the House Democratic incumbent. These were exactly the sort of opportunities that Republicans needed to win control of the House. Senate Republicans pressed Gorton's position, but without effect. A more content minority, Senate Republicans were not anxious to fight a death-battle over what they perceived to be Democratic districts. Unresponsive to the nuances of Gorton's quest for competitive contests, they agreed to the changes.

Needing to force a quick vote before the fragile agreement collapsed, Greive selected House Bill 196 – the redistricting bill previously prepared by Democratic Representative Gary Grant. He substituted the compromise plan for the entire bill and presented it to the Senate. In their caucus, the Republicans agreed to support the bill. Rather than appear too anxious, they decided to split their votes 10 to 7. Reprehensive Gorton assigned the seven "nays."

On the Senate floor, opponents of the compromise resumed their attacks. These were all Democrats, members of Greive's majority, allied with House leaders who wanted to move the negotiations into a conference committee. Greive held the support of two-thirds of the members of his 32-member Senate Democratic caucus, not a legislative majority in a chamber where 25 votes were needed to pass a bill. He tried to assuage concerns within his own party. It was a fair bill, he said. "Most who say we sold the party down the river don't know what they're talking about."[45]

House Bill 196 as amended with the Senate compromise passed the Senate on February 23, 1965, the 44th day of what was normally a 60-day legislative session. With the help of the ten Republicans assigned to support it, the bill passed 30 to 18. As a House bill, it returned to the lower chamber for an automatic vote. In accordance with the court order, the legislature had passed no other bills. The judges had scheduled a hearing for February 26th to review legislative progress.

To many House representatives, the choice seemed clear – accept the compromise bill or let the court take over the task of redistricting. When Representative John O'Brien presented a motion calling for a conference committee and new negotiations, Republican Joel Pritchard caustically observed:

> If you people think you can go over and straighten out your senators, you are mistaken. Let's not kid anybody....Who is going to be on the conference committee? I don't think you fellows over there can decide on any two to protect you.[48]

Greive and his Democratic supporters, joined by all of the House Republicans, rejected the request for new negotiations. They insisted that House members vote on the compromise.

On the Senate floor, Greive defended the bill. "This is an honorable compromise," he insisted. A"Conference is impossible. If you pull out one district you wind up pulling them all out."[49]

In the House, the Democratic leadership with their 60 to 39 vote majority could afford to lose no more than ten votes. Redistricting provided one of the sternest tests of party loyalty versus factionalism in the state's political history. Factionalism prevailed.

Gorton and the Republican leadership could count on the votes of the half-dozen dissidents who had joined to form the coalition government two years earlier. Gorton had protected the dissidents during the district-drawing process. Ex-speaker Day and the other dissidents possessed a commitment to compromise nurtured by Republicans. Even with the loss of the Democratic dissidents, Schaeffer and O'Brien could have stopped the Senate redistricting bill by unifying the rest of the Democratic caucus. They could not.

Employing a tactic they had utilized on the earlier public-versus-private electric power fight, Democratic legislators emerged from their caucus room onto the House floor where one of their leaders moved that the House adjourn. By adjourning the House, the Democrats sought to avoid a vote on the redistricting bill without asking fellow Democrats to actually vote against it. The galleries were full; Governor Evans stood in the wings, waiting for the culmination of the long redistricting battle. In a moment as dramatic as can be seen in a legislative chamber, the motion failed, 50 to 49. The galleries roared and the Republicans cheered.

The eleven Democrats who broke with their party leadership did so for many reasons. One was pressured by his employer, a large state industry. One was ideologically committed to the principle that the legislature should redistrict itself. Most did so out of personal loyalty and friendships which, in the case of Washington State politics, were stronger than party ties. A crucial and unexpected vote was provided by Ben F. Taplin, a first-term Representative from a sparsely-populated district in the southeast corner of the state. Even though Taplin would lose his seat as a result of redistricting, Republican Representative Don Moos had convinced him to support the bill. The large-framed Moos stood guard over Taplin as the Democratic leadership descended upon him with demands for further delay.

A crucial vote was provided by the first-term legislator from Greive's 34th legislative district. Representative Hays Elder, a Democrat, supported the redistricting compromise out of loyalty to Greive. Elder's experience in state politics had begun under Senator Greive, who recognized Elder's talent and brought him to Olympia as part of his legislative redistricting staff. Elder helped write the 1957 redistricting act and he voted for the 1965 bill.

Taplin agreed to a one day delay, but the loss of the adjournment vote ended the redistricting wars for that session. The following day the legislature convened to debate and pass the bill. Representative O'Brien bitterly attacked the governor for thwarting the legislative process.

He has been unwilling to permit a joint legislative conference....he has grossly abused his veto power....he has charged the House leadership with delay; however, he failed to tell that on two occasions he vetoed redistricting measures that would have stopped this agony a long time ago.[50]

Throughout the floor debate, Representative Gorton had remained silent so as not to excite more hostility. After the legislators had grown tired of talking and were ready to vote, he stood and reflected on the process about to end.

This afternoon we have reached the end of a long road that began nearly two years earlier.... In the sense that we were forced to deal with one another and have some weird and wonderful shapes and have spend more days than many legislatures, this solution may possibly have better results for the people of the state than would a solution dictated by one party.

Senator Greive, he said, had been a tough negotiator. Rebutting accusations that Greive had given in too much, Gorton said that "I hope I never have to deal with anyone who is tougher." Gorton concluded the debate with these words:

> As poor an arena as a legislature is in which to redistrict, we can say, that we have done so. You can fell triumphant in one respect. You have done the job.[51]

Aftermath

In the end, with the outcome foreseen, seventeen Democrats joined thirty-nine Republicans to approve the redistricting bill. Even though they commanded a 60-vote majority, Schaefer and O'Brien were able to hold onto only 43 votes. At a special ceremony in his office, Governor Evans signed the bill one hour later on February 26, 1965, the 47th legislative day.

The judges met eleven days later, on March 9, to review the state redistricting act. M. L. Borawick, the plaintiff's attorney, objected to the population discrepancies created by the legislature. The districts ranged in size, based on the most recent census, from 48,340 in central Seattle to 70,317 in Whatcom County, a range of approximately 1.5 to one.[52] This was the range that legislative leaders and their aides had used in setting the populations. The discrepancies, Borawick argued, had no apparent justification.[53]

The judges did not prolong the agony. "The statute does not achieve mathematical perfection," Judge Beeks admitted. Yet neither the court nor the constitution at that time required mathematical perfection.

The Fourteenth Amendment requires that the state make an honest and good faith effort to construct districts in both houses of its legislature as nearly of equal population as is practicable.[54]

From 1931 to 1957, Washington's legislative districts were not redistricted, overweighting Eastern Washington, whose legislators resisted change.

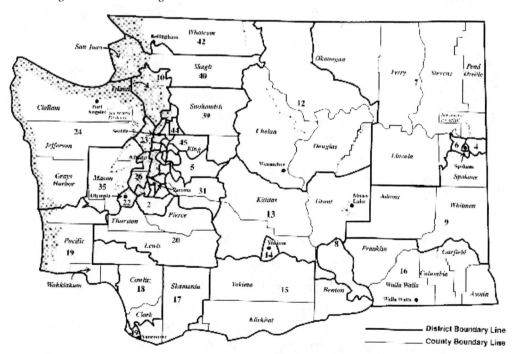

The redistricting of 1991 reflected the shift of population to the urban wet side of the Cascades.

The Washington State redistricting law, Beeks concluded, met that requirement. The judges, who had lifted their ban on state legislation a few days earlier, dismissed the case, but not before noting that the legislators would need to perform the act again after the 1970 census.[55]

Republicans gained control of the Washington State House of Representatives in the 1966 elections, moving from 39 seats up to 55.186 In 1968, they improved this margin by one seat to control the House again, 56 to 43. Democrats retained control of the State Senate, but by a narrower margin of 28 to 21.

WASHINGTON STATE ARCHIVE (OLYMPIA)
The Supreme Court appointed geographer Richard Morrill of the University of Washington to be the 'Master' drafter. The GOP won the House in the next election.

The House dissidents won fine districts, but when Republicans gained control of the House of Representatives, their role as power brokers disappeared. Wooed by neither party, the dissident faction grew lonely and ex-Speaker Day retired from the legislature.

In part as a result of the redistricting battles, Senate Democrats removed Greive as their majority leader in 1972. In 1974, he lost his bid for reelection in the district that the court master redrew. One year later he won election to the King County Council, a position he held until 1987. He died in West Seattle in 2004, at his law office, in the neighborhood where he had been raised.[56]

Slade Gorton was elected to the U.S. Senate in 1980 where he served for nearly twenty years. His party shifted to the right away from the traditions of the Republican "new breed," and he lost his seat to a progressive Democrat in 2000.

Daniel Evans served three terms as governor and five years in the U.S. Senate. He returned to Washington State and became a member of the Board of Regents of the University of Washington. Between the two Washingtons, he confessed, he had always preferred the state to the city.

Joel Pritchard was elected to the State Senate in 1968 and later served six terms as a member of the state's congressional delegation. He came home and was elected Lieutenant Governor, a post in which he served from 1989 until 1997. He died later that year in Olympia.

John O'Brien served an additional quarter century in the legislature, becoming one of the elder statesmen of the state government. Although his Democratic party eventually regained control of the state House of Representatives, he was never again elected Speaker.

Founding their state on the far edge of the continent, the citizens of Washington pursued a utopian vision that had eluded people further east – a polity free of partisanship and factionalism, in which issues of public good were decided on the basis of right principles rather than factional interests or party loyalty. To this end, they created devices such as the blanket primary, the citizen initiative and the legislative referendum. Legislative redistricting strained that vision. Redistricting is one of the purest political acts in which legislators can engage. Forced to redraw the districts that they represent, legislators in Washington State expressed little interest in population equity, the basic public good motivating the constitutional requirement. To incumbent legislators, redistricting was a tool to protect their political base, a means to advance the opportunities for their faction or party, and a device to secure their own reelection or protect their friends. Their gains inevitably produced someone else's losses, making the possibility of legislative consensus remote and the probability of division high.

To suggest that one can remove factionalism and partisanship from redistricting is to suggest that one can take politics out of politics – an illogical suggestion requiring that the essence of a thing be removed from its core. Redistricting created a fundamental conflict between the general vision of nonpartisanship and the specific necessities it entailed.

In the end, the vision and the reality proved incompatible. The citizens of Washington State could not achieve their visionary goals of nonpartisanship and fair representation while delegating the redistricting task to their elected representatives. Legislators struggled with redistricting.[57] In 1982 they passed the task to an independent commission, whose members were sensitive to the political consequences of district shifts but one step removed from the partisanship and factionalism that characterized redistricting in the Washington State Legislature.[58]

Recommended Readings

Orientation

Norman Clark. Washington: A Bicentennial History. New York: W.W. Norton, 1976.

Robert Ficken. Territorial Washington. Pullman: Washington State University Press, 2002.

John Findlay and Richard White. Power and Place in the Pacific Northwest. Seattle: Center for Pacific Northwest Women Studies and the University of Washington Press, 1979.

Joel Garreau. The Nine areas of North America. Boston: Houghton Mifflin, 1981.

Philip L. Jackson and A. Jon Kimerling eds. Atlas of the Pacific Northwest. 8th ed. Corvallis: Oregon State University Press, 1993.

League of Women Voters of Washington [Jill Severn]. The State We're In: Washington, A Citizen's Handbook. Dubuque, IA: Kendall-Hunt Publishing Co.,1984. [Rev ed., Seattle: The League, 1999].

Carsten Lein, comp. Exploring the Olympic Mountains: Accounts of the Earliest Expeditions 1878-1890. Seattle" The Mountaineers, 2001.

Thor Swanson, William F. Mullen, John C. Pierce and Charles Sheldon, eds. Political Life in Washington. Pullman: Washington State University Press,1985.

Carlos A. Schwantes, The Pacific Northwest; An Interpretative History. Lincoln: University of Nebraska Press, 1989.

Richard and Charity Yates. Washington State Atlas: The Political and Economic View of the Evergreen State.

Chapter 1 Scandinavians in Washington's Politics

Kenneth O. Bjork. West of the Great Divide: Norwegian Migration to the Pacific Coast 1847-1893. 1958?

Margie R. Lee. Kinfolk: Tracing the Footsteps of my Scandinavian and German Ancestors from Minnesota to Washington. Portland: Two Totem Press, 2007.

Odd S. Lovell. The Promise of America: A History of the Norwegian-American People. Minneapolis: Norwegian-American Historical Society, 1984.

Janet Rasmussen, editor and comp. Scandinavian Immigrants to the Pacific Northwest. Center for Pacific Northwest Studies in cooperation with the University of Washington Press, 1993.

O.E. Rolvaag, Concerning Our Heritage. Northfield, MI: Norwegian-American Historical Association, 1998.

Jon Wefald. A Voice of Protest: Norwegians in American Politics, 1840-1917. Northfield, MI: Norwegian-American Historical Association, 1971.

Arestad, S. "Norwegians in Pacific Coast Fisheries." Pacific Northwest Quarterly [hereafter cited as "PNQ"] 34 (1/48): 3-18.

Arthur J. Brown. "The Promotion of Immigration to Washington, 1851-1909." PNQ 36 (1/45): 3-17.

Jorgen Dahlie. "Old World Paths in the New: Scandinavians Find a Familiar Home in Washington." PNQ 61 4/70) 65-

72.

Frederick Hale. "Danish Immigrant Disillusionment in the Pacific Northwest." PNQ 71 (1/80): 15-23.

Jon T. Kilpenen. "Finnish Cultural Landscapes in the Pacific Northwest." PNQ 86 (1/94): 25-34.

Terye Lieren. "Ole and the Reds The America of Seattle Mayor Ole Hansen." Norwegian-American Studies 26,75-95.

Jorgen Dahlie. "Americanization: The Scandinavian Drive for Acceptance." In

"A Social History of Scandinavian Immigrants in Washington." Ph.D. WSU, 1967, 94-121.

Chapter 2: Seattle's Mayors

Charles Bender. A Report on Politics in Seattle. Cambridge: The Joint Center for Urban Studies of MIT and Howard University, 1961.

Richard D. Berner. Seattle 1921-1940: From Boom to Bust. Seattle: Charles Press, 1992.

William H Frey and Alden Speare Jr. Regional and Metropolitan Growth and Decline in the United States. New York: Russell Sage Foundation, 1988.

Walt Crowley. Rites of Passage: A Memoir of the Sixties in Seattle. Seattle: University of Washington Press, 1995.

John Findlay. Magic Lands: Western Cityscapes and American Culture After 1940. Berkeley: University of California Press, 1992.

Robert E. Horn. "The Politics of Metropolitan Integration: A Legislative History of the Metropolitan Municipal Corporations Act of 1957." MA, UWA, 1958.

Robert D. Putnam. Bowling Alone: The Collapse and Revival of American Community. New York: Simon and Schuster, 2000.

Norbert McDonald. Distant Neighbors: A Comparative History of Seattle and Vancouver. Lincoln: University of Nebraska Press, 1987.

Calvin F. Schmid. Social Trends in Seattle. Seattle: The University of Washington Press, 1944.

Roger Sale. Seattle: Past and Present. Seattle: University of Washington Press, 1976.

Carl Abbott. "Regional City and Network City: Portland and Seattle in the Twentieth Century." Pacific Historical Review 23 (8/92): 293-322.

Howard Droker. "Seattle Race Relations During the Second World War." PNQ 67 (10/76): 162-174.

Samuel P. Hayes. "The Politics of Reform in Municipal Government in the Progressive Era." PNQ 55 (10/64): 157-169.

League of Women Voters. "The Shape We're In." Seattle: Municipal League, 1955.

James P. Warren. A Century of Seattle's Business. Bellevue, WA: Vernon Publications, 1989.

George W. Scott. "The New Order of Cincinnatus, PNQ 64 (10/73): 137-146.

Susan Robertson, "CHECC—Choose an Effective City Council: A Study of an Ad Hoc Political Action Group. MA, UWA, 1968.

Chapter 3: Split Down the Middle: The Thirty Years War Over a Columbia Valley Authority

Ken Billington. People, Politics and Public Power. Seattle: Washington Association of PUDs, 1988.

Jay L. Brigham. Empowering the West: Electrical Politics Before FDR. Lawrence: University of Kansas Press, 1998.

Robert E. Ficken. Rufus Woods, the Columbia River and the Building of Modern Washington. Pullman: Washington State University Press, 1995

Charles McKinley. Uncle Sam in the Pacific Northwest. Berkley: University of California Press, 1952.

Keith C. Peterson. River of Life, Channel of Death: Fish and Dams on the Lower Snake. Lewiston: Confluence Press, 1995.

Paul Pitzer. Grand Coulee: Harnessing a Dream. Pullman: Washington State University Press, 1994.

Charles Coate, "'The New School of Thought: Reclamation and the Fair Deal, 1945-1953." Journal of the West 22 (April, 1983): 58-63.

William E. Leuchtenberg, "Roosevelt, Norris, and the 'Seven Little TVA's'" Journal of Politics 14 (8/952): 418-441.

Herman Voeltz, "Genesis and Development of a Regional Power Agency in the Pacific Northwest, 1933-1945." PNQ 53 (4/62): 65-75.

Chapter 4: Organized Labor in Washington State, 1885-2005.

Charles P. Larowe. Harry Bridges: The Rise and Fall of Radical Labor in the United States. New York: Lawrence Hill and Co., 1972.

Jonathan Dembo. Unions and Politics in Washington State, 1885-1935. New York: Garland Publishing, 1983.

McCallum, John D. Dave Beck. Mercer Island, WA: The Writing Works, 1978.John McCann. Blood in the Water: A History of District Lodge 751 International Association of Machinists and Aerospace Workers. Seattle: The Lodge, 1989.

Carlos Schwantes. Hard Traveling: A Portrait of Work Life in the Pacific Northwest. Lincoln: University of Nebraska Press, 1994.

Radical Heritage: Labor, Socialism and Reform in Washington and British Columbia 1895-1917. Seattle: University of Washington Press, 1979.

Richard C. Berner. "1948: Liberalism in Disarray." [The Boeing Strike of 1948]. In Berner, Seattle Transformed: World War II to the Cold War. Seattle: Charles Press, 1999, 202-241.

Robert E. Doherty. "Implications of the Increasing Power of Public Employee Unions." State Government (Autumn, 1976): 234-238.

Toy V. Eckard. "The Oxford Group and the Strike of the Seattle Longshoremen in 1934." PNQ 69 (10/71): 174-184.

Carlos Schwantes. "Labor's Many Faces: a Photo Essay." PNQ 86 (1/95): 83-90.

Robert L. Tyler. "I.W.W. in the Pacific Northwest: Rebels of the Woods." Oregon Historical Quarterly 56 (3/54): 3-44.

Chapter 5: A Progressive State with Regressive Taxes

Donald R. Burrows. History of Taxation in Washington. Olympia: Privately printed, 2011.

Phil Roberts. A Penny for the Governor, A Dollar for Uncle Sam: Income Taxation in Washington. Seattle: University of Washington Press, 2002.

Washington State Research Council. Research Council's Handbook. Olympia: The Council, 1961, ff.

Bureau of Research and Services, University of Washington [Governor Arthur B. Langlie]. "Revenue Problems of the State of Washington: An Evaluation of the Tax Structure and Needed Changes." Address to the 14th Annual Meeting of the Institute of State Government, 1949.

League of Women Voters of Washington. "The State League's Fiscal Issues Story 1955-1975."

Glenn R. Pascall. Washington's Tax System: Choices for the Future. Public Policy Paper # 17, Institute for Public Policy Management, University of Washington, Seattle, July 1982.

Washington State, Department of Revenue. A Progress Report on Achievements in Property Tax Administration in the State of Washington." Olympia: DOR, 1970.

Washington State Tax Structure Committee, [William H. Gates, Sr. Chair]. Tax Alternatives for Washington State: A Report to the Legislature. Olympia: The Committee, 2002.

Chapter 6: Boldt From the Blue: Struggles Over Salmon

Barsh, R. The Washington Fishing Rights Controversy: An Economic Critique 13 University of Washington Monograph Series, 1977.

Boldt, Judge George. United States of America, Plaintiff V. State of Washington, Defendant. U.S. District Court for Western Washington Civil [Action] No. 213, Final Decision, 1/11/74.

Chapter 7: Greening

Daniel J. Evans. Twelve Years: A Report to the Citizens of Washington State on the Administration of Governor Daniel J. Evans, 1965-1977. Olympia: State Printer, 1977.

Tim Egan. The Good Rain: Across Time and Terrain in the Pacific Northwest. New York: Vintage Books, 1991.

Robert E. Ficken. The Forested Land: A History of Lumbering in Western Washington. Durham, N.C.: Forest History Society; Seattle: University of Washington Press, 1987.

League of Women Voters of Washington. The Growth Management Act of Washington State: Successes and Challenges: A Report. Seattle: League of Women Voters Education Fund, 2006.

Carsten Lien. Olympic Battleground. San Francisco: Sierra Club Books, 1991.

Richard Morrill, and David C. Hodge. Myths and Facts About Growth Management. Seattle: Department of Geography, University of Washington, 1991.

Keith C. Petersen. River of Life Channel of Death: Fish and Dams on the Lower Snake. Lewiston: Confluence Press, 1995.

Joseph E. Taylor III. Making Salmon: An Environmental History of the Northwest. Seattle: University of Washington Press, 1999.

State of Washington. Office of the Governor The State of Salmon Report. Olympia: The Governor's Salmon Recovery Office, 2000.

White, Richard, Land Use, Environment and Social Change: The Shaping of Island County, Washington. Seattle: University of Washington Press, 1980.

William G. Robbins. "The World of Columbia River Salmon: Nature, Culture, and the Great River of the West." In Joseph Cone and Sandy Millington eds. The Northwest Salmon Crisis: A Documentary History. Corvallis: OSU Press, 1996.

Robert E. Ficken. "Weyerhaeuser and the Pacific Northwest Timber Industry." PNQ 70 (10/79): 146-154.

Chapter 8: The Rise of Women in Politics

Lois Austin,, Judy Eliason and Cindy Ness. "Women in the State Legislature, 1983-1993." MPAs, The Evergreen State College, 1993.

Karen J Blair. Women in Pacific Northwest History. rev. ed., Seattle: University of Washington Press, 2001.

Northwest Women: An Annotated Bibliography of Sources on the History of Oregon and Washington Women, 1787-1970. Pullman: Washington State University Press, 1997.

Elected Washington Women. Elected Washington Women. Olympia: Washington State Legislature, 1983.

Cynthia Harrison. On Account of Sex: The Politics of Women's Issues, 1945-1968. Berkley: University of California Press, 1988.

Mary Ann Irwin and James F. Brooks. Women and Gender in the American West. Albuquerque: University of New Mexico Press, 2004.

David Invent. The Missing Majority: The Recruitment of Women as State Legislative Candidates. Westport, CT: Praeger, 1998.

Katherine Whitney. Nine and Counting [On the U.S. Senate]. New York: William Morrow, 2000.

Gooding, Barbara. "Women in the Washington State Legislature, 1913-1983." Senior Thesis, The Evergreen State College, 1983.

Anne M. Commmisa and Beth Reingold. "Women in State legislatures and the States: Legislative Research." SPPQ 4 (Summer,2004), 181-210.

Jeanne A Parry. "Putting Feminism to a Vote: The Washington Women's Council, 1963-1978." PNQ 91 (Fall, 2000): 171-182.

Thorson, Winston. "Women's Victory in Washington." Colliers Magazine 44 (1/7/1911): Section 1, page 75.

Washington State Women's Council. The Needs and Concerns of Women in Washington State. Olympia: The Council, 1978.

"Women as State Legislative Leaders." In Malcolm Jewell and Marsha Whicker, Legislative Leadership in the American States. Ann Arbor: University of Michigan Press, 1994, 159-190.

"The Woman Suffrage Movement in Washington." PNQ 67 (April, 1976) 49-62.

Chapter 9: Ultimate Democracy

Carlos Schwantes, et. al., Washington: Images of a State's Heritage. Spokane: Mellior Publications, 1988.

The Pacific Northwest: An Interpretative History. Lincoln: University of Nebraska Press, 1989.

Washington State Legislature, House Republican Caucus, Capitol Buzz, an online capturing of contemporary public oriented journalism in Washington, by subject.

WSL. Final Legislative Report. Olympia: The Legislature, 1967 ff. Annual.

Washington State, Secretary of State. Initiatives and Referenda History and Statistics (1914-2009). Online via WA.gov.

Chapter 10: Redistricting Wars

Gordon Baker. The Politics of Reapportionment in Washington State. New York: Holt, Rhinehart and Winston, 1960.

Eleanor Bushnell, ed. Impact of Reapportionment on the Ten Western States. Salt lake: University of Utah Press, 1970.

Bernard Grofman, ed. Political Gerrymandering. New York: Agathon Press, 1990.

Leroy A. Hardy, and Alan Haslop. Reapportionment Politics: The History of Redistricting in the Fifty States. Beverly Hills, CA., Sage Publications, 1981.

League of Women Voters of Washington, Equal Representation: a Guide to Reapportionment. Seattle: The League, 1967.

William B. McDermott. "The Impact State Policies ." In Timothy G. O'Rourke, ed., The Impact of Reapportionment. New Brunswick, N.J.: Transaction Books, 1980.

Morrill, Richard. Washington State Legislative and Congressional Districts. Olympia: OSOS, 1972.

Washington State Redistricting Commission and the Washington State Historical Society. Redistricting: Redrawing the

Battle Lines. Olympia: The Commission, 2002.On the Worldwide Web at "Access. Washington," Redistricting Commission.

Gorton, Slade. "New Methods Urged." National Civic Review 53 (April 1964):176-181.

Jacob F. Roush. "Legislative Reapportionment in Washington State, 1890-1930." PNQ 28 (7/37): 263-300.

John P. White and Norman C. Thomas. "Urban and Rural Representation and State Legislative Reapportionment." Western Political Quarterly, 18 (11/64): 724-741.

Endnotes

Individuals, other than those in the acronyms below, are cited here by their initials

Scandinavians

1. Theodore C. Blegen, Land of Their Choice. St. Paul: University of Minnesota Press, 1955, 445-46.

2. Dahlie, Jorgen, A Social History of Scandinavian Immigration in Washington State, 1895-1910, New York: Arno Press, 1980, 1-8, 19,78,101,103,112,127.

3. e.g., Adolph Benson, "Swedish Contributions to America: A Resume." The Swedish Pioneer, v. 4, (2,(April, 1952), 13-25, or, J.R. Christianson, "Myth, History and the Norwegian-American Historical Association," in Odd S. Lovoll, ed., Nordics in America: The Future of Their Past. Northfield, MI: The Norwegian-American Historical Association, 1993.

4. e.g., Leola N. Bergman, in Americans From Norway. Philadelphia: Lippincott, 1950, claims the "settlement of Norwegians in the Far West is very much like a play within a play." Politics on the Pacific is given 11 of 300 pages. Kendric Babcock, in The Scandinavian Element in the United States. New York: the Arno Press, 1969, describes "The Scandinavian in Local and State politics" (pp.140-153). North westerner Ernst Skarstedt traces the Scandinavian's "inconsequential achievement[s] in [early] politics" here to a character "defect," and treats a lack of "brass," "nerve" and the will to engage in American "smear" politics as virtues, despite their dramatic rise in all other arenas. Ernst Skarstedt's Washington Och Dess Svenska Befolkning. Seattle: Washington Printing Co., 1908, (203-216),is as useful, as A. Fritiof Anders' earlier reliance on the 'impotence due to clustering' argument. Adolph Benson and Hedin Nolsoth's Americans From Sweden,(269), and Bergman's Americans From Norway. Philadelphia: Lippincott, 1950),(213), and Sten Carlsson's Swedes in America, 1639-1988: Technical, Cultural and Political Achievements. Stockholm: Streiffert, 1988, (322), take the same approaches.

6. Swedes in America, 322-247.

7. Benson, Americans From Sweden, 257.

8. Dahlie, 9.

9. John M. Findlay feels Frederick Jackson Turner's "thesis did not very accurately describe Washington between 1889 and 1919," which was "commercial and industrial from the start." The half of Scandinavians who chose rural space found it little different than Midwest. See Findlay, "Closing the Frontier in Washington, Edmond S. Meany and Frederick Jackson Turner." The Pacific Northwest Quarterly, 82, (April, 1991), 57-69.

10. U.S. Bureau of the Census, Thirteenth Census of the United States, 1910. Population, III, 989, table 5.

11. In 1938, 59 percent of Washington's Swedes lived in cities; 19 percent were farmers, 22 percent lived on farms and in villages but did not farm. Swedes in America, 107-119. "The Nordic Population of Seattle and Ballard," in Patsy Adams Hegstad, "Citizenship, Voting, and Immigrants: A Comparative Study of the Naturalization Propensity and Voter Registration of Nordics in Seattle and Ballard Washington, 1892 to 1900." Ph.D., University of Washington, 1982, 115-117.

12. Seattle Times, 9/4/82.

13. Hegstad,131-160, and table 16.

14. Hegstad, l81,261, and "Conclusions."

15. Dahlie's view in "The Scandinavians in Politics: Deferred Assimilation," (chp. 5), is similar.

16. The scripture reading for the celebration of "90 Years of Valhalla," (Tacoma, 1974). In the Scandinavian Archives, Pacific Lutheran University, box 24, f 1.

17. United States. Immigration Commission, Statistical Review of Immigration, 1820-1910, Washington, D.C., The Government Printing Office, 19ll, v. 15, 315-16; v. 25, 516.

18. Tacoma News Tribune, 10/1/28.

19. Washington Posten, 8/8/02. Odd S. Lovoll's "Washington Posten: A Window on A Norwegian-American Urban Community," Seattle: The Western Viking March 17, 1989, is instructive. Vestra Posten, 2/2/04. Dahlie 133,141. Vye Varden, 7/24/08.

20. Essential University of Washington theses are: Robert D. Saltvig, "The Progressive Movement in Washington," Ph.D., 1964; Hamilton R. Cravens, "A History of the Washington Farmer-Labor Party, 1918-1924," M.A., 1962; Robert L. Cole, "The Democratic Party in Washington State, 1919-1932," Ph.D., 1972; and Fayette L. Krause, "The Democratic party in the State of Washington During the New Deal, Ph.D., 1972. Scandinavians' egalitarianism and dislike of the trusts run against Central States authors' assumptions about their being "rock-ribbed Republicans" is even more tenuous in Washington.

21. Kitsap County Herald ll/05, 12/09.

22. Iverson to Congressman J.W. Bryan 2/10/15; to D.J. Davis 2/17/15. Iverson mss., UWA, 2/4. He was a member of the Distrikt-Lodge No. 1, Skandinavishi Good templar Storloge of Washington.

23. Iverson to Josiah Gideon 2/28/1924. The Americanization of Nordic names compounds the confusion of their "identicalness" with others from Northern Europe and the problem of determining numbers, as we will find in identifying legislators. All those conceivably Scandinavian have been included in the charts.

24. Iverson to the editor of the Island County Times, 2/16/15. Inversion to son, 3/2/15. Inversion 2/6.

25. Argus 3/21/18. Terye Leiren, "Ole and the Reds: The 'Americanism', of Seattle Mayor Ole Hansen." Scandinavian-American Studies 30, (1985), 82. Hansen was a second generation Norwegian.

26. Leiren, 84; Hansen, "The New Americanism," The American Review of Reviews, June, 1919, 93.

27. "It is strange," Sten Carlsson writes in Swedes in America... that so many of the leading Swedish-American politicians of this period...had clear radical tendencies. They cannot, of course, be called representative of most Swedish-Americans. The latter were generally conservative...." 114.

28. Program of the Norse-American Centennial, and of the Swedish Centenary, box 15, file 22, and box 44, file 3, of the Scandinavian Archives, Pacific Lutheran University.

29. Dahlie 136.

30. "Bylaws of the Swedish-American Non-partisan Progressive Club, and, Minutes, 1/4/34, 9/30/36. "Scandinavian Archive," University of Washington, box 21-2.

31. Seattle Post Intelligencer 1/15/34; Seattle Times 8/31/36.

32. "Finns of Southwest Washington." Sunday Oregonian, 9/3/88, 10 ff. "First the Indians--Then the Finns." Aberdeen Daily World 11/7/73; Lewis River News (Woodland), 6/16/82. The 1920 census lists 20,000 Finns as born in-State.

33. Governor C.D. Martin to Winberg 11/5,9/11/36. Winberg boxes 1, and 32; In 1936, S-ADC members Rueben Standrom ran for Mayor of Hoquiam, Carl Welander city councilman, future Congressman Martin Smith was on County Commission, and Hans Johnson narrowly lost the Third District Democratic congressional nomination to the John Coffee. Aberdeen Daily World, 10/10/36, 6/14/39.

34. Bone said to take a position would then be just "One more thump in the boiler factory." [in 1937]. H.T. Bone to Einar O. Mohn, Executive Secretary, Bellingham Central labor Council, 3/10/37, Bone mss, University of Puget Sound, box 23/2; Bone to Asplund 3/24/37. Asplund to Bone 4/5/37, Bone mss., 23/2, 23/3.

35. "Minutes of the State Convention of the Washington State Federation of Scandinavian-American Clubs, Inc.," Aberdeen, 6/18/39. Winberg mss., box 2.

36. Pat Henneford to W.G. Magnuson 6/13/42; William B. Severyns to WGM 10/15/42. Both WGM mss 3181-2, f 49/63, UWA; A.J. Abramson, president, USW, to WGM 12/6/41. WGM 3181-2, f 48/35.

37. In the 1950 Senate race, incumbent Lester Parker compared their records in the prior session: bills sponsored, 19, and 3; passed Senate, 15 and 0; passed House, 10 and 0. Parker flyer, Winberg mss; Senator Jackson to Mrs. Andrew Winberg 11/9/65. Winberg mss., box 1, incoming ltrs.

38. Smith to Bone 4/28/33 Bone mss. U.P.S., 9/2. He had married a Finn. Smith to Winberg, 9/16/36. Winberg Mss, box 2, incoming. The Aberdeen Daily World (10/12/42), noted that his "eulogy was given by Seattle soul mate Hugh DeLacey, "who found him on the right side of every issue." Senators Bone and Senator Mon Wallgren, Congressmen H.M. Jackson, John Coffee, and Warren G. Magnuson to F.D.R., 3/15/43. Henry M. Jackson mss, 3560-2, 3/15/43. Magnuson staffer Gordon Quarnstrom made a weak try in the Third in 1952; Julia Butler Hansen, a Scandinavian in 'name only,' held the seat in the in the 50's and 60's.

39. Knute Hill, "An Evergreen Politician," unpublished autobiography, n.d., [1931?]. Hill Mss, Washington State University, 2/1.

40. "I am not a Republican," he protested to the party chair when asked in to file for precinct Committeeman in Prosser--but decided he had to be. Hill, An Evergreen Politician, ibid.; Hill in the Washington Education Association Journal, February, 1927.

41. Hill to Howard Costigan, Executive Secretary of the Washington Commonwealth Federation 5/12/38 Burke mss, University of Washington, 5/99-4, and 6/119; "The Real Farm Problem," Hill in The Congressional Record, 5/16/39.

42. Hill to DeLacey 2/12/41. DeLacey note, 6/11/41. Both Burke mss, box 6/119.

43. Hill to Jackson 4/8/43. HMJ mss, 3560-2, 7/6/50. Leroy Hittle, and Jack Gorrie, interviews with the author, 12/17/89, and 1/6/90. Washington State Legislative Oral History Program.

44. HR's 4724 and 7086. See Carstein Lien, Olympic Battleground, San Francisco: Sierra Club Books, 1991, chps 9-12. Wallgren's "Alaska Fisheries Act" the first assertion of American jurisdiction to 200 fathoms failed.

45. Henry Jackson to the U.S. Senate, as he tried to amend the Science Foundation Act of 1950 to include scholarships for non-nationals. The Congressional Record, 1957, p.l855.

46. Jackson's father, a Republican and contractor, had been overruled by his son's law partner, who advised being a Democrat was a necessity. The isolationist sentiment is reflected in Einar Simonson to HMJ, 11/26/41, HMJ mss, 3560-2, 6/45; HMJ to Mrs. Pearl Simdars, 2/10/41. HMJ mss, 3560-2, 6/44. Norway's foreign policy till then was to be neutral, and never against Britain. Norwegian Information Service, "Norway in World Affairs: A Political Survey," ca 1958. HMJ 3560-3, 234/2. "Scandinavian" precincts in Everett in 1944 primary, like Beverly Hills, Beverly Park and Broadway, and

East Everett were typical. The five Republicans got 57 to 121; 41 to 87; 33 to 52.

47. Jackson, speech, 5/10/48. HMJ mss, 3560-3, 234/1. "I think it would only need another stiff note from Russia to precipitate a near panic in Norway...." Lithgow Osborne, U.S. Ambassador to Norway wrote HMJ 2/18/48. HMJ 3560-2, 5/58.

48. Speaker Sam Rayburn to HMJ, 3/29/42 HMJ 3560-2, 45/19; News Release, 9/14/43 HMJ mss, 3560-2, 48/29.

49. Jackson to Reverend H.L. Foss, 4/8/43. HMJ mss, 3560-2 3/30; Mrs. Henry Backtrom to HMJ, 4/30/41 HMJ 3560-2, 1/24. The 1940 General Election totals were HMJ 66,314, Peterson 49,209. For comparison, M.F. Smith got 60,529 to 48,700, and Knute Hill 50,493 to 48,003, both against strong opponents.

50. "Snohomish County Precinct Count, 1944 Primary." HMJ mss, 3570-2, 45/43. In the 82nd Congress, HJM co-introduced HJR 406 creating a Lief Erickson statue in Washington D.C., and dedicated it at Seattle's Shilshole Bay in 1962. Two powerful local Nordics were Howard Bargreen of Everett, Chairman of the Majority Caucus and the Ways and Means Committee in the State Senate, and Harry Henson, a legislator, Director of Licenses under Governor Wallgren, Executive Secretary of the State Democratic Committee, and a challenger for Jackson's place in 1952.

51. "How Does a Liberal View the Sixties?" Liberty was "endangered ...by the thoughtless libertarian no less than the extreme reactionary." Speech at Oberlin College, 1962 HMJ mss, 3560-3, 233/10.

52. Jackson was serious, not sober. When Congressman Noble Gregory of Kentucky wrote "Dear Scoopsie-Woopsie," the rejoinder was "Dear Nobsie Wobsie." HMJ 3560-2, 7/6.

53. Brian Corcoran, Chair, Finance Committee, People for Jackson to Mr. Norgard. n.d. [Fall, 1982]. HMJ mss, 3560-5, 320/9.

54. Asplund to WGM 7/9/37 WGM mss, 3181-2, 45/5.

55. The Washington Democrat, 9/6/40; WGM to State Senator Mary Farquharson 2/9/39 WGM mss, 3181-2 40/11).

56. "Dear Arthur" got "Dear Congressman." "One could settle and beach comb the rest of his life," Magnuson jovially wrote his secretaries, as "The Swedish King of Pogo Pogo." WGM to Mary and Claire, n.d. [late 1943]. W.G.M. 3151-2 52/5. See, "The Bachelor Senators from Washington." The Oregonian, Northwest Magazine, 1/31/54, 6-7.

57. Asplund claimed 400 members. "When Strong men Set Sail," in "The Hall of Vikings and Campaign Folder" 3/25/37. WGM mss, 3181-2, 45/5. Victor Lysell of Bellevue was elected president over Andy Winborg, with Asplund's blessing, and the locus shifted to Seattle, with all but two of the primary officers from the Queen City. Asplund to WGM 5/24/37 WGM, 3181-2 45/5.

58. WGM to Asplund, 1/15/37. WGM mss, 3181-2, 45/5. "There is no one who has rendered a greater single service to the Democratic party in our state...." Bell agreed Frank to Bell to WGM 5/22/37. WGM mss, 3181-2, 45-5 Senators Bone and Schwellenbach, Congressmen Maguson, Coffee Wallgren and Hill to Frank W. Bell, U.S. Commissioner of Fisheries, 3/18/37, and, WGM to Asplund 3/18/37; 59. Asplund to Wallgren 5/1/37. WGM Mss, 3181-2 45/5; WGM to Asplund 2/21/39. WGM 3181-2, 46/49.

60. Clara Jerstad to WGM, 5/18/38 WGM 3181-2 46/37; WGM to James A. Farley, and, to Saul Haas, 7/27, 8/6/37. WGM 3181-2, 45/28.

61. WGM to His Royal Highness Crown Prince Gustaf Adolph 7/29/37 WGM 3181-2, 45/5. WGM's glowing speech to his colleagues on the subject is in the Congressional Record, 75th Congress (1937-38), p. 8665.

62. Washington Posten, 9/23/38.

63. Seattle Post Intelligencer, 9/27/56.

64. George Ryan to WGM, n.d. [1939], WGM 3181-2, 46/35; WGM to ABL 3/21/39, WGM 3181-2, 47/1. The 1940 gubernatorial race was the closest vote between 1920 and 1960. See George W. Scott, "Arthur B. Langlie: Republican Governor in a Democratic Age," Ph.D. Dissertation, University of Washington, 1971.

65. Herb Algeo, later Wallgren's State Patrol Chief, wrote WGM after Langlie had won a fight to be seated, "The only thing that seems to worry most...Democrats is that he is going to make a good governor." 1/16/41. WGM 3181-2, 48/35.

66. Scott 5; Interview, Leroy Hittle with the author, 12/17/89. Legislative Oral History Program.

67. Scott, "Republican Governor in A Democratic Age..." 10.

68. Jack Gorrie, interview with the author, 1/6/90. LOHP.

69. Minnesota's Governor Oroville Freeman, (a third generation Swede) Nebraska's Val Peterson, Luther Young Dahl, Montana's J. Hugo Aronson of Montana (a native Swede) and Warren were among them. Democrats included Clinton Anderson governor of New Mexico and Secretary of Agriculture 1945-48. The best known Scandinavian of the 70's was Congressman John Anderson, who campaigned as an independent for president in 1980, drawing 7.7 million votes. There had been "at least" 28 "Swedish" governors by 1988, ten from Minnesota, 3 from Montana, 3 from Nebraska. 2 from Colorado, and ten elsewhere. Fewer were in congress: 13 in the Senate, and 50 in the House. Carlsson 115-118.

70. Columbia Basin News, 8/18, 9/20/56.

71. Cover story, Time, 9/3/56; New York Times, 3/29/56. Issues are summarized in the Columbia Basin News, 9/20/56; the Washington Evening Star, 10/18/56.

72. ABL, "Keynote Address to the Republican National Convention," 8/20/56, ABL Mss, 60/25. ABL's highest margin in four state races was 1952's 52.6 percent. WGM won in 1944 by 55.3 percent, and in 1950 by 53.6 percent. Not incidentally, his closest scrape until defeated by Attorney General Slade Gorton in 1980, was the 1962 race against Richard Christensen, 33, an ex-Lutheran minister playing on "American heritage" themes. He lost the 1964 gubernatorial primary to Daniel J. Evans, another 'Scout.' Seattle Argus, 2/1,22/63; Cheney Free Press, 8/28/64.

73. ABL to State Senator Al Westburg 8/4/52, Westburg Mss, 2/ "politics"; Seattle Post-Intelligencer, 6/14/55; "Traceable 'Secret' Poll Rocks GOP," headlined the P.I. on 10/12/55. Still, a poll done February, 1956 poll showed 33 percent for Eastvold, 15 percent each for Tollefson and Anderson, and 37 percent for three Democrats. The "Hundred Thousand Club for Eastvold" newsletter, 2/56 Seth C. Eastvold mss. The Scandinavian Collection, Pacific Lutheran University, box 10/governor.

74. Phillip A. Nordquist, Educating For Service: Pacific Lutheran University, 1890-1990, Tacoma: the PLU Press, 1990, 108ff. A Second Report in 1961 to the trustees says that while the president was recognized as having done a "perfectly amazing job, he "conveyed the impression that...the end justifies the means." Minutes of the PLU Board of Regents, 1-2 November, 1961, cited on 184-5. In The Lamp and the Cross: Sagas of Pacific Lutheran University From 1884 to 1965. (Tacoma: PLU Press, 1965), Walter C. Schnacklenberg characterizes the "consensus-demanding" senior Eastvold as "equally opposed to evolution, Socialism, and dancing," as a man of "unrivalled audacity" with "tastes in the direction of government and power." 113. Seth considered running for governor in 1960. Nordquist, notes for chp 8, #2, op cit.

75. T.T. to Walt Olson 6/27/55. T.T. mss., 8/corr T.T., To Governor Hugo Aronson (Montana) 1/26/57. T.T mss., l3, Personal Correspondence.; T.T. to Royal Kerch, 7/16/57. T.T. 14, Hells (2)

76. See his "Norwegian Contributions to America Life," in The Congressional Record, 5/15/53, 2656.

77. Heritage League, History of Pierce County, Washington. Dallas: Taylor Publishing, 1994; Interview of Harold Tollefson, #49,50 "Scandinavian Immigrant Experience Collection," Scandinavian Archive, PLU. Arnold J. Hagen's The

Tollefson Family, 1865-1977, (Tacoma: Western Media, 1976) list's 350 persons.

78. T.T. to Hilding Lindberg, 4/26/56. T.T. 10, governor; T.T. to Judge Story Birdseye, 2/24/56, and "To all "interested in my Gubernatorial Campaign," 7/19/56. Both T.T. mss., governor.

79. Tollefson wanted to be a federal judge. Langlie was upset with T.T. in 1953 for defying the congressional delegation. The Governor had his counsel George Boldt appointed. Walla Walla Union Bulletin, 6/14/53. "Had our own governor... done half as good... the results of 1956 would not have been quite so disastrous..... He fell down...terribly and is personally responsible for what happened...." T.T. to Dick Broz, 3/5/57, T.T. 13, personal correspondence.

80. Argus, 5/15/70. The Italian Rosellini's were also Tacoma.

81. Lowell Soike, Norwegian-Americans and the Politics of Dissent, 1880-1924. Northfield, MI: Norwegian-American Historical Association, 1991, 185-187.

Mayors

1. The Charter of the City of Seattle Adopted at the General Election, March 3, 1896, as Amended in 1900, 1902,1904, 1906, and 1908, and the Ordinances of the City of Settle From December 1, 1869 to November 1, 1907. Seattle: Lowman and Hanford, 1908; Calvin F. Schmid, Social Trends In Seattle. Seattle: University of Washington Press, 1944, 33, 53. Carl Abbott wrote in The Metropolitan Frontier: Cities in the Modern American West, (Tucson: The University of Arizona Press, 1993), "The most important contradiction...in the modern American West is that the nation's emptiest region is also its most heavily urbanized."

2. This, coincidentally, was the position of Alden Blethen (1845-1915), Publisher of the Seattle Times; The political environment is in Robert D. Saltvig, "The Progressive Movement in Washington." Ph.D., UW, 1964, 39-45, 88-103.

3. Clarence Bagley, The History of Seattle from its Earliest Settlement to the Present Time. Vol. 3. Chicago: S.J. Clarke, 1916, 367; ST 7/10/75.

4. See Richard Berner, Seattle 1900-1921: From Boomtown, Urban Turbulence, to Restoration. Seattle: Charles Press, 1991, 122-49,187-207, 211-26, and, William O. Sparks, "J.D. Ross and Seattle City Light, 1917-1932." MA, UW, 1964, 48-52.

5. The International Workers of the World, or "Wobblies," were the radical end of the Labor movement; See Norman H. Clark, The Dry Years: Prohibition and Social Change in Washington. Seattle: UW Press, 1965, chp.8.

6. In 1918, Gill was disbarred for unethical solicitation of legal work; Seattle was wild enough in both World Wars to be temporarily put "off limits" by the regional Army in and Navy commanders in World War I, and World War II.

7. Saltvig, 192.

8. Cotterill's credo is in Cotterill to U.S.S. Homer T. Bone, 2/4/35, Cotterill Papers, UW, 10/17; Cotterill to Police Chief Claude Bannick, 3/14/14. Cotterill Papers, 9-21; T.R. reflected, "If I wished to accomplish anything...my business was to combine decency and efficiency; to be a thoroughly practical man of high ideals who did his best to reduce those ideals to actual practice," something the locals were unable to do. Robert V. Friedenburg, Theodore Roosevelt and the Rhetoric of Militant Decency. New York: The Greenwood Press, 1990, 15; Cotterill instead lost a bid for the U.S. Senate, but saw prohibition pass. From 1916 to 1919 he was Chief Engineer for the State Highway Department in Governor Lister's administration, and a Seattle Port Commissioner from 1922 to 1938; Cotterill to James Allmand, 7/1/19, Cotterill Papers, 8-27; ST 3/11/36.

9. George E. Mowry's The California Progressives, Berkeley: The University of California Press, 1951 is a definitive look

at the movement's commitment to social change.

10. [Seattle] Municipal News, 7/15/11, 6/1/1912; Seattle Sun, 12/29/14, 4/26/15.

11. Seattle Sun, 6/2,10/14; See Mansell Blackford, "Sources of Support for Reform Candidates and Issues in Seattle Politics 1902-1916," MA, UW, 1967, 7-55.

12. See Dale Soden, The Reverend Mark Matthews: An Activist in the Progressive Era. Seattle: UW Press, 2001.

13. Seattle Star, 2/18,20/14.

14. Saltvig, 198; Samuel Hays, "Politics of Reform in Municipal Government in the Progressive Era," PNQ 55, (10/64), 157-69.

15. AEG to Erastus Brainerd 10/16/10, Brainerd Papers, UW, 3-8; AEG, "Austin E. Griffiths for a Clean City." n.d., [1910], AEG papers, 21-2; P.I., 8/21/12; AEG speech 11/12/32, ibid, 21-3; Saltvig, 203; Blanchard, The Street Railway Era in Seattle: A Chronicle of Six Decades. Forty Fort, PA: Harold E. Cox, 1916.

16. See Chapter 8, "The Rise of Women in Washington's Politics."

17. See Sandra Haarsager, Bertha Knight Landes of Seattle: Big City Mayor. Norman: University of Oklahoma Press, 1994.

18. ST 7/6/65; Jonathan Dembo, "Dave Beck and the Transportation Revolution in the West, 1917-1941," in Thomas G. Edwards and Carlos A. Schwantes eds., Experiences in the Promised Land. Seattle: UW Press, 1986, 339-52The[Seattle] Argus 6/20/36 compared Beck's power in Seattle to Harry Bridge's in San Francisco. See Charles Larrowe, Harry Bridges: The Rise and Fall of Radical Labor in the United States. W

19. Proposed Plan of Organization," Seattle Post Commander Ralph Potts to his staff, 11/18/33. Michael Wolfstone papers, UW; "Oath for Candidates for Public Office," and, "Inventory of Cincinnatus Candidates," Frederick G. Hamley Papers, [FGH"], UW; See George W. Scott, "The New Order of Cincinnatus," M.A., UW, 1966.

20. "Investigation by City Council of Seattle, Washington, July 10,11,12,15,17—1935," Seattle: The Council, 1935; "Majority Report and Recommendations, Department of Efficiency Investigation of Gambling, Vice, and Liquor Conditions in the City of Seattle, 7/10 to 8/10/35"; FGH Diary, 7/10,19, 8/9,10,11/35, ibid; Retired Fire Chief William Fitzgerald, interview with the author, 4/19/70.

21. "Cincinnatus Bulletin, No. 1," 2nd ed., 1/13/36, FGH Papers.

22. Lorin Peterson, The Day of the Mugwump. New York: Random House, 1961, 267.

23. Flyer, FGH Papers; PI2/23, 3/5/36; Seattle Star 2/12/36.

24. Alva Johnston, "Seattle's One Man Revolution." Saturday Evening Post, Vol. 209, 1/16/37, 6; The ABL-Beck episode is in an interview of ABL by Richard C. Berner and Robert E. Burke 8/11/61, ABL Papers.

25. ABL, "1938 Speeches," in "Political Campaigns, 1935-1938." ABL Papers. In the primary he received 51,175 votes, Meyers 27,463, and Dore 21,480; "Events Leading Up to the Adoption of the Rehabilitation Program," in "Reports and Miscellaneous Material, 1930-1939." SPL, Northwest Section; ST 2/1/76.

26. ST, 3/3/38; Gordon C. McKibben, "Non-Partisan Politics: A Case Study of Seattle." MA, UW, 1954, 53-62.

27. Robert L Morlan, "City Politics, Freestyle." NMR, 37,(1949), 485-490.

28. The new mayor quickly put Charles Doyle, Executive Director of the King County Labor Council and "the balance wheel of the local labor movement," on the city Housing Authority's Board of Commissioners. The Coast-wide Labor conflict is capsuled by Richard Neuberger in "Labor Titans Fight in the West." NYT, 9/19/37; public reaction is in George Creel's "Closed During Altercations—The Unions Fight for the West Coast, with the Public in Between." SEP,

vol. 210, 5/14/38, 104-108; Selden Menefee's "The Decline of Dave Beck," N, Vol. 146, 3/26/38, 354-55, reflects the wishful thinking of many liberals on the election.

29. ST 6/5/41.

30. ST 7/11/41, 6/5/41; ABL to FGH, 10/11/38, FGH 17-1.

31. Corporation Counsel A.C. Van Soelen to U.S. Senator Lewis Schwellenbach, 1/31/39, Van Soelen Papers, UW, 1. RFC Loan; "Draft Veto Message," FGH Papers, 18-32; ABL to FGH, 2/5/41, FGH 17-1; Author interview with FGH, San Francisco, ca 10/12/65. Scott Papers, UW. Hamley ranked first in the State Bar Exam in 1932. He became Assistant Director of the Bureau of Reclamation at Coulee Dam in 1939, ABL's Legal Counsel in November ,1940, Public Service Director in 1941 and General Solicitor of the American Association of Railroads in 1943. ABL appointed him to the State Supreme Court in 1949, and had President Eisenhower elevate him to the Ninth Circuit Court. Lockwood was the governor's first budget chief, and was the original head of the State Board Against Discrimination in 1947. He retired as a bank president. ABL was the first three term executive (1941-45; 1 1949-57).

32. SMRL, Topical File.

33. FGH to ABL 1/28/40, ABL to FGH 1/1.2/40, FGH17-1. Some 65,509 Democrats, and 40,700 Republication for Governor Martin in the primary crossed over, or back to ABL in the general election. Otherwise there was "marked stability in spatial patterning." The Seattle precinct for FDR in 1936, and 1940 were nearly identical, and had a "remarkable consistency" with issues and municipal elections. Four months later, Earl Milliken's coefficient of correlation with FDR was .910. Schmid, Social Trends, 257, 265; When he was defeated by U.S. Senator Warren G. Magnuson in 1956, he became President of the McCall's Corporation. See the author's "Arthur B. Langlie: Republican Governor in a Democratic Age." Ph.D., UW, 1971.

34. A.S. Kerry to Dr. Richard E. Fuller, 9/2/38. Devin Papers, UW, 6/13.

35. See "[The]Political History of Seattle in the 1940s: An Introduction," in Richard C. Berner, Seattle Transformed: World War II to the Cold War. Seattle: Charles Press, 1999, 3-16, and Carlos A. Schwantes, "The Pacific Northwest in World War II," JW, (7/86), 4-11; [Judge] Theodore Turner to W.F.D, 3/20/39, W.F.D. papers UW, 2-9; Devin spent $1396. Two thirds of Devin's 250 donors were in downtown professional offices; [To] "Workers in the Devin Campaign, and "Statement of Campaign Expenses" ibid., 7-1; Milliken to George G. Rogge, 1/29/41. Milliken Papers, UW, 15-1; Devin "Filing Statement," 1941, WFD, 3-15. spent $1396; [To] "Workers in the Devin campaign," and, "Statement of Campaign Expenses," ibid., 7-1; tabloid, 2/19/41, ibid., 3-5.

36. T 5/20,28/41; (Seattle) Municipal News, 2/1/42; Milliken to Barney E. Johnsen, 3/7/42, Milliken 15-15; On Milliken's indecisiveness, see the PI 3/12/41: ST 4/13/41.

37. Howard McGowan to WGM, 2/24/42. WGM Papers, UW 3181-2, 51-13. Mathewson to WGM, 2/26/42, ibid., 50-16; John Ambler to WGM, 3/11/42, Ibid., 49-54.

38. WFD [Wliam F. Devin] to Ken Colman, 3/24/41, WFD 2-41; WFD at the Washington Athletic Club, 1/30/41, WFD 3-2.

39. WFD, Opening [Campaign] Speech at the Washington Athletic Club,1/30/42, Devin 3-2.

40. WFD, "Annual Address to the City Council, 1942. WFD 3-22.

41. WFD, Desk Diary, 9/15/42. WFD 1;"Report to the City Council," 6/7/43, WFD 4-13.

42. WFD to Paul Schiffner 8/17/59, WFD Papers, 2-52; WFD's approach is captured in a speech on KOMO (Seattle), 2/13/41. WFD 3-4, and in the University district Herald, 1/31/41...

43. Councilman James Scavotto, speech, n.d. [1944], WFD 6-5. Devin said Beck demanded Scavotto's election as the price of labor peace. Devin on KOMO, 3/11/44, WFD 4-33.

44. ST 6/18, 7/8/42.

45. PI 6/15/43; ST8/9/44; "The New Charter of the City of Seattle Prepared by Freeholders." 3/45 {and passed 3/12/46] Seattle: City of Seattle, 1945.

46. In 1946, the SPD reported "serious threats," including over 100 "speakeasies and bottle clubs," and "largely un-checked" prostitution. How much "ordinary" crime was curtailed by 1952 is arguable. SPD, Annual Report, 1951, 13-51. WFD 7-26; ST5/3/58.

47. ABL to FGH, 8/25/42, FGH Papers, 17-3.

48. Interview of WFD by Howard Droker and Richard C. Berner, 11/15/72, WFD 14, acct. 2035; WFD to Mayor John Butler (San Diego), 4/9/52, WFD 2-53. This was the "Fair Employment" stage. In Olympia, Langlie signed a States Human Rights Commission into existence in 1947, with this at the top of the agenda; PI 7/11/50.

49. WFD, "Annual Message to the City Council," 6/19/50. WFD, 5-32; PI 7/11/50.

50. "Puget sound Power and Light Negotiations," [6/50], WFD 10; Frank McLaughlin, [President of PSPL] had had enough of Seattle's "volatile and unpredictable" politics. To WFD 3/31/52. WFD 1-27; WFD, "Where is Our Home Rule," Presidential Speech to the AWC, 1949. WFD, 5-29.

51. Pritchard became a State Representative, State Senator, First District Congressman, and Lieutenant Governor.

52. Fred Baker to WFD 3/12/52, WFD 1-5; WFD had presented a roseate "Picture of Seattle's Progress" (tabloid, WFD 7-18). When attacked across the board ("This Time It's Pomeroy," WFC 7-3), he went on the defensive; WFD's down-town replicated ABL's. Pomeroy's, while less conspicuous, plainly favored a less ministerial approach; Municipal News, 5/31/52.

53. Pomeroy was a UW Law School graduate, former Assistant U.S. Prosecutor and Superior Court Judge. An Epis-copalian, he lived in the South End. He found himself boxed in. For instance, the mayor could fire the Civil Service Commission—and the Council could hire a new one—without his consulting him. PI 7/13/52. For an appraisal of Pomeroy, see Charles Bender, "A Report on Politics in Seattle." Cambridge: The Joint Center for Urban Studies of MIT and Harvard University, 1961, II, 18,49.

54. Gandy sought the GOP nomination for governor in 1964, but was bested by Evans.

55. Bender, II, 59; Clinton served as the Council of Church's Recording Secretary.

56. Police Chief Frank Ramon to Clinton 6/16/60 Mayor's files, 239-2, police, 7-9/60; Ramon's inability to deal with civil rights activists and his removal finally moved Seattle to fully professional policing. See ST 7/11/65;Interview of Mayor Clinton by the author, 9/212/94, both Clinton Papers, UW.

57. ST 9/12/67.

58. Booz, Allen and Hamilton, Administrative Survey of the City of Seattle, Vol.1, in Seattle Mayors files, 239-2, box 73. GC Papers, UW; "Mayor's Annual Message to the City Council," n.d. [1957], ibid., 3, Annual Message.

59. "Report of the Metropolitan Problems Advisory Committee,"12/17/56. Seattle City Council Papers, 4, MPAC; Chapter 42, Laws of 1957; GC," Metropolitan Government that Works," The American City, 9/59, and, "Government for Growth: The Seattle Story," speech by Jim Ellis to the American Bar Association, 10/27/58, GC, 7, METRO Plan.

60. For comparison, a $7 billion bond issue approved in 1998, for a light rail system running from Seattle Tacoma Air-port to the University District did not begin construction in 2004.

61. Paul Siebert, quoted in Bender V-12.

62. GC to Albert N. Cole, Administrator, Housing and Home Finance Agency, 11/7/58. GC 8, Urban Renewal (file 2); ST 3/9/60; interview, GC and the author.

63. Described by John Findlay, in Magic Lands: Western Cityscapes and American Culture After 1940. Berkeley: The University of California Press, 1992, 10, ff, and chp. V; Joe Gandy, President, Century 21 to Harry Carr, President King County Labor Council, KCLC Papers, 1, "Century 21."

64. James D'Orme.

65. JDB to the Colorado Municipal League 6/20/68; "Testimony of Mayor J. Dorm Braman Before House Committee on Education and Labor," [Olympia], 7/13/67. JDB Papers, UW, 3, speeches. Congress' share of state and local spending was 15 percent in 1960, 19 percent in 1970, and 25 percent by 1975; Carl Abbott, Urban America in the Modern Age, 1920 to Present. Arlington Heights, Ill.: Harlan Davidson, ca 1987, 31-32.

66. JDB to Alfred Schweppe, 9/17/65. UW, Seattle Mayors, 239-3, 5, corr. out, 9-68; JDB to Ralph V. Rankin 8/19/65, and "Race Relations Speech," 1/20/66. Braman, 3, speeches; Dean Brink to Robert A. Williams 11/24/67, Seattle mayors, 239-2, 80, Model Cites '67-'68; JDB to Dr. Ezra Stotland 8/24/65. Seattle Mayors, ibid., 239-35, corr. out, ibid., 67, police department, 7-12/68.

67. JDB to Prosecutor Charles O. Carroll, 12/21/65. Seattle Mayors 239-3, 5, corr. out, 12/65.

68. JDB to Negro Voters League 8/12/68. Seattle Mayors, 239-2, 67, Police Department, July-December, 1968; Business-man's attitudes are ably dealt with in Abbott.

69. See Lane Smith et al., "Mayor Praises Negroes for City's Peace. Stability an Important Factor." ST 9/15/67; JDB, "Progress and Problems in Seattle," to University Rotary Club, 10/18/68. JDB, 3, speeches; Mark A. Sidran, "Middle Class urban Political Conflict: The Case of Seattle." BA Thesis, Harvard University, 1978, ch. V; P.I,. 4/8/68; ST 2/11/68.

70. "What Kind of a Guy is Dorm Braman?" PI 3/23/69; ST 11/18/68, 2/20//69; Interim Mayor Floyd Miller, "Annual Budget Message to the City Council,"9/29/69. Records of the Office of the City Clerk, SPL.

71. Charles W. Bender, "A Report on Politics in Seattle.' Cambridge: Joint Center for Urban Studies of the Massachusetts Institute of Technology and Harvard University, 1961, II-17, VI-14.

72. Ibid,. II-45.

73. John Rupp, President, The Municipal League, to Seattle attorneys 5/10/56. Harold Shefelman Papers, UW, 16; The malodorous result are in the author's "Special" in the ST 9/21/03. The most lucid reasons for the apathy are in Robert D. Putnam's Bowling Alone: The Collapse and Revival of American Community. New York: Simon and Schuster, 2000.

74. The League fell to under 300 members by 2000, a single-interest movements, lawyering as a business, affluence and women in the workforce undercut civic activism. Seattle Council of Churches, Civic Affairs Committee Report, in Executive Committee minutes, 9/20/54. UW

75. Argus 4/28/67, 5/5/72, 2/6/73.

76. Sidran, 34.

77. City of Seattle: Budget, Adjusted for Inflation and Population, 1940-1990

Year Budget	Actual Budget (adjusted by CPI-U %)	Budget Increase + or -	CPI-U	Population	Pop. % +or-
	A	B	C	D	E
1940	$11,533,066	-0-	0-	368,302	-0-
1950	18,625,694	$18,302,000	+21.3	467,591	+58.7
1960	112,506,457	22,457,755	+22.7	557,087	+16.1
1970	247,642,627	28,431,517	+26.6	530,831	- 4.8
1980	569,205,943	52,143,402	+83.4	493,846	- 7.0
1990	1,158,114,271	76,859,374	+47.4	516,259	+ 4.5
	$484,972,440	$99,994,049	+ 201.4%		+30.1 %

Formula: The 1940 Actual Budget (col. A), is adjusted upward decennially by aggregate inflation (col. C), to create (col. B), showing what the same service level per capita would cost in subsequent decades. The 1990 figure for col. B has been multiplied by net population growth (+30.1 %), then divided into col. A, once reduced for net inflation. Sources: Annual Report of the Controller of the City of Seattle, 12/31 of the year referenced; U.S. Department of Labor, Bureau of Labor Statistics, CPI-U, Seattle-Tacoma, Washington, 1914-1993; for population 1940-1990, Andriot and Associates, Population Abstract of the United States, Vol. 2, 1983, p. 4, for 1990: Bureau of the Census, 1990 Census of Population, General Population Characteristics, Washington, 4.

78. In 1952, and 1962; The Langlies lived at 6020 6th N.E., Devins at 5608 17th N.E., Clintons at 6234 38th N.E., Bramans at l0659 Durland N.E. Langlie and Devin belonged to the University Presbyterian Church; Clinton thought his chief distinction from Devin was that he was a Methodist; Wes Uhlman, and Norm Rice for governor, Charles Royer for U.S. Senator.

The CVA

1. See Daniel M. Ogden Jr., "The Development of Federal Power Policy in the Pacific Northwest," Ph.D., University of Chicago, 1950, and , Lawrence Rakestraw, "The West, State's Rights, and Conservation," Pacific Northwest Quarterly, XLVII (July, 1957), 89-99. For a full perspective on the institutionalization of the Bonneville Power Administration as power distributor and the federal government's controlling-anchor agency, see Eve Vogel, "The Columbia River Region: Politics, Place, and Environment in the Pacific Northwest, 1933-Present." Ph.D., University of Oregon, 2007.

2. The contradiction between desire for public development and local control is personified by the publisher of the Wenatchee World. See Robert E. Ficken, Rufus Woods, the Columbia River and the Building of Modern Washington. Pullman: Washington State University Press, 1994.

3. Best done in Herman C. Voeltz, "Proposals for a Columbia Valley Authority: A History of a Political Controversy," Ph.D., University of Oregon, 1960.

4. S. 460. The concept was first submitted by Senator Homer T. Bone in 1940, as the Columbia Power Administration. Eastern Washington congressmen Charles Leavy and Knute Hill tried till 1943. Defeated in 1946, Mitchell was congressman from the First District (Seattle) 1948-1952, when he lost to Langlie.

5. Bruce M. Haston, "From Conflict Politics to Cooperative Politics: A Study of the Public-Private Power Controversy

in the Pacific Northwest." Ph.D., Washington State University, 1970, 21, 130.

6. Seattle Post Intelligencer, June 21, 1949.

7. Langlie, Speech to the Washington State Development Association, January 10, 1950. Langlie Mss, University of Washington, 2/24.

8. "Digest of Recommendations on National Water Resources Contained in Statements Received from State Agencies, Including Governors and Other State Officials." The President's Water Resources Policy Commission, box 31, file 325, Truman Library. "Statement by Governor Arthur B. Langlie Before the Committee on Public Works," May 20, 1949, Langlie Mss, 1/32; "Statement by Assistant Secretary of the Interior C. Girard Davidson Before the House Public Works Committee in Support of HR 4286 and HR 4287 to Establish A Columbia Basin Administration," 81st Congress, July 13, 1949. "Four Western Governors Speak Their Minds on the CVA." (booklet), June 24, 1949. (McKay, Langlie, C.A. Robins of Idaho, and Vail Pittman of Nevada). Horan 134.

9. Telegram, Hugh B. Mitchell to Langlie, February 2, 1949. Langlie Mss, University of Washington, 1/9; The Governor replied, "We hold no brief for the private power interest." Langlie to Mitchell February 10, 1949, Mitchell Mss 109-15, University of Washington.

10. Circular, n.d., (February, 1950), Langlie Mss, 5a/1.

11. Langlie, Speech to the Washington State Development Association, January 10, 1950, Langlie Mss, 2/24.

12. Cain, the ranking member of Senate Public Works, introduced his CVA for "discussion" purposes, then was normally non-committal.

13. Magnuson's bill was S. 2180, Cain's S. 1631, and the joint measure HR 5472, 81st Congress, First Session; Morse to Langlie, October 10, 1949, Langlie Mss 1/13. Thor Tollefson to Langlie, February 1, 1949. Langlie 1/9.

14. Walt Horan to Kirby Billingsley, April 11,1945. "A Friendly Analysis of the Columbia Basin Bill," radio address, April 26, 1949. Horan Mss, box 131.

15. Mitchell to Horan, 2/16/49, Horan, 131.

16. Robert D. Tininenko, "Middle Snake River Development: The Controversy Over Hells Canyon, 1947-1955." Ph.D. dissertation, Washington State University, 1967, 77,78,86; A more recent investigation, Karl Boyd's Unplugging the New Deal: Hells Canyon High Dam and the Postwar Northwest," (Ph.D., University of Kansas, 2000," treats the outcome as a "national referendum on the postwar political fate of the New Deal," which it was only in a very restricted sense.

17. The Spokane Spokesman Review, November 30, 1947.

18. Radio address by Langlie, July 22, 1949, in 1949 Speeches, Langlie Mss, box 27; Telegram, Langlie to President Truman, January 24, 1949, Langlie 1/7.

19. Lee to Jack Rogers 8/18/50. CBIAC Mss, University of Washington, box 15. See Lee Testimony to Senate Committee on Public Works, 9/12/49. Nevada also wanted out of any compact.

20. Seattle Times, October 4, 1951; "Columbia Basin Inter-agency Committee Reports," May, 1949-April 1952; Remarks by Langlie, August 9, 1949, Langlie 3/9; "Comprehensive Plan for the Development of the Natural Resources of the Pacific Northwest," August 3, 1951, Langlie Mss, 6/11.

21. Jack V. Rogers, Chairman, Washington Columbia Interstate Compact Commission to Langlie, n.d., (1956), Washington State Archives, A.R.G., box 11; John S. Bragdon, memo, June 4, 1959, Columbia Interstate Compacts, Bragdon Mss, box 17, Eisenhower Library. Van Dusen, George, "The Politics of Partnership," Ph.D., Loyola University (Chicago),

1974.

22. Governor J. Hugo Aronson to Secretary of the Army Robert Stevens, October 27, 1953. Langlie 8/3.

23. The idea came from Karl Stoffel, Wenatchee newspaperman and ex-secretary to Horan, to answer their prime questions: how to get development dollars without federal control, or exporting power.

24. Holland H. Houston, "A Program For the Washington State Power Commission," typescript, n.d., (1951), Washington State Archives, A.R.G., box 38.

25. HB 561, [Chp. 227, Laws of 1949]; Seattle Post Intelligencer, January 17, 1951.

26. Langlie, Testimony to the Legislature, typescript, n.d., (February, 1951). Langlie 6/36. W.W.P. stock had a current exchange value of $85 million. The S.E.C. hearings revealed an offer for $105 million.

27. Frank McLaughlin, President, P.S.P.L, to Langlie, December 1, 1953. Langlie Mss, 7/15.

28. The speech was principally influenced by Langlie. Governor Val Peterson to Gabriel Hauge, September 30,1952. Elmer Bennett mss, box 6, Eisenhower Library; Transcript, [The nine Republican] Western Governors Conference [with the President], August 20,1952. Papers of the President, 1953-61, box 3. Eisenhower Library. Spokane Spokesman Review, September 24, 1954. See Walton Seymour, "The Partnership Policy in Regional Power Planning," The American Economic Review, XLVI (March, 1956), 521-531.

29. Two days before leaving office, Undersecretary of the Interior Elmer L. Bennett summed the administration's record as forty-nine items of "major significance," and politically, 'damned if you do and damned if you don't'" Draft Speech, "State of the Interior." January 18, 1961. Bennett Mss, box 14, Eisenhhower Library. Privately, Langlie sought a "spelling out' of Eisenhower's "Partnership Principle" when the Northwest governors met the President in April, 1954. In First Hand Report, Sherman Adams says (pp.60-62), Langlie was offered Interior first, which he denied.

30. See George W. Scott, "Arthur B. Langlie, Republican Governor in a Democratic Age," Ph.D. dissertation, University of Washington, 1971, 248-255; Time, September 3, 1956, 13.

31. Oregonian, April 16, 1954.

32. It, Cougar Dam on Oregon's McKenzie river, and Hells Canyon were the only three ever advertised as "partnership" projects.

33. John H. White to Langlie, December 23, 1953; J. Frank Ward to Thor Tollefson, March 25, 1954. Langlie Mss, box 37.

34. Spokane Spokesman Review, October 10, 1954. Of the congressional delegation, only Russell Mack sided with Langlie.

35. Lewiston (Idaho) Morning Tribune, January 22, 1954. See Axel E. Strom, "Case Study of a Hydroelectric Development: Priest Rapids and the Partnership Program," D.B.A., University of Washington, 1958.

36. I.P.C.'s move from one to three dams was to keep the BPA out of Idaho. Tininenko 91-92.

37. "Petition of Oscar L. Chapman, Secretary of the Interior, For Intervention [against project #1971 (Brownlee Dam)], December 18, 1952. Dale Doty Mss, box 18, Truman Library. Gus Norwood, Executive Secretary, Northwest Public Power Association to Eisenhower 1/7/54. GF, box 307, Eisenhower Library. See Roy F. Bessey, "Political Issues of the Hells Canyon Controversy," Western Political Quarterly, IX, (September, 1956), 676-690.

38. Oregonian, July 16,1954; Langlie to Leon M. Fuquay, Secretary of the F.P.C., October 28, 1955. Langlie Mss, 10/12.

39. Wenatchee Daily World, April 12, 1955.

40. "One of the greatest obstacles" [to returning rights to the states the federal government had "usurped"] "has been

the reluctance of the governors to take back the authority...which the administration believes is really theirs," the President wrote his brother Edgar, August 6, 1960. OF 147-6, Eisenhower Library. Louis Harris Associates, "A Survey of Public Opinion on Power in the Puget Sound-Cascade Region," claimed "A solid endorsement by the people of the harmony...between public and private electric utilities," and" steady growth for the partnership concept by locally operated Utilities," in mid-1958. Bragdon Papers, box 62, P.N.W Development, Eisenhower Library.

41. Teninenko, 4. McKay was maligned. His respectable reputation as a conservationist while governor (1949-53), emphasized coordination and businesslike management. He sponsored a Department of Natural Resources, air pollution and water storage planning, and campaigned against stream pollution. Oregon Resources Review, (November 1, 1951). See Accession 57-4, Governor's Natural Resources, 1947-53, f. 1, Oregon State Archives. A post election survey showed "relatively few were interested in the power issue," and on the candidates' positions, under half Morse's, less than a third on Magnuson's, and only one in five on McKay or Langlie. For the post-1950 period, see Bruce M. Haston, "From Conflict Politics to Cooperative Politics: A Study of the Public-Private Power Controversy in the Pacific Northwest." Ph.D. , WSU, 1970.

Labor

It is not the purpose of this paper to discuss the details, nor the pro and cons, of Initiative 1098. That information will be forthcoming from the supporters, opponents and news media prior to the November election. The official voters' pamphlet will also contain the text of the initiative, an official explanatory statement, a fiscal impact statement and short pro and con arguments from the supporters and opponents.

Washington has long been considered one of the more progressive states because it has often been at the forefront of the states in enacting progressive laws and governmental programs. For example, Washington was the first state to enact a government operated workers compensation program for injured workers. Washington was one of the first states to adopt women's suffrage and the State was among the first states to provide state equalization grants to local school districts. During the 1930s and 1940s, Washington was in the forefront of states in providing financial support for retirees with low incomes.

1. The term regressive, in tax terminology, describes the impact of taxes on families with different incomes. A regressive tax is one in which the effective rate of tax decreases as family income increases. A progressive tax is a tax whose effective rate increases as family income increases.

2. The names of these committees and the titles of their report are: (1) 1921 Tax Investigation Committee, Report of the state of Washington Tax Investigation Committee; (2) 1929 Washington Tax Investigation Commission, Report of Washington tax Investigation Commission, 1929; (3) 1957 Tax Advisory Council, Financing State and Local 3 Dembo, Jonathan, "The Washington State Labor Movement, 1885-1935.", Ph.D University of Washington, 1978.2

3. Jonathan Dembo, Labor and Politics in Washington State, 1885-1935. New York and London: Garland Publishing, Inc., 1983.

See below Table: Washington State Employment and Union Membership Statistics, 1900-2005.

4. Figures for the 2002-2005 period are not yet available. See below Table: Washington State Employment and Union Membership Statistics, 1900-2005.

5. Nonferrous mines include gold, silver, copper, lead and other non-iron bearing ores.

6. The Labor Lien Act (1899) made it easier for workers to collect their pay and debts. Dembo, Labor and Politics in

Washington State, 1885-1935, 23.

7. The official records (see Table) of the WSFL say that it had 132 affiliates in January 1902 with a total of 5,760 members. History of Washington State Federation of Labor, 1902-1904, Harry W. Call, Past President, Comp., Seattle: WSFL, 1954.

8. Table No. 1, and Dembo, Unions and Politics in Washington State, 1885-1935, 262-265.

9. New statistics for the Washington State CIO Council for the period 1937-1957 appear, and some on bodies affiliated with organized labor in Washington. I have also provided the available WSFL-WSLC per capita tax receipts, the dues they received from each of their member unions. WSFL-WSLC affiliated unions and regional bodies and trade groups pay these taxes based on their member unions' membership. See below Table: Washington State Employment and Union Membership Statistics, 1900-2005.

10. Table No. 2 and Table No. 3 in Unions and Politics in Washington State, 1885-1935, by Jonathan Dembo (New York & London: Garland Publishing, Inc., 1983), pp. 263-265.

11. The meeting had been called to campaign for the release of imprisoned labor activist Tom Mooney. Meanwhile, many WSFL leaders were distracted by the convening of the State Legislature.

12. Table No. 2 and Table No. 3 in Unions and Politics in Washington State, 1885-1935, by Jonathan Dembo (New York & London: Garland Publishing, Inc., 1983), pp. 263-265.

13. Proceedings of the Washington State Federation of Labor, Wenatchee, Washington, July 13-16, 1942; Proceedings of the Fourth Annual Washington State C. I. O. Convention Held at Olympia, Washington, March 7-8, 1942, Washington State, 1942, pp. D18-D24 (Adolph Germer Pres, Intl Woodworkers: (p. A14)

14. F. S. O'Brien, "The 'Communist-Dominated' Unions in the United States Since 1950," Labor History, Vol. 9, NO. 2 (Spring 1958), pp. 184-209, in: Interpreting Twentieth-Century America: A Reader, edited by Richard Lowitt and Joseph F. Wall, New York: Thomas Y. Crowell Co., (1973), p. 441-444. House Committee on Un-American Activities (HUAC or HCUA) was an investigative committee of the United States House of Representatives. Established in 1938, it is often referred to as the House Un-American Activities Committee. Chaired by Rep. Martin F. Dies, a Texas Democrat, from 1938-1944, the committee was supposed to investigate the activities of the Ku Klux Klan, fascists, and other Anti-American organizations and individuals. However, it increasingly focused on the presence of Communists, radicals, labor leaders and other "subversives" in government and in civil society. In 1969, the House changed the committee's name to the Committee on Internal Security. The House abolished the committee in 1975 and its functions were transferred to the House Judiciary Committee..

15. The Communist Control Act of 1954 outlawed the Communist Party of the United States and banned its members from running for public office.

1 The Landrum Griffin Act of 1959, officially known as the Labor-Management Reporting and Disclosure Act was designed to prevent improper activities in the fields of labor and management, such as collusion between dishonest employers and union officials, the use of violence by certain segments of labor leadership, and the diversion and misuse of labor union funds by high-ranking officials. The act also regulated internal union affairs, including the regulation and control of union funds and prevented members and former members of the Communist party and former convicts from holding a union office for a period of five years after resigning their Communist party membership or their release from prison. It protected union members against abuses by a bill of rights that guaranteed freedom of speech and periodic secret elections. The Act also sharply restricted secondary boycotts and organizational and recognition picket-

ing (i.e., picketing of companies where a rival union is already recognized). The Act also amended the Taft-Hartley Labor Act (1947) by authorizing states to arbitrate cases that fall outside the province of the National Labor Relations Board. Organized labor has, in general, opposed the act for strengthening provisions of the Taft-Hartley Labor Act that they opposed.

16. F. S. O'Brien, "The 'Communist-Dominated' Unions in the United States Since 1950," Labor History, Vol. 9, NO. 2 (Spring 1958), pp. 184-209, in: Interpreting Twentieth-Century America: A Reader, edited by Richard Lowitt and Joseph F. Wall, New York: Thomas Y. Crowell Co., © 1973), p. 445-446.

17. Named for its chairman, Rep. Albert F. Canwell, of Spokane, the Canwell Committee was officially known as the Joint Legislative Fact-Finding Committee on Un-American Activities in the State of Washington of Spokane (HJR Resolution No. 10). It passed the Washington State Legislature on March 8, 1947. The committee's function was to investigate groups and individuals that "foment internal strife, discord and dissension; infiltrate and undermine the stability of our American institutions; confuse and mislead the people, and impede the normal progress of our state and nation either in war time or a peace time economy."

18. Mitchell, Hugh B. (1907-1996) a U.S. Senator and Representative, was a New Deal Democrat from Washington State who believed government could and should help citizens prosper. He served in Congress in 1945-1946 and in 1949-1952. Although he supported democracy, his opponents accused him of being "soft on communism." An advocate of public power production, he supported a Columbia River Authority to manage the river resource system. He also proposed an Asian Marshall Plan to thwart the post-World War II communist threat. Mitchell lost a race for governor in 1952, and subsequently lost two attempts at a Congressional seat.

19. F. S. O'Brien, "The 'Communist-Dominated' Unions in the United States Since 1950," Labor History, Vol. 9, NO. 2 (Spring 1958), pp. 184-209, in: Interpreting Twentieth-Century America: A Reader, edited by Richard Lowitt and Joseph F. Wall, New York: Thomas Y. Crowell Co., © 1973), p. 445-446.

20. See below Table: Washington State Employment and Union Membership Statistics, 1900-2005.

21. See below Table: Washington State Employment and Union Me190mbership Statistics, 1900-2005.

22. The agreement does include significant bonuses for employees.

Taxes

It is not the purpose of this paper to discuss the details, nor the pro and cons, of Initiative 1098. That information will be forthcoming from the supporters, opponents and news media prior to the November election. The official voters' pamphlet will also contain the text of the initiative, an official explanatory statement, a fiscal impact statement and short pro and con arguments from the supporters and opponents.

1. Washington has long been considered one of the more progressive states because it has often been at the forefront of the states in enacting progressive laws and governmental programs. For example, Washington was the first state to enact a government operated workers compensation program for injured workers. Washington was one of the first states to adopt women's suffrage and the State was among the first states to provide state equalization grants to local school districts. During the 1930s and 1940s, Washington was in the forefront of states in providing financial support for retirees with low incomes.

2. The term regressive, in tax terminology, describes the impact of taxes on families with different incomes. A regressive tax is one in which the effective rate of tax decreases as family income increases. A progressive tax is a tax whose

effective rate increases as family income increases.

3. The names of these committees and the titles of their report are: (1) 1921 Tax Investigation Committee, Report of the state of Washington Tax Investigation Committee; (2) 1929 Washington Tax Investigation Commission, Report of Washington tax Investigation Commission, 1929; (3) 1957 Tax Advisory Council, Financing State and Local Government in Washington: A program for Washington, 1958; (4) 1965 Tax Advisory Council, Proposals for Changes in Washington's Tax Structure, First Report, 1966, Second Report, 1968; (5) (6)1982 Tax Advisory Council, Report of the 1982 Tax Advisory Council, 1983; (7) Governor's Committee on Washington's Financial Future, A Financial Plan for Washington, 1989; (8) Washington State Tax Structure Study Committee, Tax Alternatives of Washington state, 2002.

4. Most of the opponents to a state income tax simply say adding an income will ultimately result in an increase the total state/local taxes. Although an income tax can be used to increase the total state/local tax load, the same goal can be accomplished by increasing the present taxes. Indeed, the lack of an income tax has not kept the legislature from increasing total tax revenues. Other reasons for an income tax are: (1) to provide property tax relief; (2) to increase the elasticity (normal growth in revenues without rate and/or base increases) of the tax structure; (3) to reduce tax evasion caused by the present high rates of sales and excise taxes: (4) to reduce the total taxes paid by Washington taxpayers by shifting a portion of the income taxes to the federal government.

5. The Committee's final report is contained in Tax Alternatives for Washington State: A Report to the Legislature, Volumes 1 and 2, November, 2002.

6. Even Adam Smith in his 1776 book, The Wealth of Nations, which expounds on the benefits of the capitalistic system, supported the notion that taxes ought be imposed according to the citizens' ability to pay. In effect, Smith advocated a proportionate distribution of taxes. In the countless tax and public finance books and articles that I have read in the past 50 years, I have yet to find any theoretical support for a regressive distribution of taxes among taxpayers.

7. The gasoline tax, enacted in 1921, was the first "major" addition to the tax structure but its revenues were primarily dedicated to the growing need to pay for the construction and maintenance of state roads and highways.

8. The standard of living and level of family income, after adjustment for inflation, has gradually risen over most of the state's history. With the substantial higher personal incomes of today, compared to the income levels in 1932 (when the voters approved the income tax initiative), it is not surprising that the support for a state income tax among the state's citizens has declined considerably.

1The Board of Tax Commissioners estimated the total value of taxable intangibles in the state to be in excess of $250 million in its first biennial report. That same year the assessors listed a total of $6.2 million in assessed values of intangibles on the tax rolls.

9. Governor Rodgers was ahead of his time. There were no state income taxes during those early years. Wisconsin imposed the first state personal income tax in 1921.

10. The effective property tax rate is the relation between the amount of tax paid and the full value of the property. A $2,000 tax on a house valued at $200,000 has an effective tax rate of 1.0 percent.

1 The 1921 Legislature enacted a poll tax in order to provide revenues to help pay for the principal and interest costs of the War Veterans' Compensation bonds and permit lower state property taxes. The poll tax of $5 applied to all male state residents between the ages of 21 and 49. Some 500,000 citizens paid the poll tax during the one-year it was in effect. It brought in $2.5 million in state revenues in 1922, an amount equal to almost 15 percent of state government property taxes. However, the voters repealed the poll tax when they approved Initiative 40 by a 3 to 1 margin in

November 1922.

11. Even before the first official tax study committee, a two-day tax conference was held at the University of Washington in 1914 where the participants were seeking ways of providing property tax relief. A proposed constitutional amendment, prepared by the state's tax agency, which would have permitted an income tax, was included as an appendix to the proceedings. The Board of Tax Commissioners submitted it to the 1915 legislature but it failed to pass. Source: Taxation in Washington: Papers and Discussion of the State Tax Conference at the U of W, May 27, 28, 29, 1914, Seattle, U of W, 1914.

1 Concerning the possibility of a sales tax, the 1921 committee noted that: "a sales tax of one, two, three, or five percent, would be a very disastrous measure for this state to adopt, and in turn would not produce enough revenue to justify the cost of its collection."

12. The first successful tax amendment, Amendment 3, was in 1900 when the voters' approved a change in the tax article that allowed the legislature to exempt $300 of personal property of each homeowner. That amendment followed a state Supreme Court case in which the Court voided a law that provided taxpayers with a $500 real property exemption and a $500 personal property exemption. The Court ruled that the constitution prohibited the legislature exempting privately owned property. (State ex rel. Chamberlain v. Daniel, 17 Wash. 111, 49 Pac. 243 (1897).

13. The amendment also provided a definition of property. It defined property as "everything, whether tangible or intangible, subject to ownership." The 1929 Tax Investigation Commission expressed concern in its final report that this change in language might lead to the state's Supreme Court ruling that a net income tax was a property tax, which would mean that the constitutional uniformity and equality provisions of the property would apply to an income tax.

14. Hartley said that the private sector of the economy and county governments should take care of the unemployed and needy. He argued that proving such assistance was not a proper responsibility of state government.

15. After the voters reenacted the 40-mill limit law at several subsequent elections, the 1943 Legislature decided it was time to include the 40-mill limit in the state's Constitution. It passed a proposed constitutional amendment and the voters approved it as Amendment 17 in 1944. No arguments were contained in the voters' pamphlet opposing the measure.

16 In a 5 to 4 decision (Culliton v. Chase, 174 Wash. 363, 25 P. 82 (1933), the court ruled that an income tax was in violation of the "uniformity clause" in the state's Constitution. In reaching this decision, the Court ruled that the income tax was actually a property tax.

1 The front-page headline in the January 7, 1933 Seattle P I. claimed that "500 Schools May Have to Close."

17. State ex. Rel. Stiner v. Yelle, 174. 402 (1933).

18. For example, the number of exemptions, deductions and credits in the B&O tax has gone from 20 in 1935 to 139 in 2006. The number of exemptions, deductions and credits in the retail sales tax has increased from seven in 1935 to 148 in 2006. During the last four years numerous tax preferences have been added to the tax laws.

19. Property tax revenues produced from new construction are not subject to the 1 percent increase limit.

20. The first action on income taxes taken by the Washington legislature was passing Senate Joint Resolution 1 in 1911. That resolution ratified the federal constitutional amendment that allowed the federal government to impose income taxes. The Washington legislature supported the federal income tax because it believed that Washington would benefit by receiving more in federal expenditures than it contributed in federal taxes. The legislature thought that the wealthy eastern states would be subsidizing the state of Washington.

1 Aberdeen Savings & Loan Assn. v. Chase, 157 Wash. 351 (1930). The tax on national banks was voided by the Court for three reasons: (1) the tax was invalid on equal protection grounds because it did not apply to unincorporated business; (2) it was discriminatory by permitting the deduction of interest paid by banks but not dividends paid by savings and loan associations; and, (3) it was prohibited because Congress did not allow states to tax the income of tax-exempt federal securities.

21. Phil Roberts, A Penny for the Governor: A Dollar for Uncle Sam (University of Washington Press, 2002), pp. 96-98.

22. Hugh Spitzer, "A Washington State Income Tax--Again?" University of Puget Sound Law Review, 515(1993).

1 In 1949, Governor Langlie proposed a 2 percent gross personal income tax. He believed his proposed 2 percent income tax would pass constitutional muster. He believed the proposed income tax was in conformance with the constitutional requirements for property taxes. The rate was uniform and was within the constitutional two percent limit on property taxes (i.e., 40 mills at 50 percent value). The legislature rejected the proposed tax.

23. There was no requirement at that time to maintain a balanced budget. The requirement for a balanced budget was included in the Budget and Accounting Act passed in 1959.

24. Governor Langlie told the legislature that his 4 percent corporation tax would "effect only a slight increase in burden on our corporations." He pointed out that a large portion of the proposed state corporate income tax would be shifted to the federal government in reduced federal corporate taxes because state corporation taxes are deductible from the federal corporate tax. More importantly, Congress had just imposed a 77 percent excess profits tax on corporations to help fund the increased military spending because of the Korea War. This meant that almost three-fourths of the proposed state corporate tax would be passed on to the federal government.

25. The court also ruled the tax unconstitutional because it contained two subjects, the state's biennial budget and tax increase. Power, Inc. v. Huntley, 39 Wn 2nd 191 (1951).

26. The Tax Advisory Council submitted its first report to the governor and the legislature at the 1967 session. A two-thirds vote of both houses could not be obtained to submit the income tax to the voters. Governor Evans reconvened the Council and its second report was the basis of the proposed HJR 42 1970 amendment.

27. Having a more elastic tax structure would reduce the need for periodic tax increases needed to balance budgets. However, having a more elastic tax structure is not a panacea for completely ending future tax increases, which often occur when the economy goes into recession. There is also a need for a large budget stabilization fund in order to avoid and/or minimize tax increase during business recessions.

28. The approval of tax reform measures by the Legislature did not come easily. HJR 42 passed the House on April 19, 1969. The Senate sent an amended version on HJR 42 back to the House on May 1, 1969. A six-member joint free conference committee agreed on a compromise measure, which was approved by the Legislature on May 8, 1969. Both the House and Senate made numerous amendments to the original bill that would have implemented the income tax. Governor Evans also made vetoes in the bill before approving it. See McCaffree and Anne McNamee, Politics of the Possible: The Decade Our American Democracy Worked. Chehalis, WA: Special Printing., Gorham Press [2010].

29. There were 74 members in "The Committee for a New Tax Policy." Governor Evans organized it in October 1971. The committee included eight legislators, private citizens, leaders of business, labor, agriculture, education and tax groups, and representatives of the PTA and League of women Voters. Its charge was to make proposals to improve Washington's tax structure without increasing the total tax burden. Former Representative Mary Ellen McCaffree served as the coordinator for the large committee.

30. According to the chief staff person of the pro-HJR 37 group, C. Montgomery Johnson, "Below the top echelon of decision makers in each organization, there was little effective internal communication and virtually no involvement in the campaign by most members of most endorsing organizations." Special Edition. Chehlis, WA: Gorham Printing, [2010], 371-402.

31. The sponsors of the corporate tax measures were hoping that the Court would approve corporate income taxes by labeling them as a business privilege/ excise tax and not a property tax. Although the Court did not have an opportunity to rule on the legality of the two proposed corporate income taxes (since the voters rejected them), it had previously ruled that the 1951 legislative imposed corporate privilege/excise (net income) tax was unconstitutional.

32. The Republican Party supported the 1970 and 1973 income tax proposals after many years of having an anti income tax plank in the party's platform.

33. Statewide voter approved school M&O were $6.30 per $1000 of property value in 1977 and accounted for 34.9 percent of all property taxes. In 2009, local M&O school levies dropped to $1.79 and accounted for 18.9 percent of all property taxes that year. This downward trend could change in future years unless the state government increases its support for K-12. The 2010 legislature amended the full funding law by allowing school districts to obtain an amount up to 28 percent (higher percentage for grandfathered districts) of the state's basic support level from voter approved M&O levies. The original full funding law allowed school M&O levies up to only 10 percent (higher percentage for grandfathered districts) of the basic support level.

34. An argument often advanced by opponents of a state income tax is that the regressive impact of Washington's tax is offset by the progressive impact of the federal income tax. The counter arguments are: first, 43 of the 50 states have state income taxes despite the fact that the federal government also imposes an income tax; second, the real question is how progressive is the federal income tax. In 2010, the federal personal income rates ranged from 10% to 35%. In 2000, the rates ranged from 15% to 39.1%. However, during the Korea War in 1953 the rates ranged from 22.2% to 92%. These are marginal rates and the higher rates apply only to that portion of income over a certain level. The actual effective tax rates are lower because both the taxable income and the amount of tax paid are reduced by exemptions, deductions, tax credits and other provisions in the income tax code.

35. To eliminate the property tax is even less feasible. There is simply no other tax that could support the 1700 taxing districts relying on property taxes. More importantly, without the property tax, property values would rise quickly and many families would be unable to afford a home. Speculators could hold on to the property with little or no out of pocket costs.

36. The latest comparative state tax figures from the U. S. census Bureau show that 19 of the 40 states that imposed both retail sales and personal income had lower tax levels (i.e., taxes as a percentage of the states' personal income) than Washington.

37. Regardless of the level of expenditures, it seems reasonable that the taxes supporting those expenditures be distributed fairly among the taxpayers. Unfortunately, the use of the expenditure argument to oppose changes in the distribution of the tax burden aimed at increasing its fairness has been one of the most successful strategies used in defeating proposed income tax proposals.

38. There were two tax and expenditure limit initiatives on the ballot in 1993, I-601 and I-602. I-602 would have rolled taxes back by more than a $1 billion and require large cuts in state and local spending. It failed. I-601, which placed limits on future tax and spending increases, passed with a close vote. Much of the support for I-601 came from the

business community. Prior to the filing of the initiatives, the 1993 Legislature increased the rate of the B&O service classification from 1.5% to 2.5%, affecting some 400,000 small and large businesses.

39. At the time of its repeal, the MVET was producing about $750 million a year in state and local tax revenues. The reduction in revenues created fiscal problems for future legislatures and seriously affected several state and local government programs that were heavily dependent upon MVET revenues.

40. At the time of its passage, the Department of Revenue estimated that I-747 would reduce state and local property taxes by some $1.8 billion during the period from 2002 to 2007. Following passage of the initiative, numerous cities, counties and other taxing districts reduced staffing levels and cut programs in order to balance their budgets. Several new local sales taxes have been authorized by the legislature to help local governments in their search for replacement of lost property taxes.

41. Robert J. Landry III, "The Regressivity of Individual State Taxes From 19890 to 2000: A Nationwide Comparison" State Tax Notes, September 25, 2006, pp.899-921.

42. The largest tax preferences enjoyed by the agricultural and timber industries resulted from the current use constitutional amendment in 1968. However, both industries have been the beneficiaries of other large tax preferences.

43. There have been more than 100 business tax exemptions and tax preferences passed during the past 20 years. Manufacturers received a major tax break in 1995 when the legislature exempted all manufacturing machinery from the sales tax. The 2003 legislature passed a measure that provided the aerospace industry (primarily the Boeing Company) with up to $3.2 billion in tax reductions for assembling the 787 jetliner Washington. Two years later, it provided the timber industry with a similar reduction in the B&O tax rate.

44. The great majority of individuals I have talked to about our state's tax system think that the sales tax is a fair tax. They usually say, "Everybody pays it so it must be a fair tax."

45. Some individuals look at taxes as being a drag on the economy. They tend to ignore, or are unaware, of the positive affect that the expenditure of those tax dollars have on the state's economy. State and local government expenditures are a source of direct income to a substantial portion of the state's citizens and businesses. Those expenditures provide salaries to government employees (i.e., school teachers, police and fireman, state patrolmen, prison guards, worker at state agencies, etc.) transfers payments to various individuals (e.g., payments to the needy and infirmed) and purchases of goods and services from the private sector, which results in further multiplier impacts on the state's economy.

Salmon

1. Ex. USA-20, Joint App. 363.

2. Id.

3. FF 3, 384 F. Supp. At 350, Joint App. 100.

4. Steelhead can survive to spawn again.

5. See Ex. USA-20, Joint App. 367-68.

6. FF 6, 384 F. Supp. At 351, Joint App. 101; See Ex. USA-25, Joint App. 354-56.

7. Ex. USA-20, Joint App. 363.

8. Ex. USA-25 Joint App. 356-57.

9. FF 3, 384 F. Supp at 350, Joint App. 100.

10. Final Pre-Trial Order, docket No. 535, (hereinafter FPTO) §3-32, 3-33, Record in Cause No. 74-2414, R. 787-90.

11. Ex. USA-20, Joint App. 364.

12. George Gibbs, quoted in Ex. USA-20, Joint App. 370-71.

13. Ex. USA-21, Joint App. 399-404.

14. Ex. USA-20, Joint App. 367, 371.

15. Ex. MLQ-1, Joint App. 335.

16. Ex. JX-2a, Joint App. 341-42.

17. R. Whitebrook, Coastal Exploration of Washington 56-61 (1959).

18. "No … conveyance of lands … from any Indian nation or tribe … shall be of any validity … unless … made by treaty … pursuant to the Constitution" 4 Stat. 730 (1934) codified as 25 U.S.C. §177.

19. Act of August 14, 1848, 9 Stat. 323.

20. FF 15, 384 F. Supp at 353-4, Joint App. 106-7.

21. See id.

22. Act of June 5, 1850, 9 Stat. 437.

23. Lane Testimony, Joint App. 263-65; FF 19, 384 F. Supp. at 355, Joint App. 108.

24. FF 7, 384 F. Supp. at 351, Joint App. 102.

25. FF 8, 384 F. Supp. at 352, Joint App. 102-03; Ex. USA-20, Joint App. 371. .

26. FF 8, 384 F. Supp. at 352, Joint App. 102-03; Ex. USA-20, Joint App. 371-72.

27. Id.; 384 F. Supp. at 352, Joint App. 102-03. In 1853 an Olympia, Washington magazine exhorted the settlers to greater efforts saying "what little has been done in the business of securing the salmon, has been done solely by the Indians" Ex. USA-20, Joint App. 372.

28. Record in 9th Circuit Cause No. 74-2414, Tr. 1778-84.

29. Lane testimony, Joint App. 265.

30. FF 22, 384 F. Supp. at 355, Joint App. 110.

31. See, Dictionary of the Chinook Jargon, Ex. G-29(a) and Ex. Y-21.

32. Lane testimony, Joint App. 273-75.

33. Ex. USA-20, Joint App. 384, 386.

34. Ex. PL-16(b) at 3.

35. There is also evidence outside the record that the understanding of at least some of the United States negotiators was similar. At another council between the tribes and Isaac Stevens shortly after the treaties, S.S. Ford, a participant in the negotiations, referred to the fishing provisions of the Medicine Creek Treaty as, "Offering you for fishing privileges one-half of the waters of the rivers and Sound, offering to protect you in your rights … " Fox Island Council Proceedings, Executive Order of January 20, 1857, Executive Order File 1850-92, Records of Bureau of Indian Affairs, Record Group 75, National Archives, Washington, D.C. (emphasis added).

36. Lane testimony, Joint App. 271.

37. Ex. USA-20, Joint App. 393.

38. United States v. Taylor, 3 Wash. Terr. 88 96-97 (1887) (emphasis added).

39. Ex. MLQ-1 at 18.

40. FF 8, 384 F. Supp at 352, Joint App. 103.

41. A discussion of traps and examples are found at Ex. JX-2a, §3.13 at 112 and Fig. 46. See also Ex. PL-88.

42. Ex. MLQ-1 at 3, 19, Chart 6. Some of the trap sites became extremely valuable. In 1899, the Pacific American Fish Company of Chicago spent one million dollars to acquire control of inner Sound trap sites. Individual sites sold for between $5,000 and $55, 000 with an average of almost $20,000; by 1917, many sites were valued at over $100,000. R. Barsh, The Washington Fishing Rights Controversy: An Economic Critique, 13 (University of Washington, monograph series, 1977).

43. Ex. MLQ-1 at 18-19.

44. See Ex. PL-94(u). A suit to halt the interference was unsuccessful, United States v. Alaska Packers Ass'n., 79 F. 152 (D. Wash. 1897). The District Judge in Alaska Packers relied on a theory of treaty interpretation later rejected by the Court in United States v. Winans, 198 U.S. 371 (1905).

45. Riley testimony, Joint App. 295.

46. FF 8, 384 F. Supp at 352, Joint App. 102-03.

47. Lane testimony, Joint App. 262-63, see n. 69 and accompanying test, supra.

48. Ninth Annual Report of the Washington State Fish Commissioner's, 25, see also 26, 33-10 (1898), series hereinafter Commissioner's Report.

49. Ex. JX-2a at 60. Regulations could not be changed between legislative sessions to accommodate salmon run conditions. Regulation by statutory enactment was used until establishment of a Department of Fisheries with regulatory authority in 1921. See Wash. Sess. Laws, Ch. 7, §116 et seq. (1921).

50. Wash. Sess. Laws, 107 (1890); see Ex. JX-2a, Table 25.

51. Wash. Sess. Laws, 233 (1890); Wash Sess. Laws Ch. IX at 15-18.

52. Wash. Sess. Laws, Ch. 31, §72 (1915).

53. Cf. FF 10, 384 F. Supp. at 352, Joint App. 103-04.

54. See e.g. , Fish Commissioner Crawford's view, Third Commissioner's Report 18-21 (1892).

55. Ex. JX-2a, Table 25.

56. Id., Tables 25, 26, 27, 28.

57. Ex. USA-20, Joint App. 375.

58. See FF 10, 12-13, 384 F. Supp. At 352-53, Joint App. 103-05; and FF 35-163, 384 F. Supp. at 359-82, Joint App. 155-60.

59. See Ex. JX-2a at 64, Fig. 18, and Appendix III; cf. n. 97.

60 . Joint App. 348, see also Ex. JX-2a, Fig. 18.

61. FF 217-18, 384 F. Supp at 393, Joint App. 179-80.

62. Ex. MLQ-1 at 4.

63. R. Barsh, The Washington Fishing Rights Controversy: An Economic Critique, 24 (University of Washington, monograph series, 1977).

64. Act of June 2, 1924, c. 233, 43 Stat. 253.

65. 384 F. Supp. at 420, §5, Joint App. 230.

66. 573 F.2d at 1130, App. A-13, Petition in No. 78-119.

67. See Bergh v. Washington, et al., C74-524 S, dismissed by memorandum order (W.D. Wash. 1974), aff'd 535 F.2d 505 (9th Cir. 1976), cert. denied, 429 U.S. 921 (1976).

68. Memorandum Decision, September 12, 1976, Joint App. 427-432.

69. See Transcript, September 2, 1974 at 32-32.

70. Memorandum Decision, September 12, 1974, Joint App. 427-29.

71. Id., Joint App. 427, 434. The federal court noted that the state suit lacked the real parties in interest and involved no full-scale evidentiary hearing. Affidavits of the litigants provided the only evidence and these were not subjected to cross-examination. Joint App. 431. The Court further found that the treaty tribes had taken fewer fish both in terms of numbers and in percentage of harvest up to that point in the 1974 season than they had during the years preceding the judicial apportionrnent in Final Decision No. 1 Joint App. 430.

72. Memorandum Decision, January 20, 1975, Joint App. 444, 447.

73. Id. The Court did not interfere with the litigation between the Department of Game and the Puyallup Tribe. Id. at 449. However, since neither the federal court orders nor the parties had previously distinguished between hatchery propagated and other fish, the court refrained from making a ruling pending a request that it consider the matter.

74. The facts of the 1975 International Fishing case are set forth [in the brief for the United States].

75. App. H in Petition 77-983, Dkt. No. 1240, Record in 9th Circuit Cause No. 77-3654, R. 772

76. See Dkt. No. 1337, Copy of Notice of Trial in State Superior Court.

77. United States v. Washington, 520 F.2d 676, 693 (9th Cir. 1975), Burns, J. concurring, Joint App. at 59-60.

78. Dkt. No. 1381, Record in 9th Circuit Cause No. 77-3654.

79. Preliminary Injunction, October 27, 1975, Joint App. 450, §2.

80. Sgt. Lyle Nelson testimony, Transcript March 28, 1978, Joint App. 521, 524-25.

81. Oral ruling of Honorable George H. Boldt, Transcript October 25, 1975, Joint App. 499-500.

82. Memorandum of Facts, Exs. H, I, Dkt. No. 2077.

83. Id., Exs. A, G, Dkt No. 2077.

84. Order Re 1976 Coho Fishery, Sept. 6, 1976, §3-5, Joint App. 466-68.

85. Id., Joint App. 469-70.

86. Fisheries Advisory Board Report, Nov. 17, 1976, Joint App. 551; see also Joint App. 602-3.

87. Transcript Oct. 11, 7976, Dkt. No. 2573, see Joint App. 602.

88. Request for Determination, Dkt. No. 2574, Record in 9th Circuit Cause No. 77-3654, R. 961; B. Gruett Testimony, Oct. 11, 1976, at 193-97; L. Nelson Testimony, Transcript Mar. 28, 1978, Joint App. 521, 523-24; see Joint App.. 603.

89. FF 204, 384 F. Supp at 390, Joint App. 174.

90. 88 Wn.2d 677, 565 P.2d 1151 (1977), App. C in Petition No. 77-983.

91. Purse Seine Vessel Owners Ass'n v. Moos, 88 Wn.2d 799, 567 P.2d 205 (1977); Washington Commercial

92. See G. Sandison Testimony, Transcript Aug. 8, 1977, Joint App. 513.

93. P. Mundy Testimony, Id., Joint App. 507; see 500-10; FF 13 in Memorandum Order, Aug. 31, 1977, Petition in No. 78-119, App. A 41-42.

94. FF 10 in Memorandum Order, Aug. 31, 1977, Petition in No. 78-119, App. A 40-41.

95. See G. Sandison Testimony, supra, n. 243, Joint App. 512, and FF 11 in Memorandum Order, supra, App. A 41.

96. FF 2-3 in Memorandum Order, supra, at App. A 36-37; see 573 F.2d 1123, 1130, Petition in No. 78-119, App. A-13.

97. The State Chief of Harvest Management testified that Washington estimates the number of salmon caught by sport fishermen prior to the season and that emergency openings or closings of sport fishing are rarely used. State regulations of permissible gear, season and catch size limits largely determine what the sport catch will be. The non-treaty

commercial net fisheries inside Puget Sound are based upon the run sizes that escape ocean troll and sport fisheries. See Transcript Apr. 6, 1978 at 171-72, 174-80. Thus, the Associations' concerns, Association Br. 15, that the courts' allocation limits only commercial net fisheries is misplaced. State regulations alone determine how fishing opportunity is divided among non-treaty sport and commercial fisheries.

98. Joint App. 459-60; Transcript Aug. 8, 1977 at 58.

99. In many cases, the non-treaty fleet had already taken much of the returning runs. To equalize the opportunities, tribal fisheries were given the opportunity to take most of the run which actually returned to the usual and accustomed places. The percentage available to each side inside Puget Sound reflects this adjustment. Cf. Order re 1976 Coho Fishery, Sept. 6, 1976, §5, Joint App. 466, 468. Compare States' Brief at 11. The percentages referred to in the States' Brief are not of the total run, but only of the actual numbers of fish which reached the usual and accustomed places. These percentages are reached only after the other reductions, outlined above, are made from the total run bound for the tribal fishing grounds.

100. G. Sandison testimony, Transcript Aug. 8, 1977, Joint App. 510 at 14, J. Johnson argument, Transcript Aug. 8, 1977, Joint App. 514-15, W. Miller testimony, Apr. 5, 1978, Joint App. 530, 533.

101. Miller testimony, Transcript Sept. 22, 1977, Joint App. 519; Transcript Apr. 5, 1978, Joint App. 530-31.

102. See Joint App. 599-600.

103. Temporary Restraining Order Re Enforcement of 1977 Fisheries, Dkt. No. 3265G, Record in 9th Circuit Cause No. 77-3654; R. 230-31.

104. A series of hearing followed to determine whether preliminary injunctions should be entered. The procedural details are set out in the brief of the United States. The 1977 hearings were uniformly boycotted by non-treaty fishermen and their trade associations despite abundant notice of the proceedings. Attorneys for the Puget Sound Gillnetters and Purse Seine Owners Associations were served with copies of the United States' pleadings seeking the allocation orders. Dkt. No. 3087, Record in 9th Circuit Cause No. 77-3654; R. 6; Dkt. No. 3088., Id., R 16; Dkt. No. 3089; Dkt. No. 3090, of the tribes' joinder in that motion, Dkt. No. 3107, and of the proposed order, Dkt. No. 3178. It is noteworthy how carefully the Associations explain the process in order to mislead the Court. "No prior notice" of the Sept. 12, 1977 order "was given to petitioners." Association Br. 19. Yet an affidavit in the record showed that notice was served on Petitioners' attorneys, Dkt. No. 3467, Record in 9th Circuit Cause No. 77-3654; R. 1167, 1170. Similarly notice of the Sept. 22, 1977 hearing, was served on petitioners attorneys, Dkt. No. 3403. The Gillnetters do not discuss the extensive notice, by personal service and otherwise, given of the Sept. 27, 1977 hearing, nor the massive efforts of the United States Marshals to personally serve all fishermen with notice of the hearings which led to the order, dated June 6, 1978. See e.g. Dkt. No. 3467 Record in 9th Circuit Cause No. 77-3654; R. 1167, 1170; Dkt Nos. 4151, 4153, 4157, 4170, 4186, 4200, 4214, 4226, 4230, 4251. The latter service was made necessary only when Washington refused to mail out copies of the proposed injunction with its routine license renewal applications. See Dkt. No. 4049. A careful analysis of the Docket shows that attorneys for both Petitioner Associations have been on the parties' mailing list for service of documents since Aug. 4, 1976. Dkt No. 2324.

105. W. Lewis Testimony, Transcript Sept. 22, 1977, Joint App. 515-16.

106. Id. at 517.

107. Id. at 518.

108. G. Gabler testimony, Transcript Apr. 5, 1978, Joint App. 527, 529.

109. Id. at 530.

110. FF 26, Joint App. 482; see Transcript Apr. 6, 1978 at 325, l. 14.

111. At page 31 of their brief, the Associations' attempt to argue that their ability to cross-examine and subpoena witnesses was restricted. They failed to point out, however, that counsel for the fishermen and the Associations declined the United States' and the tribes' offers to provide the witnesses voluntarily. Transcript Apr. 5, 1978 at 114; Transcript Apr. 6, 1978 at 350; FF 12, 13, Findings of Fact, June 6, 1978, Joint App. 479-80. In addition, none of the fishermen or the Associations present through their attorneys attempted to intervene. Finally, it should be noted that an examination of the transcript of the hearing of Apr. 6, 1978 reveals that Mr. Yates, attorney for the Puget Sound Gillnetters cross-examined the various witnesses at length. Netters Association, a; party to the case, not on behalf of the Puget Sound Gill Netters Association or his individual fishermen clients.

112. W. Miller testimony, Transcript Apr. 5, 1978, Joint App. 530, 533-34.

113. Affidavits Dkt. No. 5167, 5200, 5252; Fisheries Advisory Board Report of Oct. 9, 1978; Joint App. 617, 619. See Motion, § 1-2, Joint App. 491-92. As to the state's historical policy of basing "mixed stock fisheries" on value judgments, see FF 202, 384 F. Supp. At 390, Joint App. 173.

114. F 4, Preliminary Injunction, Nov. 3, 1978, Joint App. 494-95.

115. 84 F. Supp. At 416, §19, Joint App. 225.

116. See Dkt. Nos. 5162-63.

117. Transcript Oct. 16, 1978 at 28-29, see Fisheries Advisory Board Report 78-83A, Dkt. No. 5313.

118. Larkin testimony, Transcript Nov. 3, 1978 at 12.

119. Marshall testimony, Id. at 21.

120. Id. at 14. Approximately 50 of those citations were given to treaty Indians. Id. at 24. Many of them involved federal confusion over fishing areas or compiling regulations or fishermen found outside tribal usual and accustomed places. Id. at 27-28.

121. See Whitney testimony, Transcript Nov. 3, 1978 at 7; Technical Advisor's Report Re Illegal Fishing, Dkt. 5314.

122. See Attachment to Fisheries Advisory Board Report No. 78-51. Joint App. 593. Importantly, this catch of approximately 750,000 fish represents only 9.5% of the total Washington harvest of 7,914,000 salmon. The tribes harvested additional fish from non-Puget Sound origin runs bringing their total catch to approximately 18% of the Washington harvest. The tribes do not assert that their opportunity to harvest non-Puget Sound stocks was restricted. Even within Puget Sound, the adjustment needed to raise 43% to 50% is slight.

123. 573 F.2d at 1126, App. A-3, Petition in No. 78-119.1   Ex. USA-20, Joint App. 369.

124. 573 F.2d at 1126, App. A-3, Petition in No. 78-119.

(Greening)

Women

1. T.A. Larson, "The Woman Suffrage Movement in Washington." PNQ, 67(4/76)(2), 49-62; For others who have labored long in the public vineyard, see Jean W. Schuddakopf, ed., Women of Washington: Women's Involvement in Community Concern. Gig Harbor: AAUW, Washington State, ca 1975; "Here in Washington, women hold up more than half of state government," Governor Gary Locke remarked in 1997. Officials and administrators had grown from

222 to 1,935 since 1980, from 21 to 40 percent. "Remarks of Governor Locke to the ECESW," 6/4/97, WSA, Locke, 1, sps, 6/97.

2. Governor Ferry did not think married women who had never lived in Washington should vote. Ferry papers UW, 2-A-2, letter press book, 12/1889-3/90; re SB 180; Solomon's position. See T.A. Larson, "The Woman Suffrage Movement in Washington," P.N.Q., 67 (4/76), 49-62.

3. Ruth Barnes Moynihan, "Abigail Scott Duniway: Mother of Woman Suffrage in the Pacific Northwest," in Rebel for Rights: Abigail Scott Duniway. New haven, Yale University Press, 1983, and, Duniway, Path Breaking: An Autobiographical History of the Equal Suffrage Movement in the Pacific Coast States. Portland: James, Kerns, and Abbott Company, 1914; Nelson A. Ault, "The Earnest Ladies: The Walla Walla Women's Club and the Equal Suffrage League of 1886-1889." PHQ, 42, (4/51), 123-137; and Larson, "The Woman Suffrage Movement..." 42.

4. The national nadir came on election day 1895. The Massachusetts Assembly offered a mock, non-binding referendum. Suffragettes opposed it for that reason, and few females turned out in the defeat.

5. For more on Hay's equivocating nature, see, chapter II of the author's Governors of Washington. Seattle: Civitas Press, 2010.

6. The "radicals" were led by Spokane's May Arkwright Hutton, who argued "there's no such thing as bad publicity," were open to any tactic. The Devoe and Hutton factions were both seated at the National American Woman Suffrage Association met in Seattle in 1909—and denied votes.

7. Saltvig, 314, 323-4, 350.

8. Apart from the Seattle Municipal League, the LWV was the state's strongest voice for good government through the 1960s. It has since suffered the decline afflicting almost all general interest civic organizations.

9. In 1998, Nan Campbell was elected executive of Bellevue, the state's fourth largest city, and in 2004, Kirkland, Renton and Sammamish joined Redmond and Issaquah. ST 1/9/04, 10/16/60.

10. "Bertha K. Landes, Mayor of Seattle," in Mildred Powell papers, UWA, 1/37, 6/7/26-6/2/28; See Sandra Haarsager, Bertha Knight Landes: Big-City Mayor. Norman: University of Oklahoma Press, 1994, and Mildred Tanner Andrews, Woman's Place: A Guide to Seattle and King County History. Seattle: Gemil Press, 1994, 132-34.

11. Powell radio address 2/31/38, Powell 1-30; Powell, Interview 10/13/38, Powell 1-3; PI, 2/23/39 Seattle Labor Council News 2/41; "Condensed Report of Mrs. F.F. Powell's Six Years on the City Council," Powell 1-36.

12. See the author's "The New Order of Cincinnatus," PNQ (10/1966), 141-146.

13. E.g., Charles Clise to Powell, 1/28/41, Powell 1-32, and Nat Rogers to Powell, 3/16/48, Powell 1-2.

14. See the author's "Arthur B. Langlie: Republican Governor in a Democratic Age." Ph.D., UW, 1971, 55-58.

15. She was openly pro-Devin in 1948, as he faced his first real threat in Democrat Allan Pomeroy; Powell radio address, 2/31/38, Powell 1-30[Interview, 10/13/38, Powell 1-3' PI 2/23/39; Seattle Labor News, 2/41; "Condensed Re16

16. Lamphere to Mayor J. Dorm Braman, 5/29/69, Lamphere papers, 2523-1, bx 1corr. 4-5/68.

17. The so-called "Little City Halls" were places municipal bills can be paid, inquiries satisfied, and meetings held. The coalition was one of many that sprung up to take advantage of federal matching monies for restoration and 18 improvements.

19. YHR 1/9/73; 5/6/82.

20. YHR 1/13/75, 4/8, 6/10/81; 1/10/78.

21. YHR 1/6/82. Carmichael 39, a former bank AVP was owner of the Yakima Welcome Service.

22.

23. "Vicki S. McNeill," in By the Falls: Women of Determination. Spokane: American Association of University Women, Spokane Branch, 1989, 86-87; McNeill Interview with the author, 11/20/05.

24. And the Spokane Plan Commission, the Area Youth Center, the Board of Health, the Eastern Washington Area Agency on Aging, the Homeless Task Force and co-founded of Friends of the Davenport Hotel as council woman." "Sheri Stovin Bernard", in By the Falls, 81-82.

25. Defeated in 1985, she was reelected to the Council in 1987, but resigned early to join the EWU Economics Department ,and spent much of the next four years in El Salvador and Nicaragua with her social worker daughter Julie; Bernard, interview with the author, 11/20/05.

26. DlyO 12/4/88; Mayor Eldon Marshall, interview with the author 11/8/04; Holly Gadbaw began her 20 years on the Council in 1982, and was Olympia's other female Mayor with the author 11/8/04; Holly Gadbaw began her 20 years on the Council in 1982, and was Olympia's other female Mayor, (1988-1990).

27. DlyO 12/4/88.

28. Keissling to the author, 12/8/2004.

29. YHR 9/28/04.

30. See, e.g., WSA, Minutes of the Mason County Board of Commissioners for 1973. They are almost entirely on technical queries.

31. e.g., Transcription of interview Lillian Spear with Richard Berner, Spear papers, UWA, 1-24. Naomi Benson, a compulsive activist/idealist rose through this channel to be Snohomish County PUD's manager-publicist. Naomi Benson papers, UWA.

32. Interview, Allenbaugh with the author 9/29/04.

33. Alma and John Nix, eds., History of Lewis County Washington. Chehalis: L.W. Trist, 1983, 206; Karvia to the author, 12/7/04.

34. ST 8/25/04. By 1998, Nan Campbell was elected executive of Bellevue the state's fourth largest city, and in 2004, Kirkland, Renton, Sammamish, Redmond and Issaquah had female mayors.

35. North, memo to the author, 11/17/04. She retired in 2003, at 82; Shirley Van Zandt first Executive of Whatcom County. Interview, 11/20/04; The three other "home rule" counties are Spokane, Pierce, and Clark; In 2004, women held 4 seats on the13 person King County Council, and a significant portion the large county council seats west of the Cascades.

36. Axtell failed to get the GOP nomination for U.S. Senate in 1922; On Croake, see PI, 12/29/23; TNT, 8/4/94; and Melanie S. Gustafson, "Partisan Women 1912-16," chp. 6, of her Women and the Republican Party, 1854-1924. Urbana: University of Illinois Press, 2001.

37. Hurn graduated Phi Beta Kappa from Northwestern in 1905, and the UW College of Law in 1913. Washington Alumnus, 16, (12/1924), 7-12; I am deeply indebted to Laura Asksey, whose articles "The Diaries of Reba Hurn, 1907-1908, " and "A lady in the Senate: The Political Career of Reba Hurn," appeared in the PNQ, 95 (Fall, 2004), 182-195, and in Columbia , (Fall, 2006).

38. In 1923, her Public Morals panel favored a "Temperance Day" in the public schools that was not signed by Governor Hartley; Journal of the Senate, 2/9/23, 304. A never anticipated ladies' "Cloak Room" that had to be carved out of

the senate side of the new capitol disappeared until the 70's.

39. Hurn was denied reelection as President Pro Tem in 1929.Being the presiding officer in the absence of the Lieutenant Governor, was a recognition of her ability, but not truly a "leadership" position.

40. Re: teachers: SB 66;Journal of the Senate, 2/6/23, 243; re the penitentiary, SR 9/27/24. She did oppose a mill limit, a one-third reduction in levies SR 10/22/24.

41. Arksey "Lady in the Senate…16; She was 'independent' enough for Hartley men to try to defeat her in 1926. Arksey, "Lady Senator," 8; SR 1/22/29

42. Arksey, "Lady Senator," 8.; SR 1/22/29] to rile her male peers.

43. She retired in 1946, and lived in the middle East 5 years, translating the Koran into English, and was in People to People delegations in the Eisenhower years. She died at 86 in 1967.

44. MF to Fifield, 11/10/35, MF papers, UW, acc. 497-4, 1-11; MUF to Edmund G. Brown Jr., 10/5/75, ibid, 2-24." 45 "A New Way of Life." Production for Use Association, Seattle, (1938) MF 397-4, 10-9; MF to Charles Clise 1/12/52. MF 397-4, 1-15; MF, memo to Monroe Sweetland [later director of the WCF's Oregon counterpart], 10/8/35. MF 382-1, 1-2; The WCF went into decline in continuing to follow the CP's foreign policy after the Nazi-Soviet Pact of 1939. ST 6/25/39; PI 3/8/40.

46. MF to Roger Baldwin, 2/6/41. MF 397-1, 1-14; to Roy F. Everett, 1/37/41, 397-4, 4-22; To Karen Satterlee, 2/25/41, ibid, 1-15; to The Progressive , 1/30/54, and the New York Times, 8/6/53.

47. MF, speech notes, n.d., (1935). MF 397-4, 6-4.

48. Farquharson, LOHP, 8; PI 2/24/37.

49 SB 8, SB 41; Farquharson voted "nay" on a Memorial to Congress for the Townsend Plan, "Simply a manipulation of a money system which does nothing to do away with our basic economic faults…." PI, 3/14/37.] MF to C.K. Gibbs, 3/9/37. MF 397-1, 1-5; P.I. 3/15/37; MF to Mrs. F.F. Powell, 1/28/37. MF 397-1, 1-4.

50. MF to Irving Clark, 1/16/39. MF 397-4, 2-28.

51. MF to Rev. Fred Shorter 1/19/37 MF 397-1,1-4; to Roger Baldwin. 3/26/37, ibid, 3-31; to Mrs. W.A. Roberts,1/29/37, MF 397-4, 2-29; MF to Ette C. Tripp, 2/23/37. MF 397-1, 1-5.

52. The chair of the Educational Institutions (including public and higher education could advise her professor constituents that "for the first time in recent history the University received its requested budget in the 1937 session."; "Reelect Mary Farquharson," (sheet), UW, MF 397-4, scrapbook.

53. MF to Muriel D. Poage, 1/18/39. Mf 397-4, 4-22; to Prof. S. Stephenson Smith 8/22/38. MF 397-4, 1-6; Communist Tom Rabbitt, and capable left-learning Tom Smith were backed by the WCF for the House. Albert Acena , "Notes re Conversation with Mary Farquharson, 11/14/74. UW, MF 397-4, 2-50.

54. LOPH, Farquharson interview, 9, 35; Charlie Hodde, the shrewd Democratic Speaker of the House (1949-53 Senator Al Rosellini was "always in effect the minority leader," and "gave me the impression at times that he liked it." Hodde interview by GWS, 1/12/70.

55. Gerald Dixon, the Chair of the Senate Democratic Caucus later wrote: "Although there hasn't been a Democratic majority since 1945, at which time there were 19 Republicans and 27 Democrats, we are all proud of our record in the Minority." Dixon to MF 10/13/50. 55. MF to Mrs. A.R. Todd, 1/21/41… ; MF to Monroe Sweetland, 2/20/61 MF to Senator Kieron Reardon, 2/19/41. MF 397-4, 2-28. MF UWA 1-7,

56. Their reversing of field to back Stalin, now Hitler's enemy.

57. Farquharson, LOPH, 9

58. LOPH, Farquharson; MF to Dorothy Detzer, 6/18/40.2/19/42, MF 397-4, 7-1, 397-5,1-1; to The New Leader, 8/27/45; MF oral history, 9; MF to Charles Clise 3/19/57. MF 397-4, 1; E.g., to Assistant Secretary of War John J. Mc-Cloy, 1/19/43. MF 397-5, 1-1; to Dwight D. Eisenhower, 4/21//56, MF 397–4,1-2; to Governor Dan Evans (for whom she voted),12/30/72, MF 397-4, 1/32; and Senator George McGovern, 7/1/81, MF 397-4, 3-4…" (She was elected a Precinct Committeeman in 1972 to support him); to John F. Kennedy, 1/4/60. MF 397-4, 6-2. Mary's public life is more remarkable for her sustained interest after the ego promptings and gratifications of public office were gone. She was: Vice President of The Washington Progressive League" (1939); the Board of the ACLU (1940- 41); organizing the Northwest Chapter of the Committee on American Principles of Fair Play" (1942), chair of the LWV's Committee on Constitutional Revision (1943); Director of the YW-YMCA's Students-in-Industry Project (1944): the Health and Welfare Executive Committee of the Council of Churches (1950-51); the Wage Stabilization Board (1952); The Statewide Committee for Ending the Death Penalty" (1960); chair of the Urban Nominations Committee, (1964):The Fellowship of Reconciliation (1968); The Committee for an Effective congress (1961-69); The Seattle Draft Counseling Committee (1969), and he United Farm Workers (1968-75)…58 See "Bob Grieve, Five Ball Juggler," in Scott, A Majority of One: Legislative Life. Seattle, Civitas Press, 2001.

59. LWF to Marjorie Mareso, 12/23/42. LWF, UW, 259-2, 1-2.

60. LWF, interview with Karen Blair, 7/3/83. LWF, 259-4.

61. LWF to Governor Roland Hartley, 9/9/31, LWF 529-2, 2-32; LWF to J.G. Doyle, 9/12/31, LWF 259-2, 2-1932.

62. Cornelius Hanford, Seattle and Environs. Seattle: Pioneer Historical Publishing Co., 1924, 171.

63. Forbus was endorsed by the new Women's Legislative Council. Sophie L.W. Clark to LWF, 9/20/32, LWF 259-2, 3-WLC, '31-'37.; LWF, "Radio speech" n.d., (1932), LF 259-2 Blair interview, ibid.

64. LWF, speech script n.d., [1934], LWF, 259-2, 2-1, sps; P.I., 10/14/34.

65. James T. Lawler, a member of the Taxpayers' Council, won 55,317, to 29,443; LWF to "Dear Friend" 9/15/34. LF, 259-2, 3-1, "end notes"; It was not for lack of effort. 100,000 pamphlets, "What's Your Idea of a Good Judge?" were circulated, and $1471 spent.

66. An offer to C.C. Dill, who was running for governor in 1940, was put off. LWF to C.C. Dill 5/1/40, LWF 259-2.

67. SBs 18, and 173, 1943.

68. LWF to Lt. Gov. Victor A. Meyers, 1/26/44. LWF 259-2 1-1; Journal of the Senate, 20th Legislature, First Extra Session, 2/28-3/4, 1944; Langlie's veto would "cut off the swing shift voters at war plants."

69. Langlie's close identification with losing presidential candidate Governor Tom Dewey hurt. Baker, interview with the author, 11/12/70; Hodde interview; See George W. Scott, "Arthur B. Langlie: Republican Governor in a Democratic Age." Ph.D., UW, 1971.

70. ST 1/19/49; LWF 422, Kimball; S.T. 11/9/50.

71. She claimed the Women's Legislative Council had also "always opposed the community property law." Blair interview, 7/3/83; Her opponent Hal Kimball, the community-minded publisher of the Ballard News negated the Democratic advantage at the center of the District, and took the north end two to one.

72. "Shall Married Women Work?" n.d., (1930's), LWF 259-2. 1, speeches; "Is Today's Woman a Lost Sex?" (1959). LWF 259-4, 1-sps, "Best Minds."; speech n.d., LWF 259-2-1, sps '35-48.

73. Her only objection to World War II mobilization had been "up till now women have been asked to sit by a wailing wall and knit," when they could "take over the work of men," a waste of energy that had "no place in modern warfare." LWF to Anna Boettiger, 12/18/41, LWF 259-2, 1-b; LWF to Arthur Hillman 2/1/33. LWF 259-2, 1. She was chair of the LWV's Welfare committee (1939), the Florence Crittenden Home (1942-46), President of the League of Democratic Women (1944), and the Roosevelt Women's Democratic Club, Vice President of the King County Democratic Club, President of the Ballard Business and Professional Women's Club, and Toast Mistresses, and on the ACLU Board (1958-69). The Magnolia Community Club, and was honored for "tireless dedication to community improvement," in 1960. She spoke on everything from "Educational Development in Colonial America" to "Garden Planning," to an "International bill of Rights," to "Yugoslavia's value to the United States"; King County [Democratic] Central Committee Foreign Policy Draft , April, 1960, LWF 259-4.

74. Then one of several "single member" districts, in which each Representative was elected by half of it.

75. WSA, LOHP, McCaffree, 9.

76 ST 10/16/60.

77. WSA, LOHP, McCaffree, 18,34; Evans was Floor Leader. His room mates and his co-conspirators were attorneys Charles Moriarity and Jim Anderson. Both went to the senate, where Anderson was Minority Leader, and later Chief Justice of the Supreme Court; McCaffree, "Legislative Memo, n.d., (1/63). McCaffree, UW, 2177-4-4.

78. The House was GOP, 1947-49: Under the Equal Protection Clause of the 14th Amendment; TNT2/13/63. The bipartisan Redistricting Commission Lois North sponsored passed the legislature 16 years later. Redrawing for the census pf 1970 started a year earlier with GOP members of both houses. McCaffree was chair, now that Gorton was Attorney General.

79. MEM to DJE, 7/22/69; WSLC to affiliates 7/1/68. McCaffree 2177-4, bx 4, "tips"; Labor's President, Joe Davis, withheld his cooperation until Unemployment Compensation was raised to $42 a week (SB 678), in return for closing "loopholes." LOPH, ibid. She also pushed Evan's "Washington Future" bonds, reforming the overgenerous and under funded Law Officers and Firefighters' pension system (ESHB 387), a and Department of Transportation (HB 641). McCaffree 2177-4- 4, corr, tax reform '69. The Preliminary Report of the Special [School] Levy Study Commission pointed to "undue reliance" on property taxes, contrary to the Constitution's mandate the state fund public education. (1/70), per HB893, ch. 255, Laws of 1968, 1st Ex.; Washington State Department of Revenue, "Washington's Tax System: A Comparison." Olympia: The Department, 1968.

80. WSHR, "Final Report of the Committee on Revenue and Taxation," 41st Session. McCaffree, ed., "Final Report of the [LWV] Public Policy Committee." McCaffree, 1773-1, 1. She also headed the P.T. A's Legislative Council in 1957, the Citizen's [School] Levy in 1959; "Passage of Comprehensive Tax Reform is its [the 41st Legislature's] Claim to Lasting Fame." PI, 5/12/69; Senator Mike McCormick, McCaffree's Senate counterpart, covered the Democratic Caucus. The bills were "regressive" for lack of an graduated net, and having constitutional limits. "[A] Short History of Passing Tax Reform" Memo, 5/14/69

81. LOHP, McCaffree, 11; A poll by the Republican State Central Committee in 1969 showed 45 percent "in favor" of the tax reform as presented, 39 percent against, and 18 percent with "no opinion." McCaffree 2177-4, bx 4, tax reform; See e.g., the "Proposed 1970 King County Republican Platform:" The "so-called tax reform is a tax increase." McCaffree 4 ,1-12, Republican Party." "Facts and Issues sheet," 7/11/68.

82. MEM to DJE, 7/22/69; WSLC to affiliates 7/1/68. McCaffree 2177-4, bx 4 "tips"; Labor's President, Joe Davis, with-

held his cooperation until unemployment compensation was raided to $42 a week.

83. "Facts about the Difference…"a Comparison Sheet. n.d., (1970). McCaffree 2177,4-7; "Report from Pete Francis." (2/70), ibid, voting records; ST 10/7/70, ibid; Bledsoe to MEM, 11/4/70, McCaffree 2177,4-7; Evans to MEM, 11/10/70, ibid; The House was GOP in 1947-49; Under the equal protection clause of the 14th Amendment; TNT 2/13/63. The bipartisan redistricting commission Lois North sponsored passed the legislature 16 years later. Redrawing after the 1970 census started in 1969 with GOP members from both houses, McCaffree was chair, now that Gorton was Attorney General.

84. See McCaffree and Anne McNamee Corbett, Politics of the Possible: The Decade Our American Democracy Worked. Chehalis, WA: special edition, Gorham Printing, [2010], 371-402, and the author's A Majority of One: Legislative Life . Seattle: 3rd printing, Civitas Press, 2010.

85. The GOP was in the Minority in both houses after 1934, except for 1947-49, and 1953-55.

86. Hayner was Minority Leader (1979-81, 1983-87), and Majority Leader (1981-83, and 1989-95). Honorable Mentions: Senate: Kathryn Malstrom (D), (1933-37, 1939-45)Lulu Haddon (D), (1937-45), Patrice Hale (GOP), Caucus Chair),Valoria Loveland senate Ways and Means chair, Betti Sheldon, (1993-2005), (Democratic Floor Leader). House: Maude Sweetman (1923-1929),Belle Reeves (D), (1923-27; 1930-37) Ella Wintler (R), (1939-41; 1943-45; 1947-65), Emma Abbot Ridgway (D), (1945-47;1949-57), Dr. Eva Anderson (R), (1952-62), Lorraine Hine (D), House Majority Leader, and Chief of Staff for Governor Lowry), Barbara Lisk (R), (Floor Leader) and Helen Sommers, past chair of four committees who became the senior member of the House. Notable "Firsts": House: Peggy Joan Maxie (D),(1971-77), the first African-American woman, Velma Valoria (D), , the first Asian-American in leadership, Hispanics Sharon Santos, Mary Skinner, and Rosa Franklin (D),(House 1991-93) is the first black woman Senator (1993-   ).

87. Since 2005, all five of the leaders of the Democratic Majority in the Senate have been women.

88. Belle Reeves was appointed Secretary of State in 1937 and died in 1948; Jennifer Belcher, a five term State Representative, was Lands Commissioner (1993-2001); Debra Senn was Insurance Commissioner, (1993-2001), then ran for the U.S. Senate, and Attorney General; Christine Gregoire Attorney General (1993-2005), was elected 9 governor in 2004, and 2008.

89. Preston, Department of Education, Patriotic Bulletin. Olympia: Public Printer, 1917; A teacher's certificate might be revoked for failure to teach "patriotism." R.C.S. 4855, 4846; Preston, "The Building of a State School system." S.P.I. Bulletins 23-35, 1914-20. Olympia" S.P.I. (1915ff).

90. Department of Education, Apportionment of State School Fund. Olympia: Public Printer, 1928, 28-70; Ibid, Superintendent of Public Instruction, Report for the Period 1928-1936. Olympia: State Printer, 1936,

91. Martin to PAW, 5-7-34, PAW papers, UW, 1-9; Kathryn Malstrom was also on Education. Wanamaker took Lulu Haddon's place. In 1939 PAW chaired Labor.

92. Secretary of State, Abstract of Votes in the General Election, November 5, 1940. In 1944, four superintendents of Seattle schools, and Tacoma's future one were on her Planning Committee, and all peers were invited.

93. See Ernest G. Miller, "The Management of Washington State Government: The Problem of Central Staff Organization." MA, UW, 1953, 59-62.

94. PAW, "Education and the Republican Legislature," 10/8/48, PAW, 7-9; PAW, "Address Before the First General Assembly [of the] NEA," 7/7/47, PAW, UW, 10-17; DlyO 7/8/47; S.P.I., "Financing Public Schools in the State of Washington." (1953), PAW 11-4; The Republican candidate in 1948 was State Senator Agnes Gehrman, whose late entry was

probably at Langlie's urging.

95. PAW to Worth McClure, 10/10/52, PAW 7-15; Democratic Candidate Albert Rosellini tried to exploit Catholic voters by endorsing Republican Henry W. Turner in the primary; Ed Erickson to Lloyd Andrews 2/27/56, Andrews to George McKee, 6/25/56, PAW 12-1

96. Another straw in the wind was the 1955 legislature's trimming of her budget from $192.5 million to $175.8 million; county support fell to 11.3 percent; Time. 2/6/56, "Education." Another impediment was her reinstatement of a Tacoma teacher's credentials who had refused to give the names of alleged communists to a Congressional committee.

97. 7 John Abaddoso to DLR, 9/8/74. WSA, DLR, 89, White House corr; PI 8/15/76; See Don Duncan, Jim Matassa, and Jim Simon, "Dixy Lee Ray: Unpolitical, Unique, Uncompromising," ST 1/3/94; See Scott, A Majority of One…, 77-91.

98. President Nixon asked her, "You are a Republican aren't you?" "No," Ray replied, "Neither am I a Democrat." WDW, 1/10/80.

99. Guzzo was a Republican.

100. PI 10/28/78; YHR 11/4/76.

101. TNT 1/13/77; Dly O 3/22/77. Except for the reorganization bill, most of the 25 Executive Requests were minor.

102. Asked at a press conference if she would raise taxes to offset a soft economy, she responded, "No, we will not do that. I think that's an irresponsible way to a …balanced budget." DLR, pr. conf., 7/9/80. WSA 86-7-777, bx 20, pr. rels. See also ST 2/17/77, 8/22/77.

103. "Holding Managers Accountable." DLR to Federal Personnel Management Service Seminar, Seattle, 3/14/78. WSA, DLR, 1024, bx 251-3.

104. Republican State Committeewoman Janet Tourtellote was the second woman to enter a primary for U.S. the Senate, in 1950. Interview with Maclyn Burg, 4/18/72, Women's Oral Histories, WSA; On May, See Patricia Piddock, "Catherine May: A Political Biography," Ph.D., WSU, 1992, and .May interview, LOHP, 1982, WSA. She proved women could comprehend "non-female topics," i.e., defense, atomic energy, and budgets; For Unsoeld's major contribution, see Who Gave, Who Got, How Much? Campaign Financing of the 45th Washington Legislature. Olympia: PDC, 1976"; Smith (State House 1983, Senate 1987), and a winner in Third District (and the first as a write-in candidate) was in Congress 1995-1999; On McMorris, see SR, 11/20,23/02, ST endorsement, 10/22/04, and, Washington State Legislature, Status of Bills, 2003-05 ; S-R columnist Dorothy Rochon Powers sought the seat in 1966. S-R 6/14/66, 1/10/88.

105. Marie Barovic Rosenberg, "Women in Politics: A Comparative Study of Congresswomen Edith Green, [OR] and Julia Butler Hansen." Ph.D., UW, 1973, quote from interview with Willena Butler 2/18/72, p. 71; "Julia Butler Hansen, Democratic Representative from Washington," in the Ralph Nader Congress Project. Washington, D.C.: Grossman, 1972.

106. Hansen Scrapbook, Childhood to 1946, Hansen mss, UW; ST, 12/8/52, 2/5/53.

107. Hansen chaired education four times, and was on Rules and 14 other panels over 22 years.

108. As of 1972, just 75 women had served in the U. S. House, and 10 in the senate, five for their late husbands. Of the 75, at least a third were not professionals; 24 had no previous political experience, and 17 were a "housewife," or "socialite." Half were widows, 28 successors to their husbands, and 24 one termers.] Rosenburg 1

109 See "Women in Congress: Their Power and Influence in a Man's World." Trans-Action (10/69), and "Women in Congress: 1917-1964." WPQ 19, I, (3/66,)110.

110. Congressman Tom Pelly, Interview with Rosenberg 4/2/71, Rosenberg, 163.

111. The Republican, and Democratic party papers from those years at WSU evidence dramatic differences in efficiency, which kept the GOP competitive; ST 8/20, 9/9/92; Author interviews with staffer Pierce Scranton, and Dunn, 12/03, 12/09/04; Library of Congress, "Thomas," Dunn biography, 2004; Dunn was the fifth woman to serve on the House Ways and Means Committee, beginning in her second term. She was on the 10 member transition team when the GOP took control in 1994, and George W. Bush presidential exploratory panel, raising $2 million for him in Washington in 2000; ST 1/04/05. She died at 66, in 2007.

112. See Clyde Wilcox, "Why Was 1992 the 'Year of the Woman'? Explaining Women's Gains in 1992, and, Jean R. Schroedel and Bruce Snyder, "Patty Murray: The Mom in Tennis Shoes Goes to the Senate," in Elizabeth A. Cook, ed., Sue Thomas, and Clyde Wilcox, The Year of the Woman: Myths and Realities. Boulder: Westview Press, 1994, 1-24, 49-70.

113. Author interview with Dunn, 5/2/07.

114. LOC, "Thomas," Votes (Murray), 108th Congress, Second Session; NPR interview of Murray, 11/3/98; See "Populist Opposites," ST 10/25/98; Oly 7/31/03; ST 11/3/04.

115. Library of Congress, "Thomas," Senate, Murray, "Active Legislation," and "Virtual Reference Desk"; Whirlwind Tour," Washington State Magazine, Spring, 2003; ST, 11/3/04. She was reelected for a fourth term in 2010.

116. She was Senior Vice President for Consumer Products. Her total contributions 1/11-12/18/2004 were $16,478,224, of which 62.7 percent was self-financing, 31.5 percent from individuals, and .7 percent from PACS. She refused PAC dollars in 2000, and self-financing appeared in a different light.

117. LOC, "Thomas," "Bill Summary and Status for the 107,th and 108th Congresses. The latter shows 50 sponsorships, 7 of which can be considered significant, 12 minor, and the rest resolutions and "private" bills; ST 12/18/2004.

118. Kathryn Hinch, ed., Political Pioneers: The Lawmakers. Olympia: Elected Washington Women, 1981, preface.

119. See Attachment to Fisheries Advisory Board Report No. 78-51. Joint App. 593. Importantly, this catch of approximately 750,000 fish represents only 9.5% of the total Washington harvest of 7,914,000 salmon. The tribes harvested additional fish from non-Puget Sound origin runs bringing their total catch to approximately 18% of the Washington harvest. The tribes do not assert that their opportunity to harvest non-Puget Sound stocks was restricted. Even within Puget Sound, the adjustment needed to raise 43% to 50% is slight.

(Ultimate Democracy)

Redistricting

1. Washington State, House Journal of the 24th Legislature, 108; For a parallel insider's view of the process, See Mary Ellen McCaffree and Anne McNamee Corbett, Politics of the Possible: The Decade Our Democracy Worked. Special Edition. Chehalis, WA: Gorham Printing, [2010],43-134. McCaffree was Vice-Chair of the reapportionment committee in the House.

2. James Madison, Federalist No. 10, "The Utility of the Union as a Safeguard Against Domestic Faction and Insurrection," November 22, 1787.

3. Alexander Hamilton, Federalist No. 70, "The Executive Department Further Considered," March 15, 1788.

4. Washington State Constitution, Article II, sec. 1(a).

5. Washington State, House Journal of the Twenty-Fourth Legislature (Olympia: State Printing Plant, 1935), 106-107,

324-325.

6. Quoted in Ogden and Bone, Washington Politics, 4, c 1924.

7. "After each enumeration made by the authority of the United States, the legislature shall apportion and district anew the members of the senate and the house of representatives, according to the number of inhabitants." Washington State Constitution, Article 2, sec. 3, repealed by Amendment 74, 1983.

8. See Washington State Secretary of State, Shifting Boundaries: Redistricting in Washington State , www.secstate. wa.gov/oralhistory/redistricting2/default.aspx (accessed August 11, 2005).

9. State of Washington, Session Laws, 1931, Chap. 2, Initiative Measure No. 57, Legislative Reapportionment.

10. Legislators attempted to overturn the 1930 redistricting initiative with legislation and a constitutional amendment. A gubernatorial veto, voter rejection of the proposed amendment, and a constitutional prohibition against the alteration of citizen initiatives for a period of two years existing at that time blocked their efforts. Gordon E. Baker, The Politics of Reapportionment in Washington State. Case Studies in Practical Politics, Eagleton Institute of Politics (Holt, Rinehart and Winston, 1960), 1-2.

11. See League of Women Voters of Washington, Equal Representation: A Guide to Reapportionment in Washington State. (Seattle: League of Women Voters of Washington, 1965), 20.

12. Baker, The Politics of Reapportionment in Washington State, 2.

13. State of Washington, "Official Voter's Pamphlet, containing full text of all state measures to be voted upon at the state general election November 6, 1956," published by Earl Coe, Secretary of State, 17.

14. Washington State Oral History Project, Office of the Secretary of State, R. R. "Bob" Greive: An Oral History (Olympia: Office of the Secretary of State, 2001), 12, 114.

15. Cassandra Tate, "R. R. ("Bob") Greive," HistoryLink.org, The Online Encyclopedia of Washington State History, July 19, 2004. <www.historylink.org/essays/output.cfm?file_id=5717> (accessed August 15, 2005).

16. Washington State Oral History Project, R. R. "Bob" Greive, 6.

17. Washington State Oral History Project, R. R. "Bob" Greive, 117.

18. Based on the 1950 census, the LWV initiative plan contained districts that ranged in size from 30,089 in northeast Washington (District 2) to 62,715 in the shoreline area south of Seattle (District 31), for a ratio of 2.1 to one. The bill passed by the 1957 Washington State Legislature contained districts that ranged in size from 18,942 in rural southeast Washington (District 10) to 83,343 in south Seattle (District 31), for a ratio of 4.4 to one.

19. "No act, law or bill approved by a majority of the electors voting thereon shall be amended or repealed by the legislature within a period of two years following such enactment: Provided, That any such act, law or bill may be amended within two years after such enactment at any regular or special session of the legislature by a vote of two-thirds of all the members elected to each house." Washington State Constitution, Article II, sec. 41, amendment 26, approved November 4, 1952.

20. Washington State Oral History Project, R. R. "Bob" Greive, 105.

21. Washington State, Secretary of State, "Know the Issues: Your Official 1962 Edition Voters Pamphlet," State General Election November 6, 1962, 7.

22. Colegrove v. Green, 328 U.S. 549 (1946).

23. Baker v. Carr, 369 U.S. 186 (1962).

24. William B. McDermott, "The Impact of Baker v. Carr in the State of Washington: The Relationship of Constituency

to Compliance., Ph.D., UW, 1965.

25. Thigpen v. Meyers 211 F. Supp. 826 (1962).

25. Thigpen v. Meyers 211 F. Supp. 826 (1962) at 832

26. Id., Washington State Oral History Project, Office of the Secretary of State, Joel M. Pritchard: An Oral History (Olympia: Office of the Secretary of State, 2000), 99, biographical highlights.

27. Washington State Oral History Project, Office of the Secretary of State, Joel M. Pritchard, 87, 99.

28. Ibid., 87,99.

29. Washington State Oral History Project, Office of the Secretary of State, Joel M. Pritchard, 87.1 In the 1962 general election, a total of 97 Republican candidates for the State House of Representatives running for 99 seats polled a cumulative total of 939,192 votes (52.8 percent); 92 Democratic candidates accumulated 839,644 votes (47.2 percent). The electoral outcome was 48 Republican winners and 51 Democrat winners. In the 1960? general election, a total of 96 Republican candidates polled 1,077,754 votes (48.5 percent); 95 Democratic candidates accumulated 1,144,619 votes (51.5 percent). The electoral outcome was 40 Republican winners and 59 Democrat winners. In the 1958 general election, a total of 84 Republican candidates polled 667,908 votes (40.7 percent); 97 Democrat candidates polled 972,361 votes (59.3 percent). The electoral outcome was 33 Republican winners and 66 Democrat winners.

30. Weighting the votes of House members elected in the 1958 election to the 1959 legislative session so as to eliminate differences based on district population would have produced 66 Democrats and 33 Republicans, matching the actual split of 66/33. In the 1961 session, weighted votes would have produced 61 Democrats and 38 Republicans; the actual split was 59/40. In the 1963 session, weighted votes would have produced 53 Democrats and 46 Republicans compared to the actual and closer split of 51/48. In the 1959 Senate, weighting the votes of Senate members based on district populations would have produced a party split of 35 Democrats and 14 Republicans; the actual split was an identical 35/14. In the 1961 Senate, weighted votes would have produced 37 Democrats and 12 Republicans; the actual split was 36 to 13. In the 1963 Senate, weighted votes would have produced 33 Democrats and 16 Republicans; the actual split was 32 to 17.

31. A controversial Republican amendment limiting the ability of transit workers to strike was taken in the House of Representatives on February 11, 1959, and failed by a vote of 50 to 36; weighted votes would have produced a 52 to 35 split. An effort by Democrats opposing a divisive procedure that would have given citizens the "right to vote" on efforts by public power companies to condemn facilities owned by private power companies passed the House of Representatives on February 24, 1961, by a vote of 50 to 48 (Evans vote was incorrectly recorded as a "yea" and should be counted as a "nay;" under a weighted system the majority would have prevailed by the same margin. A controversial February 16, 1961, Senate vote on a bill reforming the state liquor control board favored by the Democratic majority passed by a margin of 30 to 19; revising the vote so as to eliminate district population inequities would have produced a vote of 32 to 17.

32. State of Washington, "Know the Issues: Your Official 1962 Edition Voters Pamphlet," November 6, 1962," published by Victor A. Meyers, Secretary of State, State of Washington, 7.

33. See Daniel J. Chasan, Speaker of the House: the Political Career and Times of John L. O'Brien (Seattle: University of Washington Press, 1990). Secretary of State, Joel M. Pritchard, 100.

34. Washington State Oral History Project, Office of the Secretary of State, Joel M. Pritchard, 100.

35. See Washington State, House Journal of the Thirty-Eighth Legislature (Olympia: State Printing Plant, 1964), 270-1

The amendment provided for a House of Representatives consisting of 104 members and senators elected in single districts consisting of no more than one-half of the number of representatives.

35. Records of Howard McCurdy; later confirmed by Senator Greive. See Howard E. McCurdy, A Majority of the People: A Case Study in the Redistricting of Washington State, 1967; Washington State, Secretary of State, Shifting Boundaries; Redistricting in Washington State, The 1960s, www.secstate.wa.gov/oralhistory/redistricting2/1960s/Mc-Curdy.pdf (accessed August 24, 2005), 31.

36. Remarks by Senator Nat Washington on the Senate floor, April 2, 1963, recorded by Howard McCurdy.

37. The conditional clause tied the constitutional amendment to a specific redistricting bill, House Bill 56, which implemented the plan. Washington State, House Journal of the Thirty-Eighth Legislature, 271.

38. Washington State Oral History Project, R. R. "Bob" Greive, 114.

39. McDermott, "The Impact of Baker v. Carr in the State of Washington," 127, 140.

40. Court's Oral Opinion of May 3, 1963, 1.

41. "Reply to Answer of League of Women Voters to Appellant's Petition for Stay Pending Appeal, Affidavit of Governor Albert Rosellini."

42. Reply to Answer of League of Women Voters to Appellant's Petition for Stay Pending Appeal, Affidavit of Senator Robert C. Bailey.

43. Opinion of the Court, July 22, 1964, 2.

44. Reynolds v. Sims 377 US 533 (1964); Remark addressed to Howard McCurdy by Representative Joel Pritchard, January 11, 1965.

45. See E. E. Schattschneider, The Semi sovereign People: A Realists View of Democracy in America. (New York: Holt, Rinehart and Winston, 1960, and William H. Riker, The Theory of Political Coalitions. New Haven: Yale University Press, 1962.

46. Adele Ferguson in the Bremerton Sun, January 29, 1965.

47. Remarks by Senator John T. McCutcheon, February 12, 1965, recorded by Howard McCurdy.

48. The plan might not have failed. Later in the 1965 session, Democrats sent a less momentous congressional redistricting act to the people as a legislative referendum. Evans tried to veto the bill, but the State Supreme Court ruled 8 to 1 that the governor could not veto the bill. Subsequently, voters approved the measure. Congressional redistricting, however, was not subjected to the federal court ruling.

49. Both remarks on the floor of the Senate, February 22, 1965, recorded by Howard McCurdy.

50. Based on the 1960 census, the population of the 32nd district was 45,121. The target size for each district was 57,657.

51. McCurdy, A Majority of the People, 70.

52. Remarks by Senator Greive on the floor of the Senate, February 23, 1965, recorded by Howard McCurdy.

53. State of Washington, House Journal of the 39th Legislature, 437-38.

54. Remarks by Senator Greive on the floor of the Senate, February 25, 1965, recorded by Howard McCurdy.

55. State of Washington, House Journal of the 39th Legislature, 455.

56. State of Washington, House Journal of the 39th Legislature, 476-78.

57. Discrepancies in Senate districts, based on 1960 census figures, ranged from 1.45 to one. The Whatcom County district received an extra representative which, along with the division of districts for electing House members, produced

populations per representative that ranged from 20,848 in Lincoln and Adams County (District 9B) to 33,712 in Benton County (District 16A) 1.6 to one. Thigpen v. Kramer, 5597 Federal File, Stipulation, March 8, 1965.

58. Thigpen v. Kramer, 5597 Federal File, Plaintiffs' Memorandum Concerning Validity of Ch. 6, Laws of 1965, March 9, 1965.

59. Thigpen v. Kramer, 5597 Federal File, Court's Oral Opinion on Defendants' Motion to Dismiss, March 10, 1965.

60. Thigpen v. Kramer, 5597 Federal File, Order of Dismissal, March 19, 1965.

61. Republicans won 55 out of 99 seats with 51.6 percent of the statewide vote for all House candidates, slightly less than the 52.8 percent that had yielded 48 seats in the 1962 general election.

62. Michael Ko, "R.R. 'Bob' Greive, 84, Jumped Into Political Life Early." Seattle Times, about July 4, 2004, < www.34dems.org/biographmemoriam.htm#Grieve> (accessed September 1, 2005).

63. The legislature passed a state and congressional redistricting bill in 1981; the congressional bill was vetoed by Governor John Spellman. The courts intervened again and in 1983 the legislature allowed a temporary redistricting commission to complete the task. The 1991 and 2001 redistricting of Washington State was accomplished by commission.

Acronyms

Governors

ADR	Albert D. Rosellini
ABL	Arthur B. Langlie
BG	Booth Gardner
DJE	Daniel J Evans
DLR	Dixie Lee Ray
GL	Gary Locke
DS	John D. Spellman
MCW	Monrad C. Wallgren
ML	Mike Lowry

Elective and Appointive Offices

AG	(State) Attorney General
CC	City Councilman
CtyC	County Councilman
CtyE	County Executive
G	Governor

KCC King County Council

OSOS	Office of the Secretary of State
SPI	(State) Superintendent of Public Instruction
SR	State Representative

SPKR	Speaker of the House
SS	State Senator
IIIH	Third House (lobbyists)
SSCt	Washington State Supreme Court
USR	United States Representative
USS	United States Senator

Journals

APSR	American Political Science Review
JlH	Journal of the House of the State of Washington
JlS	Journal of the Senate of the State of Washington
JW	Journal of the West
OHQ	Oregon Historical Quarterly
PHR	Pacific Historical Review
PNQ	Pacific Northwest Quarterly
SG	State Government
WH	Western History
WHQ	Washington Historical Quarterly
WPQ	Western Political Quarterly
WSBN	Washington State Bar News

Repositories

WSHS	Eastern Washington State Historical Society, Cheney.
KCA	King County Archives, Seattle.
PLUSSC	Pacific Lutheran University, Scandinavian Special Collections Division, Parkland.
SMRL	Seattle Municipal Reference Library. (Now part of SPL).
SpL	Spokane Public Library.
SPL	Seattle Public Library, Archives Division.
TPLA	Tacoma Public Library and Archives.
TCL	Tri Cities Public Library
UPSSC	University of Puget Sound, Special Collections, Tacoma.
UWASC	University of Washington Library, Special Collections, Seattle.
UWL	University of Washington Library, Seattle.
WSA	Washington State Archives, Olympia;
(-B),	Bellingham
(-C)	Cheney
(-E)	Ellensburg
WSHSA	Washington State Historical Society Archives, Tacoma.
WSL	Washington State Library, Tumwater.
WSUSC	Washington State University Library, Special Collections, Pullman.

WWUA	Western Washington State University Archives, Bellingham.
YPL	Yakima Public Library

Oft Cited Newspapers

AR	Seattle Argus.
BH	Bellingham Herald.
BS	Bremerton Sun.
Col	The Columbian, Vancouver.
D1yO	The Daily Olympian. (Later, as "O").
EVH	The Everett Herald.
J-A	The Journal-American, Bellevue (Now the Eastside Journal).
KCLS	King County Labor Council ("Scanner")
MN	Municipal News (Seattle).
ON	Olympia News
OR	The Oregonian (Portland)
PI	The Post-Intelligencer, Seattle.
SDC	Spokane Daily Chronicle.
SR	The Spokesman-Review, Spokane.
SS	Seattle Star
ST	The Seattle Times.
TCH	Tri City Herald, (Richland-Pasco-Kennewick).
TNT	Tacoma News Tribune.
WDW	The Wenatchee Daily World.
Wkly	The Weekly (Seattle).
WS	The Washington Standard, Olympia.
WWUB	Walla Walla Union Bulletin.
YHR	Yakima Herald Republic.

Bibliography

Scandinavians

O.E. Rolvaag, Concerning Our Heritage. Northfield, MI: Norwegian-American Historical Association, 1998.

Jon Wefald. A Voice of Protest: Norwegians in American Politics, 1840-1917. Northfield, MI: Norwegian-American Historical Association, 1971.

Arestad, S. "Norwegians in Pacific Coast Fisheries." Pacific Northwest Quarterly [hereafter cited as "PNQ"] 34 (1/48): 3-18.

Arthur J. Brown. "The Promotion of Immigration to Washington, 1851-1909." PNQ 36 (1/45): 3-17.

Jorgen Dahlie. "Old World Paths in the New: Scandinavians Find a Familiar Home in Washington." PNQ 61 4/70) 65-72.

Frederick Hale. "Danish Immigrant Disillusionment in the Pacific Northwest." PNQ 71 (1/80): 15-23.

Jon T. Kilpenen. "Finnish Cultural Landscapes in the Pacific Northwest." PNQ 86 (1/94): 25-34.

Terye Lieren. "Ole and the Reds The America of Seattle Mayor Ole Hansen." Norwegian-American Studies 26,75-95.

Jorgen Dahlie. "Americanization: The Scandinavian Drive for Acceptance." In

"A Social History of Scandinavian Immigrants in Washington." Ph.D. WSU, 1967, 94-121.

Seattle's Mayors

Carl Abbott. "Regional City and Network City: Portland and Seattle in the Twentieth Century." PHR 23 (8/92): 293-322.

Berner, Richard C. Seattle 1921-1940: From Boom to Bust. Seattle: Charles Street Press, 1992.

Seattle Transformed: World War II to the Cold War. Seattle: Charles Press, 1999.

Leslie Blanchard. The Street Railway Era in Seattle: A Chronicle of Six Decades. Hanford Cornelius.

Samuel P. Hayes. "The Politics of Reform in Municipal Government in the Progressive Era." PNQ 55 (10/64): 157-

Robert E. Horn. "The Politics of Metropolitan Integration: A Legislative History of the Metropolitan Municipal Corporations Act of 1957." MA, UWA, 1958.

Norbert McDonald Distant Neighbors: A Comparative History of Seattle and Vancouver. Lincoln: University of Nebraska Press, 1987.

Roger Sale. Seattle Past and Present. UWAP, 1976.

Calvin F. Schmid. Social Trends in Seattle. Seattle: The University of Washington Press, 1944.

Seattle Municipal Reference Library. "Reports and Miscellaneous Material on Rehabilitation Program. Seattle Elections Clipping File: "Seattle Municipal and Port Elections 1933-1934."

Municipal Street Railway, 1930-1939." 1942.

Seattle Transportation Commission. Seattle Municipal Street Railway Annual Report (1932-1938). Seattle: Department of Public Works, Division of Railways.

Scott, George, "The New Order of Cincinnatus." MA, UWA., 1966.

Devin, William. M.

Hamley, Charles. (Scrapbook)   Potts, Ralph.

Langlie, Arthur B. WSA, UWASC; CC,G

Lockwood, David. (Scrapbooks); CC, DD

Powell, Mildred; CC.

*Rabbitt, Thomas. SR

Wolfstone, Micheal

The CVA

Robert E. Ficken. Rufus Woods, the Columbia River and the Building of Modern Washington. Pullman: WSUP, 1995.

Lawrence Rakestraw. "The West, States Rights and Conservation." PNQ XLVIII (7/51), 89-99.

*Burke, Robert E., Collector.

*Benson, Naomi. PUDC.

*Magnuson, Warren G. SR,USR,USS.

*Pennock, William, SR

*O'Brien, John L. WSA, UWSC; SR (Spkr)

*Farquharson, Mary, SS.

*Hansen, Julia B. SR, USR.

*Hartley, Roland H. (newspaper clippings).

 Hill, Knute. WASUSP; SR, USR.

 Hodde, Charles R; Spkr; DD; WSA

*Horan, Walter. USR. WSUSC

*Houghton, Cluck, Coughlin and Schabat

Jackson, Henry M. PA, USR, USS

 Myers, Guy Norwood, Gus

*Chadwick, Stephen F.

*Reeves, Belle C. WSA

 Riley, Edith Dolan.

 Smith, Thomas. SR, DD.

*Washington PUD Association

 Woods, Rufus

Labor

John McCann. Blood in the Water: A History of District Lodge 751 International Association of Machinists and Aerospace Workers. Seattle: The Lodge, 1989.

Carlos Schwantes. Hard Traveling: A Portrait of Work Life in the Pacific Northwest. Lincoln: University of Nebraska Press, 1994.

Radical Heritage: Labor, Socialism and Reform in Washington and British Columbia 1895-1917. Seattle: University of Washington Press, 1979.

Donald Garnel. Teamsters and Highway Truckers in the West: The Evolution of Multi-Employer Bargaining in the Western Highway Trucking Industry. Ph.D, UCB,. 1966.

Richard C. Berner,"1948: Liberalism in Disarray." [The Boeing Strike of 1948]. In Berner, Seattle Transformed: World War II to the Cold War. Seattle: Charles Press, 1999, 202-241.

Robert E. Doherty, "Implications of the Increasing Power of Public Employee Unions." State Government (Autumn 1976): 234-238.

 Robert and Robin Friedheim. "The Seattle Labor Movement, 1919-1920." PNQ 55 (10/64), 146-156.

Carlos Schwantes. "Laeftward Tilt on the Pacific Slope: Indigenous Unionism and the Struggle Against AFL Hegemony in the State of Washington." PNQ 70 (1/79), 24-34.

Harry W. Stone. "The Beginning of the Labor Movement in the Pacific Northwest." OHR 47 (6/46), 155-164.

*Democratic State Central Committee of Washington.

Northwest Public Power Association

*O'Brien, John. WSA; SR (Spkr)

*Grant, Gary. WSA; SR, SS, PC

Grieve, Robert. WSA. SS, CtyCl

 Gluck, Joe

*Rosellini, Albert D. WSA; SS, G.

Taxes

Phil Roberts. A Penny for the GovernorA Dollar for Uncle Sam: Income Taxtion in Washington. Seattle: UWP, 2002.

Washington State Department of Revenue. A Progress Report on Achievements in Property Tax Administration in the State of Washington." Olympia: DOR, 1970.

Washington State Tax Structure Committee, [William H. Gates, Sr. Chair], Tax Alternatives for Washington State: A Report to the Legislature. Olympia: The Committee, 2002.

Boldt

Andrew H. Fisher. Shadow Tribe: The making of the Columbia River Indian Identity. Seattle: Center for the Study of the Pacific Northwest, in association with the University of Washington Press, 2010.

United States v Taylor 3 Wash. Terr (1887).

Greening

Robert E. Ficken Rufus Woods, the Columbia River and the Building of Modern Washington. WASUP, 1995.

The Forested Land: A History of Lumbering in Western Washington. UWAP. 1987.

Joseph M. Petulla. American Environmental History: The Exploitation and Conservation of Natural Resources. San Francisco: Boyd and Frazier, 1977.

Dixy Lee Ray. Trashing the Planet: How Science Can Help Us Deal with Acid Rain, Depletion of the Ozone, and Nuclear Waste. Washington, D.C., Henry Regnery Gateway; Lanham, M.D. University Press of America, 1990.

Elmo Richardson. Dams, Parks and Politics: Resource Development and Preservation in the Truman-Eisenhower Era. Lexington: The University Press of Kentucky, 1973.

Joseph E. Taylor III. Making Salmon: An Environmental History of the Northwest Fisheries Crisis. UWAP, 1999.

Washington State Growth Strategies Commission. A Growth Strategy for Washington State. Seattle: The Commission, 1990.

Richard White. The Organic Machine: The Remaking of the Columbia River. New York, Hill and Wang, 1995

Mark Wyman. Hard Rock Epic: Western Miners and the Industrial Revolution. UCABP, 1979.

Jerry F Medler. "Governors and Environmental Policy." PSJ 17 (4): 895-908.

Donald C. Swain. "The Bureau of Reclamation and the New Deal 1933-1940." PNQ 61 (7/70): 137-146.

"Proposals for a Columbia Valley Authority," in McKinley, Charles, Uncle Sam in the Northwest: Federal Management of Natural Resources on the Columbia. UCABP, 1952, 443-566.

Women

Daniel J. Evans. Twelve Years: A Report to the Citizens of Washington State on the Administration of Governor Daniel J. Evans, 1965-1977. Olympia: Office of the Governor, 1/77.

The Linfield Papers. Seattle: Private Printing, 1969.

Lessons in Leadership. Seattle: The Agora Foundation, 1999. "Governor's Commission on the Status of Women. "Final Report." Olympia: Office of the Governor, 1965.

"Report of the Constitutional Advisory Council." 12/66.

Governor's Affirmative Action Policy Committee. "Report to Governor Gary Locke on Affirmative Action in State Government" Olympia: OFM, 1997.

Governors Task Force on Higher Education. Final Report of the Governors Task Force on Higher Education. Olympia: the

Task Force, 1996.

Warren, James. "'The Pioneer Roots of Daniel Jackson Evans." Portage 10 (Spring, 1989), 9,12,39.

Laura Woodworth-Nay. Women in the American West. Santa Barbara: ABC-ClioCultures in the American West Series, 2008.

Kim K. Schaefer. "Right in the Eye: The Political Style of Dixy Lee Ray." PNQ 93 (Spring 2002): 81-93.

Adlum, Merle, ["Washington Committee for a   *North, Lois. WSA; SR, SS, CtyCl.

Responsible Environmental Policy] [1970-1972] .   Ray, Dixy Lee, WSA ; The Hover Institution

Bagnariol, John, WSA, NARA (Seattle); SR (Spkr) .   Riveland, Mary. DD(3)

Berentson, Duane SR(Spkr). WSA.   Stern, Bernice. CtyC

*Evans, Daniel J., WSA; SR, G, USS.   Washington Citizens for Abortion Reform.

*Hine, Lorraine. WSA; SR (ML), GCOS.

*Hurley, Margaret. WSA;SR, SS.

Ultimate Democracy

David Broder. The Derailing of Democracy: Initiative Campaigns and the Power of Money. New York: Hillcrest Books, 2000.

Thomas Cronin. Direct Democracy: The Politics of Initiative, Referendum, and Recall. Cambridge: Harvard University Press, 1904.

Waldo Schumaker. "Thirty Years of People's Rule in Oregon: An Analysis." PSQ 47 (6/1932): 242-258.

Redistricting

Charles S. Bullock, Redistricting: The Most Politcal Activity in America.Lanham, M.D.: Rowman and Littlefielod, 2010.

Alan Heslop. Redistricting: The Key to Politics in the 1980's Claremont, CA., The Rose Intitute of State and Local Government, 1980.

Richard Morrill. Washington State Legislative and Congressional Districts. Olympia: OSOS, 1972.

Washington State Redistricting Commission/ Washington State Historical Society. Redistricting: Redrawing the Battle Lines. Olympia: The Commission, 2002.On the Worldwide Web at "Access. Washington," Redistricting Commission.

William B. McDermott . "The Impact of Baker v Carr in the State of Washington. The Relationship of Constituency to Compliance." Ph.D., UWA, 1966.

Mark E Rush. "Redistricting: The Supreme Court and American Elections." Ph.D., The Johns Hopkins University, 1990.

Slade Gorton. "New Methods Urged." National Civic Review 53 (April 1964):176-181.

Bruce M. Haston. "[The] Impact of Reapportionment on Election of the 1967 Legislature." Quorum I, Fall, 1966, 1-2.

William B. McDermott. "The Impact on State Policies." In Timothy G. O'Rourke, ed., The Impact of Reapportionment. New Brunswick, N.J.: Transaction Books, 1980.

Jacob F. Roush., "Legislative Reapportionment in Washington State, 1890-1930." PNQ 28 (7/37): 263-300.

Washington State, Redistricting Commission. "The 2000 Redistricting." The Commission, at WWW// WA. gov.

John P. White and Norman C. Thomas. "Urban and Rural Representation and State Legislative Reapportionment." Western Political Quarterly, 18 (11/64): 724-741.

Statewide Areas and Issues of Related and Ongoing Import

The Courts

Legal Foundation of Washington. "Of Shoes and Ships and Ceiling Wax: Historic Encounters wit h the Washington State

Supreme Court and the United States Supreme Court." Olympia: LFW, 1989.

Charles S. Lopeman. The Activist Advocate: Policy Making in State Supreme Courts. Westport, CT., Praeger, 1999. Sheldon, Charles H. The Washington High Bench: A Biographical History of the State Supreme Court, 1889-1991. WASUP, 1992.

Sheldon, Charles. A Century of Judging: A Political History of the Washington State Supreme Court. UWAP, 1988.

Justice James Dolliver. "The Washington Constitution and 'State Action': The View of the Framers." WLR 102: 445-458.

Justice Robert Utter, and Hugh Spitzer. The Washington State Constitution: A Reference Guide. Westport, CT: Greenwood Press, 2000.

Culture

Leonard Bloom. Removal and Return: The Socio-Economic Effects of the War on Japanese Americans. UCABP, 1949.

David Brewster. and David Buerge. Washingtonians: A Biographical Portrait of the State. Seattle: Sasquatch Press, 1988.

Roger Daniels. Asian America: Chinese and Japanese in the United States Since 1850. UWAP, 1988.

John M. Findlay. M agic Lands and Western Cityscapes: American Culture After 1940. UCAB, 1992.

Raymond O. Gastil. "The Pacific as a Cultural Region." PNQ 64, (10/73): 147-162.

L.V. McWhorter. Hear Me My Chiefs!: Nez Perce History and Legend. Caldwell, ID: Caxton Printers, 1952.

Janet E. Rasmussen. Scandinavian Immigrants to the Pacific Northwest. UWAP, 1993.

Quintard Taylor, and Shelly Ann Wilson Moore, eds. African-American Women Confront the West, 1600-2000. University of Colorado Press, 2003.

The Forging of a Black Community: Seattle's Central District from 1870 Through the Civil Rights Era. UWAP, 1994.

White, Sid, and S.E. Solberg, eds. Peoples of Washington: Perspectives of Cultural Diversity. WASUP, 1989.

Kay E. Sari. "Demographic and Racial Changes in Seattle: 1950-1975." MA, UWA, 1976.

Disclosure/Ethics

Alan Rosenthal. The Third House: Lobbyists and Lobbying in the States. CQP, 1993.

Jolene Unsold. "Who Gave, Who Got, How Much?" Olympia: the PDC, 1977.

Washington State, Public Disclosure Commission. 1998 Election Financing Fact book. Olympia: The PDC. Annual.

The Economy and the Private Sector

John B. Appleton. "Migration and Economic Opportunity in the Pacific Northwest." Geographical Review 21 (1/1941): 46-62.

Charles M. Gates. "A Historical Sketch of the State of Washington of the Economic Development of Washington Since Statehood." PNQ 79 (7/48): 214-232.

James Tattersall. "The Economic Development of the Pacific Northwest to 1920." Ph.D., UWA, 1960.

Education/Higher Education

Steve Kink, and John Cahill. Class Wars: The Story of the Washington Education Association, 1965-2004. Federal Way, Washington: The WEA, 2004.

Alan Rosenthal. Pedagogues and Power: Teacher Groups in School Politics. Syracuse: Syracuse University Press, 1969.

Walter Garms, and Michael Kirst. "The Political Environment of School Finance Politics in the 1980's." In A Decade of Conflict, edited by James W. Guthrie. Cambridge, MA, 1980.

Robert G. Raymer. "Educational Development in the Territory and the State of Washington, 1883-1908." WHQ 18 (7/27), 163-180.

Robert H. Salisbury. "State Politics and Education." In Politics in the American States, 2nd ed., edited by Herbert Jacob and Kenneth N. Vines. Boston: Little Brown, 1971.

Washington State, Governor's Task Force on Higher Education. Final Report of the Governor's Task Force on Higher Education. Olympia: The Task Force, 1986.

Washington State, Governor's 20/20 Commission on the Future of Post-Secondary Education. Olympia: Governor's Executive Policy Office, 1998.

Governors and Governing

Susie Anschell ed., Public Policy Making, Washington Style. Seattle: IGR,1968.

Thad Beyle, and L.R. Muchmore, Being Governor: The View From the Office. Durham, N.C.: Duke University Press, 1981.

ed. Governors and Hard Times. Washington D.C.: CQP, 1992.

Edmond Meany. Governors of Washington: Territorial and State. Seattle: UWA, Department of Printing, 1915.

Schlesinger, Joseph D., How They Became Governor: A Study of Comparative State Politics 1870-1950. East Lansing: Michigan State University Press, 1957.

Ira Sharkansky. The Maligned States: Policy Accomplishments, Problems and Opportunities. New York: McGraw-Hill, 1978.

George Scott. Governors of Washington. Seattle: Civitas Press, 2011.

Laura Van Assendelft. Governors, Agenda Setting, and Divided Government. Lanham, M.D. University Press of America, 1997.

Michael Berkman, and Charles Barrine. "Do Governors Matter? Budgeting, Rules and the Politics of State Policy Making." PSR 56 (12/2003): 409-417.CSG "The Governor's Powers." SG 55 (Summer 1982): 74-105.

John Leaford. The Rise of the States: Evaluation of American State Government. Baltimore: The Johns Hopkins University Press, 2002.

Sarah McC. Morehouse. "The Governor and His Legislative Party." APSR 60 (4): 923-942.

Daniel Ogden. "The Blanket Primary and Party Regularity in Washington." PNQ 39 (1/48): 33-38.

Colman Ransone, "Political Leadership in the Governor's Office." JOP 26 (2/64), 197-220.

Larry Sabato. "Gubernatorial Politics and the New Campaign Technology." SG 53 (1980): 48-52.

The Veto

Glenn Abney, and Thomas E. Lauth, "The Line-Item Veto in the States: An Instrument for Fiscal Restraint." PAR 45 (6/80): 372-377.

E.L. Bernick,, and C.W. Wiggins. "Executive-Legislative Power Relations: Perspectives of State Lawmakers." APQ 9 (4): 467-476.

Sharon Sherman. "Powersplit: When Legislatures and Governors are of Opposing Parties" SL X, # 5 (5-6/84), 9-12.

Alexander J. Walker. "The Governor's Veto Power." University of Virginia Newsletter. 55, (12/77): 3-16.

Washington State, House of Representatives. "Report on the Partial Veto Power and the 1986 Partial Vetoes." Olympia: The House, 1986.

Gary Locke. WSA, UWASC; SR, CtyE, G.

Mike Lowry,. WSA, LOC; UWASC, (Congressional); CtyC, USR, G.

The Legislature

Citizen's Conference on State Legislatures, The Sometime Governments. New York: Bantam Books, 1Alexander Heard, ed., State Legislatures in American Politics. Englewood Cliffs: Prentice-Hall, 1966.

Edward J. Clyde, and Thomas J. Lauth. Governors, Legislatures, and Budgets: Diversity Across the American States. New York: Greenwood Press, 1991.

Alan Rosenthal. The Decline of Representative Democracy: Process, participation and the Power in State Legislatures. Washington, D.C., CQ Press, 1998.

Governors and Legislatures: Contending Powers. Washington, D.C.: CQP, 1990.

George W. Scott. A Majority of One: Legislative Life. Seattle: Civitas Press. 2nd ed., 2005.

Ed Seeberger. Sine Die: A Guide to the Washington State Legislative Process. Seattle: UWP. 1997.

Toward Sine Die: A Guide to the Washington State legislative Process. Seattle: UWAP, 2nd ed., 1997.

Beverly P. Rosenow ed. "The Journal of the Washington State Constitutional Convention, 1889." Seattle: Book Publishing Company, 1962.

Claudius O Johnson. "Washington's Blanket Primary Revisited." PNQ 12, (10/52): 113-119.

Tom Loftus. "Branches of State Government: The Separation of Unequal Powers," in Loftus, The Art of Legislative Politics. Washington, D.C., CQP, 1994, 61-75.Yung-Ping, Cheng. A Historical of the General Property Tax in the State of Washington." MA, UWA, 1957.

Local government

Washington State Local Governance Study Commission. "A History of Washington's Local Governments." V. (Final Report). Olympia: The Commission, and the Institute of Public Policy, TESC, 1988.

Washington State Research Council, A Handbook for Washington's Governments, 5th ed., Olympia: The WSRC, 1981.

Newton C. Abbott. "The Evolution of Washington Counties. MA, UW, 1927.

Randall V. Mills. "A History of Transportation in the Pacific Northwest." OHQ, 65 (9/1946): 281-312.

Lobbies/Ethics

Jeffery Berry. Lobbying for the People: The Political Behavior of Public Interest Groups. Princeton: Princeton University Press, 1977.

Stephen Carter. Civility: Manners, Morals and the Etiquette of Democracy. New York: Basic Books, 1998.

E. Patrick Dobel. Pork Barrel Politics. Stanford: Stanford University Press, 1974.

Alan Rosenthal. Lobbyists and Lobbying in the States. Washington, D.C.: CQP. 2007.

The Ethics Process in State Legislatures: Disciplining Members in a Public Forum. Denver: State Legislative Leaders Foundation/National Conference of State Legislators, 1999.

Walfred Peterson. "Interest Groups and Lobbies in Washington State Government." In Thor Swanson, et. al., Political Life in Washington: Governing the Evergreen State. WASUP, 1985.

T.M. Sell. "Riding the Milk Wagon: The Effect of Money on the Outcomes of Legislative Campaigns in Washington State, 1974-1982." Olympia: PDC, 1988.

Jolene Unsoeld. Who Gave? Who Got? How Much? Everett: Working Press, 1976.

Washington State Public Disclosure Commission, Annual Report, 1974, ff. Olympia: The PDC.

Randy Ray, and Megan Mardesich, "Perceptions: Corporate Political Involvement in the Washington State Legislature." Olympia: TESC, 1976.

The Media

Timothy Cook. Governing with the News: The News Media as a Political Institution. 2nd ed. Chicago: University of Chicago Press, 2005.

Bill Kovach, and Tom Rosensteil. The Elements of Journalism: What News people Should Know and What the Public Should Expect. UCAB, 1975.

Lorraine McConaghy, and Sharon Boswell, Raise Hell and Sell Newspapers. UWAP, 1996.

Maxwell McCombs, and Donald Shaw. "The Agenda-Setting Function of the Mass Media." POQ (Summer 1971): 176-187.

Transportation

Peter Lewty. To the Columbia Gateway: The Oregon Railway and the Northern Pacific, 1889-1894. Pullman: WASUP Press, 1987.

Michael P. Malone. James J. Hill: Empire Builder of the Northwest. UOKP, 1996.

Gordon Newell,, ed. The H.W. McCurdy Marine History of the Pacific Northwest, 1966-1976. Seattle: The Superior Company, 1977.

Schwantes, Carlos A. Going Places: Transportation Redefines the Twentieth-Century West. INUP, 2003.

Railroad Signatures Across the Northwest. Seattle: UWAP, 1998.

Washington State, Department of Transportation. A History of Highways and Transportation: [The] Washington State Transportation Commission 1951-1993. Olympia: The Commission, 1993.

References

Agency directors files 1922, ff., WSA.

Governor's Office, Central Files, WSA.

Journal of the United States House of Representatives, 1853, ff.

Journal of the United States Senate, 1853 ff.

Journal of the State House of Representatives, 1889, ff.

Journal of the Washington State Senate, 1889, ff.

OSOS. Washington State Yearbook. Sammamish, WA: Electronic Handbook Publishers, 1980, ff.

abstract[s] of Votes Primary and General Elections. Olympia: State Printer, 1889, ff.

Revised Code of Washington

United States Code

Washington Public Documents. Olympia: State Printer, 1941-1968. WSA.

Washington State Legislature, Office of the Code Reviser, Session Laws, 1889, ff.

Washington State Legislature. Final Legislative Report. Olympia. Annual since 1967.

Washington State Legislative Manual. 1949, ff.

Washington State Democratic Central Committee, WSUSP. (1960's-1980's).

Washington State Republican Central Committee, Tukwila.

Oral Histories by George Scott

Frederick Baker

Ralph Davis. DD

Charles Frankland

William Fitzgerald. Seattle Fire Chief.

Charles Hodde. SR (Spkr), DD (X3).

Judge Frederick Hamley. SSCT, Ninth U.S District Court.

Harold Van Eaton. DD.

Arthur Sheridan Langlie. Son

Hugh B. Mitchell. USC, USS.

Albert D. Rosellini. SS, G.

Legislative Oral History Project I ("LOHP I"), 1989-1990.
WSA (810 pp).

Warren Bishop. GCOS/DD.

William Bugge. DD.

Gordon Clinton. M

Joe Davis. President, WSFL.

James Dolliver. GCOS, Justice.

Daniel J. Evans. (2) SR (Mel, ML), G, USS.

R.R. "Bob" Grieve. SS, CtyC.

Leroy Hittle. ST,LB.

Charles Hodde. SR (Spkr); DD.

Albert D. Rosellini (2) SS, G.

Norm Schut. ED, WFSE, TH.

"LOHP II"; 2005-2006. WSA, UW, WSU,
Special Collections.

Oral histories by Others. OSOS.

Legislative Oral History Project, WSA.

Don Eldridge. SR (Spkr).

James Dolliver. GCOS.

William Gissberg. SS.

Robert Goldsworthy. SR.

August P. Mardesich. SR (ML), SS (ML).

Mary Ellen McCaffree. SR, DD.

Joel M. Pritchard. SR, SS, USR, LtG.

Albert D. Rosellini SS, G

By the Dwight D. Eisenhower Presidential Library, (Abilene, KS),and Columbia University

George Kinnear. SR (ML), DD.

Thor Tollefson. USR, DD.